Getting Smart About

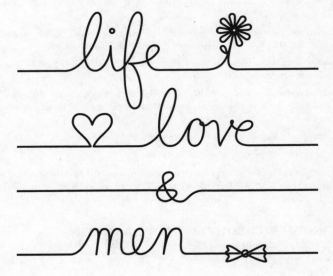

life love & men

michelle mckinney hammond

HARVEST HOUSE PUBLISHERS
EUGENE, OREGON

Cover design by Harvest House Publishers, Eugene, Oregon

Michelle McKinney Hammond is represented by the literary agency of Alive Communications, Inc., 7680 Goddard Street, Ste. #200, Colorado Springs, CO 80920. www.alivecommunications.com.

GETTING SMART ABOUT LIFE, LOVE, AND MEN

Copyright © 2014 Michelle McKinney Hammond
Published by Harvest House Publishers
Eugene, Oregon 97402
www.harvesthousepublishers.com

Library of Congress Cataloging-in-Publication Data
McKinney Hammond, Michelle.
Getting smart about life, love, and men / Michelle McKinney Hammond.
    pages cm
ISBN 978-0-7369-5940-7 (pbk.)
ISBN 978-0-7369-5941-4 (eBook)
1. Christian women—Religious life. 2. Women in the Bible. I. Title.
BV4527.M41825 2014
248.8'43—dc23

2014015592

Printed in the United States of America

14 15 16 17 18 19 20 21 22 / VP-JH / 10 9 8 7 6 5 4 3 2 1

For every woman who has desired a mentor.
When you have no one to walk with through the
difficult places in life, the words of those
who have traveled those same paths become
gold to help you follow the yellow brick road
and lead you to a safe place.
It is true there is nothing new under the sun.
What happens now has happened before, and
others have learned the lesson you're about to learn.
Listen well and take their advice.
Perhaps you can avoid some needless trials.
That is wisdom that leads to a life well lived.

Acknowledgments

To my Harvest House family and all those who make my books come alive. Thank you for being there all these years and continuing to encourage, support, and inspire me. Words cannot express my love and appreciation of you, my very special family.

To the women who have mentored me and been faithful sisters/ friends over the years. Your words of wisdom and sometimes hard advice have kept me off many a treacherous path. Your lives and stories have been beacons for me. You've been amazing examples of what life looks like when done God's way. Thank you for tackling me to the floor when I wanted to fight your counsel…for weeping with me and for me…for just holding me in silence. Thank you for listening and praying passionately when I was rendered speechless. You are my secret wealth and strength. I love you from the bottom of my heart. Thank you for being the constants in my life. Some of you are new in my life. You are my silver quickly turning to gold. Some of you are long in my life—definitely gold turning to platinum:

Denise Mitchell
Philomena "Bunny" Wilson
Terri McFaddin
Brenda Blonski
Michelle Taylor Sanders
Theresa Hayden Powell
Sheila Frazier
Charlotte Kroot
Karen McDonald

Terri Earls
Nana Addo
Nancy Hanna
Stacy Speller
Joyce Hansen
Anita Erskine
Shaneen Clarke
Adrianna Zamot

Contents

Faith Loves Company. 7

1. The Price of Entitlement. 11
   Eve

2. The Benefits of Submission 21
   Sarah

3. The Other Side of Being the "Other Woman" 29
   Hagar

4. The Power of the Past. 37
   Lot's wife

5. Making Things Happen. 45
   Lot's daughters

6. The Importance of Destiny. 53
   Rebekah

7. When Love Isn't Enough. 61
   Rachel

8. The Fight You Can't Win. 69
   Leah

9. A Mother's Influence 77
   Jochebed

10. How to Deal with Haters 83
    The Cushite

11. How to Work with Men. 89
    Deborah

12. How to Win a Battle 97
    Jael

13. The Dangers of Indulgence 103
    Samson's mother

14. How to Change Your Life 111
    Rahab

15. The Power of Connections 117
    Ruth

16. What Every Woman Needs to Know 123
    Delilah

17. Timing Is Everything 131
    Hannah

18. The Difference a Right Response Makes 137
    Vashti

19. How to Make Your Man Your Hero 143
    Esther

20. How to Live with a Fool 151
    Abigail

21. How to Avoid Relationship Regrets 157
    Michal

22. The Trouble with Secrets 163
    Bathsheba

23. When the Unthinkable Happens 171
    Tamar

24. Finding Your Balance 177
    The Proverbs 31 woman

25. How to Grasp the Impossible 183
    Mary, Jesus' mother

26. Breaking the Negative Cycle 189
    The Samaritan woman at the well

27. When Your Faith Falters 195
    Martha and Mary

28. Leaving a Lasting Legacy 203
    Tabitha (Dorcas)

Notes 209

Faith Loves Company

Through the years many Bible stories have struck me as mini adventures that I've seen mirrored in my own life. Okay, to be quite honest, a few of them had me scratching my head in wonder. Perhaps that's when it struck me that God was sharing these stories with me so that I would find myself in His story of people who learned about Him—His love for them and His power to work out difficult circumstances.

Through the Bible, God gives you and me intimate glimpses into the very private lives of the men and women He chose to reveal Himself to. And I must say their stories have left me begging for more. I'm a bit nosy and creative by nature, so images swirl in my mind as the stories unfold—especially the ones involving women from every walk of life who encountered God and were stretched beyond their resources or what they dared to believe. I wonder how they weathered the storms. How they processed their trials. How they felt when their faith was at the breaking point.

I want to know their very real emotions in the midst of circumstances that, in many cases, should have sent them over the edge. I can so relate because they're kind of like some of the situations I've found myself in. I imagine you've been through difficult times like that too. What did these women of Bible times learn? What was the point of the trials God allowed them to go through? What can we learn from them? What hope can we gain from their lives that will help us in ours?

People say hindsight is better than no sight at all. Perhaps that's true. I believe we often have the choice to learn by wisdom or by tribulation. Small wonder the book of Proverbs admonishes us to get an understanding in all our getting. Through the many proverbs, God tells us that getting an understanding and utilizing His knowledge and wisdom in our lives will bring the things we truly desire in the end with lasting blessings that will make us rich and add no sorrow. The wealth gained from lessons well learned can save us from making costly mistakes.

The more I pondered the lives of my sister friends in Scripture, the more I wanted to dig in and glean treasures from their trials and find the diamonds among the tears they cried. Although it was a different era, the underlying challenges in the trials they faced are no different than many of the ones you and I encounter. Everything from dealing with in-law drama to championing a husband whose dreams seem farfetched. Struggling with being the "other" woman or knowing how to recognize Mr. Right. Does any of this sound familiar? Or how about knowing someone whose lies put your life or livelihood at risk? Or dealing with the pain of being a widow, the challenges of being a leader in a male-dominated business sector, or being married to a powerful man whose faith doesn't match your own?

I'm sure that if you and I sat down with the women in the Bible, they would give us an earful! Through their various experiences I believe we can discover the valuable reasons and lessons in the struggles they wrestled with and the ones we face. And better yet, I believe they offer us hope in our everyday challenges and even in seemingly impossible circumstances.

It's been said that misery loves company, but I think faith does too! And seeing that we are surrounded by such a great cloud of witnesses who have walked before us on the trails we're now following, we can be assured we'll also make it because they did. I'm confident that among the many gems of wisdom we can glean from them, we'll also discover two constant and comforting themes woven into the fabric of every story they share: God is always present and God is always faithful.

So grab a cup of tea and join me in reading these personal letters from amazing women of the Bible. Let's celebrate the sisterhood of overcoming together as we discover the wisdom and timeless advice they offer.

I can't wait to get started!

1

The Price of Entitlement

My dear sister,

I may be the last person you want to hear from. You might even blame me for all your troubles—or at least have done so at some juncture in your life. That's the price I have to pay for my actions. Little did I know how far-reaching that seemingly harmless little snack in the Garden of Eden would be. But, please, hear me out. I'm praying for one thing right now—that you allow me to share my story with you. Hopefully the lessons I've learned will help you not repeat the same mistakes I've made.

Suffice it to say, you'll never be responsible for the sins of the world. That notoriety is my husband's and my cross to bear. Unfortunately, that's a lesson Adam and I learned far too late to change, so I now pass on to you the wisdom we learned from it. If you remember nothing else, remember this: *Every choice you make will affect someone other than yourself.* And the scope won't be known until after the deed has been done. I regret the way I learned this. I now know that an *informed choice* is always better than one done on impulse or in ignorance.

But let me start from the beginning to help you understand what took place that fateful day in the garden. Hopefully you will forgive me through the grace and forgiveness God gives. It's so easy to fall even when there is no reason to.

I found him sleeping—my husband, that is. He was so beautiful. So perfect. I held my breath as God stirred him awake to behold me for the first time. I was his "help meet," his "helper."[1] The one who would help him complete the assignments our Creator had given him. I'd been crafted from his rib to meet his every need save one—God's place. Even though I was made from his rib, I didn't see a scar on Adam's side. In his nakedness he was a wonder to behold. I felt no shame standing before him. I was him, and he was me. We were one. Made from and for one another. Together we were complete. Perfect complements to each other. Filling one another's spaces and, thus, making us a finished picture of God's reflection.

It seemed that all of creation held its breath to see what Adam's response to me would be. As God nudged me toward him, I saw the light of understanding in Adam's eyes. He knew! I knew too. He let out a breath and called me "woman." He gripped his side as if perceiving where I'd come from while he extended his other hand to me. He announced, "This is now bone of my bones and flesh of my flesh."[2] Yes, indeed I was. For even though we were meeting for the first time, I felt like we'd been together for an eternity already. He was so familiar. We knew each other deeply and instinctively. I could feel his soul. He was mine, and I was his. There was no question.

Adam was the perfect companion. We shared a pure love free of inhibition. We lived in a perfect world that produced food without any effort on our part. No lack, no need. Peace reigned. Truly every good and perfect gift comes from God! I wanted for nothing. I had God. I had Adam. That was enough.

Well…until I allowed myself to be convinced otherwise. "What more could you possibly want?" you wonder. In hindsight I can only say I don't really know. Perhaps there was something inside of me that couldn't bear so much perfection. I'd never encountered such a creature as I did that terrible day in the garden. I'd never heard such thoughts that he shared. There was nothing to compare it to really. God had given me access to Him and all that He'd created, which was enough…and yet I was beguiled…bewitched…bewildered…by this "outside" voice.

The serpent's voice was sweet and alluring as he told me there was more to know than what God had presented. The intriguing creature suggested God was holding out on me to remain superior with His greater knowledge. That there were secret delights beyond what I'd been privy to…things that God knew but I did not.

Perhaps this is humanity's deepest flaw. The desire for the forbidden. The belief that taking hold of it will validate us and add to who we are. This "out of reach" illusion creating a gnawing dissatisfaction for what has been freely given while robbing our spirits of gratefulness and causing us to despise the blessings of God.

Yes, the serpent beguiled me. Perhaps he'd watched me looking at that tree. It had gotten my attention long before I met the creature and discussed it. Take it from me, sin never just happens. It starts in the mind and heart and grows until it can no longer be ignored, its cravings growing more and more insistent. I admit I'd studied this special tree. Curiosity lured me closer and closer to it, inch by inch until I met the serpent there that fateful afternoon. He stoked the fire of my internal conversation about that tree. The one tree God told Adam and me not to eat from. I couldn't see any hint or evidence that it would cause harm.

Perhaps the temptation was more about me and less about the serpent than I realized. That's the conclusion I came to as I reviewed the events long after they'd transpired. Yes, there is something about the forbidden that makes it all the more desirable. The creature played on my desire. He got me to focus on the one thing that seemed beyond my reach, though it actually was not. It was only a choice away. He planted seeds of entitlement and deep resentment in my heart, and he convinced me that I should have what I wanted.

Why would God not choose this one thing for me? It seemed harmless enough. As a matter of fact, the tree was beautiful to look upon. The serpent said the fruit of it was sweet, and my flesh was stirred with desire for it. The thought of acquiring it appealed to my pride and my sense of self-empowerment. After all, wasn't this my life? Shouldn't I do as I pleased? Why should a decision of personal taste be made for me by someone else? If I wanted it, I should have it! I cast down the idea that perhaps God knew what was best for me. That if I really needed it, He would not have withheld this particular fruit from me. The serpent was right. I owed it to myself to partake if I wished. My thoughts didn't take long to manifest in actions…actions I now regret deeply.

You see, the serpent made me feel so special. I was his only focus. How could someone who harbored such deep concern for my happiness have an agenda aimed at my destruction? The thought never occurred to me. I now know he was a snare planting himself between my desire and my destiny. I allowed him to fan the flames of suspicion against God. What did God have against me? Why was He denying me something I wanted that looked so delicious? This fruit was a little thing. It couldn't be that big a deal.

Adam was nearby and said nothing. And, admittedly, I can't say that if he had reminded me not to eat the fruit I would have listened. The flame of desire burning in my heart was fanned by my questions about why God would put such a desirable fruit under our noses and then say, *Look but don't taste.* It seemed so unfair, even cruel. This was my undoing. Peace and joy left me, and I was aflame with discontent. And so I ate it. I ate the fruit God said not to partake of.

And not only did I eat it, but I gave it to my husband, and he also ate some. We were partners in sin. Not understanding the depth of our offense, we stood before one another and searched each other's faces to see if death would come. It didn't…but something else happened.

My perfect husband was suddenly severely flawed. I wondered if I were flawed too and, if I was, would he notice my imperfection. He was looking at me strangely. No longer feeling secure and beautiful, I drew back in shame, even as he did the same. Scrambling behind the nearest bushes, we tried to cover ourselves.

And then we heard Him. God was coming! Another new emotion burst inside of me. Fear. Fear partnered with shame, and I was glad I was hiding.

Can you believe it? I shake my head in sorrow even now at the memory. How could I think I could hide from God? I knew I'd have to face Him eventually, but how could I? Though the depth of my sin wasn't clear to me because it was a new experience, I knew something was very wrong. The joy of anticipation I usually felt when God visited Adam and me in the garden was gone. My peace was gone. Though I tried to portray normalcy as I crept from my hiding place, the tension in the air was palpable.

Adam spoke first. He explained that we'd hidden because we were naked. *Why had that never bothered me before?* I wondered even as I heard God's gentle voice ask a question I didn't want to answer: "Who told you that you were naked? Did you eat fruit from the tree from which I commanded you not to eat?"[3]

To my dismay, I heard Adam blame me for his actions. He didn't want to own his part in this situation! I hadn't *forced* him to eat the fruit. He willingly took it and ate it. At least I had the excuse of being deceived by the serpent. It was clear I'd lost my head in that moment with the serpent. And my own husband hadn't tried to stop me or correct me. He'd been in the garden longer than I, so he should have known better. He knew God intimately deeper. He knew all they'd spoken about before I arrived. And now Adam was saying this was my fault? How could he?

And then God spoke to me, asking me the same question. I knew He already knew the answer. I struggled to meet His gaze as I replied, "The serpent deceived me, and I ate."[4]

I could feel the weight of God's disappointment resting on me like a heavy cloak, weighing down my heart and soul. As He decreed what our choice was going to cost us, the gravity of the situation hit me. Finally. That seemingly small and personal choice had cost us—and the world—a great price. Our choice didn't affect just us. It rocked and robbed all of creation. Gone was the peace that came from living surrendered to God. My choice had robbed me of the very thing I wanted. I'd chosen an illusion. A fantasy of something I thought I was entitled to.

God had known all along that the fruit of that tree would ultimately harm me and cost me what I couldn't pay. That's why He told Adam and me not to eat it. The initial sweetness of the fruit was now bitter. And bitterness was growing within me too. I couldn't get rid of it. Even when God made the first sacrifice, tenderly clothing us with the skins of animals, I chafed beneath what I was now forced to wear because of what I'd done. As God led us from the garden, I longed for the favor and peace I once knew there. I'd never imagined being separated from God, and I couldn't comprehend what that would mean.

In the days to come, as Adam and I experienced work for the first time, the cost of our sin continued to mount. The stresses we'd never encountered when we lived within the safe confines of God's will were a constant reminder of what we had to admit was our own undoing. The earth no longer yielded food as it once did. Adam struggled to provide for us. Our relationship also suffered. The bliss we once had gave way to misunderstandings and strife. His love never seemed to be enough anymore. I felt an abyss within that I couldn't fill. And when I became pregnant, the joy of having a baby was temporarily clouded by the almost unbearable pain of childbirth.

If only I'd known what that choice in the garden would cause! I would have run from the serpent! But now it was too late. The deed was done. My choice couldn't be reversed by my hand. The consequences have left me sorrowing and longing for what once was.

The good news, however, is that it's not too late for you. Every day you make choices—to listen to the voice of God or to hear the voice of the serpent. To follow the voice of the Holy Spirit or to follow the voice of your flesh. To heed the direction of God's will or to go along with your own longings. I now know why God desires obedience over sacrifice. It's far easier to obey than to learn lessons the hard way and pay such a great cost. Oh how God longs to save you from yourself and your bad decisions. I see how you chafe beneath His wisdom and directions like a spoiled child who doubts the wisdom of her parents. And yet God alone knows what will truly fulfill you.

There are millions of questions I could ask. Why didn't Adam intervene and stop me from listening to the serpent? Why did Adam also eat the forbidden fruit? Why didn't God explain more fully why we shouldn't eat the fruit of that tree? Why did He allow the serpent in the garden in the first place? But all of that is moot now. The bottom line is that the serpent and his beguiling revealed what was already within me. I was drawn away from God by my own desires, my own lust. I didn't allow the goodness of God to be enough to keep me from falling.

My actions revealed how badly I need God to give me wisdom and the will to obey Him. It also reveals my allergy to perfection. It's as if because I'm made from dust, I seek to return to it. I think you must experience the same thing as part of humankind. Even though God invites everyone into His garden, we are frightened and overwhelmed because it magnifies all that we are not, causing us to retreat to a more familiar part of our nature—that which is apart from God.

Though we were made from dust, God breathed His life into us. We are more spirit than flesh. Our spiritual state will always be subject to physical repercussions while we're here on earth. My friend, believe me in this. I am talking to you not only has a sister, but as the "mother of all the living."[5] This is one thing that did not change as a consequence of sin. My purpose remained in spite of my sin. God's agenda was greater than my own.

That being said, you know my genes lie resident in you. You will have the same inclinations. I noticed this in my first two children. I grieve over the fact that my son Cain murdered his brother Abel. In a similar way, I'm aware that I'm guilty of bringing death to humanity both spiritually and physically because pleasing God wasn't my first desire.

So, girlfriend, I hope that you'll heed my advice and avoid some of the mistakes I made. I'm glad I have the opportunity to share with you because that eases the pain of the consequences for my sin. I'm glad I get to tell you what I've learned. God gave me everything pertaining to life and godliness, but I pressed past His provision because I believed a lie.

Don't believe the hype anyone tells you about being your own person, about being the master of your own ship. Don't believe the master tempter. You don't owe yourself anything. What you deserve you really don't want. I'm telling you this from experience.

I encourage you to stay grateful for God's blessings. Resist invitations that appeal to the spirit of entitlement within you. Embrace God's choices for you, and avoid the things He says no to. His instructions lead to abundant life, love, joy, and peace when you trust Him through His Son, Jesus Christ. God's choices for you will bear more fruit than you'll ever be able to harvest apart from Him.

And whatever you do, don't entertain serpents! They are beautiful but deadly.

I remain your sister in timely surrender,

Eve

Woman to Woman

God created us to reflect His presence and goodness by giving us entré to kingdom living. What is kingdom living? Righteousness, peace, and joy in the Holy Ghost. This is a place of surrender where we cease from striving against God's instructions and revel in His provision of every good and perfect gift. The word "Eden" means "pleasure." It's true that God longs for us to live lives filled with pleasure! He wishes for us to be successful and be in good health even as our souls prosper in Him. He's given us all things. But in the midst of this abundance, He withholds what He knows will destroy us. But He's given us the ability and freedom to choose. So if we press past Him because we're urged on by suspicions that He is a cosmic killjoy or is holding something good back, we set ourselves up for painful regrets that have lasting effects on ourselves and countless others we touch.

As Eve noted, the damage of sin is never to just one person. Others are affected because we're bound together as a body under the headship of our God. And He is a loving God who longs for us to stop living lives of disarray and return to His perfect order and plan.

The garden of living in God's will is a beautiful place of favor and provision, a place without striving where we are free to dwell as long as we surrender to Him. It's a place where fruit abounds and is available, not by our physical might or our mental power, but by God's Holy Spirit. When we yield to His instructions, we get to partake of that delicious fruit. When we resist His leading, we forfeit the pleasure of an abundant harvest. We find ourselves striving to produce what we can in our own strength. But when we're in sync with God and in His will, we produce more fruit without the stress.

The fruit of our hands and the relationships we're in can grow bitter in the midst of our do-it-yourself works. We need to resist the temptation to drown out the voice of God with our own desires and demands. Guard against the spirit of entitlement that tries to make you discontent with God's blessings. That spirit is the beginning of dangerous distractions that can lead to choices that will destroy the joy and peace you seek.

Above all, be aware that God created a void inside each one of us that only He can fill. The beguiler would lead you to believe that if you could only have this or that your joy would be complete. This is a lie that will rob you of the very fulfillment you desire and alter your garden experience with God every time.

God asked Adam, "Who told you that you were naked?" What a loaded question! In God's presence you will always have exactly what you need. Nothing less…and so much more.

Your Hope

Whatever your regrets, know this: *Not one of your experiences in life is wasted.* God uses all your mistakes and failings to reveal a greater picture of Himself and the redemption He so generously offers. Though He breaks you, He will also bind your wounds so you will become stronger than ever in Him. And yes, you will become even wiser. It is your Father in heaven's good pleasure to give you His kingdom. He wants you to experience righteousness, peace, and joy through the Holy Ghost—all the things that are conducive to leading rich and fruitful lives filled with more than you can imagine. Is it possible for your dreams to come true right here on earth? Absolutely! But only as you learn to rejoice within the safe confines of the garden God provides.

Every temptation in life is not a personal attack, but it is a direct sabotage of your God-given destiny by the enemy of your soul. As you see the larger picture of God's kingdom agenda being worked out in your life, you'll make choices based on an agenda that reaches beyond your earthly perceptions to God's heavenly vision. As His will becomes your mission statement, your decisions will be transformed to align with His heart. And that will take you to another level of living the life you hope for.

> *Be all the more diligent to confirm your calling and election, for if you practice these qualities you will never fall* (2 Peter 1:10 ESV).

Your Truth

❧ Do you think God is withholding something from you? If yes, what?

❧ How can this train of thought become an unhealthy distraction?

❧ What desires do you need to surrender to remain submitted to God's will for your life?

2

The Benefits of Submission

My dear sister,

I have so much to tell you! Where do I begin? Even now I'm gathering my memories and processing my thoughts about the many things that occurred in my life. Suffice it to say, most of it culminates in one divine principle that was hard to see at the time but, in hindsight, is quite clear. But let me start at the beginning.

My name is Sarai, and my husband's name is Abram.[1] Abe—that's what I call him—is a good man, and we had a good life. For a long time we lived among our extended family. I felt safe. Yes, "safe" is a good word for it. Familiarity bred comfort, leaving no room for surprises or the need to exercise a significant amount of faith as each day blended into the next.

Then one day Abe made the announcement that we were moving. "Moving where?" I asked. His answer was more shocking than his initial statement. "I don't know. God will let me know when we get to where we're supposed to go. He even promised me that our family will become a great nation!"

What is a wife supposed to do when her husband says something like that? Was I supposed to follow blindly without having any input? A thousand rejections and questions swirled in my head, but I kept silent. I chose to follow my husband. He'd always exhibited strength and wisdom, so there was no reason to doubt him now. Though I had my apprehensions about wandering into the unknown, to be separated from him and left behind wasn't an option I wanted to consider. If this was his purpose, his destiny, I wanted to be part of it. I believed in God and trusted Abram's faith in Him. If my Abe said God gave him a vision, I would support it despite my fears.

Abram must have had some reservations about this journey too because he invited his nephew Lot to accompany us. So we packed up and off we went. It seemed reasonable enough at first to travel with family, but now I wonder how different the journey would have been if we hadn't taken Lot along, especially in light of all the trouble he caused. It's surprising what being out of our comfort zones reveals about people—the negatives as well as the positives. We found out what Lot's weaknesses were—his fears, his greed, what he really thought about God, what he felt entitled to. Trust me, it was an eye-opening experience. Actually, it wasn't just about Lot either. I learned a lot about my husband too.

Abram, the man who heard from God that we should set off on this nameless journey with no specific place in mind and did so. Abram, the man who heard a specific promise from God and believed it. This same man was overcome by fear when we passed through the land of Egypt. Worried that I would be kidnapped and he would be killed because I was considered beautiful, he instructed me to tell people I was his sister.[2] Now this was partially true. I was Abe's stepsister.[3] But let's face it, I wasn't functioning in the capacity of a sister in my husband's life. Still, I silently did as he asked.

In Egypt people commented on my beauty, and I was promptly taken to the Pharaoh to live at his palace. I was beside myself not knowing how we were going to get out of this fix. While Abe enjoyed the benefit of receiving gifts as my dowry, I had to figure out how to stay out of the bed and heart of the Pharaoh of Egypt!

Imagine my horror when the Pharaoh and all his staff were assaulted by a terrible disease! It rendered Pharaoh too ill to touch me. I was the only person not affected in the entire court, so they viewed me with suspicion and interest. They questioned my identity. That was when the truth came out that I was, in fact, Abram's wife. The Pharaoh was upset and couldn't remove me from his court fast enough. He summoned Abram and then sent us packing laden down with all Abram had received—livestock, gold, and silver.

We definitely left richer than we came, but my wonderment wasn't about these things. It was about how God had protected me and kept me safe. To this day as I consider the alternatives, I shudder. Truly He was my shield when my husband couldn't protect me.

Now, you might be thinking that I'm a weak woman because I went along with Abe's decisions quietly. Nothing could be further from the truth! Contrary to the general belief that women in my era did everything we were told and never had anything to say, we were very strong because we had to be. I like to think I chose my battles carefully. The Egyptian terrain was unknown, so what better time to trust my husband? Abe had never steered me wrong before. And I trusted his relationship with God. Abe had wisdom too, but he was still just a man and limited by what he knew as much as what he didn't know.

I'd never seen the fearful side of my husband, and it gave me pause. I knew this wasn't the time to add pressure by questioning his instructions. He needed focus and clarity of thought to know how to navigate through this unknown land and people. He wanted to protect his family the best way he knew how, and I honored that. (I wished he'd come up with a better option though.)

In the end, God came through for us. And this happened not just once but twice! Ha! The second time was in the land called Gerar with its king, Abimelek. God closed up every womb in the household. After I was released, my husband had to pray for God to reopen them.[4] But I'm getting ahead of myself.

Children. This was my greatest difficulty. It broke my heart that I hadn't borne children. I wondered why God would promise Abram children and then not deliver. Year after year I waited expectantly...and then I gave up. I was too old. I gave my maid to Abe. How else was he going to become the father of many nations? I longed for Abe to experience the joy of being a father. This was a gift I couldn't give him, but perhaps…just perhaps…God meant to deliver the promise another way. So why should I insist Abe become the father of many nations through me? He acquiesced and, sure enough, Hagar became pregnant. And then she became insolent, arrogant, and disrespectful toward me!

I regretted my decision to use Hagar that way, and the problems that resulted were great. Suffice it to say that I never gave my husband to another woman again. I'd abdicated my position because I didn't trust God, and I suffered for it.

Eleven years later, God again spoke to Abram and repeated His promise to make Abe the father of many nations. At that time God changed Abram's name to Abraham, and He changed my name to Sarah.[5]

One night some strangers showed up. I left them to their business with Abe but stayed close enough to hear their conversation. They were talking about me having a child! Before I knew it, a laugh escaped my lips. When they called me on it, I denied it—but they knew I wasn't telling the truth. I did feel the promise they gave was some sort of cruel joke. I was now ninety years old for God's sake! And that is exactly right. It was for *God's sake* that Abe and I dared to believe again. And then I conceived our beloved Isaac.

Oh, the stories I could tell about those days. I could go on and on, sharing how Abram had to rescue Lot. The trouble between my son and his stepbrother, Ishmael. Asking Abe to send Hagar and Ishmael away. And the story he told me—only after he'd done it—about almost sacrificing the son we'd waited so long for. I don't think I would have let either of them out of the house if I'd known Abe's intention.

But then again, perhaps I would have because I learned through all our adventures that I shouldn't put my trust solely in my husband. No, I should put my trust totally in God. This is the secret of biblical submission. At the end of the day, God's direction led us to our next home. God protected me in the courts of a Pharaoh and a king. God gave us great wealth in a strange land. And God made Abraham's seed come to life in my body to produce what He'd promised—our beloved son Isaac. Yes, God and God alone was in charge! We were His children following His instructions as He brought His elaborate and, at times, seemingly impossible plan to pass.

I do want you to know that my husband never disappointed me. Even though he loved God and was a good man, Abraham was a mere mortal. He was human. Flawed. Imperfect. Incapable of doing the impossible. Yet he was yielded to the One who was everything he was not. I know some people wonder why I chose to submit to my husband—packing up to move to who knew where, saying Abe was my brother, seeing him struggle with Lot. But I knew I was ultimately submitting to God. This was where faith came in. I believed that no matter what my husband did, God was watching over us. Abram had that kind of faith. Through watching his faith in action, my own faith grew.

It is my prayer that whether you're married or not, you'll realize that putting your trust in human promises and exploits is disastrous. Expecting divinity from humanity will always disappoint. Instead, I pray that you will arrive at the simple-but-powerful faith of trusting the only One who can deliver completely—God. The God of Abraham…my God…your God.

Understanding the power of submission,

Sarah

Woman to Woman

In today's world where the battle of the sexes pits men against women and brings our rebellious selves to the forefront, the debate on submission rages on. The quest for equality often derails the importance of being a team player in our significant relationships. As each person jockeys for power, ground gets lost in the game of life. For us to once again achieve what we've lost, we must be willing to see the power and beauty in submission. We must realize that ultimately we're submitting to God. He is the One who administers the affairs of our lives. He is able to watch over whatever is committed to Him and work things out to our good.

As Sarah submitted to requests that at the time didn't make sense or seem to be the best choice, God covered her when Abraham could not. Sarah chose to allow her husband to lead her to places unknown. She couldn't afford to have all her trust placed in a fallible human though. Her trust was in Someone greater than her husband or herself—God. This faith in Him applied to all areas of her life. She trusted God to watch over them and guide them. She trusted God to keep her family in His sight.

And even though her faith wavered from time to time, she had to trust God when it came to her desire to bear children…to provide an heir for Abraham…to believe God's promise that her husband would be the father of many nations. Yes, the thought of this happening in her nineties made her laugh. It made Abraham laugh too. It was such an incredible notion. But God proved Himself even though Sarah took matters into her own hands to bring about His promise. Yes, she got the results she'd hoped for…along with disastrous consequences. Yet despite her humanity and limited faith, God honored His word to Abraham, and Sarah bore a son.

God was active in Sarah's life when she submitted to her husband by faith as unto the Lord. As we remain in the right position in our relationships, God fills the gap left by humans and brings all His promises to pass in our lives. He is a God who never disappoints!

Your Hope

No, it is not in mere men that we trust. Ultimately our faith must be placed in God. And being submissive is not about becoming a doormat. Neither is submission a passive posture. In fact, submission is an *active decision* to put yourself in a position to be blessed by God. Submission is being a team player, whether in your marriage, in your job, or in the church. It's allowing someone else to lead at critical moments to that person's benefit and your own. In marriage it is the highest form of cooperation. It is proof of your trust in God. When you're married, submitting to your husband empowers him to take his rightful positions in the family—leader, provider, and protector.

Now, life does happen. Your husband may not always be able to fulfill one of those roles at particular times or seasons of his life. This doesn't lessen who he is or what his role is in the eyes of God. When your mate is struggling, take the opportunity to strengthen your relationship by building him up and trusting God to fill in the gaps.

Submission empowers you as a couple to move in mutual cooperation, taking one another's weaknesses and strengths into consideration, so that life is balanced between you accordingly. What this looks like will vary from couple to couple. We need to never force our mates into a stereotype or mold that doesn't fit them. Each of us has been given specific gifts, and not all of us have the same strengths. Based on this knowledge, you and your mate will determine how your household will run. For instance, you may be better with money than your husband, so the area of finance may be delegated to you. He may be better at negotiating, so making large purchases may fall within his area of responsibility.

The conclusive word on submission in the Word of God is that *we are called to submit to each other*. This means no one is above or below another. Instead, we're matched strength for strength in the spirit of respecting, complementing, and honoring one another. No one is less than the other. Woman was created to be a "help meet" for man; therefore, she was created for a position of strength.

Contrary to modern belief, "submission" isn't a dirty word and doesn't call for subservience. To believe that it is those things is to fall into the trap the enemy has set for all human relationships. The devil wants to sow discord and disharmony. He wants us to be in conflict. But in God's creation, whether it be in romance or employment, there must be order for ventures to be successful. There must be an acknowledgment of roles and positions. Even in heaven there is a hierarchy. So we need to be clear on our position and make no comparisons because we submit in God's name so all praise and honor goes to Him.

When we seek power for ourselves, strife and evil wiggle into our relationships. But as we walk in the best interest of one another, we submit to one another in a way that creates harmony and synergy. Love and good fruit grow in this environment of trust and faith. As we see the power of submission at work in our lives, we're able to embrace it as a friend. Make it the silent partner in your relationships, and let it champion you to live the best life possible.

Your Truth

✤ What has made the concept of "submission" hard for you to embrace?

✤ What is your greatest fear when it comes to submitting?

✤ What happens in your relationships when you submit?

3

The Other Side of Being the "Other Woman"

My dear sister,

I hang my head as I write this because I'm "the other woman." It wasn't my intention. I wonder if it ever is when women find themselves in this position. I can only speak for myself...

I was my mistress Sarai's primary servant. That is until the day she gave me to her husband and it became apparent I'd conceived. Yes, it's quite a story.

Sarai's husband, Abram, had heard from God that he was to move away from Harran.[1] So we packed up and left. I'd heard the rumors that God had also promised Abram an heir...and I heard it from my mistress too. But years went by with no child. I saw and felt Sarai's frustration as time continued on and she remained barren. It changed her. She became sharper and more demanding. Impatient and unhappy. There were glimpses of her happier self, but the sadness lingered.

Abram felt it too. He seemed at a loss as to how to make it better for Sarai. Yes, he felt helpless. Helpless to make her happy. Helpless to give her the child she wanted. Helpless to encourage her with the faith he possessed. I could see him withdrawing from the lethal poison of her tongue. I watched his gaze focus on Sarai and then wander, perhaps when he was remembering happier times when the air wasn't filled with the tension of hope deferred.

Then one day Sarai told me I was going to sleep with her husband. I was shocked. After all, I was an Egyptian and a servant. I waited to see what would happen as Sarai talked with Abram. When she suggested it to him with the hope that I would give him the heir God had promised, perhaps his willingness was more to appease her than desire on his part for me.

I acquiesced even though I wasn't sure what the outcome would be. To be truthful, I had no choice because I was a servant. Sarai was my mistress. (I know I wouldn't give my husband to another woman so willingly, and yet I suppose desperation makes some women do strange things.)

It felt unnatural to yield my body to a man who wasn't in love with me or making promises to love me forever. But from that moment on my heart was stirred. I tried to keep my feelings at bay, reminding myself of my position, but as Abram's child grew inside me, I felt I deserved more than what I was given. After all, I was carrying Abram's offspring! I had to take advantage of the situation for me…as well as for the child that was coming. I hadn't missed the sorrow on Sarai's face when I announced my pregnancy. I had triumphed where she'd failed. Yes, I deserved to be Abram's wife. I had accomplished something Sarai could not. A little voice from deep within me said I was a better woman than she was…and a better wife for *him*. He should be *my* husband not hers.

Abram looked at me differently too. He was genuinely caring and gentle. And now with this bond between us, I found that I desired him. I found it harder and harder to serve Sarai. She had what I wanted—him. She had what I deserved. How could I serve someone I was superior to? I was carrying Abram's child. Precious cargo and an heir to all that he possessed!

Sarai knew it too. Her insecurity grew as my belly did. I felt the power of having bested her in an area she'd longed for the most. I admit

I lorded it over her. I couldn't help myself. I felt entitled to Abram. I had the right to demand more of his attention.

Abram's wife became even harder to serve as she felt her husband slipping away from her. But it was her choice...her decision! Perhaps she hadn't realized the full impact of what she'd done. At first I wasn't sorry. I was thrilled to be carrying Abram's heir. But gradually Sarai's bitterness increased, and I felt the brunt of her misery. She became impossible to please. And I no longer sought to make her comfortable. I meant to win this competition for Abram's heart.

One day I heard her complaining to Abram. *Typical,* I thought. Then I heard him telling her she could deal with me however she saw fit. I couldn't believe it! Sarai took it as a license to treat me even worse than before in an effort to, in her mind, "put me in my place." Finally I could take it no longer. I fled. I decided it would be better to die in the desert than be subject to her bitterness. But God sent an angel to me. In my undone state, I was so ashamed. I didn't feel worthy of His attention. Yet in spite of everything that had transpired, the angel was kind even though he told me I had to go back to Sarai. He instructed me to submit to my mistress's authority. In spite of the fact that I bore Abram's child, Sarai was still his wife and I must honor that. In God's eyes I had no right to claim Abram as my own. But God did say He would bless my child and increase my descendants. He even told me I was bearing a son and I was to name him Ishmael!

So I returned to Abram and Sarai. It was difficult to watch them as a couple, but I wouldn't disobey the God who had come to me in the desert. In fact, I had a special name for Him now. It translates as "The God who sees me." I still struggled with feeling rejected, and I had to tolerate Sarai, but I knew my place and I had God's promises to comfort me. I harbored those promises for the security of my child in my heart. I told Abram about my encounter in the desert, and he nodded his head in understanding. When our son was born, Abram was the one who announced that his name was Ishmael.

More than thirteen years passed, and Ishmael grew strong and spent a lot of time with his father, Abram. God came and spoke to Abram again and told him that *Sarai* would become pregnant and bear him a son. God even changed Abram's name to Abraham and Sarai's name to Sarah. And Abraham insisted that every male in the camp be circumcised, even Ishmael. I didn't know what to think about that.

And then one day it happened. Sarai…Sarah…conceived. Everything about her countenance changed. She was the Sarah Abraham had known in his younger days. Vibrant and beautiful, she now was "Sarah the mother of Abraham's heir." And life changed dramatically for Ishmael and me. My son felt his father's attention shift. Abraham still loved our son, and I tried to justify his neglect as excitement for his new baby. According to Abraham, Isaac was the promised child from God who would inherit all Abraham possessed. Ishmael didn't adjust very well to the reduced status, and who could blame him? Children don't understand the ways of adults.

My son was now a teenager who needed his father's attention more than ever. Not getting it, Ishmael teased Isaac to tears. This wasn't received well by Sarah. She said it was the final straw and announced we had to go. Abraham was powerless to go against the wishes of his wife and refused to stand up for Ishmael and me. Instead he just caved beneath the barrage of her vendetta against us. No matter how bound together we were because of our son, Sarah was his first priority. She was his *wife*. That was a bond I couldn't break. I was the outsider—and always would be no matter how much tenderness and care he showed toward Ishmael and me. Though my soul was tied to him because of what we'd shared, he was one with Sarah. He had to yield to the woman who was a part of him in covenant before God.

I could see the unspoken apology in his eyes as he sent us on our way. A thousand sorrows he could do nothing about. He had to acquiesce to his wife lest his prayers be hindered. Something inside me died with every step I took out of our home…out of Abraham's camp. As we traveled and our provisions depleted, I wept for my son and for myself. The cost of separation from Abraham was too great. I wished perpetually for simpler days before this man had been given to me only to be ripped away. I'd fooled myself thinking the situation would last forever, but it rarely does. Being the "other woman" seldom works, and even when the other woman "wins," it always comes at great cost.

The wages of anything outside God's divine order is death. Out in the hot desert sun with no water and no food left, I felt death coming to claim Ishmael and me. I couldn't bear to watch my son as the life ebbed from him. Starving and exhausted, I wept at his fate more than mine as I placed him under a tree and prayed his end would come swiftly.[2]

But again God surprised me. He sent His angel to speak words of comfort and wipe away my shame. He assured me He was a father to the fatherless as well as a provider for the forsaken. He reminded me of His promises that I'd considered too great to believe for someone of my status, but as you know, it all came to pass. He said again that my son would became a great nation in his own right. I can't say I'm proud of all Ishmael did, but I know firsthand that God is able to reconcile all things to Himself. He never gives up on anyone.

My friend, if I could leave you with one single thought it would be this: *Never fool yourself into thinking you have the right to take someone else's husband.* That is a war no woman can ever win. If you take him, you will live with shame and fear all your days. The shame you may be able to get past in time, but the fear will steal your peace. You'll be constantly reminded that stolen goods come with no guarantee of remaining yours. Loving someone else's husband brings death to your dream of "to have and to hold forever amen" a shining, gallant prince who will carry you away on his steed with sweet promises, forever loyalty, and the intent to love you as God intended. It puts an emptiness in your eyes that should not be there and robs you of the security God wants every wife to have. Yes, wait. Hold out for the husband who will be truly yours. The one God gives you.

Single-heartedly,

Hagar

Woman to Woman

So many women believe desperate times call for desperate measures. In light of the fact that there seems to be a man shortage, women have compromised themselves and gone against the grain of who God created them to be—one woman with one man. A "help meet." The missing part of his rib. Today articles and discussions on man-sharing abound as if that is a normal, perfectly acceptable part of life.

Do shifting times really call for shifting mores and ethics? I see no clause for this in the Word of God. God was cognizant of our nature and had Isaiah prophesy: "[In the last days, the 'day of the LORD,'] seven women will take hold of one man in that day, saying, 'We will eat our own bread and wear our own clothes, only let us be called by your name; take away our reproach'" (Isaiah 4:1 NASB). Nowhere is it recommended that a woman subject herself to a practice that can only end in disappointment and heartbreak. Neither is it recommended that a man take more than one wife. God said it would be problematic, and that's been proven time and time again. That situation always causes distraction, envy, jealousy, and plenty of strife.

Stories of "the other woman" are filled with loneliness and few rewards that seldom last. The adage, "If he was unfaithful with you, he will be unfaithful with someone else," resonates through the centuries. Though women compensate for what is lacking in their lives in different ways, settling for less than God's best should never be considered. Before setting out on a course of action, I pray you will *always* ponder God's design and His estimation of your worth. How much is your love, your body, your mind, and self-esteem worth to you? Do you value these things enough not to allow yourself or anyone else to diminish or destroy them? Any man who would put you in the position of "the other woman" doesn't see your true value or honor God's intention for you.

My friend, do not become the other woman. Do not allow another woman's husband to put you in that position. Make sure that loneliness never makes you settle for less than God's best for you. When you lack hope for your future keep the doors of vulnerability closed. Don't engage in conversations with married men about their troubles or their wives. This is a common access door to your heart. Know the trap and avoid it. Never believe that some love is better than no love at all or that this is all you deserve.

The power of making sure you're loved and cherished as you should be lies in your hands. You determine what you allow and disallow. Please don't let the urgency of time, your "biological clock," or the opinions of others make you settle for less than what you were created to have and to hold. Stolen water eventually turns bitter.

I encourage you to wait for God to unfold His plan for you. If He desires you to marry, wait for the man He will bring to you. The one you were specially crafted for...designed to complete and help equip him to be all God created him to be. This is God's design. This is what will bring you complete joy and fulfillment.

Your Hope

Perhaps you've made the mistake of settling for less love than you deserve. God waits to restore you, and He is well able to salvage all your wrongs. Needless to say, there are times when the consequences won't be erased by forgiveness because the evidences of our choices remain. Even then God will step in with a plan designed to remove the sting of your offense. He is faithful to minister to your damaged heart and provide fresh hope and provision for tomorrow. He remains a husband to the husbandless and a father to the fatherless.

Even as God met Hagar on the road when she ran away from the scorn of Sarah and the rejection of Abraham, God will meet you. He will instruct you on how to own your mistakes and restore you to continue on your journey with Him despite the pain and disappointment of your experience. His forgiveness is always available, along with His patient guidance on how to begin again. Only He can make sense out of your pain, help you embrace the lessons worth learning, and enable you to press past the condemnation the enemy is always so ready to throw your way. This is grace. This is God. This is the evidence of His mercy. He is well able to cover your unfaithfulness with His own faithfulness. He maintains faith in you even when you are faithless. At the end of the day He anticipated every mistake you would make and already put solutions in place. One fall does not stop His work in you or on your behalf! All He requires is your tender, repentant heart. He will take care of the rest.

Your Truth

❧ Have you been the "other woman"? What vulnerabilities left you open to that mistake?

❧ What lies about yourself did you accept that put you (or have kept you) in that position?

❧ How did you (or how can you) use God's truths to step back into His plan and will for your life?

❧ What did you learn from being in this situation? What decisions have you made in light of this?

❧ In what ways have you been tempted to consider being the "other woman"?

❧ What leaves you vulnerable and open to considering relationships that are less than what God intends for you?

❧ In what healthy ways can you deal with loneliness so you won't settle for temporary pleasure?

4

The Power of the Past

My dear sister,

My story is brief but I hope you'll take note because some lessons are best learned from what others go through rather than by personal experience. Even though my name isn't mentioned specifically, you've probably heard of me because I was married to Lot, Abraham's nephew.

When my husband came to tell me we were moving, I went along with the plan willingly. Of course I had my fears because we were going into unfamiliar territory with no specific destination in mind. I comforted myself with the fact that we were going with Abram and Sarai. Abram was strong and stable, and I trusted his judgment. If he said he'd heard from God about moving, then indeed he had and going with them could only lead to something good.[1]

And so we set out. The journey seemed endless, and I began to long for stability. So many adventures for a woman who longed for a simple family life! Each new drama took its toll. First there was a famine. That caused us to change the course of our journey and head to Egypt. Once there, the Pharaoh decided he fancied Sarai. Better she than me was all I could say. I couldn't believe Abram wanted Sarai to tell everyone she was his sister! I would never have gone along with that. Sarai is a different type of woman than I am. So when Pharaoh's people came to get her, off she went without any protest. It took a miracle from God to deliver her from that situation. The Pharaoh was so outdone when he learned Sarai was actually Abram's wife that he pleaded for us to leave. However, we didn't go empty-handed. He gave us a rich bounty of live-stock and goods to take with us. Our wealth doubled. That adventure bore great fruit.

Things were fine for a while, and I was encouraged as we continued to prosper. But, as always, with the increase came greed and dissension. When we finally found a place to settle, the land couldn't contain and feed all our herds. We'd worn out our welcome with Sarai and Abram anyway. The feuding had mounted to such a constant point of con-tention between our workers that it almost resulted in violence.[2] We decided to go our separate ways and give everyone room to grow on their own.

I would miss Sarai, but I knew it was for the best. We could no longer coexist without strained relations. The constant bickering was ruining the harmony that had existed when we'd first set out. Abram was gracious and allowed my husband to select the land he wanted. Lot chose the lush Jordan Valley, and off we went toward a fertile crescent that held great promise for a new home.

Once settled I was appalled at our neighbors. They were exceed-ingly wicked and wayward. But the land was rich in vegetation, there was plenty of water for our livestock and crops, and it was beautiful. I decided I could ignore most of the people, so I settled down on our own property. But it didn't turn out to be that simple. War broke out between the tribes all around us. As much as we tried to stay above the fray, we weren't able to escape the drama. Before we knew it, we were overrun and taken captive by the enemy. If it weren't for Abram com-ing to our rescue, I don't know what would have become of us!

Abram gathered his men and rescued our family and everyone else who had been taken captive. We even salvaged our possessions. Perhaps we should have moved after that, but I didn't have the energy. I couldn't take one more change. Lot and I settled back into our lives in Sodom. I continued to ignore the wickedness of the people around me and did my best to stay true to God. My daughters settled in as well, and I was happy when they both became engaged. The men weren't exactly who I would have chosen for them, but I was happy just the same that our family had finally grown roots and found stability.

Then two strangers came to town. Lot invited them home. He'd been at the city gates when they arrived and urged them to stay with us. Besides being hospitable, Lot knew the men's fate wouldn't be pleasant if he left them in the square. There were bands of men around who were known to attack and sexually assault travelers…well, *male* travelers, that is.[3]

Then the trouble began. The men of the city—young and old—surrounded our home and demanded we send out the travelers. Lot, acting in the tradition of our people, was compelled to protect them because they were our guests. He went outside to reason with the townsfolk. He tried to persuade them to not be wicked, even offering them our two daughters, but they grew more incensed. When they threatened to treat Lot worse than they planned to treat the travelers, our two guests opened the door and dragged Lot inside. As the mob attacked, a miracle occurred. The men outside were suddenly struck with blindness!

The visitors insisted that we get ready to leave town the next day. They said God had sent them to destroy the city. Once again I was being uprooted. As Lot went to get our future sons-in-law, I looked around my house. Though I knew it was best to heed the word of the Lord and leave, something inside of me couldn't let go. This was my home! All that I possessed was in this house. There was no time to pack. And what would I take? Too many things were too precious to leave behind.

Lot came home. Our daughters' fiancés didn't believe him, so they refused to come. Now it was morning, and I was being hurried away from all that was familiar. As our family was literally dragged up the hillside by the strangers, I felt a great sense of loss and regret. Where would we go from here? What would become of us? How could we begin again? Was this it?

I wondered if this was going to be the sum total of my life. Scampering up a hillside with nothing to show for all the years I'd invested in building the life I'd always dreamed of. The future looked bleak as I scanned the mountainside we were directed to run to. The past, for all of its issues, held more promise than the emptiness ahead. Couldn't our life in Sodom be salvaged? Was there need for such a drastic measure as leaving everything we'd owned and worked toward? Did we really have to leave all that was near and dear to us?

When the two visitors left us, they said, "Flee for your lives! Don't look back, and don't stop anywhere in the plain! Flee to the mountains or you will be swept away!"[4] But Lot was afraid for our safety, so he asked if we could settle in a nearby town. The angels agreed but told us to go quickly.

As we hurried off, I couldn't help taking one last look at the home I loved. It wasn't rebellion I felt when I glanced back for a final glimpse of our land. No, it was an overwhelming sadness...a longing for the security of what we'd created there. I'd grown used to our home and the peace and stability.

But the moment I turned my head I felt a strange sensation...an unpleasant paralysis. I couldn't move! I couldn't turn back and run with Lot and my daughters. I was stuck in my mind, my spirit, and my body. I'd disobeyed God's command through the angels, and my life ended on the mountainside.

I forfeited my future because of my insistence on clinging to that which God wanted me to let go of. Why couldn't I just let go and move on? I don't know. God had proven Himself trustworthy as we traveled with Abram and Sarai. I'd left all that was familiar to me in Harran, and Lot and I had found greater wealth and happiness by following God. Yet this time I hadn't mustered enough faith to move past the present and expect a better tomorrow. My lack of trust was my undoing. My story ended on that hillside.

Lot and my daughters moved on as I realized I'd robbed myself of the testimony of God's goodness. Of His power to restore. Of His desire to give more than I could imagine if I'd only let go.

Now I'm usually remembered as the woman who looked back and turned into a pillar of salt.[5] Not exactly the legacy I had in mind. I missed the tomorrows God had planned for me. I missed being with my husband and my daughters. But most of all I disappointed God. I'm sure He had more in mind for my life.

I'm glad God's given me this chance to share my story with you. Just as I was sure He had more in store for me, I know He has more in store for your life. If I impart nothing else, *I urge you to let go of what you're clinging to. Let go of anything that keeps you from following God* no matter how painful releasing it may be. God has something better ahead for you! Don't let the desire to keep what you have rob you of a glorious future. You will *always* gain more by obeying God. Give the things near and dear to you to God and trust Him to provide for you and give you His joy and peace. Walk before Him with open hands.

Oh, my sister, I wish I'd never looked back. I wish I had spread my arms and run into the wind expecting miracles greater than what I'd already seen. I leave you with this simple truth: *Your tomorrows will always hold greater promise.* Dare to expect it, and let nothing hold you back from receiving it!

Hoping you're looking forward,

Lot's wife

Woman to Woman

Lot's wife went through a lot (pardon the pun). She moved away from the familiar and lived a nomadic life. A natural disaster (famine) caused them an extended detour and scary circumstances (remember Sarai's time in both Pharaoh and a king's palaces?). Then Lot and his wife settled in a beautiful land but discovered the people were wicked and filled with lust. A war among the local tribes led to Lot and his family being captured and taken to what would surely be a life of slavery. What joy they must have felt when Abram rescued them! Then, after resettling in their home, two angels came and Lot was almost assaulted while defending them. Then the angels told them their land was going to be destroyed by God so they'd better run for their lives. *Whew!* That is a lot!

Even though we may not go through everything Lot and his family did, we all have our own list of regrets and disappointments that we can either learn from or be held captive by. The choice is ours. Do we sift through the remains to find the diamonds? Or do we allow the past to chain us to the spot and rob us of better tomorrows? If only we would choose to believe that every rejection is really God protecting us from something we can't see. That every disappointment is a mere detour to turn us in the direction where greater blessing awaits. Then our lives would become a series of stepping-stones that take us from glory to glory. This is God's design for the setbacks in life. But we must trust that God is able to make everything beautiful in time. To abdicate our power to move forward and, instead, sit down on the business of life robs us of what God has in store for us.

Unforgiveness, bitterness, and unresolved disappointment is quicksand. It sucks us in and roots us to the spot. It halts progress—our ability to let go and move on. A weariness blankets our souls and smothers the will to live, to move, to shake off the past, and to see the present for what it is. This weariness is subtle, insidious, and dangerous. We have a tendency to romanticize the past no matter how bad it really was. We prefer the leeks and onions we knew rather than the unfamiliar manna God serves us in the midst of transition. We resist where God is taking us because we prefer to cling to what we know. Like Lot's wife, we can all get stuck. Stuck in the past. Stuck on the idea of how life was supposed to be. Stuck on what we didn't get. Just plain ole stuck. But in those instances the only people who really get robbed are us. Life goes on for everyone around us. It certainly did for Lot and his daughters. You see, others get hurt when we get stuck too. Life isn't just about us. It's also about the parts we play in the lives of the people we interact with to complete the greater picture of God's design for us all. If we will just persevere long enough, God will bring us through the difficult places so we can reach the oasis He has in store for us.

Your Hope

The only power the past should have in your life is the ability to teach as you move forward. The past is not your present...not your future. Don't listen to any lies that tell you life seldom changes. That life will never get better. That you are doomed to repeat your story. These are all lies from the enemy to hide the truth of God's promises to you.

True, life isn't easy. But it wasn't meant to be. It was meant to prove us, purge us, and refine us to be even greater than when we started out on this journey. Yes, chastening for the moment does seem grievous, but it eventually bears the peaceable fruit of righteousness if we allow God to finish what He started in us. You don't want to stop. You don't want to lie down on the job of life. I encourage you to continue to trust God in spite of how you feel or what you see.

Awaken, shake the dust off, strengthen your body and soul, and continue on. I once heard someone say life isn't a journey—it's an obstacle course. That may be true. But the hope you have is that you can look to the one true God who will take your hand and walk with you through the roughest of terrain. If need be, He will even carry you! You don't have to be bound, or sink in desperation, or allow the things you've suffered to turn your heart to stone. You can rely on the grace God gives you to come through every situation even better than you were before.

So talk to yourself, girl. Do whatever you have to, but don't allow life to stop you in your tracks. There is no power on earth that can separate you from the love of God and the power of His deliverance. Allow Him to take your past and transform it into a beautiful future beyond your imagination.

Your Truth

❧ What events and disappointments have been difficult for you to get past?

❧ What thoughts or fears have paralyzed you and kept you from moving forward? What were the bases for those conclusions? Were they emotion based or fact based?

❧ What truths in and about God's promises will enable you to move forward with hope and anticipation?

5

Making Things Happen

Our dear sister,

Even as we write this we're hanging our heads in shame. Looking back, we see the desperation of our actions. We have no justification for what we did. So let us tell you our story so you can avoid our fate. Make wisdom your sister and embrace her words so you can avoid the snares that come during moments of fear, anger, and doubt.

Our family lived during a volatile time. From the time my sister and I were small, we were on the road. Ours was a nomadic life. When our parents finally settled, we were in a beautiful valley filled with verdant fields...and forbidden practices and beliefs. Our parents served a different God than our neighbors. Though we were taught by our parents and we tried to understand their view, we also embraced some of the values from our environment and assimilated into the society.

It was so hard to constantly go against the grain of our peers. The stress was all-encompassing. And we wondered if the things our parents upheld were even valid in this new place. So much of what they believed seemed ridiculous and outdated. How would we find husbands in this place if we followed what our parents taught? The culture in our new valley had no comprehension of the teachings and beliefs that came from the God of the Israelites. The valley people didn't follow

His staunch rules. Here no one seemed to be able to trace their principles to anything concrete, and they seemed to be doing okay.

When we asked our parents about their convictions, all they would say was the teachings they followed had been taught to them by their parents back home and were written on their hearts. They said it was the only way of life they knew.

We, on the other hand, had witnessed much more. Times had changed. People lived and related differently in this new land. So we went with the flow and got acquainted with the young men in the area. Soon we were engaged to two handsome guys. The future looked so promising!

Then they came. Two strangers. Our father, Lot, brought them home to spend the night. That night the men of the city surrounded our home and demanded we hand over the strangers so they could sleep with them. Father tried to talk them out of it, and even offered the two of us to the men in the stead of our visitors, but they refused to be placated. We were relieved that they weren't interested in us that was for sure! When the mob grew unruly, our guests pulled Father back inside the house. As the men in the crowd grew more restless and violent, they were suddenly struck with blindness. They couldn't see so they couldn't break into our home to carry out their intentions.

That's when our two visitors told us that our town was filled with wicked and evil people. The judgment of God was going to fall on Sodom and the surrounding area, so we must leave immediately. After the mob outside dispersed, Father went out to encourage our fiancés to join us in escaping the city. Not surprisingly, they found the whole thing ridiculous and thought it was some sort of joke. They declined the invitation. When Father got home, we still hesitated. Then the strangers grabbed our hands and dragged us away from the city and toward the mountains.

We ran as fast as we could as we heard loud noises and the sounds of destruction behind us. We heard people scream and saw fire and sulfur falling from the sky! When we stopped, the two strangers told us to keep going to the mountains and not look back. Mother was running in front of us still fretting about the things she was leaving behind. She glanced back, and in that moment she was turned into a pillar of salt. This escalated our terror! We kept going, not daring to stop or look back until we were safe. The strangers had told us to go to the mountains, but Father thought the neighboring village would be better. But when we got there and the people learned we'd come from Sodom, they kept looking at us suspiciously. Finally, we moved to the mountains where we'd been originally directed to go by the two angels.[1]

Safely hidden with way too much time to reflect on days gone by and the loss of our mother, the future looked hopelessly dim. All was lost. Where would we go from here? The only place we really knew was destroyed. Isolated from everyone but Father, our view became very narrow. Our fiancés had perished among the flames. Who would we marry? With whom would we bear children and preserve our family line?

So we acted. Don't ask what we were thinking because, in reflection, it doesn't seem like we were. We can only say that though we'd left Sodom, the wickedness of that place was still influencing us. Or maybe it was our biological clocks ticking, ticking, ticking until the sounds clamored loudly in our ears. Or perhaps it was simply the desperation to live life on our own terms. Or maybe it was the pressure of our own desires and expectations. In retrospect, there is no justifiable explanation for our actions. What did we do that was bad? We got our father drunk, and then we slept with him so we'd get pregnant. Our father, Lot, was so drunk he wasn't aware of what we were doing or what he was doing. Being the eldest daughter, I slept with Father first. The next night it was my sister's turn.

Unlike what we've heard happens today, our father didn't rape us, pressure us to sleep with him, or abuse us in any way. In fact, he didn't even know what we'd done until our bodies started showing our pregnancies! We look back at our shameful, incestuous actions with regret. We did what we did without realizing the far-reaching implications. Yes, we got the children—the sons—we wanted…along with some fruit we didn't anticipate.

Although we weren't around when our boys became men and had children and their children had children, we know our sons, Moab and Ben-Ammi, grew up to become mighty nations—the fathers of the Moabites and Ammonites.[2] Those two nations became ruthless enemies of our people, the Israelites. This *was not* the legacy we had in mind.

Our passion and manipulation to get what we wanted led to events and situations beyond what we'd imagined. We learned that even when we think we're in control, we never really are. Not only did our actions lead to sorrows as life played out, but the spiritual consequences were even greater. From our sons came ruthless generations giving birth to more ruthless generations, and they adopted more and more ungodly practices.

Oh my. The spirits of self-interest and preservation brought so much pain to the world. The unleashing of unbridled lust, the twisting of God's gift of sexuality, and the perverting of His plans for His people were perpetuated by our actions. For this we are deeply sorry. But one comfort remains—God can redeem what we did wrong. We know this firsthand. The same God who sent angels to take us to a place of refuge is well able to reconcile all things to Himself and grant new beginnings.

So please, sisters, resist the urge to take matters into your own hands. Release your control and the urge to make things happen. Allow God to bring all things to pass in your life. Only then will it be well established and right. Doing things for yourself and on your own bears far too many negative consequences...and even destruction...that will travel beyond your life and affect countless others.

We pray that you will be still and know that God is God. Praise Him for His good and perfect gifts that are always free of guilt and shame. Rest in Him! And regardless of what your eyes see or your natural nature wants, don't allow your emotions to exalt themselves above your faith. Birth only those things borne of God's Spirit. The ways of the flesh only lead to disappointment, chaos, and death. Stick to that which is true, and you will always be free...free to receive what God has for you, and that *always* leads to joy, godliness, and fulfillment.

Praying you trust God's ways,

Lot's daughters

Woman to Woman

There are many things that form our convictions, including beliefs, upbringing, environment, peer pressure, societal mores, observations, and experiences. All of these shape our expectations of what our lives are supposed to look like. But decisions should never be made without God being in the center of the equation. God said, "My thoughts are not your thoughts, neither are your ways my ways" (Isaiah 55:8). What *we* think should be taking place in our lives may be outside of God's plan for us.

When *we* choose to make things happen, we set ourselves up for consequences beyond our control. The control we seize to make one thing happen produces results that usually require even more control (control that we don't have), and that spirals into even greater consequences than we are prepared to deal with. Seldom do we consider the long-term results of our actions, especially when acting impulsively. And many times we can't even imagine, much less foresee, possible outcomes of the choices we make. We're so focused on immediate gratification or goals that we overlook the far-reaching effects.

When we decide to "make things happen," we are taking God off His throne and enthroning ourselves. Yet we don't have the wisdom or power or ability to reign over the circumstances we create. And because God does not share His glory with others, He allows all false gods to fall. Our efforts at becoming God fail miserably, and we are reminded once again that the one true God is God and we are not. The world may prod and press us to take life into our own hands to get our desires accomplished, but we must remember that we are in the world but not of it (John 15:19).

As members of the kingdom of God, everything we do affects everyone everywhere all the time. We are part of a uniquely connected fellowship that has a profound effect on the world. Our lives yielded to God will create lasting legacies that further His far-reaching plan for humanity. Therefore, our choices must be weighed in light of this fact and our decisions prayerfully made. We can't afford to lean on our own understanding by being moved by what we see, influenced by our peers, constrained by the urgency of time, or dependent on our own ideas of what our lives are supposed to look like. Instead we must believe and trust that God knows what is best. That the things He prevents are for our protection. What He allows are for our benefit and the further-ance of His kingdom.

God will orchestrate the circumstances of our lives to give us joy and fulfillment while glorifying Himself. When we do things His way, we will never live in regret. Truly the blessing of the Lord makes us rich and adds no sorrow.

Your Hope

Even when your way forward isn't clear, God is very much in con-trol. When your focus is on Him and your desire is to please Him, your steps are ordered by Him. He will keep you from slipping if you truly desire to be kept by Him. He knows the way you're taking. No thought, need, and longing escapes Him. But you must believe that ultimately He knows best so you can be confident as you wait for Him to mani-fest the things you long for.

As you wrestle with your desires and struggle with your faith con-cerning what you want from God, you can lean on the facts that He is good and withholds no perfect gift from you. If what you desired was truly good for you and would prove to be a blessing to you in alignment with His plans, God would freely give it. Another factor is that some-times there is nothing wrong with your desire, but it may be a matter of timing. Even good things at the wrong time can be detrimental. God weighs all the aspects of what you request from Him before granting your desire. He is careful to not give you something He knows will be detrimental in the long run. He waits until He sees that your heart is surrendered enough and your character mature enough to handle the blessings He entrusts to you.

Your Truth

❧ What circumstances in your life make your dreams look impossible?

✻ In what ways have you been tempted to take situations into your own hands?

✻ What is your greatest struggle when it comes to trusting God for your heart's desires?

6

The Importance of Destiny

My dear sister,

You might find me quite adventurous because my story begins in a rather unorthodox fashion. It started off as normal a day as any. I went out in the evening to draw water at the well as always. But when I got there a stranger was seated nearby. He got up and came over to ask for a drink of water. I knew he wasn't from our village. His clothes betrayed that he'd traveled from afar.

I noticed his camels looked thirsty so I volunteered to give them water too. To my surprise, when I'd finished, the stranger presented me with a beautiful nose ring and gold bracelets. He asked about my family. I explained that I was "the daughter of Bethuel, the son that Milkah bore to Nahor." I mentioned that we had plenty of straw and fodder for his camels and room for him if he needed a place to stay for the night.

Then he said, "Praise be to the LORD, the God of my master Abraham." He added, "The LORD has led me on the journey to the house of my master's relatives."[1]

I ran home to tell my family the news and show them my gifts. My brother Laban immediately ran to meet him and formally invite him to come to our home.[2]

At dinner the man told us his story. He said he was sent by a man named Abraham to find a wife for his son among Abraham's father's clan. The servant said he'd prayed that morning, and I had fulfilled all the requests he'd made of the Lord. He also said I was the granddaughter of his master's brother! He asked if I would be willing to travel with him back to where Abraham lived and marry his son Isaac. My father consented, and the next thing I knew I was being showered with silver, gold, and beautiful clothing. My family also received wonderful gifts.

The next morning my mother and brother asked me if I was really willing to go. Would I follow this man back to his land to marry the son of my rich relative? After all the servant had said about his prayer by the well and how I'd been the answer, how could I say no? Well, perhaps someone else would have drawn back and been afraid of the unknown. But I felt destiny calling! I felt I had to answer yes. "I will go," I said.[3]

I'll never forget the first time I saw Isaac, my soon-to-be husband. Strong and handsome, he came across the field to meet our caravan. My heart skipped a beat. I'd made the right choice! We were married right away, and he was loving and tender. I never regretted my decision to become his wife. Yes, it was a tremendous risk to take. To go to a foreign land, to meet a man I didn't know, to say yes to spending forever with someone I'd never met. Yet God confirmed in my heart that this was the right thing to do. I was born for this. I felt no fear or trepidation. I knew it was a divine appointment. This had nothing to do with romantic notions, chemistry, or any of the love notions girls dream of. It didn't have to do with the display of wealth from the servant's caravan of camels burdened down with gifts. Isaac could have been rich but cruel. No, marrying Isaac was quite simply what God had planned for my life for a greater reason than what I knew. I knew profoundly that I must go, and so I did.

Isaac was a wonderful husband. His father, Abraham, was loving and indulgent with his son, and Isaac lavished what he'd learned from his parents on me. I fretted because I couldn't bear children, but my mate never made me feel the disappointment he must have felt. Instead he loved me and prayed for me. And after twenty years of marriage, I bore twins. I figured God was making up for lost time! It was a difficult pregnancy. I was sure the babies were fighting inside my womb. When I inquired of God, He told me my children were two nations wrestling. They would become great, and the elder would serve the younger.[4] I never forgot that.

As they grew older, I'm ashamed to say I did have a favorite. No mother is supposed to love one child more than the other, but I did. Esau always seemed to find a way to grieve me. He was a man of the flesh and focused on instant gratification. He even sold his birthright to Jacob one day in exchange for porridge. He never seemed to think of the far-reaching consequences for his choices. He had no respect for purpose or destiny, and he seemed to have no concept of being set apart for something greater than day-to-day life. He chose to marry two foreign women who brought nothing but grief to our family.

I decided he didn't deserve the blessing that Isaac would give him as the eldest son. So when the time came, I devised a ruse so Jacob would get the blessing instead of Esau. I wish I could say I'm repentant, but I'm not. After all, God Himself said the older son would serve the younger son, so in my opinion it was appropriate for Jacob to get the blessing from Isaac. Of course there was a cost for my actions. Perhaps I shouldn't have "helped" God. He certainly was able to do it Himself. But fear and uncertainty got the best of me, so I brought the prophecy to pass…but paid a great personal cost.

Having found out that Jacob had stolen the patriarchal blessing, Esau devised a plan to kill him. As much as it pained me to let my dearest son go, I convinced Isaac to send Jacob to my people to find a wife. I couldn't let my husband know it was because of the blessing situation.

In that moment I fully came to know how my family felt when I left them so many years before to marry Isaac. I sensed that Jacob's leaving was bigger than the present issue at hand. It felt right. The irony didn't escape me either. I left the land of my father many years ago to marry Isaac and bear a son, and now my son was returning to the place I had left to seek a wife. It had to be significant. Even so, it was with a heavy heart that I bid Jacob farewell. With the long journey ahead of him, I knew I might never see him again. I was comforted by knowing that God had something special planned for his life.

I understood that to secure Jacob's destiny, something must be sacrificed. Could it have occurred any other way? Perhaps. But the God who knows the end from the beginning must have factored all these things into His plan. He didn't leave me ignorant of His plans for my sons. As I look back, I see the significance of His timing. The long wait to conceive wasn't about me and my longing for a child. It was about God's calendar. The sequence of events that would transpire in the years to come were part of His divine schedule that held far more significance than mine.

Though I loved Jacob from the bottom of my heart, I had to release him to his destiny. This is the greatest thing any mother can do. Perhaps my greatest regret is that I championed him deceiving his father to get the familial blessing. I knew there would be a price for that as well. I prayed that God would perfect Jacob's character so that he would be worthy of the blessings that would come.

Every mother wants the best for her children. And she wants her children to get along. However, it's important to always know what is within our power and release what is not to the true Parent of all our children—God.

As I close this note to you, I encourage you to always be cognizant of the purpose for your marriage and for your children. Instead of asking why something happened, we should ask God what He wants to accomplish through the events that unfold in our lives. The details of our lives are bigger than us and firmly in God's hands. The moment we decide to live for ourselves, we cut ourselves off from the great adventure of following God's will.

I wish I could have been privy to all that occurred once Jacob left home, but what I do know is that whatever transpired after that served as a catalyst to bring him into the fullness of the purpose for which he had been created and born. What I was not able to instill in him, God, by His Holy Spirit, would. This was my confident hope and prayer for my youngest son.

As much as we would like to control the outcome of our children's lives, we need to understand we can't. Our children's lives are ultimately in the hands of God because, above all, His destiny calls.

Your sister in destiny,

Rebekah

Woman to Woman

Every woman dreams of the day when her knight will arrive to carry her off to the land of happily ever after. The various reasons we long for marriage in today's culture seldom have to do with the purposes of God. As we wait longer to marry, our roots are deeply set in place. This doesn't make it easy to uproot ourselves and move across the street, not to mention going to a land we don't know to marry a man we've never met! I wonder how this scenario would play out today.

Rebekah showed courage when she accepted the invitation to follow a stranger back to his land to marry an unseen suitor. This displayed massive trust in God. Rebekah cast off trepidation to sign up for a great risk that obviously reaped great rewards. What could have compelled her to say yes to the stranger's invitation? Was there a great sense of knowing in her being that this was the right thing to do? Her family graciously left the decision up to her, though this was contrary to their culture. Rebekah chose to go...

We all have choices, and it is up to us to make the best ones through prayer and communion with God when it comes to love and life. Our decisions will affect all of our tomorrows and beyond. They also affect the lives of others—our children, our communities, our cities, our nations, our world.

When we get to the place where we understand that God is interested in strategic alliances for His kingdom purposes, we'll see marriage and even motherhood in a different light. We discover that purpose has little to do with emotion, though great joy often results in fulfilling it. To prayerfully submit our lives to God, giving Him permission to uproot us if need be in order for His will to be manifested is just the beginning of the exciting journey God has prepared for us. Only those who dare to say yes receive the great rewards.

Your Hope

Every day you get the opportunity to say yes to God. In small or largely significant ways you are asked the question time and time again. Are you willing to step outside your comfort zone? Are you willing to make the sacrifice that is needed to invest your life in God's kingdom and trust Him for an abundant return? Each one of us will be tested in the area of trusting God with our tomorrows...as well as with our loved ones and with the things we hold dearest. Yet God is not insistent. He's a perfect gentleman. He waits for your heart to align with His will. If you are wise, you will willingly follow Him knowing the outcome will always be greater than your expectations.

The resounding message of the entire gospel found in each individual story is the fact that you will never regret making a move for God. Every God-given opportunity is greater than you know. The hidden blessing is greater than the obvious. As Rebekah went to meet Isaac, I'm sure she didn't know what a divine match made in heaven this union was. Little would she suspect that she would give birth to the father of a great nation! She didn't know that her father-in-law, Abraham, was the recipient of a divine promise that she would play a part in fulfilling. You never know what awaits you in God's destiny for your life.

What a lofty thought to consider how your contributions play into the greater plan of your amazing God. And yet He chose you and uses you to fulfill His purposes. Every encounter is a divine opportunity to step into the center of your destiny and watch your world explode with purpose. This is the path to fulfilling your destiny and leading a life of joy.

Your Truth

❧ What impacts the decisions you make in life?

✻ What are your top three priorities? How do those priorities affect your choices?

✻ What do you sense concerning your destiny and God's plan for your life?

7

When Love Isn't Enough

My dear sister,

Mine is the story of a fairy tale gone awry in the worst way. It started off well enough. Boy meets girl. Love at first sight. We both knew we were made for one another. How could God have planned it any better? That this handsome man would come from afar and yet be from my family served to confirm that we were a match made in heaven. What woman wouldn't love a man so sold out to her that he would work seven years of his life to earn her hand? I loved him, and he loved me. We lived and breathed for one another. A year was as a day, and nothing could abate our passion for one another.

I vividly remember when the dream turned into a dark and twisted nightmare. I still remember the moment my father called my sister, Leah, and me before him. He announced that it would be Leah who would occupy *my* marital bed. I was speechless! How could my own father do this to me? He knew how much Jacob meant to me and I to him. It was as if Father had taken a knife and stabbed me. No consolation or explanation could make up for the pain I experienced. I hated my father! But how could I hate someone I was supposed to love? Someone who was supposed to love me, cherish me, and protect me? He went on to explain it wasn't correct traditionally for the younger daughter to marry before the elder. That Jacob could have us both, but things must be done properly and in order. Amid my protests, Leah was taken away to be made ready for the marriage suite.

I was left to weep uncontrollably for what seemed like a lifetime. The moment I'd dreamed about and pictured in my mind was ripped asunder. I couldn't be consoled. My maids restrained me until I fell into a fitful sleep. I cried for myself. I cried for Jacob who would learn of my father's decision too late. The cruelty of my father's deception cut me deeply and left a wound that never healed. My trust in his love was shattered and couldn't be repaired. I saw him as a tyrant who used people for his own purposes. This was confirmed the next morning.

Jacob, upon discovering it wasn't me he'd married but Leah, confronted my father, who calmly told him he could have me as his second wife if he gave him another seven years of service.

"What do we mean to him as daughters?" I wondered. "Are we merely bargaining chips to get what he wants in life? With no regard for our feelings or desires? Our happiness? Our peace? What type of father does that?" Something inside of me died that day. I never saw my father the same way. I also questioned God. If He was who I was told He was, how could He let something like this happen? Jacob had told me about his encounter with God on the way to our area.[1] I was filled with a fear and awe I couldn't explain. No one else I knew had ever spoken of having such a real experience with God. But now I was disappointed. Was this how the God of Jacob treated His followers? I wanted no part of that kind of God.

I hurt so deeply inside I felt like screaming. Instead I bore the pain in silence, allowing it to eat away my joy like bitter acid. A week after marrying Leah, when all the nuptials were completed, Jacob agreed to work for my father another seven years, so Jacob and I were finally married. But I would always be his second wife.

Yes, I had Jacob's love, but it seemed an empty prize as I watched Leah bear son after son. Not only had God allowed her to circumvent me in marriage, but I now had to sit by and watch her give Jacob what I could not. My guilt wouldn't allow me to admit there were times I hated her. I don't know if it was this God of Jacob's plan or my own bitterness that closed my womb. In my despair I blamed Jacob. He in turn reminded me that he wasn't God.[2] And I wondered again what his God had against me.

I resorted to having my maid sleep with Jacob so I could have a child through her. Leah followed suit. The competition raged on with our maids giving Jacob two sons each. Finally, I bore my own son. He was beautiful! "God has taken away my disgrace," I said. I named him Joseph. I should have been satisfied, but my son felt like a consolation prize in comparison to the many sons Leah had. So I also said, "May the LORD add to me another son."[3]

It seemed almost ridiculous that my sister would be unhappy because she felt unloved while I was thoroughly loved but pining for more children. Don't ask me why I couldn't seem to be content with the lot I'd been given. So many women dream of a man loving them the way Jacob loved me—and yet it wasn't enough. In my time, bearing children was how society measured a woman's worth. A child was evidence of love and a blessing that love produced.

When Jacob decided it was time to go back to his homeland, I felt a mixture of excitement and fear. I would finally be free from my father who was selfish, and deceptive, and had failed me. But I was also going to the land of Jacob's God. And though Jacob clung to Him with fervent belief citing how God had helped him increase his flocks supernaturally in spite of my father's efforts to sabotage his ability to gain wealth, I remained unconvinced of His benevolence.[4] When I watched my only son playing apart from his siblings, I wondered what the future would hold for my son and me. Who would take my part?

So our little family, Jacob, Leah, me, and our children and servants packed up and moved. While my father, Laban, was shearing his sheep, I took his household gods and hid them among my things. What possessed me to steal my father's gods? They were part and parcel of everything my father held dear. I don't think my father had ever had anything he prized taken from him. And since he'd done that to me, I decided to do it to him. I wanted him to feel the sting of losing something precious. And then there was Jacob's God. He hadn't been fair to me either, I decided. I wasn't sure I wanted to be completely vested in Him, so I took the idols for extra reinforcement. Not that I knew if they'd ever worked or done anything, but just in case it wouldn't hurt to have them along. Needless to say, those were famous last thoughts.

Indeed, the household idols were precious to my father. He caught up with us in frantic search of them. And though I overhead him telling Jacob the God of his father had warned him not to harm our family, I was too entrenched in my thinking to change. Jacob was indignant at being accused of thievery and said if anyone in his entourage had stolen the idols, they would be put to death. I quaked in fear—but not enough to confess. I stole away to my tent and hid the objects inside the packs on my camel. And then I sat on them. I knew Father wouldn't search there because I told him it was my time of the month so he wouldn't ask me to get down. My father was none the wiser.

Ah, but the power of our words…

After Jacob was reconciled with his brother Esau, we continued to travel until we arrived in Shechem. There Leah's daughter, Dinah, was assaulted and her brothers took revenge, so Jacob's God told him to move us to Bethel. Then we moved on toward Ephrath. At that time the child inside me was ready to be birthed. I knew I didn't feel as well as I should, and I reflected on what Jacob had said in haste about the household gods. I'd never forgotten his vow and wondered if it was my undoing. Even as I delivered my son Ben-Oni I knew I wouldn't be given the gift of seeing him become a man.

In my final moments I had many regrets, but it was too late to do anything about them. I asked the God of Jacob that I hadn't trusted for so long to forgive me. I should never have compared Him to my earthly father. That was an unfair analogy although I had accused Him of not being fair. Perhaps if I'd embraced Him, my life would have turned out differently. As for Leah, I prayed that she would have what had eluded me—peace. I should never have said that love isn't enough because in the end it is all we have. The love we give and the love we receive.

Is it God's fault when we aren't happy? I would have to say no. My own outlook was my worst enemy. Leah was praying for what I could not appreciate. I had what she wanted and couldn't see the blessings because I was focusing on what I did not have. I should have been celebrating what God had given me. Looking back I conclude that truly love is enough.

Wishing you love and contentment,

Rachel

Woman to Woman

Every woman has dreams of their Prince Charming coming to carry them away. Oh, the excitement when he finally arrives! We look into each other's eyes and know in that moment that this is it. We were made for one another. We join hands and face the future with joy and hope. Then life happens. Disappointments, betrayal, rejection, perhaps even unfaithfulness. We struggle with where things went wrong when they seemed so right.

With Rachel, two key figures were the catalysts for her disappointment. Her father and God. It doesn't get any more critical than this. If God and our fathers let us down, what is left? Who do we turn to for support and strength? There are millions of questions we ask ourselves when we feel forsaken by God. Many more questions we imagine when our fathers, the first men in our lives who are supposed to love and protect us, do something that violates that trust. Our earthly fathers are supposed to represent our heavenly Father, and to feel betrayed by both leaves us with no hope for restoration. This is where Rachel found herself, and it led to a lifetime of disappointment, heartbreak, and great sorrow.

On the surface we wonder what Rachel's issue was. It wasn't Jacob's fault he had to marry Leah first. He made it clear he loved Rachel, so what was the problem? Laban is the one who threw Rachel under the bus by giving what she valued most to someone else. And to add insult to injury, God not only allowed someone else to marry her man, He shut Rachel's womb.

Have you too felt betrayed and denied of something closest to your heart? I pray you'll realize it's for a purpose, and based on your response you'll either heighten your pain or replace it with joy…and even fulfillment. What Rachel had was overshadowed by what she didn't have. This is a mistake we commonly make. We must remember that God factors in what we can and cannot handle in the equation of our lives. He knew Rachel couldn't bear a lot of children, and yet His plan was to birth a nation through Jacob. Leah was necessary in Jacob's life in order to bring God's heavenly agenda to pass for His kingdom purposes. And yet Jacob loved Rachel and made no apology for it.

To be able to be grateful for what we do have without getting distracted by discontentment over the things we can do nothing about is one of the greatest things we can master. It is also one of the hardest. At the end of the day we must own the fact that we have more power over our responses to circumstances than we usually care to exercise. God uses even the flaws of humanity to carry out His plan. Our lives are under His control. When we know this for sure, we can aggressively choose to rest in Him and trust Him to work all things for our good.

I firmly believe Rachel didn't have to die prematurely in childbirth. But her bitterness caused her to make choices that set her up for her untimely demise. Her heart condition coupled with the words of her mouth were her undoing. The book of Proverbs tells us that the foolish woman destroys her house with her own hands.[5] Have you heard the adage that "others are praying for what you already have even while you're looking elsewhere for more"? All Leah wanted was Jacob's love. But for Rachel love wasn't enough.

Where does it end for all of us is the question that has to be settled. The enemy of our souls would keep us grasping for things beyond our reach hoping to cause us to nurture ungratefulness, which eventually kills our faith and our joy. This is a battle every woman must fight…and can win with God's help.

Your Hope

You may not always understand the way God moves in your life. At times His denial may even seem cruel. But I encourage you to always trust that He knows best. That He has considered what you can handle and, based on those calculations, He determines the path that is best to fulfill His purposes and your destiny. When you can't see God's hand, trust His heart toward you, which is always focused on working all things for good. The more you are able to rest in Him and trust His motives, the happier and more fulfilled you'll be.

How can you do this? By rehearsing all the times God showed up for you. Constantly nurture a heart of gratitude and acknowledge that God knows best. Remind yourself that He sees what you cannot, and choose to believe He is ultimately saving you from greater distress and disappointment (yes, even when it doesn't feel like it). God denies you nothing that is good and will deliver you from what is not. Make sure you let your faith override your feelings.

Your Truth

✣ Who has disappointed you, and what has been the lasting impact?

✣ In what ways have you struggled with unfulfilled desires?

✣ What will help you trust God more and release your struggle to Him?

✣ How can you make the shift in your heart and mind to rest where God has you?

8

The Fight You Can't Win

My dear sister,

I don't know what you've thought about me based on Rachel's story. You might have felt sorry for my sister and resented me because my father gave the man she loved to me for a husband. Or you might have felt disdain toward my attempts to win Jacob's love. Perhaps I was right, perhaps I was wrong in loving him. Either way, there are valuable lessons to be learned from every experience in life. Hopefully hearing what I suffered will help you sort through your own circumstances when life seems unfair.

When Jacob came to town and I met him for the first time, I hoped that he'd be the one for me. But then I saw the way he looked at Rachel. It always seemed to happen that way. Rachel was beautiful, and I was, well, let's just say I was average. I was okay to look at, but nothing to write home about. I was used to living in Rachel's shadow even though I was older. Rachel was young, lively, and effervescent.

Yes, Jacob was hopelessly besotted with her, and she with him. He told my father he would agree to work seven years for Rachel's hand in marriage. Can you imagine? He literally sold himself for her. When the wedding night came and my father informed me that I would take Rachel's place, I have to admit I had conflicting emotions.

Part of me worried about how my sister would feel. I knew how much she loved Jacob, and I knew how much both of them had anticipated this day. It seemed cruel to take that away from her. I couldn't bear the thought of her pain or the anger she would surely direct toward me. Would she ever forgive me? Would she realize that our father was really to blame—not me? After all, we were taught to obey father's orders no matter how unfair he seemed.

Another part of me thought this would be my chance to win Jacob's heart. Father assured me that he would work everything out with Jacob. That having Jacob marry me first was best. It went against our tradition for a younger daughter to marry before an older one. Jacob would understand. After all, he could have us both. What man wouldn't want that?

But then again, what woman would want to share her man? No one really stopped to consider that.

My heart was in my throat as I waited for Jacob in the dark in the marital tent. Finally he came in full of wine and fell into my arms, declaring his love for me. Though I knew his words weren't meant for me, I pretended they were. I gave myself fully to him with all the passion within me. In the darkness I was almost convinced that things would work out fine. But morning came soon enough, and Jacob's look of shock and anger was a knife in my heart. He was horrified that I was in his marriage bed and not Rachel. That he had loved me so fervently in the dark instead of his beloved. He fled from the tent and found my father. I could hear their voices outside. Jacob's was filled with fury; my father's was much calmer as he put forth his proposal that Jacob could marry Rachel too if he agreed to work another seven years. However, Jacob would also be required to finish the traditional marriage week with me first.

I dared not look Jacob in the eyes when he returned. I didn't know whom I felt the sorriest for—Jacob or me. Jacob because he was forced to be with a woman he didn't want or love. Me because I was forced to be with a man who didn't want me or love me. I tread carefully trying to make the situation positive for him. He would come to love me. He would see that I would be an outstanding wife. Though I was not his first choice, I would make him see I was his best choice.

In essence that turned out to be the truth, but it took a lot longer than I thought it would. Though Rachel was beautiful and all a man could ask for, I was the one who was more fruitful. Rachel was barren, but I was fertile. So while her beauty was his pride, what I gave him was even more valuable—sons…heirs…the fulfillment of God's promise to him. With each one I thought, "My husband will love me now!" I lived to earn his love. He rejoiced at the birth of each child, but the light in his eyes never changed when he looked at me like they did when he looked at Rachel.

After my fourth son whom we named Judah, I was resigned to the fate of being in a loveless marriage. I decided to take my solace in the God of Jacob. Perhaps it would have been funny if it wasn't so painfully sad. I had sons and no love; Rachel had love and no sons. She refused to be comforted. The irony couldn't be missed. Though she had his love, their love produced nothing. She wasn't able to have what she wanted most—Jacob's children. She gave him her maidservant, who bore him two sons. I also gave him mine, and she also gave birth to two sons. Everyone around Rachel was conceiving and birthing sons except her. I saw the way she watched my sons, and my heart broke for her.

And then finally she conceived and bore Jacob a son. She was ecstatic. But the contest was far from over! I conceived again. The joke was that I was birthing the nation that Jacob's God had promised him. I wondered in my heart if it was really true. If the contest between Rachel and me was based on what we produced, I won that easily…but with little satisfaction. Rachel gave birth to two sons, but I gave birth to six sons and one daughter.

Over time we made peace with what we had, I suppose. Jacob worked hard for my father, Laban. Too hard, in fact. We all agreed with him the day he announced that we should leave and make our way back to his homeland. I was happy to leave. Our father had taken advantage of him long enough. I was anxious to see his people and hear more about the God he served. I'd drawn comfort from his God when

I struggled with wanting Jacob's love. I'd learned no amount of doing good, serving him, or producing sons for him would win his heart. I sought solace in prayer and giving thanks for what I had. I believed in God's love and how He had pitied me and regarded my low estate—and then blessed my womb. To make up for the love I didn't receive from my husband, God gave me children that would love me and fill my heart. Of course they couldn't play the part of a surrogate husband, but they did fill a place in me that yearned for fulfillment. Rachel struggled to have children, but she had the love of her husband. In my eyes God was being fair.

Perhaps Rachel didn't see it that way. She continued to cling to the gods of our father. In fact she stole our father's household gods when we left. I'm sure this was her undoing. Jacob didn't know this side of his favorite wife's heart. In his vehement defense of his household, he cursed whoever had taken them, declaring that whoever had stolen them would not live. He was confident in doing this because he so firmly believed that no one had done such a thing.

Time passed and we traveled on, but at the end of our moving, with Jacob's land in sight, Rachel died in childbirth. I considered the damage that words can do. She'd told Jacob, "Give me children, or I'll die."[1] She died in childbirth. It made me wonder if the thing we think we'll die without is the very thing that will kill us. This put my love for Jacob in perspective. No, I would not die without his love because God sustained me. I would no longer perform for love because nothing I could do would ever be good enough if I didn't have Jacob's heart. I would no longer contend with another woman for the heart of my husband because that was a fight I couldn't win. In the end it seems everyone loses to some extent when we look back and view the scars and pieces of ourselves that we lost during the fight. Some pieces we never get back and the wounds never heal.

At the end of our lives, I had Jacob to myself. Rachel was gone. Time had softened his heart and made our relationship easy and without the noisy expectations that once robbed us of our peace and joy. If I knew then what I know now, would I have fought so hard for his attention and performed to gain his love? Perhaps not. In the end Jacob was mine alone, and the end was much better than the beginning.

Your older and much wiser sister,

Leah

Woman to Woman

These days there appears to be a man shortage in many areas, and women have become more desperate than ever. Countless articles have been written that examine the advantages of "man sharing." The Bible tells us that in the last days "seven women will take hold of one man and say, 'We will eat our own food and provide our own clothes; only let us be called by your name. Take away our disgrace!'"[2] Though this may be becoming a popular, modern-day approach to solving the insurmountable problem of not enough men, it will create an even greater problem. We were not created to "share" men. The Word clearly states that a man will leave his mother and father, cleave to his wife, and the two shall become one.[3] This oneness can only be achieved between one man and one woman—not multiple partners. Anytime we do things out of God's order, we suffer the consequences of our actions. From the beginning it was God's will for one man to have one woman. As time progressed, men took their lives into their own hands. For the sake of economics and political alliances, they married more than one woman. Through the Bible we can see this practice has always caused confusion. Contending with another woman to gain the affections of a man is a fight no woman ever wins. And if it seems like someone does win, the scars that remain are never worth the prize and we don't know the far-reaching consequences that woman will go through.

The onslaught of low self-esteem that overwhelms a woman who becomes embroiled in such a hopeless contest is too costly. If children are involved, the strife and division will be overwhelming and far-reaching. As we saw from the saga of Rachel and Leah, and then what happened between their sons, jealousy is a terrible thing. (Remember the story of Joseph and his brothers selling him into slavery? It was no secret that his mother had been favored as well. This planted seeds of bitterness that bore terrible fruit in the years to come. Check it out in Genesis 37.)

Here is what every woman needs to know: *There is nothing you can do to make a man fall in love with you.* There is no rationale for why a man chooses to love whom he does. He can't be swayed from his choice but by his own inclinations. To try to make the women he's chosen look bad in his eyes is a setup for greater rejection for you. To try to out-perform her will heighten your heartache. The man's love has little to do with what you do, but it has everything to do with who you are— who you are in his eyes and who he sees himself as when he's with you. Depending on where he is in his life, he may or may not be able to see your value or appreciate the woman you are. If he is a boy, he will pick a girl over a woman. If he is broken, he will choose someone who is broken because your wholeness will hurt his eyes and bruise his ego. The only way not to get caught up in a contest that will have no good out-come is to know your own self-worth in God's eyes and love yourself enough to settle for nothing less than the best God has for you. One man loving you God's way.

Your Hope

The comfort in this fight you can't win is that God is intimately interested in your love life. He has a purpose for every relationship. He has a kingdom agenda for each and every one. They all feed into an intricate tapestry that makes up the picture of what His kingdom looks like and how it functions. Sure, love between a man and a woman should include chemistry, passion, romance, and emotions. But always remember that God has more in store.

Jacob, Leah, and Rachel's lives were intertwined and, at times, con-voluted, but it was evident that God's hand was very much involved in the events that transpired. He had a purpose for Leah as well as for Rachel. Leah gave birth to the sons who would form some of the major tribes of Israel, including the priesthood and worshippers. Rachel's son was part of the line of our Savior, Jesus Christ! Her son was a "redeemer" of God's people as well, in a sense, a prophetic forerunner of Jesus. There was purpose stamped all over the union of Leah and Rachel with Jacob. We will never fully understand why the story unfolded the way it did. We can speculate that because God knew of Rachel's divided heart that kept her father's gods and her lack of physical fortitude to bear many children, He didn't want the tribes of Israel polluted by idol worship. Perhaps because God knew of the strength of Leah to withstand rejection and be a fruitful wife despite her emotional pain He ordained the alliance between Jacob and her. Although we can't say definitively, we do know that God is a God of process. He will ultimately bring about His plan by doing whatever He desires to do in and through our lives.

In the knowledge that when we follow God He will work in our lives, we too can come to the place Leah reached—refusing to wrestle or perform for that which we can't force to occur. We can come to that place where we choose to simply worship the Lord and leave our cares in His more-than-capable hands. And He who is faithful will work all things to the good for all concerned in accordance with His will and His higher purposes (Romans 8:28). And the end result for us will always be joy and contentment.

Your Truth

❧ What has been your greatest struggle in your search for love or being in love?

❧ In what ways have you wrestled for or tried to perform to get the results you wanted? What was the outcome?

❧ In what ways have you stood in God's way in your love situation? What place do you need to get to so you can experience peace and embrace God's will?

9

A Mother's Influence

My dear sister,

Mine is a heart-wrenching tale of the sacrifices I made to secure the destiny of my child. And yet I tell you the story with a singing heart! Greatness is born out of adversity. But let me start at the beginning.

Usually a mother is excited to know that a child is growing inside her, but I was filled with fear. As a Hebrew living in Egypt, being pregnant was not the joyful event it should have been. The Pharaoh was worried that the Hebrews were multiplying and might become too powerful, so he issued an order that all Hebrew male babies were to be killed at birth. Can you imagine the dread that every Hebrew wife lived with? How could we bear to carry a precious life for nine months only to have it snatched away the moment it was delivered? We cried out to God as this cruelty was implemented.

After my initial trepidation, the peace of God descended over me. I sensed my story would be different. I wouldn't allow anyone to rob my child of its God-given destiny. Because the Hebrew midwives didn't cooperate with Pharaoh's edict, my son was born...and lived. The first time I looked into his face, I knew that he was a child of promise. There was something about him. I sensed the hand of God upon him.

I couldn't let him be murdered. I had to protect him. I knew God had entrusted him to me for the preservation of His call on my boy's life.

So I hid him. For three fearful months. Though I had peace within, my mind warred against my faith. And when I could hide him no longer, I wrapped him carefully, settled him into a basket I'd prepared and made watertight, and I placed him among the reeds in the Nile. In this way I was obedient to the law of the land. Pharaoh had demanded that all male babies be cast into the Nile. I simply chose to make sure my son would float. I knew the Pharaoh's daughter bathed in that area...so there was hope she would save him. I sent my daughter Miriam to watch over the baby to make sure he was all right. Then I released him into the hands of God.

As I'd hoped, Pharaoh's daughter plucked him out of the river and chose to adopt him![1] God blessed me by having the Pharaoh's daughter hire me to nurse my child and keep him safe until he was weaned. God is gracious that way! I learned through that experience that whatever I was willing to release to God, He was well able to give back to me in His special way. Being able to nurse my son during his infancy was a sacred gift I never took for granted.

Releasing him to the house of Pharaoh was difficult, but I was comforted with the fact that God had placed him there. The purpose of God would yet be revealed in his life. I didn't know if I would get to see it, but I knew I had done my part. Did it ever cross my mind that my dear son would be the deliverer of the Israelites from the bondage of Egypt?[2] Or that my son Aaron would become a prophet and the head of the Levite priesthood?[3] Or that my daughter, Miriam, would rise up as a prophet, a leader of the Israelite women, and a worship leader?[4] No, I was simply a mother who wanted the best for her children. I was a mother who desired to teach them about the God I knew and loved. I wanted to instill within them the importance of serving Him wholeheartedly. I often shared the story of how we ended up in Egypt in the first place and about the many things God had spoken about and done for us as a people.

I wanted my children to know their history. I wanted them to know they came from greatness, and they should never believe they were less than anyone else. I wanted them to know they had the power to change their world with the help of the living God. We had endured much because God was preserving us for an even greater future. My children would sit and listen to me with awe as I told them stories about Joseph, who had come down to Egypt to prepare the way for us. The exodus we made to Egypt to escape the famine and how God had preserved us as a people.

I didn't want them to be fearful. And I didn't want them to resign themselves to the fate of being slaves. I knew that slavery started in the mind. No mother in her right mind would allow her child to accept a victim mentality. I was very purposeful in the things I imparted to my children. I prayed that one day they would do great things for God and make me proud. The specifics I didn't know. I only had this knowing and hope in my soul. I suppose that's what they call mother's intuition. I viewed raising my children as an assignment from God. It was what I lived for and where I drew my fulfillment. I believe God honored that, and it did my soul good.

What advice do I offer to women about to give birth or thinking about having children? Don't just birth children! Instead, birth the purpose of God. Your job as a mother isn't done until you've given your children a sense of their destiny, of how they should look to God for His purpose for their lives. Help them identify their gifts and breathe life into them.

Children are so impressionable. We have them for only a short time before other influences begin to whisper in their ears. We must use our time with them wisely. When we're holding them to our breast, whisper visions to them. Plant the seeds of dreams before they go to bed at night. And always greet them with open-ended possibilities every morning. This is the purpose of mothering. I embraced this purpose in the face of terrifying circumstances. But no one said raising children would be easy, but they are worth the fighting and the risks we take to raise them to become healthy, wise human beings excited to serve the Lord.

God has entrusted our children to us. They aren't born just for our personal pleasure or to populate the earth. No, we're to raise them so they become responsible members of the kingdom of God who enthusiastically live for and carry out the plans of our holy God.

I have done that.[5] I understood my assignment and completed it. It was a privilege and an honor to bear my three children and rear them for the glory of God. May you be blessed to do and experience the same.

Maternally yours,

Jochebed

Woman to Woman

Sometimes motherhood feels like a thankless job, and yet it just might be the most powerful position in the world. The human race would not exist without mothers! Mothers incubate, carry, and deliver every person on the face of the earth. That is beyond incredible. Without the seed there would be no life, but without that seed being carried to full term there is no life either. After the conception, pregnancy, and birthing process, the real work begins. Nurturing, grooming, and growing up a child into full maturity.

Three times Jesus asked Peter if he loved Him. Each time Peter answered yes, Jesus asked Peter to care for His lambs and, finally, His sheep. He specified that Peter care not just for the mature but also for the babies of the flock. In this same way God entrusts children to mothers and fathers with the same charge. Parents are assigned to bring up children trained in the way that they should live with the promise from God that when they get old they will never depart from it (Proverbs 22:6).

In many cases mothers become disappointed because of misplaced expectations. Their children become surrogate mates or are pushed to fulfill their mothers' dreams instead of viewing them as assignments placed in their charge by God to be prepared for release to the world. As I read through the Word of God, I find the stories of mothers called to release their children for greatness. It wasn't just Jochebed who had to release her children. There was Rebekah, who had to send Jacob away to secure his destiny. Hannah had to leave her child in the keeping of Eli at the temple in Shiloh for him to become the prophet he was born to be. David had to go live in the palace with Saul. Mary had to release Jesus to the world. Do you sense the pattern? Birth. Nurture. Release.

The book of Proverbs instructs children to heed the instructions of their mothers and the law of their fathers (Proverbs 1:8). Mothers are traditionally the parent who spends the most time with the children. Mothers are given the insights to notice their children's giftings and the wisdom to help their children develop and refine them. Mothers are given the supernatural ability to sense things about their children no one else can perceive. As a mother trusts in the Lord and leans not on her own understanding, she will be led and prompted by the Holy Spirit on how to carry out God's will for her children. Though it may seem thankless at times, the Word confirms that women's contributions will be spoken well of in their families, communities, and beyond. In due time we will receive due praise (Proverbs 31:28, 31). The lives of your children well lived and exemplary should be thanks enough because God is the true Rewarder of the faithfulness we give to our assigned tasks.

Your Hope

Sometimes it isn't clear what will become of your children. Releasing them is scary. What if they end up taking the wrong direction or fall into the wrong hands? Any number of things could go awry when you take your hands off. And yet you must. Every person must eventually rise and fall on his or her own merit.

Can you imagine how Jochebed felt when she placed that basket containing her precious cargo of a son in the Nile River? It was a "trust God or die from worry" moment. But God has promised that He is well able to keep what is committed to Him. You must also believe that when it comes to your children. I've observed that it seems the greater the gift the more opposition to it will be birthed. Remaining sensitive in the Holy Spirit is essential to following the plan of God. Hearing His voice and obeying are key in the process of surrendering and recovering what you release. When you give everything to God that He asks for, He inevitably will give you back way more. You can't beat Him in giving! And yet you can't reap the extraordinary until you're willing to release to Him the things that are dearest to you. In that moment He knows He can trust you to handle the blessings He wants to give to you.

Then another amazing thing occurs. You realize you can trust Him too. God never disappoints. Imagine that Jochebed only had saving the life of her son in mind. In return for her sacrifice, that son she released became a prince in the house of Pharaoh and later became a deliverer of the Israelites living in Egypt. Could she have seen any of that coming? I think not. When she said yes in obedience to God, she opened the door for exceedingly abundant blessings above what she could even think to ask for.

Yes, letting go is difficult and even scary. But as you keep the purposes of God ever before you, making that the priority of your heart, the rewards will come. As a mother, sister, or simply as a woman, you were created to give birth to something. As mothers, the first release comes from our bodies, but further release is required from our hearts.

Your Truth

❧ Do you have a sense of purpose? What are you giving birth to in this season of your life?

❧ What struggles do you experience in the area of releasing things to God?

❧ What will it take to help you let go? What is your hope as you release to God what is dear to you?

10

How to Deal with Haters

My dear sister,

Perhaps this is something all women go through, but that doesn't make it any easier. I don't know what I expected when I married Moses. I was a foreigner. And not just any foreigner who could blend into his world. I was a black woman...a Cushite.[1] I could tell from the stares when he brought me home that our marriage wasn't the norm. The Hebrews didn't marry outside their people. It was frowned upon. And yet here I was—married to one of their leaders. I decided I would not say much and avoid any unfruitful confrontations.

My husband's brother, Aaron, and sister, Miriam, weren't pleased about our marriage. I perceived that they felt I was replacing them. That I would now be the one whispering in Moses' ear to render my opinions and influence how he did things. No, those two weren't happy at all.

Aaron and Miriam conspired to bypass Moses and step out on their own. They decided they were able to hear from the Lord without my husband's involvement. But in the middle of their insurrection, the Lord God intervened. He called Moses, Aaron, and Miriam to the entrance of the tabernacle. The Lord came down in a cloud and berated Aaron and Miriam for daring to ignore His servant Moses with whom

He had a special relationship. "The anger of the LORD burned against them."[2] In the wake of His leaving, Miriam found herself stricken with leprosy. Aaron desperately pleaded with Moses to ask God to heal Miriam. God agreed to heal her, but He said Miriam had to wait for seven days.

Because of the leprosy, Miriam had to live on the outskirts of the camp until the eighth day. We all waited for her restoration before continuing our journey. Throughout this entire experience I said nothing. However, I did marvel at the justice of God. Miriam had a problem with me because of the color of my skin, and now she would find out how it felt. God could have dealt with her in so many ways, but he chose to afflict her skin. She found out how it felt to be ostracized because of something she couldn't control. I couldn't harbor hard feelings against her because I pitied her. I had dealt with prejudice all my life and learned to adjust or ignore it when people didn't accept me because of my race. But for Miriam to suddenly find herself in this predicament had to be traumatic.

I held my peace from beginning to end. And that is the key to dealing with people who hate or refuse to accept people who are different. If you experience bias against you, I encourage you not to sink to that person's view and conduct. Don't try to defend or explain yourself. Those responses only escalate the problem and give the person an excuse to justify his or her stance. What should you do instead? Refuse what the person says and turn the person over to God. Release the person to His judgment. In my case, I'd silently prayed that God would consider the situation between Moses' siblings and me, judge between us, and render the appropriate consequences. Miriam was especially hard on me, so I trusted God to deal with her accordingly. I kept my hands and my heart clean before God.

Did I feel bad about the disdain leveled at me? Yes, of course! I am only human. A hundred retorts went through my head. Words remained unsaid that could have hurt her back by insulting her. But I chose to take the high road for the sake of my husband. I knew Miriam couldn't fight with someone who refused to join her in the fray. As for Aaron, I think he had absorbed some of his sister's bile, and sadly it infected him. But Miriam was the instigator obviously since God dealt with her so severely and only chastised Aaron.

When God called Moses, Aaron, and Miriam before Him, He spoke to Aaron and Miriam and reminded them of His close relationship with Moses. That He spoke face-to-face with Moses. God then asked them, "Why then were you not afraid to speak against my servant Moses?"[3] How could they come against him knowing his special relationship with God? Didn't they understand their brother's position? This was when I learned a vital lesson. *God defends His own.*

God takes it very personally when someone attacks those He loves. He considers it an attack against Himself. Therefore, He will contend with people who contend against His loved ones. There was no need for me to defend myself. God would fight my battles when I entrusted them to Him. And so I stood still and watched His judgment unfold on Moses' and my behalf. Because of my relationship with Moses, I was given the same covering he enjoyed. The very hand of God protected and kept us.

After this turn of events everyone in the camp held their peace. All murmuring against our marriage was silenced. No one wanted to experience what Miriam had. I smiled to myself inwardly. I suppose God knows whom He can trust to bear specific burdens. He gives His grace for our individual journeys. We should never have to apologize for who He created us to be or feel the need to defend ourselves.

This truth may save your life, dear sister. There will always be people who don't see your value or recognize your worth. Understand that others may try to superimpose their insecurities over you and try to rob you of your security. They may despise your confidence. The very thing they envy about you is what they'll try to destroy. *Be still before them and let God handle it.* Give God room to intervene. Don't cast away your confidence in Him. He is with you even when you feel alone in your struggle. He will take your part when you walk with Him.

Unapologetically, I am

The Cushite

Woman to Woman

The art of silence is difficult to master, but the discipline will save us much heartache and drama. When someone attacks or rejects us, it's natural to want to defend ourselves. But this saying is true: "We should never have to explain ourselves to anyone." The people who love us don't need it, and those who don't like us won't believe us anyway.

It is sad but true that people can be cruel. And women seem to have a knack for ripping a person's heart out in subtle ways that can destroy the other person's confidence and self-esteem...usually so they'll feel better about themselves in the face of their own insecurities. When attacked, we need to examine the roots behind personal comments people make before we allow them to affect our emotional and spiritual health.

To master our emotions and not allow them to run rampant takes a will that is totally surrendered to God. Self-control is part of the fruit of the Holy Spirit (Galatians 5:23). As a wise friend once said to me when I was struggling with a situation, "You can't walk by feelings and expect a faith outcome." Our feelings may cause us to react in ways that we would not if we took the time to carefully weigh the situation.

What's the bottom line? *Never respond when you feel angry, fearful, or hurt.* When we do, we usually respond in the wrong way and make choices that exacerbate the situation. So when experiencing any of these emotions, this is when we need to wait on God for His input. Knowing that He is ultimately in charge of every situation will help us maintain our peace. Knowing who we are in Him keeps us confident— not in our ability but in His. Being mindful that we are His children will keep our esteem high because our identity is wrapped up in His presence within us. The arrows that fly from people's mouths in our direction can only bounce off when our spirits are fortified and hidden in Christ. This releases us to view the attacker with pity or, perhaps, even sorrowful understanding.

So love and bless those who insult and spitefully use you (Matthew 5:44). Trust God to deal with the person trying to put you down or rock your world. Allow yourself to grow more fruitful in self-control during your time of affliction. Remember, we all reap what we sow. You can only control what grows in your own garden, so plant the right seeds.

Your Hope

No ifs, ands, or buts about it. *God is your defender.* His banner over you is love (Song of Solomon 2:4). When we run to God we are safe. Remember from the start that the battle is the Lord's. He will take up your cause and fight for you. He will not turn a deaf ear to the words hurled in your direction or turn a blind eye to what unfolds in your life. He is ever present. He feels your pain. He knows the way you take. He won't take it lightly when others come against you unjustly.

Your posture when under attack affects how and when God will move for you. Jesus, the Lamb of God, stood silent before His shearer when they hurled insults at Him (Matthew 26:63). Someone was always accusing Him of heresy or attacking His identity. He never allowed their taunts and lies to sway Him or pull Him out of character. He submitted Himself to death in the face of betrayal and slander. While hanging on the cross and still being subjected to people's heartless insults, He prayed for them! "Father, forgive them, for they do not know what they are doing" (Luke 23:34). Even as He died in excruciating pain He was standing in the gap for those who reviled Him.

Perhaps you don't feel you have the strength to bless your enemies. Remain silent and talk to God. Be still and commune with God when you're capable of nothing else. He will fortify you and, if He desires, give you the words to say. Waiting for God's fullness is what troubles us at times. Sometimes God's justice is swift and other times it seems that He's forgotten what occurred. But your God never sleeps or slumbers. He does all things well and effectively.

And when He repays an offense, it isn't just for your personal satisfaction. It's also for the one who offended you so he or she may be corrected and possibly repent and turn to Him. God allows pain to correct people. He allows wounds to restore people to Him. This is why He asks you to forgive those who hurt and despitefully use you. First of all, forgiveness releases you from being bound to your offender. Second, it releases you to celebrate the restoration of the offender after God has dealt with him or her. God is a God of reconciliation. His correction and discipline are designed to encourage people to turn to Him, to trust Him for salvation and righteousness, and to turn to Him for the restoration of broken relationships.

In the midst of all that occurs during offenses, be comforted by God's love for you and His ability to make all things right. He alone can be your defender and the One who works righteously on your behalf.

Your Truth

❧ What is your usual initial reaction when someone hurts or insults you?

❧ What is the hardest thing for you when it comes to forgiving those who hurt you?

❧ What has been the outcome when you haven't held your peace and allowed the Lord to fight your battle? What did you learn?

11

How to Work with Men

My dear sister,

Let me tell you some truths that will help you and make your life easier. I'm sure life in many ways hasn't changed much since my time. Sure, technology and other advances have been made, but people are basically the same as they've always been. From where I sat under my palm tree as a judge for the nation of Israel I saw a lot. I know that women have always worked hard to make a mark in the world and exercise their own significance. I don't think that struggle will end anytime soon. And yet it doesn't have to be that way if you know what your strengths are.

I was a prophetess and judge over Israel, a highly coveted and lauded position.[1] I was also wife to Lappidoth, and my husband was a great light to me. Perhaps because of my leadership style, I was also known as the "Mother of Israel." And, indeed, I saw my people as my children and desired to lovingly guide them rather than exert the power granted by my position. It wasn't my job to do what the people could do themselves. It was my calling to influence and inspire them to rise up and do what God created them to do. I believe this is the essence of a woman's power: *to influence the people in her sphere to rise to the occasions before them and fulfill their God-given destinies.*

We women have the ability to sense the fears and weaknesses of the people in our lives and then inspire them to meet the challenges with confidence. I believe this is God's gift to us—to be able to see the end of the matter and discern the intent of people's hearts.

Because the Hebrews hadn't been following God's commands, we were under the rule of Jabin, the king of Canaan, when I became judge. Sisera was the commander of his army and oppressed us cruelly. Hope was gone because we were weary from oppression. One day I sent for Barak. I knew he was reluctant to face our enemy because they were harsh and intimidating, but I had a message for him.

Now here is an important truth: *It is never a good idea for women to bark commands at men.* Instead, we need to appeal to the part of them that desires to do what God has called them to do. Approaching them with respect, if we gently put them in remembrance of who they are and what they are capable of doing, we will be more successful. This approach releases them to solicit our help because we haven't challenged them or questioned their strength or ability.

When Barak arrived, I gave him the message from the Lord: "The LORD, the God of Israel, commands you: 'Go, take with you ten thousand men of Naphtali and Zebulun and lead them up to Mount Tabor. I will lead Sisera, the commander of Jabin's army, with his chariots and his troops to the Kishon River and give him into your hands.'"[2]

Because I was a prophet and judge, Barak said he would go into battle, but only if I accompanied him. I agreed because I understood that it was my place to assist him—but only to a certain point. I accompanied Barak to the battlefield but left the actual conquest up to him. I'd given him my full assurance that God was with him, and this was enough impetus for him to gain the confidence he needed to move forward.

Sisters, this is where our power lies. *We can gently and respectfully point the men in our lives in the right direction, but then we need to release them to do what they do best.* They have muscles and abilities to flex that we do not. When we allow them to own and exercise these aspects of themselves, they excel.

I did let Barak know that because of his hesitancy to go into battle without me, a woman would be given the honor of killing Sisera. Still, he wanted me to go with him. Barak recruited his army, and we went out to the place of battle.

Our army faced Sisera and his army, and "the LORD routed Sisera and all his chariots and army by the sword."[3] But Sisera escaped. Then, as I'd prophesied, a woman named Jael slew the general.

When Barak and I returned, I gave credit where credit was due and praised him for his contribution to defeating our enemy. He had led his troops into battle and fought well, routing those who were coming against us. We experienced a great victory! There was no need to jostle for credit and accolades because the battle was fought and won with God's help. God's grace allowed us to finish victoriously.

Barak and I wrote a song and sang it to our people…a song of victory, of praise for the warriors and everyone involved in the battle, and of great joy to God for making our success possible.

In a world where everyone is fighting for power and recognition, it's important to know where our true power lies. As a woman, I never felt I had to flex my muscles, raise my voice, or hammer people over the head with constant reminders of my position in order to get things accomplished. My position came from God. I was appointed by Him to influence the nation of Israel. I wore my title loosely and focused my passion on fulfilling my God-given assignment. My job was to decide, guide, inspire, and empower. I was very much a woman, and I had no desire to be a man or act like one. I allowed the men around me to be men. I did not fill in the blanks for them or do what they had been assigned to do. I resisted the urge to fix what they should fix and encouraged their desire to rise to the occasion and be who God called them to be.

I had no need to laud my credentials or throw my weight around. Had not God Himself qualified me for service? I quietly did what I needed to do with love and gentleness, and I was given respect and consideration in return. I wasn't in a contest with the men and women around me. Neither did I consider myself special because of my unique position in our patriarchal society. That was not my focus. I exercised my skills and talents to achieve the contribution God called me to make. I understood that the greatest power a leader can possess and exercise is the ability to release everyone to be and do what God has called him or her to do. Whether you're active in business or your home, your leadership or influence shouldn't make others question who they are and what they have to offer. Instead, your contribution should solidify their understanding of their gifts and calling and help them succeed.

Whether you're single or married, God has given you the discernment to know the strength of the men in your sphere of influence and speak into their lives in a way that enables them to better see the vision God has called them to. And if you're married, you have even more to offer to that special man in your life.

When we women embrace our assignments in the lives of the men around us, whether it be wife and lover, sister, aunt, grandmother, or friend, we fulfill God's call on our lives as His women. This is when we can live at peace and in complete fulfillment knowing we've lived up to the full measure of who we are to be as women. We have nothing to prove to anyone. Our call is simply to be who we were created to be by utilizing everything God has equipped us with to fulfill that call. In that there is great reward. Does that mean everyone will be happy with your decision? Probably not. This is why you must make pleasing God versus pleasing man your focus. Whether we are being a source of wisdom and influence with men or women the aim is always the same—to maintain our femininity while exercising our strengths, whether in the marketplace or at home. Single or married, the charge is the same. To be an agent of positive change. This is the ultimate fulfillment.

Respectfully,

Deborah

Woman to Woman

In today's world powerful women intimidate many men, so it is with great interest that I examined the life of Deborah. She was a woman in authority in a male-dominated society. She commanded generals but with such grace and femininity that Barak asked her to accompany him into battle. She was respected and acknowledged as judge of Israel, but she was also given the sweet moniker of "Mother of Israel." I'm sure this reveals her style when dealing with the people who sought her counsel. She was also a prophetess of God, seeing beyond the obvious in people's lives and speaking what was not as though it were, thus motivating them to fulfill their destinies and live up to their purpose.

Firm but gentle, she spoke into their lives without bruising egos or throwing her weight around. It's important for women, especially those in high positions, to avoid the desire to toot their own horns. We want to leave enough room for others to be impressed by us without our help. We need to let our work and accomplishments speak for us. Men love successful women. They love to brag that their women are about something significant. What they find unattractive is when women keep reminding them of who they are and what they've accomplished. Men don't want to feel like they're in competition for significance. Being impressed with yourself is also unattractive.

I also want to point out that God didn't create women to work as hard as we do. I believe we work so hard because we aren't allowing men to do their jobs. If we relinquish control of some of the things we strive with and allow men to take their rightful positions, our lives will ultimately become easier and a lot more stress free. Although we love the song "I'm Every Woman," we weren't created to do everything or to be Superwoman. In our fear that men will not do the things we need them to do for us, we tend to try to do everything ourselves. We need to step aside, let them do their things, and applaud them for it. Men live to be a woman's hero, but we're guilty of not allowing them to do so far too often, whether because of our fear of disappointment or our pride in self-sufficiency. The bottom line? *Women should not be in competition with men.* In the kingdom of God there is no battle of the sexes. The woman was made for the man because he needed help and companionship. Men are generally physically stronger, but they are weaker in the gifts that have been given to women. This creates perfect balance when everyone stays in their lanes, so to speak, and rejoices in how they were made. Woman is the divine complement of man. The period at the end of his sentence. As we women release the men in our lives to be who they were created to be, they will come into the fullness of manhood and become the partners we long for them to be.

Your Hope

It's never too late to make adjustments and start afresh in any relationship. If you're a businesswoman and need to adjust your approach in working with men, go ahead and do it. God has given you the power to empower. That ability is powerful and shouldn't be taken for granted.

If you're a wife who has grieved her husband by being a control freak, I urge you to let go. This will be scary at first for both of you. He won't know what to do at first. Let him know you believe in him and his abilities to be the main man in your world. Have an open and honest discussion about what he wants you to do and what he wishes you would let him handle. Remember, Barak asked Deborah to go to war with him. When a man feels safe enough by knowing you respect and trust him, he'll be honest about what he can and can't do. Here is where the strength of complement comes into play. You work together on finding the balance for both your strengths and weaknesses in your relationship. This is not based on the "roles of the sexes" but on an honest assessment of your abilities, his abilities, and the best way to make your relationship work at optimum level for both of you. This is your partnership to run the way you mutually choose to do so.

If you're a single woman, you're free to get this right before entering marriage. Your ability to allow a man to be a man is the most attractive feature you can have. Celebrate being a woman. It's only difficult to be a woman if you spend your time and energy trying to be a man. Allow yourself to be vulnerable. Admit your needs and weaknesses, and allow the man in your world to assist you with his advice and help. Men need to feel needed. As I always say, "It's wonderful if you can fix your own car, just don't do it when a man is around who can do it for you." Is that dumbing down or taking advantage of him? No, it is giving him the room and opportunity to feel just as good about himself as you feel about you.

A man loves a woman based on how he feels when he's with that woman. What does that mean for you? If you allow your man to be your hero, your knight in shining armor, he'll feel empowered to be the man God created him to be. God has given you everything you need to be the woman He created you to be. Resist the urge to do more than He asks of you. Embrace the peace that comes with letting go and trusting God to work through your man to meet your needs.

Your Truth

✻ In what ways do you struggle with balancing the strengths and weaknesses in your man/woman relationships?

✻ What is your greatest fear about letting go and allowing the man in your life to take the lead?

✻ What battles would you like the man in your life to fight for you? What would you need to do for that to happen?

12

How to Win a Battle

My dear sister,

I guess you could call me a reluctant heroine. Truthfully, I didn't see it coming. I got up, and it seemed to be a day like any other day. I went about my daily routine. And then he showed up. I recognized him at once. Sisera. King Jabin's general was running across the field toward me. My heart leaped in my throat. My husband wasn't at home. What should I do?

I'd heard the fighting. And though my family wasn't at odds with King Jabin, my heart went out to the people of Israel because I'd heard of Sisera's cruelty to them. I knew the Israelites had rallied troops for battle, but we lived outside the fray. Why was Sisera here? What was going on?

Then he was at my tent. He crumpled at my feet, so weary was he. Between gasps he told me how he'd narrowly escaped the battle and asked if I would hide him. He didn't know how far back his pursuers might be, but he hoped he'd escaped notice.

A sudden calm came over me. I knew what I had to do. I heard myself telling him not to be afraid. I would take care of everything. I invited him in. I covered him with rugs. He asked for some water because he was parched from running. I served him some warm milk and reassured him that he was safe. That he had no need to worry or fear. His enemies would never find him here. He should relax, sleep, gather his strength.

He agreed and told me if anyone came looking for him to say that he wasn't here. I nodded, careful not to speak because words might betray my heart.

He gratefully drank the milk I'd given him, and I could see sleep overtaking him. I waited until I heard the low rumble of deep snores that signaled the depths of sleep. Then ever so softly I crept toward him. My heart was pounding in my ears. I slowed my breathing as I picked up a tent peg and mallet. Positioning myself over him. I knew I had one chance. If I slipped or made a mistake it would be the end for me. Quietly I placed the peg against his temple. With all my might I lifted the mallet and swung down, pounding the peg straight through his skull, pinning it to the ground. I stood up. The deed was done. Sisera the tyrant was dead.[1]

I heard the sound of horses approaching. I felt a moment of fear. What if it was Sisera's men? I took a deep breath and went outside. An Israelite man rode forward. He said his name was Barak, and he and his men were searching for Sisera. Had I seen him? I nodded and led him to where Sisera lay.

It wasn't until after they took him away that it totally sank in what had taken place. It shook me to my core. Perhaps it was the Hebrew God who empowered me the moment Sisera had appeared. Left to my own devices I would never have attempted such a thing. The Hebrew warriors looked at me with shock…and even awe. They'd fought hard and chased their enemy, and now I stood before them. A woman who had felled their fearsome foe. They couldn't believe I'd used a tent peg. But it was nothing special or new to me. I'd driven tent pegs into the ground many times when we moved. It was part of my job as home-maker. My arms were strong from chores. I hadn't given whether I could carry out my plan a second thought. Quite by instinct and sec-ond nature I'd selected my weapon of warfare. I stuck to what I knew.

In that moment I learned we can live an entire lifetime and then one moment can change everything. The accumulation of everything

I'd ever done up to that moment seemed to coalesce, and I did what needed to be done. I moved without thinking. There wasn't enough time to draw back in fear. This was my moment to do something.

I believe every woman has a moment…if not many…like this. Where the life of someone or something dear to us is at stake. Then we'll rise up and win the war the enemy is waging against who or what we love. In that moment it doesn't matter who gets the credit. What only matters is that the battle is won.

I believe we win battles by being our authentic selves. I did nothing out of the ordinary—for me. The tools and place were familiar. How many times had I driven tent pegs into the ground? How long had I had this tent? I didn't flex different muscles or seek glory. I simply did what I had to do in a manner I was used to. And, my sister, that was enough.

Grateful for the victory,

Jael

Woman to Woman

In a world where women are tempted to flex their muscles and authority to prove their power and ability, we've managed to do little more than become a generation of weary women. I'm convinced that women who say it's difficult to be a woman today find it hard because they're too busy trying to be men. Jael stayed in "her lane" in the face of a potentially life-threatening situation. She operated within the area of her strengths, maintaining her femininity all the while.

No drama, no shouting, no posturing. Jael simply went about doing what she was comfortable with. She knew how to serve men. And she did that. She didn't challenge Sisera or reveal her hand. She quietly went along until she could put her plan in motion. From Jael I learned that battles can be won quietly. In other words, we don't have to go about proving a point or showing people who we are and what we're capable of. We just need to stay focused and work toward the desired end result.

There is no evidence that Jael was interested in claiming credit for defeating Sisera. She did what was necessary and explained it to Barak. I believe that when we embrace who we are as women, we become more confident and effective. The innate gifts God gives us are the most effective tools we have to secure our lives and the well-being of our loved ones. When I think of women like Rosa Parks, who started a revolution by quietly taking a seat on a bus and refusing to move, I see the strength that manifests in every woman who decides to function within the bounds of who she is and how she was created.

We don't need to imitate men to be successful or get ahead. If we do, we aren't being genuine and we'll encounter resistance and resentment. When we remain our authentic selves and focus on trusting God and following the Lord, we will succeed.

Your Hope

The burden to be "super woman" places a tremendous strain on you, especially because it's not something God calls you to do. He calls you to be. To be whole and holy in Him. That is your only charge, which actually covers a lot of ground. It is in the *being* that we end up *doing* all that God desires. As you embrace and act within who you were created to be in Him, God will rise to your defense and orchestrate your victory.

He created you in such a way that when you operate within your strengths and give your weaknesses to Him, He steps in to make up the difference. He will create favor for you and provide a way out of no way. He will give you the grace and ability to do whatever He has assigned to you. Isn't it a relief to know that after you've done all you can, you can stand still in your God and see His plan unfold? When you trust God completely, you can relax in His care.

Life is never about who takes the credit for victories because all the glory goes to God. It is not by physical might or intellectual power that you achieve things. It's by the Spirit of the living God who knows and sees all things from beginning to the end. In His infinite knowledge He moves on your behalf and guarantees that all things will work to the good. Why? Because He loves you and you are called according to

His purpose. When you are in alignment with Him, He will fight your battle. And He always wins!

Your Truth

✗ What battles have you taken into your own hands? What happens when you do things in your own strength?

✗ In what areas have you grown weary of fighting?

✗ What have you taken on that is not your battle to fight?

✗ In what ways do you struggle to maintain your femininity in the face of struggles?

13

The Dangers of Indulgence

My dear sister,

Suffice it to say that when I got the news I would bear a son in my old age I was elated. God was truly good! I immediately told my husband, Manoah. Trusting what I said was true, my husband immediately entreated the Lord, asking for guidance in raising this special son blessed by God. The news was so incredible! I was chosen by God to have a son who would be a deliverer of our people. We were both so excited. We felt honored and privileged to be entrusted with such a precious gift. To birth a man-child was an honor; to birth a man-child chosen by God to deliver the Israelites from Philistine oppression was beyond comprehension.

When our son was born, he was so beautiful I could hardly believe he was mine. My husband and I raised him in a state of awe. His was a special call, the angel said. No razor was to touch our baby's head because he was to be dedicated to God as a Nazirite.

Perhaps we were too much in wonderment of our son, Samson.[1] I confess we spoiled him. We'd waited for a child for so long that we indulged him. Manoah was quite focused on following the specific instructions on raising our child of promise. And, yes, we were faithful to follow all the Levitical guidelines to keep Samson in line with his priestly duties. But we were lax on other disciplines that proved to be as important if not more so. Our Samson was incredibly strong physically and equally as strong willed. He seemed bent on having what he wanted at any cost. And for the sake of peace, many times we gave in despite our reservations about the choices he was making. We loved him. We couldn't bear to withhold what he wanted or face his displeasure.

Samson had a lust for life—including beautiful, exotic women. The day he told us he'd selected a wife from among our enemy the Philistines, my heart broke. I protested but he was resolute in his choice. "Get her for me. She's the right one for me." Again we folded when we felt like we should have stood firm. My husband and I decided to keep quiet and pray for the best.

With dread in our hearts we went to meet our future daughter-in-law. The events that unfolded were like a bad play. Samson, ever the one to enjoy a good joke or riddle, challenged the guests at a feast he hosted with a difficult one. They were to give him thirty sheets and thirty changes of garments if they didn't answer correctly. This didn't sit well. Eventually the guests threatened Samson's bride. She, in turn, pleaded with Samson for the answer. After his bride-to-be cried for several days, Samson gave in. His fiancée quickly conveyed the information to the guests, who wasted little time in giving Samson "their solution" to the riddle. Samson became so angry at their cheating that he went down to the Philistine town of Ashkelan and slew thirty men. He took their clothing and gave them to the feast guests as their payment. He then returned home still fuming. He descended into a black hole of anger and bitterness, and no manner of trying to comfort him prevailed against his ire.

When he finally snapped out of it, he returned to the Philistines to get his bride—only to discover she'd been given to his best man! Needless to say, this did nothing to abate my son's already foul mood. He tied three hundred foxes together by their tails, added firebrands in the knots, and turned the animals loose in the fields of the Philistines. The Philistines retaliated by burning down the home of Samson's wife and father-in-law with them in it! I'm ashamed to say my dear son then retaliated by slaughtering more Philistines. Then the Philistines marched against our people. To prevent war, all the Israelites delivered Samson to the Philistines. Then Samson broke free and took the jawbone of an ass and killed a thousand more Philistines![2]

My boy sure created drama! When I review the past, I confess there were many things in his childhood that we probably shouldn't have overlooked. Many things I should have said. Examples I should have set. But now all I have are regrets. By indulging our son, we let him believe he should and could have anything he wanted—whether it was within God's will or not. He was unbridled. He loved the wrong women. Danger appealed to him.

Don't get me wrong. We were proud of Samson for some things. For all the fuss he created, he was appointed by God to be a judge for our people during our days of captivity under the Philistines.[3] But he let his passions rule him in many ways.

I would have thought he'd learn his lesson from so many consequences, but he was wise in his own eyes and not open to correction. I can't place the blame on him alone. I placated him far too much. Instead of focusing on his divine purpose, I dwelt more on my desire for confrontation-free love between Samson and me. I didn't realize I wasn't helping him prepare for his destiny. I watched his downward spiral from afar with my heart breaking. The rumor mill produced many stories about Samson's dalliances. I heard that one time he spent the night with a Philistine prostitute and barely escaped a deadly ambush.[4]

But it was Delilah who was his undoing. Why he didn't realize she was playing the same trick over and over on him that his wife had, I'll never know. By then it was too late to speak reason to Samson about his choices. Delilah fooled my son through her ways of seduction. This time he fell and never recovered. Finding out that Samson's strength was in the length of his hair (which represented his dedication to God), Delilah had his head shaved and exposed my son to bondage like he'd never known. Even now I weep over his untimely demise. Bound and blinded by the Philistines, Samson was led away like an animal and put into prison.

My Samson was defenseless because the Spirit of the Lord left him.

For so long he'd taken God's presence and blessings for granted. Perhaps because we never allowed him to suffer the consequences of his actions when he was a child, he grew up believing there were none. Perhaps I didn't do a good enough job of teaching him that *God* was his true strength. I should have told him that the length of his hair was merely a *sign* of his consecration to God. Oh, how he loved his hair. It was a source of his pride, along with his physical strength. He never understood his true strength came from the anointing of God. Shorn like a sheep, he suffered great humiliation. And this time he couldn't escape and no one could rescue him. Then came the day the Philistines took my son out of prison to make sport of him.

When Samson was tied to two pillars in the temple for Dagon, perhaps the light finally came on in his mind, illuminating his understanding. Samson turned to God and prayed for strength for one last feat. Then he pressed against the columns until they gave way. My son killed more Philistines in this last act of revenge than he had before. But he paid a great price. He was also killed in the carnage.

I wonder if things would have turned out differently if I'd been more firm. If I'd been more centered on his purpose and destiny instead of just him as my beloved son. Samson became a celebrity in his own mind instead of a servant of the living God. Thinking back, every battle my son fought was for his own agenda. Not one of the battles he picked and fought were for God's glory. He was selfish and self-centered.

What else can I say? In my pain, I share with you woman-to-woman the cost of overindulgence when it comes to raising children and interacting with the people you love. *To not speak the truth to them under the guise of love is really an act of hatred that can lead to tragedy.* We aren't responsible for another person's actions once they reach maturity, but if we know we've done all we can to impart God's truth and equip them to do the right thing, we can be at peace even if they stray from what is right.

I learned these lessons too late to help my Samson. In a way I feel I loved my son to death instead of to life. I've asked for and received God's forgiveness. Thankfully, He's allowed me this opportunity to share with you what I've learned. What is the main advice I'd like you to remember? *Actively show your children (and other people you love) how to serve God and help them prepare for serving others.* Jesus said that those who seek to save their own lives will lose it (Matthew 10:37-39). I pray you won't have to learn this the hard way like I did.

Regretful but wiser,

Samson's mother

Woman to Woman

Sons are the pride of every mother. Husbands are the loves of their wives. Friends are the security of every person. However, it is important to know that love doesn't go along with everything. Love rejoices in the truth. Love is relentless. Love is not indulgent. Love doesn't enable bad and self-destructive behavior. Love goes for the best in the beloved. If need be, love will break to bind and crush to strengthen. The potter isn't kind to the clay. He slaps it into shape until it becomes a beautiful vessel. Love puts that lovely vessel through the firing process. This may look cruel, but the end result is an object of great and lasting beauty that is also useful.

Never mistake love for indulgence. Don't be fooled into thinking you secure a relationship by choosing not to rebuke or correct a loved one. The Bible clearly tells us that the Lord rebukes and chastens those He loves (Revelation 3:19). Discipline of our children is a sign of love. God's Word also tells us that the heart of a child comes into the world seeking correction. That foolishness is bound up in the heart of a child, and the rod of correction will drive it far from him (Proverbs 22:15). Parents are encouraged to not withhold correction from their children. They won't die when you correct them. Physical discipline may well save them from death (Proverbs 23:13-14). The bottom line is that from God's perspective those who spare the rod of discipline hate their children. Those who love their children care enough to discipline them (Proverbs 13:24)

Why is discipline so important? Because mothers are called to discern God's purpose for their children, identify their gifts, train them up in the way they should go, and provoke them to good works. We are to teach them in the ways of the Lord, which is wisdom. We can't mother correctly if we're trying to be our children's friends. We must parent! (Friendship may come later in life when your child is mature enough to know and understand the boundaries of giving you honor while walking with you as a friend and confidante.)

I recall my mother telling me, "You may not like me right now, but you will love me later." She was right. I grew to appreciate her strictness when I saw the things she saved me from. While some of my friends grew up in more lenient households, their lives were shipwrecked later in life, while the discipline my mother instilled in me kept me out of harm's way and led me to be discerning in my choices. My mother is now my closest friend, but I admit I didn't like her much when I was a child.

"Faithful are the wounds of a friend, but the kisses of an enemy are deceitful" (Proverbs 27:6 NKJV). Whether we're mothers or not, the spirit of motherhood is part of us. And these discipline principles don't just apply to children. They extend to our family members and friends. Speaking the truth in love when we see someone doing the wrong thing or headed in the wrong direction is an act of love. We are our brother's and our sister's keepers. It is up to us to speak the truth gently to those we care about. We can't force them to make the best choices, but we can present the options and reason with them. Should they fail to take our counsel, we need to also be there to love them through the consequences. Our consolation is twofold: at least we gave them the ability to make an educated choice and their mistakes can't be charged to us. We never need to say "I told you so." The pain of the consequences is usually enough to tell them they've made a mistake.

Short-term gratification usually doesn't lead to a lasting great result. And this is a lesson that doesn't need to be learned by personal experience of the outcome of bad choices. It can be learned by example and choosing wisdom.

Your Hope

When children go wayward, mothers shouldn't feel as if they failed. We are all born with free will and the ability to make our own choices. You can pour all the right things into your children, and they may still go left when faced with choices that appeal to their desires rather than what they've learned. That is when you especially apply yourself to prayer that God will redeem them from their wrong choices. Remember, the Word says "train up a child in the way he should go, and when he is old he will not depart from it" (Proverbs 22:6 NKJV). This suggests that most will attend the school of hard knocks a few times. That is the way of human nature—finding things out the hard way.

Discipline and speaking the truth extends beyond parent/child relationships. "As iron sharpens iron, so a friend sharpens a friend" (Proverbs 27:17 NLT). Think of the times you've seen friends making wrong choices and you've tried to tell them what they were doing wasn't a good idea. They may have gotten angry and even decided not to speak to you for a time because you wouldn't support their actions. Needless to say, when the outcome was exactly what you predicted, they had to suffer the embarrassment of their stubborn insistence. At this point, as a true friend you need to be there to help them pick up the pieces of their shattered expectations. The beauty and hope in this situation is the power of God's restoration when we choose to embrace it.

"We all, like sheep, have gone astray" (Isaiah 53:6). We all make bad choices. We all mess up areas of our lives despite receiving the wise counsel of people in our lives. Thankfully God faithfully mends, restores, and reconciles us back to Himself. Whether it's loved ones or yourself, a great goal is to not let the folly of bad decisions lead to irreparable harm (or death, as in the case of Samson). You'll grieve when you see the fallout of the not-so-great choices your loved ones make, but always remember that God is able to keep what is committed to Him. Release your loved ones to Him knowing He is well able to exchange beauty for ashes.

Your Truth

❧ What is your greatest struggle with speaking truth to your loved ones?

❧ In what ways have you made concessions that might be harmful to your loved ones? Is there anything you can do to adjust the counsel you gave?

❧ In what ways can you renew your thinking to embrace the value of speaking the truth in love?

14

How to Change Your Life

My dear sister,

I pray my story will give you hope. I know what it's like to feel bound to a life you long to be free of. I can't say I was someone's victim. I lived the life I created for myself; nonetheless, I longed to be free. I wanted to change my circumstances so desperately, but I couldn't see any way out. As a matter of fact, the more I dreamed of a new life, the more deeply entrenched I seemed to become in the life I was living. I was empty. Merely existing. Going through the motions. Doing what I had to do to survive.

I won't lie to you. I was a harlot, a prostitute. Everyone knew it. It wasn't something I tried to cover up. My clientele consisted of the powerful and upwardly mobile, which afforded me the good things in life. I was beholden to no one. My home was nice and in a prime location. I lived well. But then again, that might depend on your definition of living well. To acquire all the trappings of a fine life but lose yourself in the process isn't really living. Not at all. This is the state I was in when God sent me deliverance.

How many times had I breathed "God help me" under my breath, not knowing if anyone was really listening? I didn't have a direct channel to any specific god, but everyone in town was buzzing about the

Israelites. They were conquering and taking possession of land, and they were headed our way! People said the God they served was awesome and fearsome. I heard that He parted the Red Sea so the Israelites could escape the Egyptians. The Israelites said their God ensured their victories. They won great battles against fierce and "invincible" kings who attempted to stop them or conquer them. And now they were headed to Jericho. Hearts in the city were melting in fear. No one knew quite what to do so we simply waited. We were paralyzed by angst and in awe of their God. We hoped our city walls would keep them out.

I didn't know what to make of the Israelite advance and hadn't taken the time to think about how it would affect me. Then one night two men showed up at my door. These men were very different from my usual customers. They only wanted shelter.

That's when I devised my plan. It was risky, yes, but it was a risk I was willing to take. In no time at all the news spread that foreigners were at my house. I was used to being the topic of gossip, so I didn't panic when the king's men showed up asking about Israelite spies. I diverted their search to the city gate.

After they left, I went up on the roof where I'd hidden the Israelites under stalks of flax. I told them I would help them escape on one condition: They must exclude my family from the destruction their army would cause when they conquered Jericho. The men agreed and told me to hang a scarlet cord in my window as a signal to their warriors to avoid my home. They gave me their word that whoever was in my house wouldn't be attacked or killed. So I got out a long rope and let them down the city wall in the dark of the night.[1]

The next day I gathered my family and told them the plan. They all agreed. Some were apprehensive, wondering how they would survive the loss of all they had worked so hard for. Leaving everything behind. I reminded them it was just things. What was more precious—life or material possessions that could be replaced?

I knew this was my chance for a new life. I didn't know what the future would hold, but I was well acquainted with my past and my present, and neither one was desirable. There had to be something better! Perhaps if I made this God of Israel my own He would move on my behalf and give me the life I'd always dreamed of. I was willing to take the chance. To let go of everything. I hoped against hope and waited for the Israelites to return.

And return they did. All of them in full force. We all watched with apprehension as they did a strange thing. For seven days they walked around the city outside the wall. They walked in silence. The wait felt interminable. No one knew what to expect or what to do. The city was frozen in terror, waiting for what we knew not.

And then it happened. On the seventh day they marched as usual, but when they'd made their rounds this time they didn't retreat. They stopped and gave a fearsome shout. It resounded and echoed off the desert. The wall—our fortified wall the men of Jericho had prided themselves on building—came tumbling down as if they were brittle rocks weakened by time.

The rest of the day is a blur. Everyone in my household was whisked away by the same spies that had come to my house earlier. They took us out of harm's way before the battle began in earnest. In one day my life was changed forever. I found myself living among a people I had never met. Some were wary of me and my kindred, but they relaxed at the assurances by their leader, a man named Joshua, who told them I was the one who had helped the spies escape when they were trapped in Jericho.

I settled into my new life, and then I met a wonderful man named Salmon. He not only introduced me to the Israelite God, but he also introduced me to true love. We were betrothed, and I gave birth to a son we named Boaz. When Boaz was grown, he married Ruth, a foreigner from Moab. I hope I can take a little bit of credit for that. Since I was an outsider who married an Israelite, I figure that's why he was willing to marry one too, which under normal terms wouldn't be accepted among the Israelites. Perhaps I helped carve a special place in his heart for her. Like me, Ruth also left everything behind to pursue the God of Israel and the chance for a new beginning.

I believe we all come to a place in life where what we've been experiencing is no longer enough. We long for something that gives life purpose and meaning. Something that says, "Yes, life is worth living."

Opportunities to make a contribution that bears lasting fruit that blesses people other than ourselves. That's what I lived for. And God answered the cry of my heart and blessed me…but only after I deliberately chose to take a leap of faith. To fly in the face of the rationale that because the outcome was uncertain, I should remain with what I knew. I defied my fear to trust God.

I fell into His arms, and He caught me and set my feet on high places. And now I have a legacy I can be proud of. My grandson Jesse sired a son named David, who became king of Israel. And Jesus of Nazareth was also born of my family line. Would I have ever dreamed that I would be part of the lineage of Jesus Christ, the Messiah? Absolutely not!

When we dare to take a leap of faith, only God knows where we'll end up and what will happen. So this is my challenge to you. Assess your life and have the courage to trust God and embrace the adventure He has for you. He'll bring about change and add more meaning to your life. I can attest to the fact that what you gain will exceed the risk. So go for it! Do it to the glory of God!

Still amazed,

Rahab

Woman to Woman

There comes a time in every woman's life when she searches for meaning and a reason for being. The norm becomes no longer acceptable. Our spirits are stretching and desiring a breakthrough. Something new. A higher level of living that is evidence of God in our lives. That He is active and spiritual growth is taking place within us. That we are bearing fruit—fruit that not only sustains us but also blesses others.

Then there is the personal satisfaction we get from experiencing progress or movement in our lives. Life doesn't remain the same in God. He is always moving forward. When we feel stuck we experience a sickness in our souls because we weren't created to stagnate. We were created to grow and bear fruit in due season. Whether that fruit is an accomplishment, a relationship, a child, a new place to live, or a dream come true, we must experience something different. We must give life to something; we must produce something that affirms we're alive and significant. "Hope deferred makes the heart sick, but a longing fulfilled is a tree of life" (Proverbs 13:12).

What we must realize is that change doesn't just happen. It occurs in cooperation with God as we take advantage of the opportunities and open doors He presents to us. I believe this adage: "When opportunity meets preparation, success happens." Many times the silent seasons of the soul when we find ourselves despairing and longing for change are those times of preparation that open our hearts to embrace the opportunity for change when it comes. Until the pain of staying the same becomes greater than the pain of change, most of us won't move or dare to do anything different. Our comfort zones inhibit us from taking risks. Often we complain about wanting change, but we don't exercise the courage needed to utilize our faith and take the leap required to move forward, break a cycle, or press past where we are.

Taking a chance is required to achieve or reach anything that is of substance and meaning. If we want a breakthrough, then we've got to break away from something in order to get to the other side of what we desire. Simple yet complicated because where or how far we'll reach isn't fully known. It's the mystery on the other side that often causes us to draw back. The "what ifs" of life can paralyze us and cause us to cling to the familiar no matter how unsatisfying or undesirable it is. Like Rahab, we must be radical and seize the day. We need to go forward with the passionate faith that God wants the change for us even more than we want it. "If God is for us, who can be against us?" (Romans 8:31).

Your Hope

No matter what mistakes you've made or what failure you've experienced in your life, God stands ready to give you a new beginning. He abounds with new mercies every morning that are pregnant with the promise of the life you really want down deep inside. After all, He placed those desires in you. And He is faithful to fulfill your longings. The timing becomes the issue. Often it seems the wait for change is interminable. Never assume that God *is not* working on your behalf, lining up the circumstances for your good to produce the end result you both desire.

Don't despise the growing pains, and don't shrink back from taking a risk. This is where you get to exercise your faith. God will always make provision for the vision He gives you. Therefore, you can move forward with confidence knowing that He is walking with you and will assist you to the other side of the promise or dream He has given you where you'll experience new and greater fulfillment. Embrace the adventure! It's not for the faint of heart, but the reward will be greater than your trepidation.

Your Truth

❧ What changes would you like in your life?

❧ What can you do to help make it happen? What do you need to surrender to God?

❧ What holds you back from pressing forward? What are your fears?

❧ Where have you placed your confidence for finding meaning and fulfillment?

15

The Power of Connections

My dear sister,

I know that many of you have told my story over and over again. I realize I've been an example to many women on how to find a godly man like my Boaz. But I'd like to submit a different train of thought. It's wonderful to have men who are special to us, but I'm also very aware that we can have our men today but they may be gone tomorrow. Whether it be through unfaithfulness, divorce, or, as was true for me, death. As a widow I learned that my life and my joy can't be reliant on the presence of a husband. This was my experience. Things change. Life happens. What we thought was a permanent fixture can be gone in a snap...without notice....never to return.

My first husband came from Bethlehem in the land of Judah. He was an Israelite. His family moved to Moab to escape famine. I felt fortunate to become part of their wonderful family. So did my sister-in-law, Orpah. It was nothing short of a miracle because we knew the Israelites didn't usually mix with other peoples. Their religion forbade it. Perhaps they thought they would never return to Judah. Whatever the reason, I was thankful. Different from the men of Moab, our husbands were very kind and very devoted to their God. They continually rehearsed all the things their God had done for them as a people and often spoke in fond remembrance of their land.

My mother-in-law's husband died before I married into the family. Then more tragedy struck. Orpah's husband and my husband died. My mother-in-law, Naomi, was heartbroken.[1] She couldn't be consoled and wondered if they'd angered God by leaving their homeland. When she heard the famine was over and her friends were doing well again, she decided to go back. Orpah and I said we'd go with her, but Naomi discouraged us. She said we would remain husbandless if we went with her. Orpah returned to her family, but I wouldn't be dissuaded. I told Naomi I would not leave her. I felt we had a divine connection I didn't want broken. I'd pledged my life to her son, and now he was gone. Naomi had no one, and neither did I. All the more reason to stick together. My purpose for going with her wasn't to get another husband. It was to stay connected to her. To her God. To her people. How could I let her go alone? She'd been far too good to me. The fear of the unknown was not greater than my need to go with her. So we set off.

When we got to Bethlehem, people were so happy to see her! But Naomi declared to them all that she was broken and bitter. It broke my heart to see her in this state. I felt the need to do whatever I could to lift her spirits and take care of her. She'd returned defeated because of all the losses she'd endured. I tried to do what I could to help her realize the faithfulness of God. All was not lost. She had her health and strength, a place to live, and a person who loved her very much (me).

I wanted to make sure we had enough food, so Naomi suggested I go out to glean in the fields. As I was gleaning, a worker said the owner of the field wanted to meet me. The owner introduced himself as Boaz and invited me to sit and eat with him. He was such a kind man. He told me I could eat as much as I wanted and continue to glean in his fields. He instructed his workers to watch out for me and treat me kindly. I didn't find out until much later that he'd also told them to leave some sheaves in the field for me to collect.

That night when I told Naomi about my encounter with Boaz it was the first time in a long time that I saw the spark of excitement in her eyes. She praised God for the connection I'd made. It was as if her hope had been reignited.

I remained in Boaz's fields gleaning through the wheat and barley seasons. Then Naomi told me it was time to ask Boaz to be my redeemer. He was Naomi's next of kin on her husband's side and, according to their custom, he should marry me to preserve our family lineage. I couldn't believe my ears. Would Boaz consider taking me, a Moabite, to be his wife? We were despised in Israel. I knew if he hadn't instructed his workers to make sure I was safe I would have been shunned or worse. Then Naomi told me Boaz's mother was Rahab, who had been a prostitute in Jericho. "So he knows what it's like to be an outcast," I thought. His mother had also been a foreigner who had probably been subjected to the stigma of being disregarded because of her background.

Naomi said Boaz was her next of kin. This was a God connection. I was sure of it! If I followed her instructions, I would be a married woman in no time. And so I did everything she said. I made my way to the threshing floor, and after he'd retired for the night and fallen asleep there, I lay down at his feet. He awoke later and noticed me. He was so surprised! He was even more pleased when I stated my purpose. He was very thoughtful and told me he would immediately take care of everything. However, there was one small problem. Someone else who was also kin was entitled to redeem me first. Boaz said he would sort the matter out. He then instructed me to stay until right before dawn so no one would trouble me or see me leaving the threshing floor. He sent me home laden down with provisions.

Naomi was anxiously awaiting my return. When I told her what Boaz said, she rejoiced and assured me that all would be well. And it was. Boaz, true to his word, sorted out everything and claimed me as his bride. I could hardly believe it! I felt as if I were in a dream. Me, a Moabite and widow, was marrying one of Israel's most eligible and wealthy bachelors! And all because I chose to stay connected with my mother-in-law. She in turn connected me to my new husband.

Boaz and I had a beautiful baby boy we named Obed. Naomi was elated, and the legacy of our family continued.

I never heard anything else about Orpah after she returned home. I think of her often and shiver at the thought that I too could have chosen to remain behind and fade into the oblivion of the familiar. Oh, what I would have missed! Perish the thought. Neither did I anticipate all that would occur simply because I couldn't bear to part with Naomi. I take this as evidence that God uses people to bless one another. That there are minimal degrees of separation between people and our destinies. Our connections afford us the ability and opportunity to embrace and fulfill our purpose in life. Without those connections we'd be left to fend and flail for ourselves. Like a well-proportioned body, we all come together at the right time to connect and discover the next step toward the fulfillment of God's plans for us. Don't miss this, my sister. *We can do nothing alone.* The greatest blessings come in unexpected packages and through those we might not expect as we reach out and stay connected through the joys and trials of life.

Together we make it. Together we stand. Together we forge new beginnings. There is wisdom in a multitude of counsel. We need each other, so stay connected!

Grateful for sisterhood,

Ruth

Woman to Woman

I've heard many women say it's difficult to have great female friendships. That women can't trust other women. Yet I've been blessed to have rich friendships with women over the years. I treasure every one of them, but the ones that impact me the most are my older women friends. The wisdom they impart and the insights they give on the issues of life have helped me in too many ways to count. These friends are the same ones who broadened my world by connecting me with key people and great opportunities. For instance, my mentor connected me to someone who helped me publish my first book.

God has wired us to be interdependent with each other while being completely dependent on Him. He uses people to assist us in our life journeys. We need one another to survive. We need one another to be fruitful. [2] We are the body of Christ. The Word explains how we need to work together by likening us to a physical body. The hand can't say to the foot, "I have no need of you" because every part in the body is necessary. This principle of connection is the essence of what took place in the garden. Adam needed to be connected to another human to complete the assignments God gave him. Though the man walked and talked in the cool of the evening with God, Adam needed to be joined to someone of his kind to be more fruitful in life.

Jesus understood the value of connections. He said, "I am the vine; you are the branches…apart from me you can do nothing." [3] Our entire existence and capacity to flourish relies on our connection to God and the relational exchange that affords us. In Him we live, move, and have our being. Apart from Him we are nothing, but in Him all things are possible! [4] There are endless scriptures that stress the importance of relationships and that we are not islands unto ourselves. King Solomon, renowned for his wisdom, said, "Two are better than one because they have a good return for their labor." [5]

Ruth would never have met Boaz without Naomi. But Ruth didn't attach herself to Naomi for what she could get. She chose to walk with Naomi because of what she could give to her mother-in-law. Ruth genuinely cared for Naomi. I believe that "networking" isn't effective if it is only for the sake of networking. The connections must be genuine in terms of relational sentiment as well as vision to be fruitful. Two cannot walk or work together effectively if they are not in agreement. When our heart motivation is that of giving, we will always receive more than we give.

Your Hope

Relationships can hurt as much as they can help. People fail us, reject us, betray us, make mistakes against us, and walk away from us. However, we are made for relationships—with God and people. When life rocks us, God wants us to experience not only His comfort but also support and comfort from family and friends. Loved ones are extensions of God's arms and the natural reflection of His care in real and tangible ways.

For every disappointment you experience, God has a blessing in store from an unexpected source. As you focus on being a blessing to others and connecting in such a way that you weather some trials together, blessings are sure to come out of your broken times. Stronger bonds are forged amid adversity. Don't let the setbacks of life pull you away from relationships. Instead, let the challenges push you forward so you can discover even greater things about God and yourself.

Never look for a blessing from the place where you planted. The root travels, but it is still connected to the seed. So definitely plant, but never demand fruit from it. Look for the increase from God as He breathes over your labor of love. He will surprise you far beyond what you can imagine. Remember, the fruit you bear will only be as good as your connections, so embrace your relationships passionately and generously. Through them is where real wealth and fulfillment of purpose are found.

Your Truth

✤ What motivates you to connect to others? What holds you back?

✤ How have you invested yourself in others? What results have you experienced?

✤ What have you gained from connections in the past? How do your expectations affect your connections?

16

What Every Woman Needs to Know

My dear sister,

I know…I know. You think I'm a wicked woman. But hear me out. Perhaps I used my womanly wiles to the wrong end, but that doesn't mean I don't have wisdom to share. I won't waste your time justifying my actions by playing the victim or saying that a woman has to do what she has to do to make it. I chose my lifestyle quite purposefully, and I did what I did well. My thoughts were of maintaining a great life, seeking immediate pleasure, and getting ahead. I didn't think of eternal consequences; I lived for the day. Mine was a life lived as fully as possible in the moment.

Samson was a fine specimen of a man. Large and strong. Beautiful with flowing locks. There was something almost savage about him.[1] Others quaked in fear when they saw him, but I was filled with desire. He was also high profile—a powerful judge among his people.[2] After our first encounter, he came to live in my house. We were both creatures of pleasure, and we fed each other's passions. Since he was an Israelite and I was a Philistine, the sense of danger heightened our excitement of being together.

I'll tell you what Samson found intriguing about me, and you can apply the information however you'd like. I was "all woman." You see, a man wants a feminine woman...not a woman who acts like a man. I made myself soft and alluring. I stroked his ego at every turn. I encouraged him to believe that everything I did was for him. From the way I dressed to the food and drink I served, it was to please him. He believed he was my only focus. Because he was head over heels in love with me, my wish was his command. I took care of him, built up his confidence, and loved him passionately. It took a while, but I finally finagled the secret of his great strength out of him.

A man won't reveal his innermost being to a woman until he trusts her completely. The more vulnerable we are, the more a man feels we need him, the safer and stronger he feels. I allowed Samson to be the king of my world. Because he believed he was my everything, he felt he could trust me. His trust made him open to revealing his heart and telling me his innermost secrets.

Yes, I am known as the woman who took an amazingly strong man down. I leveled him to nothing. And then I let him be carted off like an animal. All that is true. I sold my soul for money...money that couldn't possibly equal the value of his life. And I paid the price of my actions by leaving a less-than-desirable legacy. Evil temptress is not my favorite way to be remembered. But I can attest to one thing: I knew how to get a man and keep him. Perhaps I can redeem myself by sharing a few things with you that may help you in your marriage or committed relationship.

Modern women have lost the *art of femininity*. When used properly, human intimacy—physical, mental, and emotional—can make romantic relationships heaven on earth. So here goes...

Every man longs for a woman who is interested in him. In what he does. In his hopes, aspirations, and everyday adventures. So draw him out. Get him to talk and then listen...really listen.

Every man longs to be your hero. Samson loved it when I spoke in awe of his strength. It made him feel like a king. Let your man rescue you. Your relationship should not be a contest where you feel the need to display your strength or self-sufficiency. That is not why he is there. He is there to cover your softness. Allow him to be your man. Let him do things for you. This lets you embrace and revel in the freedom of being feminine.

A man falls in love and stays in love based on how *he* feels when he is with you. Appeal to all his senses, stimulating them in different ways to keep him intrigued. *For his sense of touch*, take care of your skin. Keep it soft and supple. *For his sense of smell* always be scented faintly with oils or perfumes that make him want to draw closer. Fill your environment with smells that he'll find pleasing and inviting. Fill the air with scents that intoxicate him.

To appeal to his sense of taste, serve him food that makes him hungry for more—but only from your hand because the flavor or way you serve is so unique. You want your cooking to taste like home to him. You want to leave him comparing everything else he tastes to the delights he samples with you. *For appealing to his sight*, be feminine and natural, using just the right amount of enhancement, and add a touch of mystery. Dress well. A real man likes quality. Never reveal too much. Leave some things to the imagination. Wear fabrics he'll enjoy touching. Don't use too much makeup because he doesn't want to wear it when he kisses you.

And how could I forget *his sense of hearing*? Words of respect, encouragement, and love are what he needs to hear. Play soft music in the background to soothe his spirit and make him forget the cares of the day. A man is extremely sensitive to the sound of your voice. Avoid harsh attitudes and anger that will cause him to retreat. Whisper something pleasant in his ear. Tell him you love him. You want to be his oasis in the middle of the desert. Let your gentle reassurances and confidence in him fill him up and recharge him to face the fray another day.

If every wife acted like she was her husband's mistress, she could be confident that her husband would never feel the need to find someone like me. Never let the business of life kill your sense of romance. A man must have it. If he doesn't get it, he will seek it elsewhere. Whether he channels that energy into another woman, his job, or a sport or hobby, rest assured that he will refocus somewhere to get the fulfillment he seeks. My best advice? Be your husband's girlfriend always, especially when you become his wife. Don't make him long for the woman he married.

Did you see that there wasn't anything earth shattering or complicated here? Simply enjoy being a woman. These womanly traits will come naturally to you if you let them. Yes, femininity is an art, but it is also a part of you, of who you are as a woman. When a man taps into your softness, it disarms him. His secrets become yours. He will reveal the deepest parts of himself to you because he trusts you completely.

I did learn one lesson. I don't recommend you take advantage of your guy's weaknesses like I did. I robbed Samson of his strength and liberty. There is a price to pay for everything. I must say there isn't a sadder sight than seeing a broken man. Strength gone. Betrayed. Resigned. You'll never get a man back once you have broken his spirit. He may stand before you again, but his eyes will be empty, his posture bowed, his spirit quenched. And trust me—you'll want the man you once knew back...but you won't find him. There is no reward big enough for destroying a man. It's too great a loss. This I learned too late. I hope you won't make the same mistake.

Left with memories only,

Delilah

Woman to Woman

The most powerful gift God gives women is femininity. Men have fought wars over it. Sacrificed kingdoms for it. Performed feats to win women's admiration. The softness of a woman is her allure. It's like a harbor offering safety in a man's life. He's drawn to it. Without it he is tossed to and fro by the affairs of life. When the right woman is in a man's life, he operates at his peak capacity, producing fruit and flourishing. When the wrong woman is in a man's life devastation results. His spirit may be corrupted and his moral fiber may be compromised. She can even sidetrack him from his destiny.

God created the woman for the man...to help him be the man God created him to be. To help him complete his God-given assignments on earth. This is a powerful position that we should never pervert or use for personal gain. The innate giftings women possess make us highly influential in the lives of our husbands and the men God puts in our lives. The things we whisper to them are the ideas that stick with them.

When a woman deliberately messes up a man's mind, he may get confused or even fail to function. He may become paralyzed or cast aside integrity to carry out her wishes. Obviously this wouldn't please God. Jezebel influenced her husband to be corrupt. He suffered, she suffered, and the kingdom suffered for her manipulation. She met a horrible end and left a terrible legacy in the aftermath that affected her children and her children's children.

We don't know what became of Delilah after she led Samson down the garden path to defeat. Perhaps she was in the stadium that collapsed. Whether she suffered physical death right away or death by living long with guilt and regret, neither is a desirable outcome. What can we gain from women like her? God gives us gifts that must be exercised in godly ways to bear the best fruit in the lives of our husbands, our households, and our communities. We impact the world not just through what we do individually but also how we impact the men within our sphere of influence.

Three things are basic to men when it comes to romance. They want to be well respected, well fed, and well loved (in the intimate sense). God gives us special gifts and attributes that can inspire men to live up to what God asks them to do. The husband's assignment toward his wife is to love, cherish, and protect her. Those gifts are built into his fiber; therefore, he needs to be needed by his wife. When a husband is emasculated at home, he may go rogue. His judgment may be impaired and ungodly actions may follow.

As in the garden, there is a price to be paid for influencing our husbands the wrong way. While husbands will be judged for not being in the positions they were called and created to stand in, wives will be judged for their actions. As Eve received the consequences of her actions so will we. Our place of influence next to our husbands wasn't created to be used for our own gain. We are to be partners with our husbands to further the purposes of God. Personal agendas lead to actions in the flesh that can lead to the deterioration or even death of relationships. Following God's ways always leads to life and fruitfulness. This was the assignment given from God to the man and woman in the Garden of Eden. Be fruitful and multiply, subdue evil, and exercise dominion over every living thing. When we line up with God's plan, we will experience kingdom living on earth at its best. Along with a relationship that glorifies God, we will experience righteousness, peace, joy, and marriage at its best.

Your Hope

In a world of fractured relationships and selfish agendas we can find our way back to the garden if we choose to renew our minds (Romans 12:2). The world has made our romantic relationships contests that no one can win. It has promoted the concept that women are powerless unless we take control. Nothing could be further from the truth. Our relationships with our husbands were meant to be powerful partnerships that further God's purposes on the earth. It is His desire that we walk in unity and experience harmony.

Our marriages are the reflection of the relationship between the members of the Godhead (God, Jesus Christ, and the Holy Ghost). There is no striving between them. Nothing separates them, and they are in agreement with their agenda. Everything they do individually feeds into their agreed-upon goals. This is why Jesus said apart from the Father He could do nothing. He only says what He hears the Father say and does what He sees the Father doing (John 8:28). The Holy Spirit testifies of and reveals the Son. They counsel with themselves and operate in complete harmony. Out of that unity powerful things occur. That is our charge to imitate.

When you work for our own gain within your marriage, unity is broken and strife is created. The world system has done a good job of pitting men and women against one another and making them believe they must fight for their positions or rights. But as a believer and follower of Jesus, you are of a different kingdom where that mindset doesn't work (John 17:14). It is only when you are authentically functioning true to the way God wired you that you will reap the rewards and fruit of investing in your husband's life. Whether you are married or single, God places men in your life that you can impact in a positive way…not so much by what you do but by whom God created you to be.

Your Truth

🌿 What mind-sets do you struggle with when dealing with men? In what ways do your thoughts and attitudes hinder you from being your best feminine self?

🌿 What effect have you had on the men in your life? In what ways have you helped strengthen or weaken them?

🌿 When have your goals interfered with getting the results you wanted in your marriage or committed relationship?

17

Timing Is Everything

My dear sister,

I pray my letter gives you hope. I feel as if my story is made for those who have come to the place where they question the faithfulness of God and wonder if He is really able to deliver the desires of their hearts. Trust me when I say I know how you feel. It seemed I had everything a woman could ask for—a husband who loved me, a good home, no financial worries...shouldn't that be enough to make any woman happy? Still I yearned for the one thing I didn't have—a child. I felt terrible and ungrateful.

My husband, Elkanah, didn't seem to care if I ever had children. But then again why would he? He already had children with his other wife, Peninnah. And much to her amusement I remained childless. Every year we would go to Shiloh to worship and sacrifice to the Lord. The irony of not finding peace at this place of rest didn't escape me. Peninnah would remind me that she was going to thank God for her children. I struggled to think of what I could give thanks for. Every year we came to offer our thanksgiving, and I would find myself feeling so bitter to the core that I couldn't even eat. Elkanah would ply me with a double portion to offer to God. My husband would ask me if his love wasn't enough to make me happy. How could I tell this dear sweet man that it was not? Did his love mean more to me than ten sons?[1] Who said I wanted ten sons? It was enough to hope for one.

God had shut my womb, and I didn't know why. My speculations were many but none made sense. The more I tried to make sense of why God would withhold the one thing I desired so much, the more frustrated I became. I finally decided I would stop trying to figure it out. It only led to me feeling worthless, especially when I compared myself to Peninnah, who seemed to be more fruitful than most. How could I compete or measure up to that? It destroyed my self-worth to the point that I couldn't receive and enjoy my husband's love. Though I talked to myself seeking reason and calm, the pervading thought I had was that if I only had a child I would be so happy.

I finally came to the end of myself. I struggled to be free of the longing. I couldn't bear it any longer. I went to the house of the Lord at Shiloh and bowed before God and cried out to Him with all my heart. I must have looked like a crazy woman as I emptied myself to the depths of my soul until I was speechless. The priest Eli thought I was drunk, but I assured him I was desperately reaching out to God for the request of my heart. I told God if He would just give me a son I would give him back to Him. That was the best offering I could give. Eli told me, "Go in peace, and may the God of Israel grant you what you have asked of him."[2] His words resonated in my soul, and a peace came over me that I hadn't known for a long time. I felt as if a boulder had been rolled off my shoulders. I rose and went back home feeling free of all that had weighed down my spirit.

And then it happened! God opened my womb, and I was with child. Elkanah and I were elated. Finally God had granted me my request. Our beautiful little Samuel was born. I remembered what I'd promised God, and after I weaned Samuel I took him to the Lord's house and presented him to Eli. It was bittersweet. To release what I had wanted most back to God wasn't easy, and yet I knew I must. I gave my Samuel to God with a trusting heart that He would keep my treasure safe and make my sacrifice worthwhile. My reward was seeing Samuel grow up to be a mighty man of God and an awesome prophet.[3]

Perhaps that is what all the delay was about. I merely wanted a son, but God wanted a prophet after His own heart. And as you know by now, it's impossible to out give God. He blessed me with five more children after that. He truly made me fruitful out of my affliction.[4] I will be honest with you. Had God given me Samuel when I first wanted a child, I would not have given him for service to the Lord in the house of the Lord. I would have kept him.

I wonder if sometimes God keeps us from having something until we come to the place where we are ready to release it for His glory. I suppose it takes some of us longer than others to get to that place. But, oh, the freedom when we finally get there! Truly God will give us the desires of our hearts when they align with His desires and plans. We must never deceive ourselves into thinking that the things we desire in life only benefit ourselves. My son Samuel wasn't just a gift to me; he was a gift to the world. He crowned two kings and spoke into their lives in ways that affected our nation.[5]

In my wildest dreams I would never have thought I would give birth to someone so phenomenal. But God knew. And He waited patiently until I was ready to give Him what He wanted. Then He gave me what I wanted. My conclusion? *All things in God's time, in God's way, for God's purposes.* We think way too small. Our tiny vision sometimes hinders our blessings. We need to ask God to enlarge our view.

So, my dear sister, do not grow weary of waiting on God. Know that He uses time as part of His design to develop something great in your life. Stand ready with open hands to give back to Him what He gives to you. Your rewards will be great.

Still praising Him,

Hannah

Woman to Woman

"Hope deferred makes the heart sick" (Proverbs 13:12). God knows this, and yet in our lives He allows seasons of waiting that can seem interminable. "What is He waiting for?" you might ask. He is waiting for you. I often say, "When God doesn't get you out of a situation, it's because He is waiting to get something out of you." When we come to God, we become part of a plan that is much greater and bigger than we are. This affects each of us personally in the sense that our desires now become part of the tapestry of God's design. This means that life may not go according to our schedule because He factors it into His plan, which often demands more critical timing. This is exciting when we're aware of it and frustrating when we forget.

We women are a major part of God's kingdom plan because of the influence we wield, what we bear, and the things we give birth to beyond children. We need to understand our strategic part in God's intricate workings. Hannah only saw her desire for a child from her personal viewpoint. Her longing for a child would also garner her approval from her spouse and community. It would be a stamp of her worth. But God wanted more. He saw a woman He trusted to release her child to Him. And since God is a gentleman who won't force His will on people, He waited for Hannah's heart to get to that place of willingness. Though it was painful for her to wait so long to realize her dream, the joy she finally experienced far outweighed her suffering.

"You do not have, because you do not ask. You ask and do not receive, because you ask wrongly to spend it on your passions" (James 4:2-3 ESV). When we come to the realization that God has selected us and included us in His plans, we are able to see the occurrences in our lives from an entirely different perspective. This rearranges our hearts to embrace a bigger picture of kingdom living that leads to peace, joy, and fulfillment in Him, as well as the assurance that the things we wait for will be entirely worth the wait.

Your Hope

In opera, "it isn't over until the fat lady sings." Because we are believers in Jesus, we have eternity so it will never be over...period! While we're here on earth, we're bound by time. But in God's economy there is never a need to rush. Perfection takes time. Remember, it is all right for you to have desires, just make sure those desires don't have you.

Give your desires to God, who is able to do all things well. His plans for your life will amaze and astound you. It will fill your heart with joy and laughter! All that is required on your part is to trust Him and be available. You don't have to make anything happen—God will do that in the fullness of His timing.

As you walk before Him with open hands and give Him your expectations He is able to transform your desires into an even greater design that fits into His plans. One you probably didn't even think of. One that will ultimately give you more joy than you imagined possible. Don't try to figure out or rationalize what God is doing and why it's taking Him so long. You'll only frustrate yourself. His ways are beyond your ways, and His thoughts are higher (Isaiah 55:8-9). Learn to rest in Him. In moments of impatience, go back and give Him your desire again. Do it as many times as you have to. In the end God will prove Himself faithful—just you wait and see. Keep in mind that people think way too small, and God wants to do something exceedingly and abundantly above all you could ask or think for you. Get ready to be surprised by His joy.

Your Truth

❧ What is your response to delay in your life?

❧ What is your motivation for what you want? How can God be a part of what you desire?

❧ In what ways do you need to release your desire to God? What should your new perspective be?

18

The Difference a
Right Response Makes

My dear sister,

Where do I begin with my story? In hindsight I didn't handle my situation well. Perhaps I thought too highly of myself. I was lulled into my high-minded state because I enjoyed being so celebrated. It was no secret that I was the pride of my husband. A trophy wife or arm candy, you might call me. I just say my husband married well.

I was beautiful, and he took great pride in showing me off. I made him look good. I heightened his pay grade. My husband was a powerful king. He'd conquered lands from Ethiopia to India, but a man's self-worth reaches beyond his material acquisitions to the woman he is able to wed. In a sense, a wife is a man's real wealth. She is what he measures his masculinity by. The more beautiful and out of reach she is to other men, the greater prize he believes he's won and the greater he views himself in the eyes of those he competes with.

I was such a woman and I knew it. Ahasuerus spoiled me. I was surrounded by plush accessories in my luxurious apartments within the palace. I reveled in my world. But as you know, possessions aren't enough for any woman. We want our husbands close by.

King Ahasuerus was a powerful man with big dreams. He played as hard as he worked. I was happy enough for him when he won his last mission to subdue yet another vulnerable nation, but I was left to amuse myself for months while he celebrated with his male friends. I distracted myself by throwing my own party, but it wasn't my preferred mode for spending my time. Therefore, I'm sure you can imagine my mood when I was *finally* summoned by him to put on my crown and come to display myself to his guests. First, it was against the law for a woman to show herself in public that way. Second, I was hurt and angry that it had taken him six months to ask for my company! And his snubbing of me was very public. Everyone in the castle...and probably outside the walls too...knew my husband had not called for my presence. I could see pity in the eyes of the servants, maids, attendants, and slaves.

And now the king had requested my presence. How could I face everyone with any dignity or pride if I obeyed as a slave or maid would. After all I was the queen! I deserved respect. As badly as I wanted to see him, I refused to let him treat me like a possession around just for his convenience. Besides, I'd also heard "the king was merry with wine."[1] I refused to enable his drunken behavior.

In retrospect, I admit that my fear of the opinions of others won out over my desire to see my husband. Though I was flattered that he wanted to show me off, my hurt and anger at being disregarded for so long stopped me from pausing to consider my actions. Suffice it to say that my refusal to appear before my husband and his guests became one of the most famous denials in history! I never thought my choice would turn into a national scandal.

Apparently my refusal to immediately go to the king was seen as a public affront. The king was upset, and soon the rumor mill had spread it throughout the palace grounds. The king's colleagues took it quite personally. Before I could consider the best way to respond and apologize, I was ousted from the kingdom and banned forever!

Why such a drastic fate? The men were paranoid and afraid! They managed to convince the king that if their own wives heard of what I'd done, the disrespect throughout the kingdom would become contagious. They would no longer be able to manage their own households. My actions would embolden the wives in the kingdom to not heed the voices of their husbands. The men were worried they'd lose their authority and power. So the king's "wise men" recommended I be made an example for all women to see and understand that failure to obey would not be tolerated, thereby squelching any temptation they might have to consider such a thing. In his anger, my husband concurred, and what had been a six-month separation became a lifetime.

Now I see my mistake clearly. I never considered for a moment that I could be replaced. In hindsight it does not escape me that the first things I admired about my husband became the aspects I despised. His power, his commitment to his work, and his love for his people I found sexy—until I felt ignored.

I'm not saying that what my husband did was right. It wasn't. In fact, it was wrong on many levels, the greatest being that he knew he was asking me to break the law. But the part I have to own was the way I responded. Sometimes it's not *what* we say but *how* we say it that destroys relationships. I could have asked for a private audience with the king so I could share my concerns. He would probably have seen the error of his ways if I'd made a personal and private appeal to him.

I never considered what an affront my refusal would be to him or that it was done in such a public forum. After all, my husband was the king. I undermined his authority in front of everyone. I took away his power. I bruised his ego and set him up for public ridicule. I didn't consider how I could respond that would empower or enable him to release me from his request with dignity and generosity.

Yes, I embarrassed my husband. And for that I'm truly sorry. And once the damage was done, I was given no opportunity to apologize or attempt to reverse it. I sacrificed my relationship and position for the right to be right. I lost my partner by standing on a minor principle. Was it worth it in the end for me to assert my right? No. I picked the wrong battle to fight and lost the war. Would it really have been so terrible to do what he asked and speak to him in private about it later? Not at all. Any consequence then would have fallen on his shoulders.

Why do I write to you today? To encourage you to never make

decisions in the midst of hurt or anger. If you're upset, delay your response until you've calmed down enough to hear and respond to wisdom. With everything in you, whenever possible, pursue peace and understanding (1 Peter 3:11). Proving your point to the detriment of your work or relationships is never worth it. You will lose more than you gain. This is what I've learned, my sister. I hope you'll heed this wisdom through me instead of finding out on your own.

Banished and alone,

Queen Vashti

Woman to Woman

A man's ego is a terrible thing to bruise. The repercussions usually extend much further than we think they will. The Word of God tells us that "a brother offended is harder to be won than a strong city. And contentions are like the bars of a citadel" (Proverbs 18:19 NASB). To publicly put your man on "front street" is an even worse no-no.

As we've seen before, a foolish woman destroys her house with her own hands—or, in this case, with her mouth (Proverbs 14:1). It pays to be wise in relationships. To be quick to listen and slow to speak. The thing about words is once they've been spoken they can't be taken back. The world was created with words. Words have tremendous power. They can make or break relationships. No relationship is free of offense, but how we respond to them makes all the difference in the world.

Even when we're right, we need to be careful. Being right doesn't necessarily guarantee we'll win the battle without scars. When facing a situation when we're feeling hurt or angry, it's always best to hold our peace until a sense of calmness returns. Responses made in anger tend to be the wrong ones. And they usually do more damage than we know.

If our goal is to seek peace and in times of conflict work toward reconciliation, we must remember that "a gentle answer turns away wrath" (Proverbs 15:1). Perhaps this is why the Word of God encourages us to, above all things, get understanding or wisdom. Understanding can settle a lot of issues *before* they become areas of contention.

Vashti was married to a powerful man...a king. There are certain considerations that come with being with a man who is influential and powerful. First, he is probably always busy. He didn't become powerful or important by sitting around and doing a lot of socializing, unless it had to do with his business. Have you too noticed that usually what attracts us to someone also ends up being what causes the most problems? For instance, if a man is available for romance all the time, later the woman he's dating may get annoyed that he's so laid back...and may even complain that he's lazy. That powerful man with all the money is busy making money!

We need to know and understand our husbands. We don't want to provide excuses for any bad behavior, but having understanding will help us give better responses when something bothers us. We want to build our marriages, not destroy them.

In marriage, pride should never be part of the equation. Proving a point shouldn't be either. Speaking the truth in love and offering solutions that will help both of you grow together is optimum.

Another important principle is to never betray the trust of your partner in public. There is a reason we call it a "personal life." Keep your issues between the two of you unless there is a need for counseling. When you invite others into the arena of your relationship, you become vulnerable to the pressure of the opinions of others. Those on the outside looking in will never extend the grace you will for your partner because they don't love him like you do...and he is not their assignment to love.

Be careful in your interactions and always be considerate. Never take for granted that you can't be replaced. Forgiveness is difficult and never assured on a human level. Make love your highest goal, and fashion all your responses accordingly.

Your Hope

With God in the midst of your relationship there will always be the capacity to mend what has been broken. Our God is a God of reconciliation. As you trust Him to be the keeper of your relationship, you can weather any offense and get to a place of understanding so you can share from your heart with a transparency that will empower your partner to hear what you're saying.

Being gracious and exercising the grace God extends to you keeps you looking beyond the fault of your partner to see his needs. When you look at his heart, you can make a much calmer assessment on how to approach any given situation and find a lasting solution that will bring you closer together. When you lack wisdom on what to do, ask the Holy Ghost. He will instruct you and reveal the hidden things that you might overlook with your natural eyes (James 1:5).

As a woman who knows God, you should listen to the still small voice within before listening to the voices without. Purpose to respond instead of react during tense times. But just in case you mess up, you have what Vashti did not—the Holy Spirit. He will do a work of reconciliation. He is able to mend the breach and bind up the brokenhearted. He is able to make everything beautiful in its time (Ecclesiastes 3:11).

Your Truth

❧ How have you reacted when your mate or a loved one has offended you in the past? What were the results?

❧ What do you need to work on when it comes to how you respond to an offense?

❧ In what ways do you need to be more sensitive with loved ones when they do something that you don't like?

19

How to Make Your Man Your Hero

My dear sister,

So much can be accomplished by simply being who you are. Though every woman dreams of who and what she'll become, in most cases the lives we end up living are vastly different. My story is an example of exactly that. Many years before I was born, Israel was conquered by the Babylonians and my ancestors were taken to their land as captives. I was an orphan being brought up by my cousin in Susa. My dream was a simple one. The best I hoped for was to become a wife, a mother, and perhaps do some sort of business should my husband deem fit. But that's not what happened.

Sometimes I still think I'm dreaming. Can you imagine? The town was abuzz with the gossip of Queen Vashti being banished. The word was out that the king was looking for a new wife. And then one day I woke up to find myself being escorted to the king's palace with a lot of other young women. I was ushered into the suites of the harem and surrounded by attendants whose jobs were to teach me court manners and make me more beautiful. I was told I was being prepared to meet the king to see if I would be chosen as the next queen.

Hegai, a eunuch, was in charge of the harem. Not long after I arrived, he had me assigned to the best place in the suites and gave me seven attendants. I was given the finest of garments, oils, perfumes, and food. He doted over me and instructed me in all things related to the king. After a year of beauty treatments, the evening arrived when I was to go to King Xerxes (another name for Ahasuerus). Hegai personally oversaw every bit of my preparations. He finally clucked his satisfaction and ushered me out of my quarters. Before I knew it I was at the door of the king's private apartments.

I was so nervous. What if he didn't like me? What if I was banished to some other part of the harem like some of the other girls who had visited him earlier and been rejected. Hegai assured me this would not happen, but how could I be sure? I had to trust God. I whispered one last prayer under my breath and entered his chambers. To my surprise he was not the fearsome king I'd heard of. Rather, he was a gentle and loving man. Though he was not one of my people, I found myself being drawn to him.

It was all like a dream. I pinched myself when the king told me I was going to be his queen! How could I, a Jew, be chosen to be the queen of the Babylonian nation? *The sooner I wake up the better!* I thought. But no, it was true. I was chosen to be the queen of Persia!

Time passed, and I settled in to my new role. From the beginning my cousin Mordecai told me not to divulge my heritage, so no one at the palace knew I was Jewish. I still heard from him occasionally and followed his advice.[1]

The gravity of my situation didn't sink in until the day my cousin Mordecai sent a message to me of the utmost urgency. He said the lives of my people were being threatened by a mandate set forth by the king. Haman, my husband's good friend, hated my cousin because he refused to bow down to him as the king had decreed because Mordecai would not worship anyone but God. And now Haman was getting his revenge. He influenced the king to issue a death decree against all the Jews within the kingdom. Mordecai wanted me to go to the king and plead for its reversal.

That was when it hit me. Yes, I was the queen, but the king hadn't called for me for quite some time. People couldn't just boldly charge into the throne room uninvited. They had to be summoned by the king. If they did appear, the king could decide to grant leniency by extending his scepter. If he didn't, the person was put to death. I sent a message to Mordecai explaining this, but he said it was my duty. Perhaps I'd been called to be queen in the kingdom for such a time as this. He even said if I didn't do anything about the situation, God would have someone else rise up to save the Jews but my family would perish.[2]

What was I going to do? Would I also perish with my people once the king and others in the court discovered I was Jewish? I couldn't be certain. For the preservation of my people and myself I would have to take the risk.

I decided to respond to the panic I felt by fasting and praying before attempting an audience with the king. I took three days to quiet my spirit and settle my soul with God before making my way to the great hall. I dressed carefully that day, choosing what I knew he liked best. This dress, that fragrance…not so distracting he couldn't stay focused on why I was really there but inviting enough to make him happy to see me. With my heart pounding in my ears, I made my way to the great hall. Positioning myself at the entrance, I watched my husband taking care of affairs of state. The air gradually changed as people became aware of my presence. I stood quietly. Suddenly the king stopped his conversation and looked in my direction. A smile lit up his face, and he extended his scepter and beckoned me to come closer to him. I came forward and touched the tip of it. His expression was warm and filled with genuine pleasure to see me. This was reassuring.

My husband asked me what I wanted and said he'd give it to me— up to half of the kingdom.[3] My heart leaped at such a generous offer, but something within me put my heart in check. I would accept none of the things he offered. In that moment they were but mere distractions to what truly mattered. Neither would I state my case at this moment. It had been a while since I had seen him, so I would make no request lest he feel I had come for what I wanted and not for him. So I invited him to dinner. He loved food and attention. I would lavish him with both. And then it came to me—invite the enemy also! The king seemed pleased that I invited his friend. The stage was set. My heart was steady, and I knew in my spirit that time would allow the story to unfold in accordance with God's plan.

That evening spirits were high as my husband and Haman, the enemy of my people, ate and drank and exchanged stories to entertain me. Again the king asked me what would I have. Again I felt restrained to pose my dilemma. Not just yet. It was better to wait until I felt God's release to broach the topic. So I invited the king and his friend to yet another evening of dining. The light in my husband's eyes told me this pleased him. He felt loved and wanted—not because I wanted something but simply because I enjoyed the pleasure of his company. He was used to everyone having an agenda or a wish to ask for when approaching him. This was refreshing to be wanted for nothing more than himself. He and Haman left in high spirits looking forward to the morrow.

They returned the following evening. Haman wasn't in high spirits, but he was not my focus. During dinner the king shared that after leaving my quarters the night before he'd been unable to sleep. He had the chronicles of the kingdom read to him and discovered that he'd never rewarded my cousin Mordecai for uncovering a plot against his life. He'd asked Haman for suggestions on what to do for someone whom the king wanted to honor. Then the king had ordered Haman to carry out the task of publicly celebrating Mordecai.

"Ah," I thought. "Now I understand Haman's demeanor."

The king was in a particularly great mood and feeling very generous. Again he asked me after a sumptuous dinner with fine wine what I would like. Again he said it would be given to me even if it were up to half the kingdom.

Then I felt released to lay my dilemma before him. I was careful to couch my request in a manner that made the decision completely his to make. I told him if it pleased him and I had found favor with him, I would ask that he spare my life and the lives of my people. I told him that if my people were merely going to be sold as slaves I would not have troubled him, for what could be greater than being in service to the king. But because our lives were being threatened by a terrible enemy I would prevail upon him for intervention.

King Xerxes' eyes grew dark with anger as he asked me who dared to threaten my life. I pointed toward Haman, who looked as if he were about to faint. My husband was so incensed that he excused himself to walk in the garden to recover his faculties. It was then that Haman threw himself upon me on the couch where I was reclining to beg for help. At that moment the king returned and flew into a rage at the sight of Haman clutching my gown. He ordered his attendants to take him away and hang him on the gallows Haman had prepared for Mordecai.[4]

A wave of relief swept over me and the floodgates opened. I wept as I told him the terror my people faced. He swept into action and released a mandate for my people to defend themselves. He stripped the household of Haman of their status and gave the properties to me! My husband was my hero! He rose to the occasion and defended me. I felt safe, secure, covered, and loved. He could have ignored my request so easily, but God created favor for me. Then the king did another wonderful thing. Because of his integrity and service, my cousin Mordecai was elevated to Haman's position and given the king's signet ring for authority. I also asked Mordecai to oversee the possessions the king had given me.[5]

In my eyes I did nothing special. I was simply the woman God created me to be. I was a wife who loved and served her husband. Who was sensitive to his needs. Who was responsive to his heart. He felt safe with me, and I with him.

Unlike Vashti, I didn't wait for an invitation to approach my husband and king. I humbly appeared before him looking my best. And he received me warmly. Well, not just received but celebrated!

I believe when we make bringing gladness to the hearts of our husbands, bosses, supervisors—anyone in authority in our lives—this will always be the case. Who would not want to reward the person who made sure his or her needs were met? Perhaps this sounds simplistic in your sophisticated world, but I believe it to be a universal truth. Simply be who you are, do what you can, and God will do the rest. He will direct you as you trust Him completely and resist the urge to move according to your own understanding. Then be willing to step out in faith when God instructs. As we obey Him He will send His favor before us. After all, the hearts of kings are in His hands.

A daughter of God above all else,

Queen Esther

Woman to Woman

Many are called but few are chosen. This is why it's so important when dating to let the man choose you. When he considers you his reward, he will go to great lengths to protect his heart's desire. And once you have his heart, be gentle and kind. Don't take advantage of your status. Manipulation isn't attractive or godly. Simply be and grow into the woman God created you to be. Being who you are is far more powerful and fruitful.

Esther wasn't a sophisticated head of state. She was a woman and a wife before she was a queen. On her own, she had no major strategy for saving her people. She sought God's counsel and help. She appealed to her husband's heart and inspired him to come to her defense. She did this not by demanding but by understanding his needs and giving him an opportunity to grant her heart's desire. She focused on his needs instead of her own. This took great courage and discipline. Because she surrendered to God first through fasting and praying, she trusted God to move, create favor, and come to her defense. This was the God who had parted the Red Sea! Influencing a king to save His people was nothing for Him. He was King of kings. Once Esther's heart was settled on who had her back, she was ready to approach the king.

She realized she was breaking protocol, but her trust in God, along with Mordecai's encouragement, spurred her forward. God would prepare the way for her. And indeed He did. The evidence of God's favor calmed her spirit and helped her pace herself in the situation. First she would make sure her husband's needs were met before she made her request. Though he made her a generous offer, he must not be found wanting in any way before she made her request. Her surrender to God helped her focus on the real issue and heed His guidance. Now was not the time to be distracted with tempting offers that weren't related to the outcome she needed. She made sure that she gave before she asked for anything.

When people don't like us they won't help us, and that can really hurt us in the long run. The Bible tells us when the king smiles there is favor (Proverbs 16:15). Our gifts make room for us to act by inspiring people to want to do something for us. When we curry favor, we will win friends and influence people. This works across the board, whether in personal relationships or in the marketplace. If the people we need favor from are distracted by what we haven't done, we won't get the help we need.

Remaining aware of and sensitive to the needs of the people we make requests of is vital to creating good will. Through prayer and tapping into our intuitive natures, we can discover the best ways to nurture people who are significant in our world and approach them with what we need. And when it comes to our husbands, oh what a simple-but-delicious meal can do. It doesn't just feed their stomachs, but the love and care we put into it feeds and fortifies their spirit. Husbands fully satisfied will be the heroes of our dreams!

Your Hope

Where have all the good men gone? I believe they are alive and well. The real question is, how do you find one and win his heart? I believe it is the influence of the right woman that makes a man the right man. An African proverb sums this principle up well: "The man is the head. The woman is the neck. Wherever the neck turns, the head turns." When voting for politicians, we scrutinize their spouses as well because we know their influence is significant. I wonder if Queen Vashti would have cared about the plight of the Jews. Probably not, and she most certainly would not have put her life on the line for them. Perhaps that is why she had to be removed—to make room for Esther to come on the scene and be put in place to rescue God's people. In God's view relationships are often strategic alignments to move His plans forward.

When you are in the center of God's will, nothing can keep you from experiencing joy and satisfaction in your relationships and life in general. God will grant you favor when you allow Him to lead you and instruct you. He'll give you the wisdom you need to accomplish His will and overcome challenges.

The hope you have in any situation that threatens your security is God. He will always have a plan to deliver you. It may not be obvious to the natural eye. It may not be a sophisticated maneuver. It may be as simple as a conversation over dinner. God goes before you to do the groundwork and prepare your husband or whoever you're making your request of. It is not by might or power that the details of your life are worked out. It is by the Spirit of God being released to do what He does while you remain your authentic self and following the Lord. So be the woman, the wife, the sister, the friend, and the employee you were created to be. Leave the rest to God.

Your Truth

❧ When you're confronted by emergencies in life that threaten your security, what is your usual first response? Do you need to change it? If so, to what?

❧ How can you serve the person to whom you want to make a request of?

❧ How can you remain authentic in who you are as you seek a solution to the problem or issue at hand?

20

How to Live with a Fool

My dear sister,

Trust me—I'm not exaggerating when I tell you I had the misfortune of being married to a fool. Perhaps his parents had an inkling of what was to come because even his name meant fool. I'm not good at dressing up the truth. It is what it is. So yes, my husband was a fool. Why would I marry such a man? you ask. All I can say is that in the flush of romance I ignored a lot of warning signs. Perhaps I just focused on making it work. He was the husband I was given to by my parents, who thought he was the right choice for me. It became apparent later that wasn't the case, but I committed myself to being the best wife I could be.

Nabal wasn't a fool about all things, obviously. He made a good living, and we lacked for nothing. But he was short on patience and even shorter in handling his temper. He had no regard for the people who worked for him or around him. I bore my husband's shortcomings as patiently as I could. I tried to look beyond his faults to see his needs so I could help. I covered for his lapses as best I could. But the day came when Nabal's foolishness almost cost us everything.

David and his army were in our area, and the young commander sent his men to ask us for some provisions. My husband, with his rough nature, was quick to refuse and insulting to boot. Upon hearing about the exchange between Nabal and David's representatives, I was warned by one of our servants that David might respond with anger and consider taking what he needed by force. I hurriedly gathered together provisions and sent them ahead of me to David. I didn't tell my husband at the time because I needed to circumvent impending catastrophe.

When I reached David, I bowed low and asked for his pardon as I stood in the gap for my husband. I could see the commander was angry even as I told him my husband was a fool like his name indicated, and I would take full responsibility for what he'd done.[1] I offered David what I'd brought hoping it would placate him and divert his ire. I also reasoned with him that needless bloodshed shouldn't be on his hands in light of what God had called him to do.[2]

David calmed himself and blessed me for my discernment. He thanked me for the provisions and granted my request to overlook Nabal's insults. I breathed a sigh of relief and made my way home.

Nabal was involved in festivities late into the night. He was drunk and in such a merry state that I didn't want to approach him. I waited until the next morning to tell him what had transpired the day before. When he heard I'd taken provisions to David he got so irate that he fell down and became as a stone. Ten days later he died.

Shortly after this, messengers from David came. They said, "David has sent us to you to take you as his wife." I couldn't believe it even as I accepted! This is how my mighty God exchanged my fool of a husband for a king of a husband.

What do I want to pass on to you? Let me just say this. Telling a man he is a fool will get you nowhere. The secret to living peaceably with a man like that is to know who and what you're dealing with and work around him. Give that man to the Lord and then stand in the gap for him when need be. Pray for him and trust God to keep you safe above your husband's foolish choices.

When I met David, I took responsibility for Nabal's foolishness. People have asked me why, and I simply say that at the end of the day he was my husband. We were one whether I agreed with the way he did things or not. Did I usurp his authority by taking provisions to

David when he'd already said no? Maybe, but I believe God always chooses the greater good and examines our heart's motives. I did what I needed for the sake of our entire household. Many lives were at stake, and a judgment call had to be made in the interest of everyone involved. Nabal thought only of himself and his own ego when he reacted the way he did. I chose to cover us all as well as I could. Is the way this unfolded God's preference? No, it was not. God put husbands in charge of households. And yet He covered my actions and went before me as I approached David and asked for his favor.

I feared Nabal's response when I had to tell him what I'd done. But God is a God of mercy who searches every heart and judges accordingly. I believe God honored my desire to cover my husband and our household. When I spoke to Nabal the next day, I didn't accuse him or lay any blame on him. I just quietly explained what I'd done to pursue peace. When Nabal died I had to accept that it was for the best. I accepted my fate as a widow. I won't lie to you. In some ways I breathed a sigh of relief. The stress of living with a fool kept me on edge all the time because I never knew what he'd do next to derail our stability. God was with me!

Imagine my surprise when David sent for me to become his wife! I knew he had appreciated my efforts to forestall disaster, but it never occurred to me that I'd done anything he'd remember. I guess he was touched by the fact that I put him in remembrance of his calling and advised him to walk in light of that. But isn't that what any woman with integrity and wisdom would do?

My advice to you, dear sister? Don't despair if your husband isn't living up to your expectations. Don't try to prove your point. Live quietly and as peaceably as you can. Allow God to be your mediator and deal with your mate. No one will do it more effectively. And don't allow yourself to sink to a petty level and return kind for kind. Sometimes fools bring out the fool in others. Instead, choose the path of wisdom and hold your peace so that your mate can hear the voice of God.

Yes, at times you will have to make a judgment call and step in. Before acting, though, make sure you have the peace of God and His backing so He'll cover you. One caveat: My situation was pretty unique.

God will probably not have your foolish man drop dead so suddenly. However, God is well able to kill the foolishness in your husband and replace it with wisdom.

The secret to maintaining peace and hope is, as the book of Proverbs says, to "not answer a fool according to his folly, or you yourself will be just like him."[3] Don't try to be the Holy Ghost in your man's life. Leave room for God to deal with him. Allow time for your husband to respond to God.

Our God is faithful. This I learned in the midst of difficult times. So hold on, my friend. God is on your side. He will strengthen you and take your part.

Living in peace at last,

Abigail

Woman to Woman

Not every relationship is easy. There are times we see loved ones doing the wrong thing, and every instinct within us screams to correct them. The frustration when our counsel is ignored tears at the fiber of our relationships. Knowing when to speak and when to be silent can be a challenge. What we have to remember is that their choices are not our responsibility. As the old folks say, "Everyone has to walk in their own shoes." God has His own way of dealing with each person individually.

We can't point out the errors of their ways to fools. Well, we can but they won't believe, comprehend, or receive what we tell them. Only the Spirit of God can penetrate their understanding or teach them through experience to change their way of thinking.

How do we maintain our peace in the midst of the chaos of fools? By releasing them to the hand of the Lord. Trying to hold on or fight to make our points with foolish people will rob us of our sanity. Instead, we need to ask God to give us insights into why our foolish people do what they do. Why do they react the way they do? Ask for His help to look beyond the faults and see the need. The root of foolishness is usually fear or pride. When we know the root, we can better deal with the fruit.

Even so, we don't want to give license to or allow abuse. If that is taking place in our relationships, we need to distance ourselves. Sometimes fools can't or won't correct themselves or get help until they experience loss...or maybe never. It takes the intervention of God to straighten out a fool, and the fool has to be willing to listen to God. We can't take it personally if we can't penetrate the foolish haze or get through to them.

In many instances fools are masters at making others feel as if they are the ones at fault. Don't buy into it. We need to surround ourselves with solid counsel that will keep us rooted in what is true and what is right. We don't want to lose ourselves in the fray.

Foolishness is a distraction from righteousness. It pulls us away from the fear of the Lord, which is the beginning of wisdom (Job 28:28). We're instructed to ask God for wisdom and embrace wisdom like a sister. I love the fact that God personifies wisdom as a woman (Proverbs 4:7-9)! Remember that wisdom is not common. Cling to the Source of wisdom, and surround yourself with a multitude of sound counsel who draw on God's Word for guidance. There is safety there. "Plans fail for lack of counsel, but with many advisers they succeed" (Proverbs 15:22).

Your Hope

God is well able to keep you if you are submitted to Him no matter what is going on around you. Like Abigail, if you remain discerning in the midst of chaos and foolishness, God will bring you out. The key is staying centered in Christ so that you can hear His instructions on the way you should take. There may be a time when you need to stand in the gap. At times God may instruct you to hold your peace. In that moment God Himself will fight your battle and be your protection and defense.

As in the case of Nabal, God may deliver you from your fool or replace him physically or spiritually. As you release that person to God wait for Him to intervene on your behalf.

Part of the beauty in the story of Abigail is that she was beautiful and discerning. Yet I'm sure in the middle of what she dealt with when it came to Nabal's foolishness she didn't feel very lovely at all. Her self-esteem may have suffered. God took care of her by making her beautiful and wise in the eyes of David. Through David, God gave back everything that was taken from her through her marriage to Nabal. God won't leave you feeling forsaken or trapped in a situation that grieves you or puts your well-being at risk. As you submit to Him and trust Him for the right outcome, He will intervene and assure you of your worth. He will guide you and lead you on a path that leads to the peace and joy you seek. The wisdom God gives will always lead to a life rich with fulfillment and honor. So let me repeat Abigail's advice. "Cling to the Source of wisdom, and surround yourself with a multitude of sound counsel who draws on God's Word for guidance. There is safety there." Then stand back and see the love, grace, and mercy of the Lord. You will be the wiser for it.

Your Truth

❧ What is your usual response when loved ones reject wisdom?

❧ In what ways do you try to get them to see reason? What is the outcome?

❧ What is your greatest struggle when dealing with those who refuse to embrace wisdom? What can you do to preserve your own wisdom?

21

How to Avoid Relationship Regrets

My dear sister,

Let me save you from becoming or remaining loveless all your life. There are seeds that get sown in the heart of a woman that must be rooted out if you want to be happy. Though your negative feelings may be justified, they will not serve you well if you cling to them.

The first time I saw David I thought he was the most beautiful man I'd ever seen. I'd heard how he slew the Philistine giant called Goliath. Everyone was talking about it. My father brought David to the palace, and David would sit and play music for my father. His music sounded as if it were from heaven itself.

How I loved him! I would watch him and imagine being his wife. Everyone could see it in my eyes. I thought it was a dream come true when my father offered him my hand in exchange for the foreskins of a hundred Philistines. David went above and beyond the call of duty by presenting him with two hundred![1] I was so happy.

I became the wife of the man of my dreams. Afraid of David's success my father feared he'd try to take over the kingdom. His inner demons made him so paranoid he wouldn't rest until David was dead. I heard of a plot to take his life, so I helped my husband escape.[2] I wept as he ran off into the night because I didn't know what the future would bring. I was now married to a man on the run.

My father was angry that I'd helped David escape, of course. Not long after that, Father gave me off to another man as if David was already dead. I resigned myself to the fact that I would never see my love again. My husband Paltiel (I called him Palti) was a good man who loved me. But I would often hear of David's exploits and wonder if he missed me as much as I missed him.

Years passed, and by the time I saw David again he had six wives and six children. He demanded that I return to him. My brother Ish-Bosheth sent men to take me to David. Poor Palti. He wept and followed me until Abner, the commander of the army from the house of Saul, sent him away.[3]

Again a man who loved me was forcefully taken from me. I was returned to David, a man I had loved passionately long ago, who now had six other wives. He had also changed. I was no longer the single focus of his love. *He had the time to acquire six wives and have six children, but he never sent anyone to get me before this*, I thought. My heart couldn't reconcile this hurt. I couldn't be comforted. Even after David became king my bitterness grew.

David led his army, and they defeated many foes. They fought the Philistines, and David became obsessed over recapturing the ark of the Lord that had been taken by the Philistines in battle long ago. He wouldn't give up until he got it back. "If only he'd been that determined to get me back after I was given to another," I thought. When David was successful and brought the ark home there was a great fanfare.

When they returned with the ark, I looked out my window and saw my husband dancing out of his clothes with the young maidens following him.[4] I was filled with contempt. I thought he was a hypocrite. How could he lose his dignity over a box and yet not find it in his heart to be that concerned over a person who had risked her life to save his? Was I not precious enough for him to pursue? How dare he be so happy when I was so hurt! I stood in the doorway waiting to deflate his balloon.

I was ready when David got home. What kind of king was he with his ridiculous display. Losing his dignity by dancing naked in the streets in front of the slave girls of his servants. The sparkle of excitement in his eyes turned dark as he answered. He said that when it came to God he would lose all of his dignity without reserve. And those same maids would give him respect.

I realized in that moment that I had crossed a line. I'd chosen the wrong fight. My husband took my words as an insult against God. Our relationship was never the same after that. I remained loveless and childless for the rest of my days.

I wish I hadn't let my pain fester. Perhaps I should have asked David why he never came for me. Why I wasn't important enough. Why he waited so long and used me as a bargaining chip in negotiations for his kingdom? After all, he'd gone way above what was required when he wed me…or had he? Was it only for principle that he'd killed two hundred Philistines to gain my hand? Had he ever loved me? Had he not loved me and missed me like I had him? And why after so long had he disrupted the life I'd made for myself after suffering such a severe loss?

But I never asked the questions, so I never got answers. He may have had good reasons…or at least justifiable ones anyway. I'll never know. All I knew was that I felt misplaced and unloved. I was unable to let go of my pain, and finally it surfaced. When everyone was congratulating him on finding the ark of the Lord and bringing it home, I was condemning him. My bitterness made me a killjoy.

I never lived past that moment really. It was as if life went on without me. All the bitterness I harbored not only didn't bear fruit but it robbed me of the little bit of joy I could have had in my lingering years. Instead all I had left was unspoken regrets.

I allowed my unresolved offense to destroy my life and my relationship with a man I'd once loved and prayed to have. My sister, I beg of you to not do what I did. If you love your man, talk to him. Talk until any and all pain is resolved. Staying silent and unforgiving only destroys any hope of reconciliation.

And never insult a man over his devotion to God or the other things

that are important to him. You'll lose him. If you're currently discon-
nected with your love, seize the opportunity to reconcile with him now.
Make haste. Don't allow the misunderstandings and unspoken issues
to fester between you any longer. Life is too short to live without love
or the presence of God. These are the only two things that make life
worth living.

Mired in regrets,

Michal

Woman to Woman

I'm sure you've heard the saying that "hell hath no fury like a
woman scorned." And it's true! A woman who feels unloved can allow
her pain to fester until it becomes a ball of cold resolve to give no
honor or respect to the person who hurt her. And yet this is a very self-
destructive path. Offenses occur in every relationship, although they
vary in degrees. Some offenses are unacceptable, but thankfully that's
not true in every case. We need to make every attempt to come to a full
understanding of what occurred. We should avoid leaving our emotions open to the danger of assumptions. Of assuming facts or thoughts
or beliefs that haven't been confirmed. The record of assumptions that
have turned out to be correct is not good. In most cases the conclusions
we come to are not accurate. To harbor ill will and bad feelings based
on information we don't have is the death knell to any relationship.

Love that is true and committed insists on communicating no matter how painful the conversation may be. It is willing to wrestle with
the truth until it gets to the heart of the matter. If Michal had asked
the right questions, she may have gotten an unexpected answer from
David that could have eased her pain and hurt. We don't know why
he delayed...and never will because she never asked. Similar scenarios
occur in relationships every day. People walk around with hurt feelings
over words or situations that could easily be put into healing perspective with loving conversation. But when we let offenses grow in our

hearts, it kills our respect for the other person. And once respect is gone, desire quickly follows. Many a marriage suffers under the weight of two strangers living together under the same roof.

The depth of pain that must have kept Michal from rejoicing with her husband over recovering the ark of the Lord had to be deeper than deep. She missed the joy of celebrating one of David's most important victories. She was too focused on her own pain, jealousy, and bitterness.

Michal wondered how David could desire anything more than her after all she'd invested in him. She'd gone against her family for David. She'd given all and sacrificed all, including a husband who loved her, to be in this unenviable position where she felt overlooked, displaced, and taken for granted. These aren't easy emotions to handle. We women are natural nurturers, but we also have the capacity to stuff a lot of hurt and pain away in the name of "keeping life moving ahead." In the process of being strong we can shoulder a lot that we shouldn't, so we move on, dying inside by degrees. And yet we aren't called to live in pain or be victims. God is close to the brokenhearted and well able to heal all hurts. And that truth can set us free. Free to forgive offenses. Free to breathe. Free to reconcile our pain and release it. Free to live and love. Free to be fruitful.

Your Hope

When we come to God bearing the broken pieces of our hearts, He is faithful to bind us up and free us from the pain that crushes our spirits. Relationships are complicated and difficult to navigate without God's loving intervention and help. When we lack wisdom on how to navigate through the twists and turns of matters of the heart, God's followers can call on Him for counsel. He is the relationship expert. He is the giver of wisdom. He will give you the grace to follow His instructions.

There is a reason one of the attributes of love mentioned in 1 Corinthians 13:4 is patience or longsuffering. No one is exempt from disappointments in any human relationship. This is why God encourages us to speak the truth *in love* (Ephesians 4:15). If someone offends you, go to them and share how you feel. Seek reconciliation. "Bear with each other and forgive one another if any of you has a grievance against someone. Forgive as the Lord forgave you. And over all these virtues put on love, which binds them all together in perfect unity" (Colossians 13:13). As much as you have it in you, pursue peace in all things. The Message version of Philippians 1:9-10 encourages you to "not only love much but well. Learn to love appropriately. You need to use your head and test your feelings so that your love is sincere and intelligent, not sentimental gush."

Love isn't just a feeling; love includes commitment. A decision to remain committed to that commitment. Love is willing to confront to maintain a healthy relationship. Love sees problems clearly but also seeks solutions. It empowers you to do the right thing. The best thing you can offer your loved one is honest, loving communication. Only then will your relationship grow stronger. No matter how deep the hurt, there is always hope for reconciliation when you reach out and do the work to dismantle assumptions and make a clear path for understanding as God gives direction.

Your Truth

❧ How do you usually respond to rejection?

❧ When you're offended what steps can you take for reconciliation?

❧ What keeps you from confronting and speaking the truth in love? What fears do you need to overcome so you can stop suffering in silence? How will you do that?

22

The Trouble with Secrets

My dear sister,

You may believe I'm responsible for the trouble that came my way. That it was my fault for bathing on the roof. But it was late evening and that was the custom in my day. I'd like to think I should have known someone was watching me, but I was too absorbed in my toilette to notice. And later when the king's men came to my door and told me I was summoned to the palace, I wasn't sure why. A million questions went through my mind, including, "What could the king possibly want of me?"

When I entered King David's chambers I was struck by how handsome he was. He was gracious and attentive, making sure I was comfortable. I was extremely nervous. He offered me food and drink that looked sumptuous. And just when I relaxed and let down my guard, he took me. Yes, he took me. I didn't cry out because how could I say no to the king? When he was done, he instructed me to tell no one. That this would be our secret. Then he sent me home as if nothing had happened. But I wondered if such secrets are ever really secret. I could tell by looking in the eyes of the guards who escorted me home that they knew.

I thought of my dear husband who was away fighting for the king.

I hung my head and asked God to forgive me if I'd contributed in any way to what took place. Uriah, my husband, was a sweet and simple man dedicated to his work, his country, his king, and me. How would he feel if he knew what happened? It would hurt him deeply. I resolved to never tell him.

Then the dawning came several weeks later when my menses didn't come. The secret was now screaming to be announced. I was pregnant. I sent a message to King David. He said he would take care of everything.

The next thing I knew, my husband came back from the war zone. "Ah, that's the king's solution," I thought. I laughed without mirth. The king didn't know my husband very well. Uriah wouldn't indulge in pleasure or comfort as long as his men were still fighting. He was fiercely loyal.[1]

Then Uriah received his orders. He was being sent back to the battle. He died shortly after that during an attack. I suspect it wasn't as simple as that. That's the thing about secrets. One secret begets another.

After Uriah's death, David sent for me and we were married. It was the buzz of the palace—especially when my abdomen began to swell. The whispering was ceaseless, but I kept my peace. The time came to give birth, and David and I had a beautiful baby boy.

And then Nathan the prophet came to inform David that our secret wasn't a secret to God. The prophet announced that because of what David had done, the sword would never depart from his house, David would suffer humiliation, and the child born to us would die. David admitted he had sinned, and Nathan said, "The LORD has taken away your sin. You are not going to die."[2] But the consequences of David's sin would remain.

When our baby became ill, David and I prayed fervently that God would change His mind...but He didn't. Our son struggled to live, and seven days later our sweet baby boy died.

My first child was gone. Sorrow consumed me. Though I knew God didn't blame me, I blamed myself. Perhaps I should have resisted David more. Cried out or done something more to stop him. Now the guilt I felt over the deaths of my husband and my son were overwhelming.

I blamed myself though a part of me knew I had no basis for shame. Once again I knew David and I were the main topic of gossip within the palace walls. I wasn't sure if I would ever recover from such a massive weight on my soul.

David rose from his fasting and praying and came to console me. We grew close in the midst of our pain. I became pregnant again and gave birth to another son. God pronounced His love over this babe we named Solomon. But the stain of what had occurred between David and me colored our lives for the rest of our days.

After time had passed, David's son Amnon raped his stepsister Tamar. Though David was angry, he never dealt with it properly because his own guilt stopped him from confronting his son. After all, what could he say? His son would only say that his father had done a similar thing. Tamar's brother Absalom never said a word to Amnon about the assault either, but he never forgot. He never forgave David for not addressing the issue when he told him either. Two years later Absalom followed through on his secret desire for revenge and killed Amnon. Years later, in an attempt to overthrow David, this same Absalom slept with David's wives in clear view of everyone on the roof of the palace, which fulfilled Nathan's prophecy of David's humiliation.[3] It was as if Absalom wanted to give his father a dose of his own medicine while exacting his revenge for David ignoring the plight of his sister.

The revolts and murder and chaos that occurred after that until the time David died made me pause to think so many times how damaging sin and secrets can be. The impact of them remains long after the deeds. No amount of forgiveness can remove the scars. I have no doubt that the wages of sin is death.

I think the consequences of David's sin affected him deeply. I'm sure he imagined many times what his life would have been like had not that fateful day occurred when he sent for me. How different his family and his kingdom might have been. David's sins made him lax with disciplining his sons. He was hesitant to correct them because of his own guilt. Though God had forgiven him, I'm not sure David ever really forgave himself.

While it is easy to beat ourselves up about our choices and the deeds we've done, we must move on. It was up to me to ensure the future of my son Solomon. During David's last days and with Nathan the prophet's help, I reminded David that our son Solomon was to be made king even as yet another insurrection was being planned by another of David's sons. David agreed, and Solomon became king.[4]

My Solomon was a wise and powerful king who would have made his father proud. I'm grateful to God that something beautiful was created from the chaos David and I created and had a hand in. I thought our situation was beyond redemption, but God stepped in.

If ever there was a lesson to be learned in all this, it was the devastation that one secret can do. I often wonder what I could have done differently. Should I have told my husband what happened when David brought him back from war? I don't know. I'm not sure that would have changed anything. He would have been powerless to confront David or, if he did, I'm sure he would still have met his death too early.

There is only one thing of which I am absolutely certain: Our sins will be found out and every hidden thing will be revealed. And when that moment comes, it can be excruciating. But it is only the truth that will set us free. The truth enables us to own what we've done and go to God with a transparent heart and a contrite spirit. In His great mercy He forgives us and redeems us from our failures and mistakes. Only He can take the worst of situations and turn them around for the good. I say this to encourage you to live a life of transparency and accountability. There is a high price to be paid for our secret sins because as quiet as we try to keep them, they all eventually are told. Our subterfuge only delays the inevitable outcome of our actions. We will collect the wages of our sin, and there is only one way around that whether we try to keep it secret or not—God. When we ask Him for grace, mercy, forgiveness, and restoration, He will grant our requests. But only as we choose to walk in His light.

Thanking God for His great mercy,

Bathsheba

Woman to Woman

The old folks used to say, "You can run, but you can't hide." This is true! Sometimes life takes us down paths we don't anticipate. We end up doing things we said we would never do. Then our shame overwhelms us so we try to hide. We keep secrets that corrode our souls because, in our hearts, we know that God knows. Our secret becomes an open door for fear to enter into our hearts as we shiver in dreadful anticipation of being exposed. How, when, and by whom we don't always know, but deep down we know it's inevitable that the truth will come out. It always does.

We've watched the news enough times when someone in ministry or politics has been exposed for secret, unethical practices. The devastation to the family and ministry as people are forced to endure the public glare of scrutiny can be intense. We don't know what takes place behind closed doors after the TV cameras have left, but I'm sure it is not the polished and calm veneer people put forth for the public. No. In fact, I'm sure there is pain, anger, resentment, hurt, and bitterness. The lack of respect and the betrayal that disintegrates relationships are like a slow cancer causing inevitable loss and, in many cases, death of precious relationships. Life is never the same after that. The former glory has been tainted forever.

When secrets are outed, a huge question asked of or about the guilty party is, "What else don't we know?" Secrets destroy the foundation of trust in relationships. Once that trust has been destroyed, it's hard to continue the relationship. Yet it seems we all still hope our secrets will remain undercover though time has shown us differently. The commercial with the tagline "What happens in Vegas stays in Vegas" is a promise everyone smiles at, but the truth of the matter is that our secrets follow us everywhere we go.

No secret is ever a secret anyway. God is watching! And He only delights in the truth. He refuses to dwell in darkness. He will not enter into our sin areas and cover us. When we belong to Him, He pulls us toward the light where He can meet us and cleanse us. Although it may be hard for us to face the glare of our own mistakes and we would rather avoid the embarrassment, we must be willing to own our stuff no matter how shameful it is. We must be willing to be authentic with God. After all He already knows. He knew what you were going to do before you did it so He is not shocked by it. He stands ready to forgive and restore you. He still loves you!

It's so easy for those who keep secrets to turn to more lies to keep the deception going. One lie begets another, and soon we are trapped in a web of deceit. No good thing ever comes from sin. And secret sin creates a private hell of severe bondage. Only God and His truth can set us free.

Your Hope

The beauty of David and Bathsheba's story is that though the consequences of their actions seemed severe, God extended His mercy in gracious ways. Out of the chaos that arose from David and Bathsheba's actions, God blessed them with another son who became renowned for possessing great wisdom. Solomon was a credit to his parents, the nation of Israel, and God.

God uncovers our sin in order to cleanse us. He lovingly washes us with His Word and pours on healing oil to soothe the ravaged places in our souls. Secrets hurt and leave scars. Our heavenly Father knows this, and for this reason He won't allow painful secrets to fester when we're truly surrendered to Him. He must remain true to His Word that every hidden thing will be revealed (Matthew 10:26). But with the truth comes the freedom to get back on the path of redemption and restoration in Christ. God throws our sins into the sea of forgetfulness once we bring them to Him (Hebrews 10:17). It is we who go fishing and reel them back in.

The sad part of David's story is that he let his own sins hinder his ability to address the sins of his family members. Self-condemnation did its work well. This is the residue that often remains like fine dust over our souls after we've done questionable things in the dark. Our shame follows us. But if we're open and receive God's forgiveness and acceptance, if we embrace His grace and find the courage to own what we've done, shame loses its power. If we use our mistakes to redefine our commitment to God and live in His truth, we are free to apply what we've learned to help others. The lessons we learn equip us to teach and strengthen others.

Transparency is a powerful teacher. The Word tells us that Jesus was tempted in all manner like we are so He can relate to everything we go through. In the same fashion, our willingness to be vulnerable and share our mistakes and failings with others and the lessons learned become powerful tools to encourage change in the lives of others. As we take our wounds and turn them into teaching opportunities, no experience in our lives is wasted. "We know that in all things God works for the good of those who love him, who have been called according to his purpose" (Romans 8:28).

Bathsheba became part of the lineage of Christ. I can't say how that would have occurred if David had chosen to crucify his flesh and do things God's way. Perhaps Uriah would have died in battle without David's orders, and the king would have been free to ask for the hand of Bathsheba in the same way he was able to marry Abigail after the death of Nabal. Sometimes we sully God's plan, but He will work around us when necessary. At any rate, despite all the drama, God worked out the details for His purposes.

This is where your focus needs to be after repentance too. Ask yourself these questions. "What lesson did I learn from this choice I made and the outcome?" "What does God want me to get out of this situation?" "How can I use what I've learned to help others?"

When you walk in the knowledge that God is able and willing to redeem all of your failings and create beauty from ashes, you can walk in the assurance that the negatives too shall pass.

Your Truth

❧ What secret sin are you wrestling with? How has shame kept you from owning your mistake or problem appropriately?

❧ What is your greatest struggle at this time in light of what you've done in the past?

❧ What do you need from God right now to redeem your current situation and revive your hope?

23

When the Unthinkable Happens

My dear sister,

Violated. I was violated. There's no pretty way to dress it up. If it had been done by a stranger it might be easier to understand. But it was my own flesh and blood. My brother whom I loved. He took what was most precious to me. The depths of my pain went even deeper when my father turned a blind eye to what had happened. I know I'm not alone in my experience. I know your story might be similar to mine. If it is, I also know it colored everything in your world. That's what rape and incest do.

Too often it starts out innocently enough. I trusted my stepbrother. I'd admired him from afar for a long time. He was always kind and a bit flirtatious, but it caused me no alarm. After all, he was my brother, and brothers protect their sisters. Or so I believed. Oh sure, there was talk that he liked me, but I figured he'd either get over his crush or ask our father for my hand. That was done in my day.

Our father was King David. I was a princess and Amnon a prince. There was never any reason to assume the worst of him. We'd grown up together. There had been the usual rivalry among our mothers, as would be natural any time a husband has many wives. That's why I don't believe it was ever God's design for a man's heart to be divided between women or for a wife to share her husband with another. That would be too much for the heart to bear. However, it was the reality of my time and family, and we learned to cope and live harmoniously together...until this travesty.

When I was told by my father that Amnon was ill and had requested that I come to serve him food, I went willingly. When I entered his chamber I thought it odd that he ordered everyone out, but I still didn't get it. And when he asked that I serve him in his bedroom, I thought he might have something of a personal nature to tell me and didn't want to be overheard.

But when I drew near he grabbed me and said, "Come lie with me, my sister."[1] I struggled even as I tried to speak reason to him. I told him such wickedness was not done in Israel. And where would I go in my shame since I would no longer be a virgin? I even suggested he ask our father for my hand. But Amnon would hear nothing of what I had to say.

He raped me. I remember it as if it were yesterday. And worst of all, the love he'd professed immediately turned to hatred. His eyes changed. They became cold. He brutally cast me off and ordered me from his chambers. He turned a deaf ear to my pleas for him to not put me out, for him to not do such a detestable thing. But he called his attendants and said, "Now throw this woman out of my presence, and lock the door behind her." And the young men did.

I went from being the lovely Tamar to being "that woman who was ruined." Had Amnon forgotten I was his sister? His own flesh and blood? Someone he should have loved and protected? I had been a virgin, and now I was no more. What man would wed me now that I was sullied? Used and cast off. The hope I had of marrying and settling down to have a family was irreparably altered. My future was shattered. In sorrow and mourning I ripped my robe and covered my head in ashes. I went weeping to my brother Absalom's house. But Absalom told me not to speak of it. He also told me, "Do not take this matter to heart." I heard my father was angry when he heard what Amnon had done, but he too did nothing. I was left to live in desolation in my brother's house. I was disgraced and displaced. I know Absalom meant well, but he couldn't understand the depths of my pain and shame.

But Absalom never forgot either. Two years later he took revenge against Amnon for what he'd done to me. Absalom held a great feast and invited all our brothers. Then he had his servants rise up and kill Amnon once he was drunk with wine.

And what did my father do? He wept for Amnon! I wonder if he ever wept for me. Did he not realize that I died inside when Amnon raped me? Did he not see that Amnon's violation murdered the daughter he knew? That my innocence and future were torn from me? No, I don't think he did.

After murdering Amnon, Absalom went into exile for three years so I was left to fend for myself. The death of Amnon did nothing for me, although I was grateful Absalom finally came to my defense. Amnon was gone, but I was still very much alive to suffer with the memory and consequences of what he'd done.

I don't blame myself for what occurred. It wasn't my fault. I trusted Amnon purely, and I was betrayed. Although difficult in my culture, I reminded myself that what happened didn't affect my worth no matter what anyone thought. I was sorry for the way it affected our family. Bitterness crept into Absalom's soul, and it caused him to kill his brother, rebel against our father, and ultimately led to his untimely death. The damage was so far reaching. I wish the rape hadn't happened, of course. But it did, and the fruit Amnon's actions bore was excruciating and the repercussions seemingly endless.

No one ever spoke of my situation again. It was the elephant in the room. As time went by the sting of it lessened somewhat. But innocence can't be replaced. I learned to take my pain to God and live each day one at a time. Life went on. I could choose to allow that one incident to define me, reign over me for the rest of my life, and die by degrees every day. Or I could choose to deal with the pain, trust God, and move forward. I chose to live.

I'm sharing my story with you so if you've been violated you will know you're not alone in your feelings of betrayal and heartbreak. I have no answers except to encourage you not to let this be the end of your story. Turn to God and let Him heal your brokenness. Then choose to live and use your pain for good. Perhaps every woman has a secret wound. Don't hide your plight. I pray my scars are tools that will help you find freedom. Rise, my sister, and be downcast no more.

Praying for your healing,

Tamar

Woman to Woman

Most little girls dream of a prince coming to carry her away. Of having a man in her life who will love her, provide for her, and be a fierce protector. To have that dream marred by violence and defilement is heartbreaking. Shameful acts shatter the spirit and can leave the abused one bereft and inconsolable. To attempt to ignore what happened or to live in silent pain and isolation is to cut yourself off from life. Rape and incest are violent crimes against a person's soul. All three stories in the Bible that speak of this heinous offense were followed by violent acts from the men related to the women. Dinah was raped by the prince of Shechem, a stranger who then decided he loved her and wanted to marry her. Her brothers were so incensed by what occurred that they used deceit to murder the prince and all the other men in his city. They retrieved Dinah from his house and took her back home. Although we hear no more about Dinah, because of the culture of the day it's safe to speculate that she lived in isolation and never married. The next story is the brutal rape and murder of a Levite's concubine (Judges 19). This started a war against the tribe in Gibeah whose men had done the awful crime. That war almost caused their extinction. And then, as we've seen, there was Tamar.

Each woman was defended, but could more violence mend a broken heart, heal a ravaged soul, or bring someone back to life? No. The most heartbreaking thing about this type of defilement occurs even today—most women keep silent. The shame and fear that they will be blamed for what occurred means many offenders walk free while their victims become the walking wounded bound by damaged emotions and physical trauma.

I conducted a seminar in London one year. We were having an interactive discussion about heartbreak and disappointment. One of the ladies stood up and shared about being raped by an uncle and how she'd worked through it. One by one more ladies stood and shared that they too had been violated. For many it was the first time they'd told people what had happened. These women gathered together, held one another, and wept. As they comforted each other and turned to the Lord, it became a great time of healing. It still is one of the most powerful moments I've ever experienced in ministry. Jesus and the truth sets us free, ladies! Coming into God's light dispels the darkness. Realizing you're not alone in your pain is a major step in healing. Friendships were formed that day through the common bond of brokenness, and it was clear the mending had begun.

Although we follow God, we're not exempt from tragedy. We are not of the world, but we are in the world; therefore, terrible things will happen (John 15:16). And yes, bad things do happen to good people. We must remember there is strength in numbers. We are part of a body that has been charged with weeping with us when we weep and laughing with us when we laugh (1 Corinthians 12:24). The women around you will understand your pain better than most men will. Dare to be transparent; don't keep silent. Recognize and embrace that your value has not been diminished by what someone did to you. Arise, my friend. Shake off the dust, strengthen your arms, and take your place as a beloved daughter of God worthy of restoration and wholeness.

Your Hope

God tells us to cast all our cares on Him because He cares for us (1 Peter 5:7). He promises to bind up the brokenhearted. To pour soothing oil on our wounds. To rebuild and restore us. We can't do any of these for ourselves. The Holy Ghost is at work in us as we surrender all that we are and all that we have experienced to God. He is the Healer and Comforter in the midst of circumstances that don't make any sense to us. Who can say why anything happens or why God even allows negative events or actions? We can choose to cling to His promise that all things work to the good no matter how awful the challenges seem to us (Romans 8:28). I think of the woman who lost her son to a drunk driver so she formed Mothers Against Drunk Drivers (MADD) to battle against impaired driving so many others might be spared from what she experienced. Talk about turning a wound into a helpful tool! And there's the man who started *America's Most Wanted* because his son was kidnapped and murdered. He has helped thousands of people recover children and relatives who were abducted or lost.

The hope you have is not just how God gives comfort, but also what He can use your pain to accomplish. "Vengeance is Mine, I will repay" says the Lord (Romans 12:19 NASB). That doesn't mean you wait around for the hammer to fall on those who hurt you. That would actually do little to alleviate your pain. But what can revive you is using what you've experienced to help someone who is struggling with similar issues. I've been on the giving and receiving end of this type of sharing. I'm so thankful God allows me to assist in the healing process.

Whatever your experience, don't let it take over and ruin your life. Don't let it break you. Instead, let it make you stronger. Don't let it define you; let it refine you. Let it make you a tool in God's hands for healing, for His glory, and for restoration. Tribulation brings out experience that will build your faith to the point where you will not be ashamed because you have proof of God's love and the grace He gives to overcome all things (Romans 5:3-5).

Your Truth

❧ In what way have you been violated or betrayed?

❧ What has been the most difficult part of letting go of the offense?

❧ How have you utilized your support base to help you?

❧ In what ways have you chosen to refocus your pain for a positive end?

24

Finding Your Balance

My dear sister,

I'm sure many of you have heard of me...and even been intimidated by me. Please don't be. The list of my attributes looks impressive even to me, but let me help you put things in perspective so you too will know you can be virtuous. A woman of excellence. In and of myself, I can do nothing. I believe that less is more, and a simple life is one of order—God's order, which leads to peace, joy, and fulfillment. I am not Superwoman, nor do I try to be. I live not to impress but to please God by being all that He designed me to be. In light of that, I take one day at a time, doing what I can and knowing the morrow will come. Whatever I didn't complete today will be there to do tomorrow. God is faithful to redeem the time when needed if I stick to His plan.

My priorities are clear. My relationship with God comes first. He is where I draw my strength, the wisdom I need to make the best decisions, and the guidance to navigate the challenges that are sure to come. I feed myself—my soul, my mind, my spirit, and my heart—in His presence. He is the beginning and the end of my days. I seek Him early to fortify myself for the day. As He feeds me knowledge of Him, I receive and overflow to feed and nourish others. He fills me with the love I need to love others appropriately and well. His voice is the one

I seek for direction and counsel. He helps me put myself and my day in order.

Then there is my husband as my next priority. We are one. Loving him is loving myself and vice versa. Our bond is strong. He is my friend, my lover, my confidant, my life partner. I keep no secrets from him. We are co-captains navigating life together. His heart trusts in me and I in him. He is my pride and joy. I enjoy making him look good. I make sure his home is a sanctuary where he draws strength and solace. This frees him to be a man of integrity in the marketplace so he garners much respect. I put him first before my children because they will grow and leave. He is my partner for life. I make sure we keep romance alive so we will never be strangers. I celebrate him, and he celebrates me. He releases me to be all that I want to be. The foundation of our home is built on trust and love. It is solid.

Next are my children. They are grounded and well-behaved because they see two parents in love who are united in their decisions concerning them. We agree to disagree in private and always present a solid front to them. We realize our children are our assignments from God that we're charged with preparing for life. Discipline is important. I don't try to be their friend. There will be time for that when they are responsible adults. Right now God calls me to be their parent, and that's an awesome responsibility that I will be held accountable for. I work to prepare them now to respect authority before they are released to the world where grace might not flow as freely as it does at home. I listen. I hear. I see. I'm aware of as much as possible concerning them. I hold them accountable for their actions. I lovingly instruct them in God's ways and pray they won't depart from it.

Next come the people in my life. When I first got married, I focused on my home and my husband. I took the time to secure the foundation of our lives together before focusing on anything else. Then our children came along, and I took the time to nurture and train them. But as time went by and they matured, I had more and more time to devote to others in need. I planted vineyards and taught my sons about business. I sewed sashes for merchants and taught my daughters. As they grew up and married, I extended my arms to the needy outside of my home. Life was a work in progress and unfolding organically. No season was forced. I was blessed to have servants. I treated them kindly and gave them instructions that did not grieve them but helped them do their jobs well. I mastered the power of delegation; therefore, I was never worn out and depleted. The people around me were empowered because they were clear on their roles and assignments.

Order is important. No one in my household felt ignored or unimportant. I took each day one at a time. I focused on the assignments God gave me for that life season. As women, it's important to know the season we're in…and the purpose of that season. As you know, seasons do change and more rapidly than we anticipate. I recall a time when my children needed me to do everything. But now they've gone on their way. There was a season to nurture and a season for release.

I stayed within the sphere of influence God gave me and used the gifts He bestowed to bless others. I discovered that I gained as much from them as they did from me. I didn't try to do everything. I got help when I needed it, and didn't overextend myself because then I wouldn't do my work to the best of my ability. My first purpose was to be the woman God created me to be, exhibiting and living the fruit of the Spirit. In order for me to do that, I had to keep my life in balance. I can't be loving, joyful, peaceful, patient, kind, good, faithful, gentle, and exercise self-control if I'm depleted from doing too much.[1] I learned to free myself from needless distractions and false obligations so I could be free to deal with the things that really mattered.

Understanding our purpose is essential in making the best choices for every season of life. Without an end goal in sight, we can wander aimlessly. A clear sense of purpose keeps us from giving into distractions that might lead to nowhere fruitful.

No, my sister, you see I'm really not that impressive. I'm a woman like you doing my best to live as God directs. A balanced life is a simple life that reaps great rewards. And that is excellence at its best.

Isn't it interesting that with all you've heard about me and all the accolades I'm given, you still don't know my name? As much as I'm written about and held up as an example, I'm never identified? That's because I've never sought fame or recognition. I give God the glory for what He enables me to accomplish. Although I didn't seek it, I am blessed by my family's appreciation. With God's help I live a stress-free life filled with joy, peace, and fulfillment. I wish this for you too.

I believe people call me,

The Proverbs 31 Woman

Woman to Woman

God has entrusted a lot to us. The pressure in our competitive world is to try to be all things to all people and still keep who we are intact. The word "virtuous" means "excellent" in the context of chapter 31 in the book of Proverbs. Excellence requires focus, discipline, and an understanding of purpose. The world puts a lot of pressure on us to spread ourselves thin by being involved in many things. But how many of those things are God's design for us should be our overriding concern. We talk a lot about being worn-out. Everyone is way too busy, too tired, and too mentally and physically spent. Jesus said His yoke is easy and His burden is light (Matthew 11:30). Perhaps we need to consider that if our way is hard and our burdens are heavy we've taken on more than God wants us to.

Unfortunately it's easy to allow secular thinking to pollute what God says about how we should view our husbands, children, and careers. This subtle attack rocks and dismantles the family structure, which is the very foundation of society. Sound families make safe communities and economically secure cities. Small wonder the attack is against the household. When our priorities are in order and we don't have the desire or need to make names for ourselves, we can clearly set life goals that are achievable. Being in agreement and setting realistic timetables helps everyone work toward realizing their dreams. This makes life at home full of anticipation, hope, and joy.

Understanding the seasons in life frees us from anxiety. The race is over because it never began. We pace ourselves according to who we are and the season we're in. God is not in a hurry so He isn't rushing us. We can take time to enjoy where we are. To revel in our experiences.

To enjoy our husbands and their dreams. To kiss those fat cheeks on our babies and enjoy that fresh baby smell. To enjoy a slower schedule before it picks up in activity. We spend far too much time reminiscing over times gone by that we didn't appreciate while we lived it because we were too busy trying to get ahead. In the end we regret not smelling the roses along the way. Single or married, understanding the season and its purpose enables us to be present. Only when we are present can we seize the day and get all there is to get out of it. And that, my friend, is true excellence.

Your Hope

Plan your work and work your plan, but don't do it without God. Every good idea is not a God idea! Some good ideas can lead you down a path that takes you away from your desires and God's best for you.

Stay focused. Is this a season to focus on getting your home in order? If so, your career and all the rest will still be waiting for you. Is this the time to focus on your children? Then do it to the best of your ability. They won't be children forever, and time marches swiftly by.

Are you in tune with your husband's needs? A happy man is a successful man. Be his inspiration and his muse. Be his lover and his friend. Give him his props and respect him. Every man wants to be his woman's hero, so give your husband room to be yours. Wield your power appropriately and guard his heart and your marriage.

And what about you? The people in your home will only feel as good as you feel. Take the time to put on *your* oxygen mask—commune with God—before trying to save everyone else. A friend of mine, Lindsey O'Connor, wrote a book entitled *When Mama Ain't Happy, Ain't Nobody Happy*. That is so true. Women are often the heartbeat of a home. Be your own best friend by making God your everything. From your relationship with Him, all others will flow as they should. To know and love God is to tap into His heart and mind. To glorify Him is to give an accurate reflection of who He is to those around you in your home, your community, and everywhere you go. Then your husband and children, family and friends will arise and call you blessed.

Every day is a new opportunity to start anew if need be. No one is perfect. But there is also no one like you. You are uniquely you, created to do what you do through your unique gifts and talents. Release yourself to God's creative direction. No family is the same. There is not a right or perfect way to do things because we're all wired differently and have different needs and preferences. Thankfully, God's standards leave a lot of room for individual expression. Set your pace according to what He has put inside you.

Whatever your God-given assignments, rest assured that He will be with you every step of the way and equip you for your journey. He'll never ask more of you than you can give. He will always provide the strength and grace you need. He is faithful to meet you with new mercies every morning (Lamentations 3:22-23 NKJV).

In those times when you feel your life is thankless, remember that God is with you. Seek His praise rather than focusing on people, who are fickle. As you strive to keep God's standard in everything you do, His rewards will come. And no one argues with excellence. Excellence is a force to be reckoned with. It makes itself known without any help from you. Do everything as unto the Lord and then rest in Him (Colossians 3:23). He is your great and exceeding reward.

Your Truth

❧ What is your greatest struggle in establishing balance?

❧ Are there any obligations or distractions you've embraced that might not be part of God's best for you? If so, what are they and what will you do about them?

❧ What life season are you in? What is God's purpose for you right now? What does He want you to focus on?

25

How to Grasp the Impossible

My dear sister,

If my story doesn't increase your faith, I don't know what will. When the angel Gabriel greeted me, I thought I was dreaming. His announcement to me that I was going to give birth to the Son of God was even more incredible than Gabriel's appearance. I asked him how could this be? He told me it would be by the power of the Holy Spirit.[1] This was far above my comprehension, but interestingly I didn't doubt what the angel was saying. I was surrendered to God, and I wanted so badly to be used by Him. I felt honored that He would choose me to receive such a miraculous gift! When I submitted myself to God and said yes to His will, I felt an overwhelming peace inside. I knew that, yes, it would be so—as crazy as that sounded.

The angel also told me that my cousin Elizabeth, who had been barren all these years, was also having a child in her old age. I decided I should go to see her. I was so grateful that God wasn't asking me to walk through this experience alone. He'd given me Elizabeth as a confirmation to what Gabriel had told me.

My main worry was how Joseph would take the news. I was a virgin, which was very important in my culture. How would I explain that I was with child but still pure? How would I explain this in a way

183

he would understand and accept? How would I make him believe I hadn't been unfaithful…that this was truly a miracle of God? Even if he believed me, he would bear a lot of weight from my state. How would his family respond? People would count the months and figure out I was pregnant before we were married. In my culture at the time, this could place my life in jeopardy. If it was determined that I was an adulteress, I could be stoned to death.

I approached Joseph and told him about the angel. He seemed hesitant to believe me. I decided there was nothing I could do to convince him. If God was truly in this, He would deal with Joseph and make it right. And God was faithful! He sent an angel to Joseph to confirm what I'd told him. Joseph later confessed that he'd considered sending me away secretly to save me from disgrace. After the angel told him to not be afraid to marry me because my child was conceived of the Holy Spirit, the matter was settled in Joseph's heart and we were married.[2]

Then came the time we had to report to Bethlehem for the census. It was a difficult trip because it was near my time of delivery. Joseph and I ended up staying in a stable because all the inns were full. Such a humble place for the King of kings to be born, but there was also something so right about it. After Jesus was born, shepherds came to pay homage. They said angels had sent them![3] Amazing stories were no longer questioned by Joseph and me. Some wise men came from the East to pay tribute to our son too. I could go on and on telling you more incredible experiences, but I would be writing forever!

Joseph and I had more children after that, but life with Jesus was certainly unique! Even though I knew He was the Son of God, Jesus was also my son. His passion for God at even a young age and His knowledge of God's Word astounded everyone. And then He started performing miracles. From turning water into wine at a wedding to healing people, wherever He went reports of lives being changed soon dominated conversations.

I was so proud of Him. I knew the religious leaders had problems with Him. He certainly went against the status quo and all the rules the Pharisees and Sadducees had added to our faith. He rocked the religious system and went against the strict adherence to the letter of the law to address the heart of why God is God and why we worship Him. The religious leaders said the claims Jesus made were heresy. *But how can they argue against the miracles?* I wondered.

My heart hurt for my son. He was so misunderstood. And yet He took the abuse and betrayal without seeking to defend Himself. He merely said He knew who He was. Often He was accused of breaking the Sabbath law and hanging around with the wrong types of people— tax collectors and sinners.[4] After He raised up His friend Lazarus from the dead, the mood of the Pharisees grew even darker.

I started worrying about Jesus' safety. He reassured me that He would be all right and tenderly reminded me of who He was. Although that was comforting, it was still worrisome. When Jesus was still a babe, the Holy Spirit came upon a man named Simeon, and he told me that my son's life would be filled with trouble and that a sword would pierce my soul.[5] And indeed it was. Jesus was the Son of God, the Lamb of God, but in my heart he was also my child.

To see Him being reviled, abused, beaten, and then crucified was more than I thought I could bear. Oh the torment! Despite what I knew to be true in my heart, I had to fight to keep my faith in those horrendous days. John, one of Jesus' disciples, held me close but I felt as if I'd died with my son on that cross. How could I bear to go on in life without Him? This couldn't be happening!

After darkness fell over the land, my son cried out to God and then died. I watched them take His body down. I couldn't bear to see Him being placed in the tomb. I clung to His words through my tears. He'd said He would rise again at the third day, but on the day of His death everything seemed hopeless. I asked the same question I'd asked when the angel appeared. "How can this be?"

Again the knowing reverberated deep in my spirit. "All things are possible with God."[6] The agony He was subjected to couldn't be erased from my mind. Between bouts of weeping I rehearsed all that He had done. He raised Lazarus from the dead. He said He was the resurrection and the life. He said He would rise again. He performed healings and other miracles. Why was I doubting then? And so I chose to wait expectantly.

And then it happened just as He said it would. He rose from the dead. On the third day. The two other Marys went to the tomb, and an angel told them Jesus had risen. They were running back to tell the disciples when they met Jesus Himself![7] When they got back they told the disciples Jesus said to meet Him in Galilee. Oh the joy most of us felt because we believed.

Did I need more proof of God's power? No! Jesus had proven Himself in miraculous ways over and over again. I had no excuse for not having faith. I was a living, breathing example of God's miraculous abilities.

Please take my message to heart in your life. No matter what you've been struggling to birth, no matter what things may look like, even when it seems the thing dear to you is dead and gone, God is able to breathe life into your situation. He will manifest His power in ways that will astound you. Get ready to receive your own miracles!

Convinced of God's power,

Mary, Jesus' mother

Woman to Woman

We were created to defy the odds in life. From the moment Eve stepped into the garden the devil knew he was in trouble. He knew of the influence she would have on man and the world. She was born to be a conduit of faith and life. Every time a child enters the world it is a miracle. To be able to birth life, to literally receive a seed and nurture it into the full manifestation of the handiwork of God, is an amazing gift we often take for granted. But to literally birth the Son of God? Wow! Small wonder Mary was in a state of awe when the angel Gabriel appeared.

"Why Mary?" you may ask. She found favor with God. She was pure in body and heart. She had childlike faith to believe God for the impossible. She was willing to serve God with joy even if saying yes to what He asked would invite trouble and criticism from others. But let's not rule out her relationship with Joseph, to whom she was betrothed. Joseph is listed in the generational lineage of Christ. Joseph was of the house of David, which God had said would go on forever. God is so meticulous in His dealings, that in His selection of the mother of Jesus He chose someone who was espoused to a descendant of David.

Based on that criteria, would any of us qualify for a miracle in our lives? Yes! Why? Because in Christ we are reborn, we are new creations (2 Corinthians 5:17). We've been given a new beginning as well as being added into the generational lineage as a child of God! We are now espoused to Christ and primed for receiving and participating in miracles. "How can this be?" we ask as we stretch our faith to believe in what looks impossible. Whether we long to birth a child, an aspiration, a dream, a loving relationship, a financial blessing—whatever it is, God still performs miracles for those whom He loves.

Our lives may look barren, but when we decide to agree with God and obey His instructions, He moves on our behalf. I recommend you ask God to send someone who will partner with you in faith for your miracle. Ask God for someone who will champion the word He has given you regarding your desire. Actively engage with God to bring your hope to life.

You don't need to advertise what you're hoping for. Your desired miracle isn't always for the masses to know while it's incubating. Ask God if and when He wants you to share. Nurture your dream quietly with faith. Like Mary, harbor God's promise for you in your heart. Trust God to confirm to the necessary parties their involvement and roles in your endeavor. Understand that every miracle has a set time to be delivered, but continue to move ahead. Be still and know that God is in charge. In the fullness of His time, His will is fulfilled.

We have an amazing capacity to walk by faith because of the intuitive qualities God has placed within us. Looking through the "hall of fame" in the Word, we see women facing extraordinary odds and coming out victorious (Hebrews 11). Time and time again God opened the wombs of barren women or saved them from catastrophes. When God made barren women conceive, I believe He was sending more than just a message about the ability to bear children. God is the God who can bring about the impossible! He will bring miracles into our lives if we say yes to Him and make ourselves available to be used as He desires.

Be aware that there is a price to pay for receiving and participating in miracles. We must release God's gifts to us back to Him. They have been entrusted to us to nurture and build upon for the glory of God. Fruitfulness is contingent on our availability and posture before Him. Our willingness to sacrifice enables us to receive unspeakable joy and fulfillment as we become partakers in God's divine plan.

Your Hope

Every person has a moment in their lives when they face seeming impossibilities. This is when God does His best work as you yield yourself to Him. Like Mary, to take the posture that you are open to God and all His possibilities sets you up for the miraculous to occur. And yet how compassionate and sensitive God is. He knows it is fearsome to believe for the impossible alone. He often provides "an Elizabeth" to walk with you. A spiritual midwife, if you will, who confirms the promises of God and will help you birth your promise.

Though women are intuitive by nature, it is still challenging to exercise faith in the face of a situation others might question. You may find yourself back in the garden with the serpent whispering, "Did God really mean what He said?" Even when you're clear about what He said, there is a tendency to question, to second-guess. Faith simply says yes and follows God's directions no matter if it goes against the grain of your intellect. In the fullness of time God's promises will manifest.

Your Truth

❧ What miracle are you believing God for today?

❧ What specific things are challenging the miracle you're working toward?

❧ Who is your support to reinforce your dream?

❧ What is the hardest part of waiting for God to manifest His promise? What can you do to silence any doubt?

26

Breaking the Negative Cycle

My dear sister,

Now that I know what I know, I feel compelled to share my story with you. I'll never forget the day I met Him. Jesus. So lost in myself and in my own thoughts I paid Him no mind. I'd purposely gone to the well at the hottest point of the day because I knew no one would be there. I'd grown weary of being judged and found wanting by my community. I was tired of their stares and whispers. I kept to myself, maneuvering around the masses to keep my peace.

There He was. I groaned inwardly. I wasn't in the mood for conversation. And then He asked me for a drink. I knew from His clothes that He wasn't one of us. He was a rabbi…a Jew. I was a Samaritan. In those days our people didn't interact. And yet He asked me for a drink! In my day the exchange of a drink wasn't a casual thing. It was an invitation of friendship. Was He trying to approach me? What manner of woman did He think I was?

I confronted Him, reminding Him that His kind didn't mix with the likes of mine. He refused to be put off. He said if I knew to whom I was talking to I would have asked Him for a drink and He would have given me "living water."[1]

"Who is this man?" I thought. His talk seemed so arrogant. And what was this "living water"? I challenged Him. I asked how He'd give me living water since He had nothing to draw water with. I also asked Him if He was better than our ancestor Jacob, who had provided our town well.

Then He said something about the water He gives would satisfy my thirst perpetually. It made no sense but the idea sounded good. If I never thirsted again, I wouldn't have to come back to this place. And I was thirsty...for more than just water. I was dry in my soul. Weary from the disappointments of life. I licked my lips just thinking about water that could satisfy my deepest thirst. Could it satisfy my thirst for love and contentment? I wondered. Could it satisfy my thirst for peace? I wrestled with so many issues all the time and found no rest. Jesus looked so calm and sure of Himself sitting there. I wanted to be like that.

I told Him I wanted His water. He told me to get my husband and come back.

Oh. Now that was a different matter. "What should I tell Him?" I wondered. "What will He think of me if I tell Him the truth about my situation?" I decided to skirt the issue by keeping it vague, so I told Him I had no husband. He said I was right. And then He told me my entire history with men! Yes, He was right. I had had five husbands, and I wasn't married to the man I was currently with. I exhaled. Five failed marriages. Disappointment after disappointment. I had suffered tremendous losses. I'd given up on love. Resigned myself to the fact that I would never really be happy. Men weren't reliable. I couldn't count on them to give me joy—only pain. I couldn't live with them, and I couldn't live without them. So I'd made a vow. I would never set myself up to be hurt again. I wouldn't marry again. I would keep things less complicated that way. This way I could handle my expectations. I wouldn't expect a future with a married man.

And now here sat this man calmly telling me everything I'd ever done. His demeanor was nonjudgmental and he talked like He was just stating the facts. "Ah," I thought. "He has to be a prophet. Perhaps He can answer my questions about God. Where was God in the midst of all my distress?"

So we talked. He told me many things about God that I'd never heard before. For instance, that it didn't matter who, what, or where a person is. God is looking for worshippers who will follow Him and be authentic to His principles in the way they live.[2] That I could do, I decided. I could respond to someone I knew really loved me. I could give Him my all. Suddenly I realized my thirst was gone, and I was filled with joy.

The man's traveling companions returned. They looked suspicious of our interaction, but I no longer cared. I dropped my water jar and headed back to town. I had to share this news! I felt so free. Even those who shunned me needed to hear what this man Jesus had to say. I told them what He'd said to me. They all saw how my countenance had changed, so they followed me back to the well to see who had such an effect on me. When they heard Him speak, they too believed He was the "Savior of the world."[3] It was no longer about me and what I said; they saw for themselves that He promised us all a new beginning.

From that time on I was able to face the people from my village with new eyes. I was free! I was no longer bound by my past or destined to repeat it. Their opinions no longer mattered. I had a new identity. No more repeats of wrong choices or disappointments. I would be a true worshipper of God. I was free to live in the light of His love. He quenched my thirst. My search was over.

No longer thirsty,

The Samaritan woman at the well

Woman to Woman

We all thirst for something, be it love, joy, peace, fulfillment. Sometimes in our search for these things we get lost in a hopeless cycle of disappointment after disappointment. We look for satisfaction and love in all the wrong places. For the Samaritan woman at the well, she was still thirsty six men later. It wasn't until she had an encounter with Jesus and opened her heart to Him that her destructive cycle was broken.

I believe when Jesus asked her about her husband He touched on the core of her issue. She was forced to face the truth of her situation and come to grips with the fact that the choices she'd made weren't working for her. She owned her part in what had taken place in her life, and she knew she needed something different. She acknowledged that she was at a critical point. She could continue the way she was living or she could accept Jesus' invitation.

I believe the well was more than just a place to draw water. I believe it represented her life. How many of us have also found ourselves at the well of life still thirsty, depleted, longing for more as we search for the place of breakthrough and renewal? We long for a fresh start free from the mistakes of the past.

The woman at the well almost missed it. She was ready to cut Jesus off. But with tender mercy He persisted in His conversation with her. How many of us may be cutting off our blessings today because our eyes are too clouded by hope deferred?

When people fail us, we often make vows to protect our hearts. But often these lead us to an even deeper place of isolation and bondage. Friends offer advice but their patience gets depleted when our lives don't change. They don't have the grace to weather all that we suffer when it seems to go on indefinitely. Then we give in to the idea that something is wrong with us. Our self-esteem plummets and we settle for far less than God's best.

Only when we turn back to God and bare all we know before Him, choosing to be true to Him and worshipping Him in the midst of our struggles will He bring His river of refreshing and cleansing renewal. Then He fills our mouths with testimonies that will help others find their freedom in Him too.

Did Jesus single out the Samaritan woman at the well because He knew she attracted men and had influence? Perhaps. God uses all of us to touch people no one else can reach. This is one of the reasons why He wants us to be whole and holy—so we can be blessed to bless others.

Your Hope

God is near to the brokenhearted (Psalm 34:18). He knows just what you need and how to restore your wounded spirit and bruised emotions. He is tender and faithful to catch all the tears you cry. None will fall to the ground before Him (Psalm 56:8). His tender mercies are new every morning, and He comes bringing healing as often as you need it (Lamentations 3:23).

He allows you a time to grieve, but He also has your recovery scheduled. He comes with instructions to set you on the right path. When you are willing to be open to doing things His way, the habits that have kept you bound will fall away. Your life will be transformed when your mind is renewed to embrace truth from God's perspective (Romans 12:2). That truth will cause you to make the necessary changes that are needed for you to have the new life you desire.

You can spin your own rationale for your bad decisions, but when you see things the way God does and begin to worship Him in Spirit and in truth, being authentically who you are and open to God's way of doing things, your life will change. All that you thirst for will be realized.

Your Truth

✼ What does your heart thirst for?

✼ What disappointments have caused you to make vows to protect your heart? What cycle(s) needs to be broken in your life?

✼ What has God revealed to you about yourself that will help you make a positive difference in how you move forward?

27

When Your Faith Falters

My dear sister,

My sister and I decided we would tell you our story because it flies in the face of a lot of your modern-day faith theology. This was our experience.

Our family was close with Jesus, and our brother considered Jesus a great friend. We loved Jesus, and Jesus loved us.[1] So when Lazarus got sick, it stood to reason that we'd send an urgent message to Jesus and expect Him to drop whatever He was doing and make haste to join us. But days passed without a reply from our friend. We heard nothing…nothing…and then our brother died.

We were beside ourselves. What had happened to Jesus? Where was He? Where was the Healer? Jesus had dined in our home on countless occasions. We spent a lot of time with Him and were counted among His strongest followers. My sister, Mary, had even poured her life savings in precious oil out on His feet and then wiped them clean with her hair. Where was Jesus when we needed Him most?

I thought of the time when Jesus and His disciples came to dinner. I was so excited as I made preparations to feed everybody. I was running around, worried I wouldn't get it all done, when I noticed Mary sitting at Jesus' feet drinking in every word He said. I needed help, and was just sitting around! I asked Jesus to tell her to help me, but He told me I was in the wrong. That I was too anxious and troubled by too many things. He pointed out that Mary had chosen the better thing that would be the most lasting. She was sitting at His feet, hearing His words, and hiding them in her heart.[2] Words of faith and God's faithfulness. His power to move in every situation. This could not be taken from her, He said. "Well," I thought, "where is all that faithfulness and power now?"

If Jesus really loved us wouldn't He have come when we sent word? Why didn't He come and heal our brother? Mary agreed. In our grief we questioned God. How could He allow such a loss? It didn't seem fair. Everything I believed about Jesus was rocked to the core. I couldn't reconcile the fact that He loved us and yet ignored our cries when we really needed Him.

And now Lazarus was dead. Hope evaporated. Despair and grief...and yes, bitterness, set in.

And then He came. Four days after our brother died Jesus strolled into our town as if it were an ordinary day. Mary and I were told He was at the edge of our village; I rose and went to meet Him. With every step I took the questions I'd wrestled with about His absence filled my mind. As soon as I reached Him I couldn't restrain myself. I vented my disappointment in Him. "Lord, if You had been here, my brother would not have died!"

Jesus didn't seem shaken by my outburst. He calmly replied, "Your brother will rise again." How could He say that at a time like this? His words didn't comfort me. Of course he would rise again. I believed what Jesus taught about the last days when everyone would rise. But I wanted Lazarus alive right now!

Then Jesus told me He was the resurrection and the life. He said anyone who believed in Him will live, even though they die. He asked if I believed Him. I wasn't sure what to believe. Well, actually I did know what I believed, it just wasn't going to serve me well at the moment. I knew Jesus was the Messiah, but now I wasn't sure about His claims regarding life and resurrection. I told Him I believed He was the Messiah, the Son of God.

My shoulders slumped and I turned away. All I knew was that brother was dead, and Jesus had failed us in our hour of need. Perhaps Mary could make sense of it since she was the one who sat at His feet. I went home and got Mary. On the way back to Jesus I wondered at how unmoved He'd seemed considering Lazarus was supposed to be His close friend.

Poor Mary was in such distress. All that she believed about Jesus had been shattered. She said she was thankful He'd come but disappointed He was too late. When we got to Jesus, Mary echoed my sentiments. "Lord, if You had been here, my brother would not have died." This time Jesus looked upset. He asked to be taken to the tomb. He wept openly as we walked. The crowd following us was divided in sentiment. Half the people were moved by the deep grief Jesus displayed that reflected His love for our brother. The other half ranged from annoyed to angry. "Could not this man, who opened the eyes of the blind man, have kept this man also from dying?"[3] My sentiments exactly!

At the tomb Jesus asked for the stone to be rolled away. Was He going to go in? This wasn't how things were done. I told Him the body would really smell by now. He didn't seem to care. He again asked that the stone be rolled away. Once that was done, Jesus sighed deeply and looked toward heaven. I will never forget what He said. "Father, I thank You that You have heard Me. I [know] that You always hear Me; but because of the people standing around I said it, so that they may believe that You sent Me." Then He looked toward the tomb and said, "Lazarus, come forth."

I thought, "What is He doing?" And then wonder of wonders, there was Lazarus shuffling out of the tomb! Complete mayhem reigned. People were screaming, weeping, and praising God. We could hardly believe our eyes. Jesus calmly instructed some men to unwrap the burial cloths and free Lazarus.

Our brother was alive! Imagine our shame at doubting Jesus. Now I could tell He'd been deeply hurt by our lack of faith in Him. The accusations I'd hurled at Him replayed in my head. How I wished I could take them back!

Later when Mary and I talked, we agreed that we'd learned

something we'd never forget. And we hung on to that lesson again and again in the days and months that followed when we encountered things that challenged our faith. It even replayed in our minds on the day Jesus was crucified. We comforted ourselves with the words He'd spoken to us. *He is the resurrection and the life!* He proved that to us. In the death of His friend Lazarus, Jesus revealed His life-giving power. He was indeed the Son of God! Mary and I decided we would never fear death again. And since that day we never again doubted His words. All things are indeed possible with God.

Looking back, I wonder if Jesus stayed away on purpose when He first got our message. Did He realize our faith wasn't where it could be? Did He allow this situation to demonstrate the power of God so that our faith would grow? I believe so. Although learning this lesson didn't feel good at the time, my faith was truly solidified. I saw with my own eyes the dead brought to life. Now nothing seems beyond repair. I was forever changed. I know for sure that God hears *every* prayer I pray *every* time I pray. And when I don't sense His presence or He doesn't answer the way I'd hoped, I rest assured that He is on top of things and doing what He knows is best. I trust Him to answer the cries of my heart above and beyond what I know to expect.

Living and uplifted by faith,

Martha (and Mary)

Woman to Woman

I find details of Martha and Mary's tale extraordinary. Yes, they sent an urgent message to Jesus prevailing on Him to come when their brother became ill. They took care to remind Jesus that this was Lazarus, the friend He loved. The Word of God takes great care to confirm that, indeed, Jesus really did love Lazarus and his sisters, Mary and Martha (John 11:5). So Jesus stays away from Bethany until Lazarus has been dead for four days. Read it for yourself. That is what it says! "*So* when he heard that Lazarus was sick, [Jesus] stayed where he was" (John 11:6). Jesus loved them *so* He stayed away.

This is a hard story to understand. How can God love us so much and yet choose to delay taking action when we're in a crisis? And this is exactly what Jesus did. He deliberately stayed away until He knew Lazarus' body would be decomposing. He told His disciples that Lazarus was only sleeping, and He was going to wake him up (John 11:11). This flies in the face of our rational thinking. "What's going on?" we wonder. When the disciples didn't get it, Jesus told them plainly that Lazarus was dead and that He was glad for the delay in returning to Bethany because now God would be glorified and people would believe God had sent Him.

As much time as Jesus spent with Lazarus, Martha, and Mary, He knew their faith wasn't where it could be. Perhaps through their friendship they had let familiarity temper their belief in Him. After all, this was their buddy Jesus. We too can grow casual in our belief in God's power. We've read and heard so much that instead of building our faith the knowledge streamlines into a sophisticated belief system that suits our intellect. We rationalize what God is capable of based on what we know.

Martha was trapped by what she knew, and she couldn't see past it. Her conversation with Jesus shows how stuck she was. She'd put God in a tidy little box based on what she knew. She knew Jesus was the Son of God and the Messiah, but she didn't grasp that life resided in Him—physical and spiritual. And when Lazarus died, her faith faltered. When Jesus didn't come right away, she had no knowledge or hope that more was to come...until the last days, anyway. Jesus didn't come until after the situation with Lazarus was a wrap. He was too late and irreparable damage had been done. How could anything be redeemed now?

Jesus gives us a huge insight when He told the disciples Lazarus was sleeping. Death was a *temporary* state. There was nothing final about it. And He wanted to shatter the limitations they put on God. He wanted to show them that God was greater than their assumptions and belief. Was anything too hard for God? No! And this was the lesson they needed to learn in preparation for the difficult days to come.

I believe their lack of faith hurt Jesus deeply. He longed for them not only to hear him but to comprehend and believe the words He'd spoken. Jesus did not weep over the death of Lazarus. He knew the end of the story concerning him. I believe Jesus wept over Martha and Mary's lack of faith. How disappointing to spend so much time with them and then discover their faith was still so limited. Even so, Jesus loved them. Even so He was willing to once again reveal who He was—the Son of God who was able to do what He said He could do. As one of my favorite songs says, "He's able!"

God longs for us to be women of solid faith who won't be swayed to doubt by difficult circumstances. He wants us to continue to fearlessly believe in Him. This is why He encourages us to walk in the company of other people who hold the same faith in the one true God. As we mature in our faith, we tend to have fewer highs and lows. We don't panic as often, and we draw on the strength of past experiences where God came through for us. We finally arrive at that place of constantly reflecting on God's Word no matter what our eyes see. In Christ it is never too late for a situation to be redeemed! Our circumstances are never dead to the Lord. Just sleeping. Just waiting for that amazing moment when God breathes new life into that situation that looked hopeless. When God revives the desires of our hearts, it is as a tree of life to us that solidifies our faith in God.

Your Hope

We all come face-to-face with situations that assault our faith and make us wonder where God is. He is right there beside us in the easy times. He is right there beside us in the hard places. He longs for us to embrace faith shamelessly and believe for the impossible. "Now faith is confidence in what we hope for and assurance about what we do not see" (Hebrews 11:1).

Our faith must be present and immediate so it activates our attitudes, our conversations, and our actions as God works His will into the scene. We call those things we hope for that are not as though they are. We say out loud what faith announces in our spirit. Like Jesus, we only want to say what God tells us about our situations. The only reality we care about is what God says. Not what others think…not what we see. Only what God speaks and teaches. He said, "Let there be light," and there was light (Genesis 1:3). Darkness couldn't remain once God called for light!

The Word says that except a seed fall into the ground and die, it cannot bear fruit (John 12:24). In some instances in life, death of a sort is required for good to come out of a situation. All that is wrong has to fall away to make room for the fruit God desires to grow within the circumstance and the people connected to it.

Faith must keep growing and stretching. It doesn't stay in the same place. Greater miracles await! God wants us to have death-defying testimonies. This is one way He works in our lives to draw people to Him and give them hope. He selects you and me to face dramas and traumas because He can trust us to stand firm and wait on Him. Even when we despair and doubt, God uses our desert time to encourage us to seek Him so He can quench our thirst.

"It's impossible to please God apart from faith. And why? Because anyone who wants to approach God must believe both that he exists and that he cares enough to respond to those who seek him" (Hebrews 11:6-7 MSG). This is so often our greatest unspoken fear. That God doesn't care enough about us and what is going to respond helpfully. But when we truly believe He loves us and wants the best for us, we release our faith and believe for the best possible outcome. No matter how dead the situation looks, we believe it can be revived or transformed by God. Why? Because all things are possible with God (Matthew 19:26). He continually defies the odds in our lives to reveal His glory. To blow our minds with awe-inspiring wisdom and silence our doubts that He is who He says He is. God is the Rewarder of those who diligently seek Him.

My friend, you can trust God to be faithful and always be with you to replenish your faith. To grow it from the size of a mustard seed into a mustard tree. He wants your faith in Him to grow so that you will exercise your authority as you should. Your faith should produce works for the kingdom of God. "Faith without works is dead" (James 2:26 NASB). As you grow, so does your testimony of what God is able to do. If your relationship, your marriage, your dream, your career has died before your eyes, listen to what the Spirit of the Lord is saying. He is able to resurrect and redeem the most impossible-looking situations. When God shows up in your situation, death can't remain. He is the truth and the life. When He steps into your situation, positive change is inevitable.

Your Truth

❧ What situation in your life appears to be dead or looks impossible?

❧ What is causing your faith to be shaken in this instance?

❧ What do you believe God is working out in your life at this time?

❧ What is the best posture you can take in this moment?

28

Leaving a Lasting Legacy

My dear sister,

I am a woman of few words, so I'll get straight to it and tell you what I experienced and what I know. I've always had a heart for the poor and for widows. God blessed my life abundantly, so I've been able to share what I had with others. My heart bled for my sisters who lost their husbands and could no longer afford the basics. What could I do to help? I sewed and made them coats and clothing. I quietly helped when I could, and it made my heart glad.

Giving to others, whether it be a listening ear, a meal, a shoulder to cry on, or creating garments was my joy. When I grew ill, I prayed that I might remain a little longer because I worried over those the Lord had put on my heart to care for. But my body wasn't as strong as my will. I felt life draining away. Then I died...although I'm not sure I was actually aware of it. For me it seemed like I fell into a deep sleep because the next thing I knew I heard a man's voice telling me to get up.[1]

I felt a hand in mine, and then I was sitting up in bed. The apostle Peter told me what had happened, and I couldn't believe it. Neither could those who had gathered to mourn my passing. My friends had called the apostle to my house hoping for a miracle. And now that it had occurred, they could hardly believe their eyes!

Oh the rejoicing that broke out! Singing, clapping, and tears of joy filled the air. The news traveled fast, and many believed in Jesus because of this miracle. I was so glad. God used my death even more than He used my life! That gave me great satisfaction.

Even though I was brought back from the dead, I knew I wouldn't live forever. Oh, but I'm thankful that God allowed me more time to go on making a difference. I prayed that the seeds I sowed in people's lives would return fruit long after I'm gone. This miracle from God gave me great assurance that nothing I do in His name is in vain.

It wasn't until that time that I stopped to think of the importance of legacy. Most people live for just today, but the day passes. Life comes to an end. What we leave behind will speak volumes on how we lived and what we accomplished. The memories of our deeds and heart attitude are the things that will remain. Most other facts will fade away.

Helping the needy fed my soul and made me feel wealthy. I used the gifts God gave me to honor Him and do what I could to ease life for the people around me. I lived for the satisfaction and joy people revealed when they received my small gifts. I was humbled and thankful when I noticed smiles of thanksgiving or tears of appreciation. I loved that God let me be an extension of His grace. I prayed others would feel His love as profoundly as I did.

I'm filled to overflowing with gratitude for all the Lord has done for me. That He would take notice and raise me from the dead so I could continue to serve Him was a great gift beyond what my words could express. My service was all I had to give to God. It was my offering to Him, my way of saying thank You for all that He has done for me.

Oh, my sister, I pray that you will find your joy and satisfaction in the simplicity of servanthood. Your obedience to God sets the atmosphere for miracles Waiting on the Lord is never about standing still. Be in active service to Him while you anticipate the full manifestation of His goodness and blessings. Teaching people about God by helping them is one of the highest honors God bestows on us and yields the greatest blessings. The world is such a selfish and self-serving environment. Most people are making sure they're getting ahead and are afraid that others will steal what they have. Resist the urge to focus on what you have and, instead, focus on what you can give. Embrace the heart of God. Let your heart beat for what His heart beats for. This is the secret to true and lasting peace and fulfillment.

Grateful to be in His service,

Tabitha, also known as Dorcas

Woman to Woman

Have you heard the saying that "people don't really care what you know; they only want to know you care"? Our actions speak volumes about what we truly value. Where we spend our time and money reveals much about the condition of our hearts. We're all called to be the manifestation of God's care for us to others. He allows us to be extensions of His loving heart here on earth. When we feed the hungry and clothe the naked, God counts it as if we're for Him personally (Matthew 25:34-40).

Serving others proves our love for Jesus. He asked His disciples to do two things as proof of their love for Him. "If you love me keep my commandments" (John 14:15). And when affirming His love for Peter despite His disciple's denial of Him, Jesus said, "Feed my lambs…take care of my sheep" (John 21:15-16). What is the difference between lambs and sheep? Sheep are adults in control of their faculties and able to feed themselves. Lambs are still babies who need assistance and care to survive and grow. God is asking us to tend to His whole flock. From new believers to the mature in the faith, we're to be involved in their lives. Even mature believers need encouragement and help from time to time.

We're called to help bear the infirmities of the weak, to laugh with those who laugh, and to weep with those who weep. These are the moments people will treasure when they think of us. Jesus wasn't wealthy when He lived on earth. He didn't dispense millions of dollars to anyone. He didn't drive fancy cars or wear fancy clothes. He was moved with compassion for the sick and dying, the lonely and destitute, the sinners and the hopeless. He made His care known through loving gestures and words that gave life, and healing, and hope. Throngs gathered to see Him and hear His teachings because they were changed by them. People were affected by His presence (physically and, by faith, spiritually) in their lives.

Jesus gives us the same opportunities to make a lasting impact in the lives of those we meet. When people see us extending God's grace, charity, and love to them and others, they're encouraged to consider their own faith journeys.

Tabitha (Dorcas) so deeply touched the lives of those she came in contact with that they were unwilling to be separated from her. When Tabitha was dying, they sent for the apostle Peter to come as quickly as he could. When Peter arrived they shared their stories of how much Tabitha had blessed their lives and what she'd done for others. Peter was so moved he raised her from the dead so she could continue to serve and represent Jesus.

Even though we may not be resurrected in such a dramatic fashion when we die, our works done in the name of Jesus will live on through the people we've helped. The greatest testimony we can leave is that we gave honor and glory to God by reaching out to help those around us.

Your Hope

Are you wondering what you can really do or give to others? The answer is simple: give yourself. Give of your time and your talents. Give of the gifts that come naturally to you. Be flexible and ready to help moment by moment. God will give you what you need when you need it to help others. He provides the seeds, the soil, and the necessary energy. You provide the willing heart and helpful hands.

You can't be a cheerful giver if you're worried about how your own needs will be met. When you take care of God's business, He will take care of yours (Proverbs 28:27). There is a reason He says it is more blessed to give than to receive! God desires fruit from your life, and He's given you the ability to use His power to share His love and grace. As you yield yourself to Him, He will reward you for carrying out His instructions and being His agent of change and blessing.

What do you want for your life? Give it to others. When Abraham prayed for the household of the king that was struck with barrenness, shortly thereafter Sarah become pregnant. When Job prayed for his friends, he experienced restoration and riches far beyond what he had originally. When Jesus laid down His life for us, He gained the whole world.

As so many of the women of the Bible point out, there is no way we can out give God! And on top of the joy of giving, we stand to gain so much more when we pour out ourselves for the benefit of God's kingdom. Leaving a legacy of God's goodness as the memory of your character is something that is the greatest period you can have on the sentence of your life. To live selflessly will reap rewards beyond your lifetime. People may forget the specifics about your possessions or achievements, but they will never forget how you made them feel. The greatest blessing of all is what you will have to present to God when you finally see Him face-to-face. Works that not only blessed others but pleased Him. Works that will pass the test of fire. What a great blessing it will be when Jesus says, "Well done, good and faithful servant!…Come and share your master's happiness" (Matthew 25:21).

Your Truth

❧ In what ways do you serve the people around you?

❧ How can you be the heart and arms of God to people in need?

❧ How can you use your gifts and talents to help others without spending a lot of money?

❧ What burden for helping people has God placed on your heart?

❧ How will you make a difference right where you are?

Notes

Chapter 1—The Price of Entitlement

1. Genesis 2:18 KJV and NIV.
2. Genesis 2:23.
3. Genesis 3:11 NCV.
4. Genesis 3:13 NIV.
5. Genesis 3:20 NIV.

Chapter 2—The Benefits of Submission

1. Genesis 12.
2. Genesis 11:11-13.
3. Genesis 20:12.
4. Genesis 20.
5. Genesis 17.

Chapter 3—The Other Side of Being the "Other Woman"

1. Genesis 12:4.
2. Genesis 21:15-16.

Chapter 4—The Power of the Past

1. Genesis 12:4.
2. Genesis 13.
3. Genesis 19.
4. Genesis 19:17.
5. Genesis 19:26.

Chapter 5—Making Things Happen

1. Genesis 19:30.
2. Genesis 19:36-38.

Chapter 6—The Importance of Destiny

1. Genesis 24:27.
2. Genesis 24:12-31.
3. Genesis 24:58.
4. Genesis 25:22-23.

Chapter 7—When Love Isn't Enough

1. Genesis 28:10-15.
2. Genesis 30:2.
3. Genesis 30:23-24.
4. Genesis 30:32-43.
5. Proverbs 14:1.

Chapter 8—The Fight You Can't Win

1. Genesis 30:1.
2. Isaiah 4:1.
3. Genesis 2:24.

Chapter 9—A Mother's Influence

1. Exodus 2:9-10.
2. Exodus 3:10; 12:31.
3. Exodus 7:1; 28:3.
4. Exodus 15:20-21; Micah 6:4.
5. Numbers 26:59.

Chapter 10—How to Deal with Haters

1. Numbers 12:1.
2. Numbers 12:9.
3. Numbers 12:8.

Chapter 11—How to Work with Men

1. Judges 4:4.
2. Judges 4:6-7.
3. Judges 4:14.

Chapter 12—How to Win a Battle

1. Judges 4.

Chapter 13—The Dangers of Indulgence

1. Judges 13.

2. Judges 15:3-15.

3. Judges 15:20.

4. Judges 16:1-3.

Chapter 14—How to Change Your Life

1. Joshua 2:12-15.

Chapter 15—The Power of Connections

1. Ruth 1:3-5.

2. Romans 7:4.

3. John 15:5.

4. Matthew 19:26.

5. Ecclesiastes 4:9.

Chapter 16—What Every Woman Needs to Know

1. Judges 13:5; 14:5-6; 16:6.

2. Judges 15:20.

Chapter 17—Timing Is Everything

1. 1 Samuel 1:8.

2. 1 Samuel 1:17.

3. 1 Samuel 3:19-21.

4. 1 Samuel 2:21.

5. 1 Samuel 7:15; 10:1; 16:13.

Chapter 18—The Difference a Right Response Makes

1. Esther 1:10.

Chapter 19—How to Make Your Man Your Hero

1. Esther 2:20.

2. Esther 4:13-14.

3. Esther 5:3.

4. Esther 7:9 NASB.

5. Esther 8:1-2, 8-9, 11.

Chapter 20—How to Live with a Fool

1. 1 Samuel 25:24 NASB.

2. 1 Samuel 25:26-31.

3. Proverbs 26:4.

Chapter 21—How to Avoid Relationship Regrets

1. Samuel 18:27.
2. 1 Samuel 19:11-12.
3. 2 Samuel 3:15-16.
4. 2 Samuel 3:20.

Chapter 22—The Trouble with Secrets

1. 2 Samuel 11:11.
2. 2 Samuel 12:10-14.
3. Ibid.; 2 Samuel 16:22.
4. 1 Kings 1:11-48.

Chapter 23—When the Unthinkable Happens

1. 2 Samuel 13:11.

Chapter 24—Finding Your Balance

1. Galatians 5:22.

Chapter 25—How to Grasp the Impossible

1. Luke 1:26.
2. Matthew 19-20.
3. Luke 2:8-17.
4. Matthew 9:11.
5. Luke 2:34-35.
6. Matthew 19:26.
7. Matthew 28:1-10.

Chapter 26—Breaking the Negative Cycle

1. John 4:10.
2. John 4:21-24.
3. John 4:42.

Chapter 27—When Your Faith Falters

1. John 11:5.
2. Luke 10:41-42.
3. John 11:37 NASB.

Chapter 29—Leaving a Lasting Legacy

1. Acts 9:40.

For more information about
Michelle McKinney Hammond,
her books, or her ministry,
log on to
www.michellehammond.com

For booking information, click on the booking tab at:
www.michellehammond.com

Twitter: @mckinneyhammond
Facebook: Michelle-McKinney-Hammond
YouTube: heartwingmin

· · · · · · · · ·

HARVEST HOUSE PUBLISHERS
EUGENE, OREGON

To learn more about books by
Michelle McKinney Hammond,
and to read sample chapters, log on to:
www.HarvestHousePublishers.com

· · · · · · · · ·

Michelle's books are available at
your local Christian bookstore and other book outlets.

How to Get the Best Out of Your Man
The Power of a Woman's Influence

Get the Relationship You Dream Of

Do you want more passion? More unity? Want your man to rise to the occasion? Bestselling author Michelle McKinney Hammond shows you how to create a stronger love that will bring you joy and fulfillment, as well as resilience for weathering the challenges every couple encounters. Through a unique look at the life of Esther, you'll gain:

- ideas for inspiring and supporting your man
- a better understanding of how men think and operate
- specifics for helping your partner meet your needs
- innovative ways to bless him…and let him bless you
- suggestions for using these principles to improve other relationships

If you want to build and enhance your love relationship, let your man be your hero. You'll reap the rewards!

How to Get Past Disappointment
Finding Hope

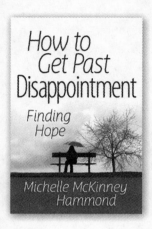

An Unforgettable Encounter

The Samaritan woman always welcomed the heat of the sun once she sat on the edge of the well and splashed her face with cool water from the bucket she drew up. This place was her oasis of peace and refreshing. But not today. A stranger was sitting in her spot. A Jewish rabbi...

Drawing on the dramatic story of the "Woman at the Well" found in John 4, bestselling author and dynamic speaker Michelle McKinney Hammond invites you to move beyond life's disappointments and experience God in a new and deeply fulfilling way. Through powerful, relevant biblical teaching, she encourages you to...

- ❧ let God's love help you face your hurts and forgive when necessary
- ❧ look beyond disappointment to embrace new beginnings
- ❧ release your expectations to discover even greater blessings in God's plan for you

As an added bonus, Michelle includes insightful questions and uplifting affirmations to help you live the life God wants you to have.

Also available
How to Get Past Disappointment DVD!
Let Michelle lead your group in six dynamic, 30-minute sessions.

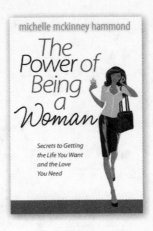

The Power of Being a Woman

What Are You Looking For?

Romance? Healthy relationships? Success? Bestselling author and businesswoman Michelle McKinney Hammond can help. After exploring the positive attributes God gives to you as a woman, Michelle goes on to help you discover your own unique gifts and talents. With this firm foundation, she reveals how you can move forward confidently, using your new understanding and skills to

- ✸ influence rather than challenge
- ✸ master the balance between your personal and professional life
- ✸ experience harmony and passion in love
- ✸ effectively achieve your goals
- ✸ move mountains with your faith

Enthusiastic, outspoken, and entertaining, Michelle lives what she teaches. Let her help you experience the vibrant life God planned for you!

> *"[Michelle] calls a truce between the genders with her biblically based perspective on the art of being a woman."*
>
> TODAY'S CHRISTIAN WOMAN

More Encouraging Books by
Michelle McKinney Hammond

101 Ways to Get and Keep His Attention

The DIVA Principle

Getting Smart About Life, Love, and Men

How to Avoid the 10 Mistakes Single Women Make

How to Be Found by the Man You've Been Looking For

How to Be Happy Where You Are

How to Get Past Disappointment

How to Get the Best Out of Your Man

Lessons from a Girl's Best Friend

The Power of Being a Woman

The Real Deal on Love and Men

Right Attitudes for Right Living

A Sassy Girl's Guide to Loving God

Sassy, Single, and Satisfied

Sassy, Single, and Satisfied Devotional

Secrets of an Irresistible Woman

What to Do Until Love Finds You

Why Do I Say "Yes" When I Need to Say "No"?

A Woman's Gotta Do What a Woman's Gotta Do

DVD
How to Get Past Disappointment (180 min.)

Aboriginal Autonomy

Issues and Strategies

H.C. COOMBS

Edited by Diane Smith

CAMBRIDGE
UNIVERSITY PRESS

Published by the Press Syndicate of the University of Cambridge
The Pitt Building, Trumpington Street, Cambridge CB2 1RP, UK
40 West 20th Street, New York, NY 10011-4211, USA
10 Stamford Road, Oakleigh, Melbourne 3166, Australia

National Library of Australia cataloguing in publication data
Coombs, H.C. (Herbert Cole), 1906-.
Aboriginal autonomy.
Bibliography.
Includes index.
[1.] Aborigines, Australian, - Government relations. [2.]
Aborigines, Australian - Politics and government. [3.]
Aborigines, Australian - Social conditions. [4.] Aborigines,
Australian - Economic conditions. [5.] Aborigines,
Australian - Land tenure. [6.] Aborigines, Australian -
Ethnic identity. I. Smith, Diane (Diane Evelyn). II. Title.
323.119915

Library of Congress cataloguing in publication data
Coombs, H.C. (Herbert Cole), 1906-
Aboriginal autonomy: issues and strategies/H.C. Coombs;
edited by Diane Smith.
p.   cm.
Includes bibliographical references (p.   ) and index.
1. Australian aborigines–Government relations. 2. Australian
aborigines–Politics and government. 3. Australian aborigines–Land
tenure. 4. Australia–Ethnic relations. I. Smith, Diane (Diane
Evelyn). II. Title.
GN666.C657   1994
994' .0049915–dc20
                                                94-10309
                                                CIP

A catalogue record for this book is available from the British Library.

ISBN 0 521 44097 1 Hardback
ISBN 0 521 44637 6 Paperback

Transferred to digital printing 1999

There is little in the history of the decade since the referendum about which white Australians can feel complacent, but the way ahead is clearer and the ferment of ideas necessary to open that way has begun. Above all, Aborigines are developing the sense of a common identity, the institutions of political action and the intellectual and spiritual leadership which will give increasing authority to their claim to move along this way by their own efforts and at their own pace. Hope for the future lies essentially in their growing capacity to maintain these trends. That capacity would of course be more effective if it were matched by an increasing desire and determination among white Australians generally to welcome and support Aboriginal initiatives.

H.C. Coombs
Kulinma, 1978

Contents

Foreword by Michael Dodson   ix

Preface   xi

Acknowledgments   xv

The Aboriginal World View
1 The making of Aboriginal identity   2

Aborigines and the Land
2 The future of the homeland movement   24
3 Warlpiri land use and management   32
4 The implications of land rights   39

Aboriginal Lifestyles
5 Economic, social and spiritual factors in Aboriginal health   54
6 Aboriginal education and the issues underlying Aboriginal
    deaths in custody   66
7 Aboriginal work and economy   76

Aborigines, Resources and Development
8 The ideology of development in the East Kimberley   86
9 Aborigines and resources: from 'humbug' to negotiation   100
10 The McArthur River development: a case in point   111

Aborigines, Law and the State

11 The Yirrkala proposals for the control of law and order   118
12 Aboriginal political leadership and the role of the
        National Aboriginal Conference   131
13 Aborigines and the Treaty of Waitangi   143

Asserting Autonomy: Recent Aboriginal Initiatives

14 Aboriginal initiatives on the land   156
15 Initiatives in Aboriginal political organisation   171
16 Education: taking control   187

The Recognition of Native Title

17 The Mabo decision: a basis for Aboriginal autonomy?   200

Conclusion

18 Negotiating future autonomy   220

Appendix: The Eva Valley Statement   231

References   235

Select Bibliography of work by H.C. Coombs   241

Index   247

Foreword

In August 1993, I attended a national meeting of Aboriginal and Torres Strait Islander representatives at Eva Valley in the Northern Territory to discuss issues arising out of the High Court decision on native title. On the morning just prior to the commencement of the meeting, Nugget Coombs, who had been invited to attend, arrived to wish us well and briefly renew acquaintances with many old Aboriginal and Islander friends. There were warm greetings and well wishing until shortly Nugget departed to allow us to proceed with our business. A young Aboriginal man of perhaps 16 or 17 years inquired of me as to 'who was that old man?' My response was, 'That old man must be respected; he is the whitefella's most senior Elder'. Nugget himself asserts the powers of elders may not amount to more than '... a right to be consulted and listened to with respect'. We may not agree with many of the views put forward by him in this book; however, what he has to say demands our respect. In reading the thoughts and words of this man we must listen to what he has to say. It may just transpire that Nugget is right about the solutions and the way forward.

I doubt, however, if anybody has the correct answer to overcoming the enormous disadvantage visited upon Aboriginal and Torres Strait

Islander people. The bureaucratic apparatus which shrouds Aboriginal and Islander affairs precludes a solution. It is the bureaucracy that obstructs and hinders indigenous development and in particular, indigenous self-determination and autonomy. This is not to suggest all bureaucrats are the problem. On the contrary, many, including Nugget, have struggled to turn around the mindsets that have restricted Aboriginal and Islander aspirations.

The remarkable thing about Nugget Coombs is that he could be doing other things. He could be quietly enjoying his retirement after years of service to his country. He chooses not to do that; he chooses to continue to raise his voice in calling for the rights of indigenous peoples. Nugget is merely asking that we Aboriginal and Islander people be given control over our own lives and the things that dominate them.

These are no one else's views. This is fearlessly Nugget Coombs. He makes it clear he speaks for no-one but himself. I suspect we will, having read his book, find that in some way or other Nugget is speaking for all of us.

Michael Dodson
Aboriginal and Torres Strait Islander Social Justice Commissioner

Preface

This book is a personal document. In form it is a selection of essays I have written for various occasions since 1978 about issues central to the autonomy of Aboriginal Australians and continues the record of my involvement with those issues after the publication of *Kulinma* in that year. That book carried the sub-title, *Listening to Aboriginal Australians*. One of my critics in the bureaucratic conflicts over Aboriginal affairs policies of the time was heard to remark, 'It sounds more like Nugget listening to himself talk about Aborigines'. There was some point in the criticism and it could be repeated in relation to this volume also.

Neither book has authority to speak for Aborigines, nor is it a record of views sponsored by them. It presents my own thoughts as they developed on issues and as they were confronted by Aborigines and Australian society. They are the thoughts of a white Australian of Celtic origin, educated and trained initially as a teacher and progressively as an economist, central banker, public servant and academic. One who came late, almost by accident, to a position of responsibility affecting Aborigines and whose knowledge of Aboriginal people has been derived primarily from the work of professional anthropologists and other writers with experience of them. Fortunately, that knowledge has been supplemented and developed by personal contact and experience with Aboriginal men and women in their groups and communities over 25 years of fairly frequent visits and other forms of communication. Because the focus of much of my work has been predominantly with Aboriginal Australians, this book does not deal with the many important issues regarding self-determination that have been, and continue to be of great importance to Torres Strait Islander peoples; though many of the topics mentioned here will have relevance to them.

Collectively, the essays consider the forms and significance of Aboriginal autonomy and especially its crucial role in contemporary Aboriginal identity. As they have been written about closely inter-related issues and events, there is a degree of overlap and repetition. Some essays, which have appeared previously in published form or presented at workshops and conferences, have been revised to remove some, but not all overlap. In the majority of cases, they have simply been edited to obtain consistency of style and format. Chapters 1, 14, 15, 16, 17 and 18 have been written specifically for this book in an attempt to express the present state of my views about a range of issues currently affecting Aboriginal autonomy.

The order of the essays is not chronological, but has arisen out of their placement within sections that address a general theme relevant to the role and expression of autonomy within Aboriginal society. Thus, Chapter 1 provides a general introduction to the formation and strength of traditional and contemporary Aboriginal identity. It introduces the concept of autonomy which I suggest is a key component of that identity and highlights the central importance of Aboriginal practices of nurturing and socialisation in regulating individual autonomy. Chapters 2–13 describe various aspects of Aboriginal people's relationship with the land; the nature of their social world and preferred lifestyles; their approach to the environment and the use of resources; and the significance of Aboriginal political organisation and law. Chapters 14–16 present overviews of some recent Aboriginal initiatives to maintain autonomy and control in important areas of their identity. Chapter 17 locates the issue of Aboriginal autonomy within the current debate and negotiations following the High Court's Mabo judgement. Finally, the Conclusion looks to the future, to consider how Aboriginal auto- nomy and the diversity of lifestyles might be secured through a formal Act of Self-determination.

I have been motivated to prepare this present volume by my deep affection for the Aboriginal friends I have made, by my conviction that they share a rich heritage important to the human race and by my profound concern that the society to which I belong continues to perform so badly in its relationships with them that we are, all of us, shamed in the eyes of the civilised world.

At the time *Kulinma* was being compiled, after a decade of involve- ment, I believed that real progress was being made and that an optimistic political consensus was emerging; a consensus that the way forward was towards increasing autonomy for Aboriginal people, towards increasing recognition of their right to preserve and develop their own traditional culture, and to choose freely a way of life in Australia in which the land and access to resources necessary for its achievement would be progressively returned to them.

However, the growth of that political consensus was rudely interrupted. There was a sudden realisation in the early seventies that supplies of oil were not unlimited and that the world could be held to ransom by those who, by 'the arrangements of society', owned the limited resources. The world was made aware that there were limits to the basic natural resources which our industries and our militarists squander; limits which, in some important instances, are uncom- fortably close to exhaustion.

This awareness has stimulated changed attitudes towards conser- vation of resources and the need to protect the environment. These changes are polarising the world and its people. There are those who see the recognition of limits as a signal for a dramatic reform of human relationships with nature, so as to respect and maintain its infinite diversity for all time. There are others who have been, or wish to be, involved in the profitable exploitation of these resources; who see those limits as an invitation to greedier exploitation and greater short-term profit. In this polarisation the hope for a consensus by which the rights of indigenous peoples to land and resources can be restored to them more justly appears so far to be a victim. Greed, contempt for future generations and willingness to exploit racial antagonism in order to resist change have become, with honourable but few exceptions, the mark of the policies of those who desire to control the world's resources.

We in Australia may still have the opportunity to build a society in which mankind recognises itself as a part, not the master, of nature and in which men and women of different races and cultures live in creative diversity, valuing and protecting that diversity in nature and in humankind. To the achievement of that society this book is dedicated.

Acknowledgments

In putting this book together I was greatly assisted by Diane Smith, whose contribution was far beyond the normal role of an editor, providing a constructive contribution to the content and structure of the book. I was also assisted by Ettie Oakman (secretary) and Mickey Dewar (research assistant). Without them I doubt whether the task would have been accomplished and I thank them.

The acknowledgement of help in content is difficult. I have been fortunate throughout my working life to be involved in issues about which I have felt intellectually and emotionally deeply committed. I have been equally fortunate to be able to work in association with others who shared that commitment. Some have been women colleagues with whom I have shared ideas and uninhibited comment. I mention in this book several who have been important in the conception and the realisation of this and other books. Of these, none has been more fruitful than the thirty-year partnership I have enjoyed with Judith Wright, which began in relation to the role of government in the arts in the early sixties and has continued to enrich my experience in relation to the environment, economic policy and Aborigines. Indeed, it is difficult for me to identify much which was not, to a greater or lesser degree, the product of that partnership. Often, in the manner of the male, it has been taken for granted. To Judith and my other women colleagues, I acknowledge my indebtedness and record my gratitude.

I gratefully acknowledge the assistance of my friends and colleagues from the Centre for Resource and Environmental Studies and the Centre for Aboriginal Economic Policy Research at the Australian National University, Canberra, and from the North Australian Research Unit, Darwin. I am also grateful to those concerned for permission to publish the essays in this form: including the Centre for Resource and Environmental Studies of the Australian National University, the Aboriginal Studies Press of the Australian Institute of Aboriginal and Torres Strait Islander Studies, the Friends of the National Library of Australia, the Australian Broadcasting Corporation, and the Australian Government Publishing Service.

My special thanks go to the Northern, Central and Pitjantjatjara Land Councils, Tangentyere Council, Yolngu Association and their staff, and in particular, the peoples of Yirrkala (East Arnhem Land), the Pitjantjatjara lands and the Kimberley region, both black and white, who over the years have shared their vision of the country and their worlds with me.

H.C. Coombs

The Aboriginal World View

1

The making of
Aboriginal identity

A CERTAIN HERITAGE

In the early eighties I worked with Maria Brandl, an anthropologist, and Warren Snowdon, a teacher and political activist, on a project to prepare for the Minister for Social Security, Senator Margaret Guilfoyle, a volume to help public servants and others involved with Aboriginal people and their children understand something of those among whom they were to work. The volume was called *A Certain Heritage* and was dedicated

> ... to those public servants in Australia who seek to understand Aboriginality and to accommodate it. (Coombs et al. 1983: iii)

Maria, who alone among us was a professional anthropologist, was our guide in developing an awareness of the existence, the strength and the persistence of that heritage among the various groups of Aborigines. She also made it possible for us to recognise how little public policy and its programs, including those in which we ourselves had been involved, were based on an understanding of the content of that heritage and how, so far from accommodating Aboriginality, they worked to weaken and destroy it.

2

The book reviewed the Aboriginal heritage – social and cultural – recognising many components which have become, at least to some degree, part of the public image of Aboriginal people. They include:

- a sense of identity and having a shared experience with other descendants of the original inhabitants of the continent; an experience which incorporates a memory of an ancestral heritage and of the agony of colonial dispossession;
- a sharing of that ancestral way as a distinctive vision referred to as the Law or the Dreaming, which is still widely maintained and renewed by an ordered ceremonial life and which, even when apparently lost or destroyed, remains at least as a vivid reminder of the bitterest of their dispossessions;
- a conviction that they hold and maintain a special familial relationship with the land and indeed with the earth, its creatures and the universe generally; a relationship which persists despite white dispossession, so that rights and obligations under it continue unimpaired in Aboriginal minds; and
- a consciousness of a close pattern of relationships with and obligations towards others with whom they are related by kinship; a pattern which can comprehend and incorporate people from 'far away', other living creatures and aspects of the physical and spiritual environment.

Contemporary experience and the work of other later anthropologists confirmed for me the significance of these components and have enriched my knowledge of their role in Aboriginal life. That work has, in recent years, focused my attention on:

- some elements of apparent contradiction within the scale of values characteristic of Aboriginality and the degree to which, and the means by which, these are reconciled;
- the demands on the time, behaviour and dedication which the Aboriginal way of life imposes on those who wish to live by it; and
- the degree to which those demands can be met within a society such as that of mainstream Australia in which direct access to the earth's resources is no longer generally possible and which is dominated by an economic system from which almost all must 'earn a living', most generally by employment.

My thinking about these important matters has been greatly influenced by the work of anthropologists, but also by ideas which have emerged from that of ecologists who have studied both the genetic inheritance which Homo sapiens brings into the world and the degree to which, the purposes for which, and the means by which that inheritance is adapted to the experience of individuals within the environment into which they are born. In some ways, the most important contribution of ecological thought to the issues with which we are concerned is perhaps the least attended to. Homo sapiens and our hominoid ancestors have lived on the earth for millions of years for all of which, with the exception of the last few thousand, the lifestyle was essentially that of a hunter-gatherer. Accordingly, says ecology, humankind's development has progressively been adapted physically, mentally and culturally to that lifestyle, acquiring remarkable efficiency in its practice.

Within just the last few thousand years, probably under the pressure of increasing population relative to readily available resources, humankind could no longer rely solely on the yield of hunting and gathering. Land and resources became increasingly the private property of powerful individuals and latterly, corporations. After passing through phases of itinerant pastoralism, humankind has become increasingly sedentary as herders, agriculturists, craftsmen and at last, predominantly as traders and employees. The inherited character appropriate to the life of a hunter-gatherer was not, and is not, necessarily well adapted to the various lifestyles required for these latter occupations. The record of social change within western society and its contemporary institutions bears witness to the colossal effort which has been required to adapt men and women to life in the industrial and post-industrial world. Indeed, our social institutions can be seen as a gigantic structure to socialise people so that they conform to the needs of the economic system and the related institutions of our society. People are now separated from the natural resources the system uses, their work controlled by a division of labour which isolates them from its purposes and from those for whom they work. They are encapsulated into factories, offices, shopping centres, into suburban and city dwellings, with their peculiar forms of

4

personal isolation and loneliness. It is an astonishingly successful socialisation but not one achieved without major cost:

> Life ... has become a symbol of the fact that man can become adapted to starless skies, treeless avenues, shapeless buildings, tasteless bread, joyless celebrations, spiritless pleasures – to a life without reverence for the past, love for the present or hope for the future. (Dubos 1965: 278)

This assessment is in some respects exaggerated, but it is not without truth or relevance. It is sufficiently accurate to lend support to the ecologist's hypothesis that if the habitat and lifestyle of any creature (including Homo sapiens) deviates significantly from the conditions of life in which its species evolved, the health – physical, mental and emotional – of that creature will be impaired possibly to the point of its extinction (Boyden 1970). Thought given to the almost universal evidence in contemporary human society of social disorder, violence and escape through drug abuse and suicide; to the breakdown of family and community; to the disruption of local, national and international socially accepted order; and to the widespread decline of concern for others, at least lends plausibility to that hypothesis. There is reason to doubt seriously whether the socialisation practices our society has established to fit men and women to the needs of our institutions are compatible with their health. Events in Los Angeles, in Bosnia-Herzegovina, in Israel, Iraq and Iran, in China, Bougainville and East Timor are not the work of sane or healthy men and women.

Whatever we may conclude about the validity of this hypothesis for the rest of the world, here in Australia it must call into question the insistence in our policies towards Aborigines that their future requires that they abandon the Aboriginal way of life and actively seek to become assimilated into our industrial urbanised society, accepting its work ethic and related values, acquiring its skills and ceasing to exist in any significant sense as a distinctive people within Australian society.

ABORIGINAL SOCIETY – AUTONOMY AND NURTURE

This book is a response to that call: to consider Aboriginal society and its 'way' as it exists after 200-odd years of attempts to destroy and change it; to consider its dominant qualities and its capacity to survive; and to assess whether the Aboriginal desire for it to persist is still strong. If it is, then it calls for action to explore the possible character of an Aboriginal society within the wider Australian society and the changes in white Australian attitudes and policies which such co-existence would call for. It also requires an exploration of the basis for possible reconciliation between black and white Australians within a multicultural society.

My thinking about these issues has been that of a white policy adviser trained initially in arts and economics, with a long and diverse experience as a public servant and administrator. That experience has been supplemented by short, but fairly frequent visits to Aboriginal communities where I have come, over 25 years, to be welcomed and to some degree accepted as 'belonging'. During that time, I have drawn heavily on the work of those anthropologists who have been more closely involved with Aborigines than I. Since the writing of *A Certain Heritage* with Maria Brandl and Warren Snowdon, the most important of these for me have been Bill Stanner, Annette Hamilton, Nancy Williams, Fred Myers, Peter Sutton, John von Sturmer, Marcia Langton, Robert Tonkinson and Diane Smith and, more recently, Deborah Bird Rose.

From them and my own personal experience of Aboriginal men and women in their groups and communities, and in their relationships with the mainstream, I have become convinced that the drama of Aboriginal response to contact with white society is expressed in terms of its effects on two dominant components in Aboriginal values – components which, to some extent, seem incompatible or mutually constraining. The first of these is the need Aborigines feel for personal autonomy or independence. The second is the willingness and duty felt by individuals to care for and nurture others among their kin and those with whom relatedness is established.

These two crucial components of Aboriginality – autonomy and nurture – are, I believe, deeply based in the long existence of their ancestors as hunter-gatherers. In the sense I use the word, autonomy is an attitude of mind, a willingness, desire and a capacity to be alone and independent in certain contexts; to be able to assess complex

6

information about the immediate and changing environment; and to formulate and trust one's own judgement in action. Such capacities had obvious survival value to the individual hunter, but also to the small kin-based hunting and gathering groups most commonly preferred in such societies. In these groups, the capacity to share resources and information, to divide responsibility and to protect, care for and teach others was vital to group survival. In other words, family and group solidarity were supported by individual autonomy and that autonomy was, in turn, regulated by wider social responsibilities.

ABORIGINAL KNOWLEDGE

Most societies develop a shared model or mental picture of the universe and the relationships between themselves and its constituent parts. The model used by Aborigines is a metaphor using the structure of their own family-based society; a metaphor which is extended to comprehend all living creatures and indeed the physical universe itself which to them is also imbued with life, consciousness and a capacity to communicate. Their society is composed of men and women, male and female; as are all animals and other species. Often that society is divided also into two moieties, perhaps originally based upon the division into the groups from which marriage partners are chosen by their respective members, but also having many other connotations. My limited experience in this matter is based primarily upon what I understand of the Yolngu communities of East Arnhem Land, but while differences exist between Aboriginal tribal or language groups, most seem to have similar structures formed of linked pairs. Thus, every Yolngu Aboriginal is male or female and Dhuwa or Yirritja. Membership of these named moieties is determined by parentage and marriage in accordance with customary rules. Important social responsibilities tend to be divided between male and female and between members of the two moieties, in ways designed to achieve balance; a quality highly valued in Aboriginal society. For example, a man or woman may be the 'boss' or owner for a particular ceremony, but its conduct must be planned and supervised by a 'guardian' or 'manager' from the other moiety. Relationships, functions and obligations within the pairs are mutual, reciprocal and, ideally,

7

evenly balanced. Such division based upon 'balanced pairs' with reciprocal responsibilities and mutual accountability pervades the life of Aboriginal groups and its organisation.

Aboriginal people's relationship with nature is essentially familial. The obligations to care for, bring up and protect members of their immediate and extended family include not only people from 'far away' with whom relationships have been established, but also subsequent generations, all living creatures and inanimate aspects of the group's habitat. Thus, the obligations to nurture that are imposed on young men at their successive initiation ceremonies and on women from birth, refer not merely to their human kin, but to the whole family of nature.

For many Aborigines the earth is female and the mother of all: having given birth to the spirit ancestors who incorporated within themselves the qualities of all species; having travelled the earth creating and giving names to its natural forms and creatures; prescribed the relationships and behaviour appropriate to them; and left in spirit form the 'seed' of the creatures which would, in succeeding generations, inhabit the earth. Important within this created pattern was the design of a vast repertoire of knowledge and ceremony which it was the primary function of Aboriginal people to perform in perpetuity. The performance of these ceremonies was both a record and a celebration of the ancestral acts of creation and a representation of the names, locations and qualities of the physical forms in which they were now embodied. It was also a kind of sacrament by which some of the creative power of the ancestors continued to be entrusted to men and women, to oblige and enable them to fulfil and perpetuate the ancestors' purposes.

This structure is widely referred to in various forms of Aboriginal English as the Dreaming, although the corresponding words in their own languages are not the same as those used to refer to the images and experiences which come to them in sleep. The word is used (in Aboriginal English) to refer more specifically to:

- the ancestral beings who walked the earth creating its physical features, and to living species and the laws of their existence;
- the creative acts themselves;

8

- the time in which these events occurred; and
- the relationships linking individual human beings and other created species, places or events.

Thus, the Dreaming is an Aboriginal 'model for and a celebration of life itself' and can be understood as a kind of map, a logos or principle of order, a poetic key to reality (Stanner 1979). It is a system in which each 'part' is both part of the whole and a system in itself (Rose 1992). It is a description of the world in terms of metaphor and provides a framework on, within and around which can be integrated the vast collection of observations and hypotheses which Aborigines have derived from living and interacting with their environment, in profound personal intimacy over thousands of generations. Its vast repertoire of names, songs, stories, dances, designs, paintings, sculptures and engravings, interwoven and embodied in ceremonies, served as a storehouse of Aboriginal culture. The ritual performance and repetition of these ceremonies serve also as an effective mnemonic for their group and individual memory.

This system of knowledge is the equivalent for Aborigines of western science with its accumulated knowledge, its hypotheses and accepted paradigms of explanation. This equivalence, however, masks significant differences as well as exhibiting interesting and relevant similarities between the two bodies of knowledge. Both are based upon direct observation and experience of nature. There is nothing in the 'logos, or principle of order' offered by the Dreaming which would require an Aboriginal person to reject the evidence of his senses or of his reason. But there is an important difference in the Aboriginal approach to the things or experiences observed. Western science seeks to examine these in their most basic components; to reduce them to their irreducible atoms. It seeks also to quantify the qualities of these units and the patterns within which they are related. Aborigines do not share this reductionist approach, believing that things and events in nature can properly be observed only in their contexts, as part of their environment. Nor do they share the assumption underlying the quantification process that the things being counted are in some sense identical and unchanging during the events being considered. They apparently perceive that concentration on quantity inevitably excludes qualitative aspects of those events from observation and reflection; that such aspects of knowing may be vital to their understanding.

To some extent this difference reflects Aboriginal unfamiliarity with numbers and mathematical processes. Recent developments in Aboriginal education have drawn attention to the similarity between the recursive character of the names and structures employed by Aborigines in their accounts of relationships between the members of their own successive generations, and the structurally similar pattern of names and relationships within the western numbering system. This recognition of similarity has certainly made the transition to numeracy easier for some Aboriginal children, but doubts about the validity of the simplification of experience necessary to render it capable of manipulation by mathematical processes may present more fundamental difficulties and in some contexts, legitimate scepticism.

Emphasis on quantification tends to remove from fields of interest to western scientists certain natural processes and events which cannot readily be quantified. The recent development of 'chaos' theory has drawn attention to aspects of nature which cannot usefully be conceptually organised in mathematical form. Even more recently, scientists have become aware of patterns in chaos which can be recognised and explored in terms of metaphors, but perhaps only of non-mathematical kinds. The existence of the 'El Nino' effect in weather formation is perhaps an example of such patterns in 'chaotic' events.

Aborigines recognise these patterns and welcome metaphors to describe them which seem useful. A good example is the linking of natural events, apparently unrelated causally, which seem to be grouped in time: 'March flies are telling you that crocodile eggs are ready'. 'When the brolga sings the dark catfish starts to move' (Rose 1992). Such linkages are seen by western scientists as a form of the *post-hoc ergo propter hoc* fallacy and therefore to be rejected. It was, however, much relied upon by their pre-Baconian predecessors and is still of great interest to Jungian psychologists, contemporary weather forecasters and obsessive gamblers. To Aborigines, such patterns are valuable sources of knowledge, or at least of interesting and valuable hypotheses for action: the test is whether they yield crocodile eggs and catfish.

Both bodies of knowledge are essentially hypothetical and what is accepted as knowledge is the result of negotiation between respected practitioners. Aborigines tend to emphasise the need to negotiate the content of knowledge in particular environmental and social contexts and see negotiation as a continuing process, never finally finished, but to be activated as required. Hypotheses cannot be proven, but in both societies they are tested by much the same kinds of criteria: for internal consistency, for apparent power to explain the processes involved, for apparent capacity to predict, and in both societies for aesthetic qualities (in western science for simplicity and elegance, and in Aboriginal knowledge for the aptness and memorability of the metaphors employed).

Both bodies of knowledge are conservative and change is generally marginally achieved by slow accretions or interpretative modification. Aborigines, I feel, are generally better at recognising change as an integral part of natural processes and of being able to see it as the working out of a longer-term pattern or as evidence that 'patterns in chaos', while perhaps never wholly knowable, can be recognised and used as a valuable basis for action. It is within this world view and system of knowledge that individuals are socialised and become Aboriginal.

SOCIALISATION FOR THE ABORIGINAL 'WAY'

Genetic adaptation over many generations is generally modified by cultural practices, especially by the socialisation of the young and by the division of responsibility for aspects of that socialisation between the sexes and within kinship groups, where some interesting differences emerge. Thus, young Aboriginal boys traditionally were and still are encouraged to assert their personal autonomy and initiative; to roam freely in small anarchistic 'gangs' acquiring mundane knowledge and skills by observation and imitation, with little formal discipline or instruction. Girls, on the other hand, were from the beginning incorporated into female groups for child-care and for food gathering, and were generally supervised by their natural or classificatory mothers and older female siblings. Their socialisation for the roles they were to perform as adults began early and progressed naturally, with its emphasis on nurturing. Traditionally, women also had an independent ceremonial life and, separately from men, had rights and responsibilities in relation to land. It seemed, however, that it was only after the period of child-care and socialisation was complete that older women appear to have acquired significant authority in the other, more general affairs of the group. But there is evidence of change in recent decades.

The socialisation of boys proceeded on a significantly different pattern. The wild, anarchistic freedom was suddenly ended and the boy subjected to an intense period of organised discipline and instruction conducted by the adult male members of his immediate and related kin group. Bringing together young candidates from various groups lent extra authority to this important rite of passage and helped widen the scope of the mutual support system it was designed to establish. It was in such initiation ceremonies that the anarchistic autonomy of young boys began to be constrained. This constraint was directed to establishing in them the responsibilities attendant upon gaining religious knowledge and an obligation to nurture and to share with others with whom they were connected.

In essence, the initiation ceremony is a test by ordeal in which the initiate is expected, with support from appropriate members of his kin, to demonstrate courage and fortitude as proof of his suitability for membership of the cult of men. This involves accepting painful physical changes and markings to his body which seem, perhaps, to simulate aspects of women's role in giving birth and nurturing as symbolic evidence that the initiate, along with his fellows, has the capacities and accepts the responsibilities for the continuance of and care for succeeding generations.

In addition, initiation is his introduction to a lifelong process of acquiring knowledge through the performance of ceremony: knowledge of the Dreaming, of the creative activities of the spirit ancestors, of the lands and pathways along which they travelled and of the evidences of their presence left as they have gone down into the earth or up into the sky. This religious knowledge is recorded in the songs, stories, dances and rituals which they will acquire progressively by performance and will help pass on to their juniors. Similarly, young women were introduced by their female kin into the knowledge and ritual of women's religious life; though via different processes and ceremonies to those of men (Bell 1983; White et al. 1985). This process of ceremonial socialisation is conceptually unending; the most senior is a learner as well as the bearer of wisdom. The ritual is both a celebration and a mnemonic; the means to achieve continuity and group identity over time.

It is in his performance in these and succeeding ceremonies that an initiate's capacity to subordinate his personal autonomy to the needs of others and to the continuity of their society will be made evident, and his progress to seniority in the Law achieved. Although this process is referred to as the Law, it does not dominate simply by compulsion or prohibition; qualities which our society regards as the essence of the rule of law. There seems to be no decalogue of commandments or instructions; the stories told are in the nature of parable or cautionary tales, encouraging behaviour in which caring for others is presented favourably. No one is given general authority to tell others what they must do. Personal autonomy is unimpaired, although those who exercise it in order to 'look after' and care for others are held in high respect.

All human societies, if they are to survive, must to some degree subordinate the individual right to unfettered autonomy. In most societies this is achieved by establishing a hierarchy of authority within which coercion in some form is exercised and often enforced by violence or its threat. What is unusual about Aboriginal traditional society is that it appears to have chosen to achieve that subordination primarily by a comprehensive socialisation, so that the subordination is internalised, supported by social group pressure and comes to be acted upon apparently voluntarily by the individuals themselves. In this progressive manner, personal autonomy is conjoined with wider social and tribal obligations.

Throughout this process of acquiring knowledge it seems common for a man to experience internal conflict between his need for personal autonomy and the demands implied in the expectation that he will care for others. To resolve this conflict men, from time to time, exercise what Hamilton (1981) has described as the deepest and most significant freedom in Aboriginal society: to resolve the potential conflict by simply moving away.

MOBILITY

Mobility seems necessary to satisfy Aboriginal psychic needs. Knowledge of the seasonal location of water and of bush tucker made mobility a condition of survival for hunter-gatherers. Its value was amplified as relationships established in initiation ceremonies widened the territory in which mutual rights exist, for food, ceremony and for marriage partners. All Aboriginal societies require that such partners should be outside close kin and some, like the Pintubi, stress that they should be 'from far away'. There are obvious economic values in this widening of territorial rights, but sometimes it creates problems in reconciling benefits and responsibilities which have become competitive. In such circumstances, the exercise of this 'most significant freedom' may become a convenient tactic.

In the lives of some of the most significant Aboriginal men I have known, there have been periods when they have 'walked out' and undertaken long and difficult journeys, adopted new activities in different societies or territories, returning after many years to pick up the threads again among their kin. I think of Phillip Roberts who as a youth left the Roper River, joined Bill Stanner's paramilitary irregulars during the Second World War, remained to work as a liaison between the medical staff of the Northern Territory Department of Health and Aborigines in the campaign to bring leprosy under control, and continued in a similar capacity with the Council for Aboriginal Affairs when it was set up by Harold Holt after the referendum in 1967. I remember being worried when the Council was being wound up to be replaced by the Department of Aboriginal Affairs, lest Phillip's remarkable capacities might be lost and I was seeking alternative employment for him. He refused. 'It is time', he said, 'for me to go back'. When I asked what he would do, he replied, 'sit on the bank of the river and think'. In fact, when he returned he found the clans of the Roper River in familial disputes for dominance and saw no role for himself there. He moved to Kakadu Park where he married and continued to be consulted by governments and community leaders. I met him again shortly before his sudden death, in a happy exercise of reminiscence about our work together, planning a reunion with Barrie Dexter, Jeremy Long and others when next he would be in Canberra; a reunion which, alas, never was held. I think of the journey he made to the Macassan and other islands in search of evidence that Aboriginal women and their children, returning with Macassan men after the latter's visits to Arnhem Land, had taken with them ceremonies, songs and stories which he assured me were now incorporated into the island life.

There are many Aborigines of whom such unexpected odysseys can be told: people such as Johnny Watson and his fellow stockmen of the Kimberley, who drove cattle throughout the north and centre, but to whom the Stockmen's Hall of Fame seems forever closed; Yami Lester, the blind seer of the Pitjantjatjara lands, who spent his years of exile in Adelaide as an interpreter for white courts of justice, but returned to his families and became an honoured leader; Dick Roughsey, blue water seaman, artist, teller of tales and rediscoverer of the rich heritage of Aboriginal rock art in the tablelands of Cape York; and Mudrooroo, the author of *Wild Cat Falling* (1965), who found his way to an Indian ashram to absorb the wisdom of the Buddha and returned to incorporate elements of it into that of his own people.

The opportunities for such constructive escapes were, for Aboriginal women, obviously more limited. The demands on them for nurture and child-care were more immediate and insistent, but they existed occasionally for women whose childbearing was complete or those who had been exiled into white contexts. In my limited experience I think of Oodgeroo Noonuccal, poet and fighter in the Aboriginal cause; of Vai Stanton, elder and leader of the anti-grog campaign among the 'paper-bark' people; of Nganyintja, the founder of Pitjantjatjara homelands and of Aboriginal education for their homeland children; and of Marcia Langton, academic and *la pasionaria* of the Aboriginal revolution. These and other women have made similar journeys, some geographically more limited, but all as courageous and as politically significant as those of men. More generally, older Aboriginal women throughout white occupation have been 'keepers' of women's Law, teachers of the young and a focus for Aboriginal resistance against the forces of social disintegration.

DECISION MAKING AND LEADERSHIP

Sometimes the reliance upon internalising the commitment to care for others appears to render Aboriginal society ineffective in the conduct of its collective affairs and in the decision-making processes necessarily involved in them. Outside the established ceremonial arena there is often no generally recognised focus of leadership. Within small family-based groups the authority of the 'elders' was commonly respected, but in larger groups the power of the gerontocracy amounted to little more than a right to be consulted and listened to with respect. Decision, so far as it was achieved, was by the progressive evolution of consensus. Even so, what may appear to be a consensus was often simply *nem con* (nobody objecting), with the absence of objection often indicating indifference rather than concurrence. Decision was sometimes left to those personally seeking leadership status, but general indifference was often quickly transformed into hostility at the first sign that the person's motivation was that of status or power.

Sometimes, failure to achieve consensus provides the incentive and the opportunity for a group to divide. Myers' (1986) account of the progressive break-up of the enthusiastic group of Pintubi who left Papunya (in the early 1970s) to establish a new community of their own at Yayayi, into smaller and smaller 'settlements' moving progressively westward towards the traditional lands of their ancestors, is instructive. Quite small communities frequently are organised into a series of largely separate camps, coming together for special purposes. The same motivation underlies the dramatic multiplication of homeland or outstation centres since the movement first became clearly apparent in the late sixties and early seventies. It also contributes to the unwillingness, or inability, of Aboriginal groups to satisfy the white bureaucracy's demand for evidence of their firm intention to settle and stay as a condition of receiving infrastructure and support services for those homelands.

16

In some circumstances, Aborigines seem able to accept decisions originating from external sources more readily than they can those proposed from within their own society; for example, where authority for the decision must be accepted 'as a fact of life', where the person making it has an external competence or expertise recognised and valued by the group or has standing with that group derived from a practice or reputation for looking after them, and where the decision does not impair personal autonomy or intrude into matters clearly within the Aboriginal domain. Thus, there is no doubt that despite its exploitative character, the relationship between some individual white pastoralists and Aboriginal groups resident on the land concerned was often more respectful of Aboriginal priorities and values than many of the better-paid alternatives which have succeeded it. That relationship introduced Aborigines to cattle work and an associated pattern of activities which made use of their traditional knowledge and skills, in which they showed natural aptitude, which involved them in the exciting new horse-based source of mobility, and which offered status based upon performance. At the same time, it allowed them to maintain their contact with the land and the creatures with which they identified and, especially in the long annual 'stand down' period, left ample opportunity for ceremony, instruction of the young, visits to sacred sites and to distant kin; that is, for opportunities to fulfil the multiple obligations involved in being Aboriginal.

Humane and intelligent pastoralists like the Parkinson family of Willowra did not seek to restrict those opportunities, but recognised their importance to group cohesion and therefore to the continuity of their workforce. They demonstrated their entitlement to respect by their competence in the cattle work itself, including aspects of it beyond Aboriginal experience, but of which they became aware. Above all, they and their families in the homestead provided food for resident Aboriginal families, cared for the sick and the injured, and helped when Aborigines sought a school for their children and various other services. Clearly, in Aboriginal terms, they were entitled to respect as competent men and women who 'looked after' others. In general, the relationship between Aboriginal workers and such station owners was a kind of symbiosis and its destruction was as much due to the appearance of a technology based upon fenced paddocks, bore watering-points, motorised post-war transport, together with the capital and impersonality of the absentee corporate management, as it was to the demands of Aborigines for equal pay and the intervention of the Arbitration Court in 1966 to make equal pay effective from December 1968.

A somewhat similar relationship seems to be emerging between Aboriginal-controlled organisations like land councils, resource agencies and their white employees. These employees have knowledge and skills which their Aboriginal employers value and respect, and are content to accept their role as employees. These qualities justify to Aborigines acceptance of their decisions as those of persons who 'care for' others. The contemporary role which appears to puzzle Aborigines most is that of the career-driven official; the bureaucrat who is the instrument of a distant and often incomprehensible authority. 'Why do they come here?' I have been asked. 'They do not like us, they are unhappy here and cannot wait to be allowed to leave!' or, 'What do they do here? We only see them when suddenly they want a meeting for us to agree to what they will do anyway; for the rest, they sit in their air-conditioned offices. They say they are here to help us. We feel they are here to stop us!'

The strengths and weaknesses of Aboriginal reliance both on socially internalised autonomy and on responsibility to care for others are demonstrated in their attempts to deal with the destructive impact of alcohol abuse. In predominantly Aboriginal communities such as homelands, antagonism to grog is almost universal, strongly felt and expressed. Where it is within their power, most such communities ban the entry of grog into their territory. This does not prevent abuse. Those who wish to drink are told they must do so elsewhere. Personal autonomy is preserved but those who offend, while usually forgiven, may be summoned before a community meeting and 'shamed', especially those who do so on Aboriginal land. Advocacy for official government action usually concentrates on opposition to any increase in liquor licences and the need for more stringent control of the practices of suppliers.

It is difficult to assess the outcome, but it seems clear that social control is most effective in small communities and where Aboriginal Law and ceremonial life is strong. Indeed, in places where that practice has declined, especially among the young, participation in group drinking sessions sometimes seems to develop as an alternative cult where achievement of manhood status is marked by acceptance into a drinking group, rather than into that of the ranks of initiated men. On the whole, Aboriginal concern and action in this matter compares favourably with that in white society, especially where Aboriginal political activity is strong, but remains a major handicap in their re-establishment of an autonomous Aboriginal society. It is, nevertheless, an area in which Aboriginal action and mutual support have made impressive ground.

COMPETING AND CONFLICTING SOCIALISATION

Little has been said in this introductory chapter about the impact of government policies upon the way in which Aboriginal society operates and especially upon its vital capacity for autonomy and the provision of nurture. During the period of open warfare between white settlers and resident Aborigines for control of the land and its resources, the attitude of government authorities in the various colonies was either that it was a matter they had neither the desire nor the capacity to control, or was one in which their purpose was to validate the settlers' hegemony once it had been established. As disease, murder and starvation by isolation from natural resources eliminated the great majority of the population, token protection of the declining number of survivors became the official rationale. Not until the 1930s did it become apparent that missionary activities and publicity had brought an end to indiscriminate killing and that Aborigines were not going to 'die out'.

Despite some developments in the Northern Territory stimulated by the influence of A P Elkin, professor of anthropology at Sydney University, on J McEwen, then Minister for the Territories, it was not until after the referendum in 1967 and the entry of the Commonwealth into Aboriginal affairs more generally, that there was any serious thought given to how an Aboriginal minority might be accommodated. I remember Prime Minister Curtin establishing in 1941, a Commonwealth–State Ministerial Council to be presided over by himself to consider the development of northern Australia, and also establishing a committee of officials to work on that council which had included among its terms of reference 'the welfare of the native peoples'. As chairman of that committee I arranged a discussion amongst officers responsible for Aborigines in the various States and the Northern Territory about how this aspect of the terms of reference was to be handled. I was reminded promptly that the Commonwealth had no constitutional status in that matter except in relation to the Territories and that in the Northern Territory it was the exclusive concern of the Department and the Minister of the Interior. As a result, the powerful influence exercised by post-war reconstruction activities in relation to health, education, training and development on the native peoples of Papua New Guinea (PNG) was not matched for Aborigines in Australia. A collaboration was quickly established between post-war reconstruction and the PNG civil administration, especially in the use of the Commonwealth Reconstruction Training Scheme, to speed the movement towards independence and development. The official attitude in Australia was to deny Aboriginal participation in the war, or any impact of it on them sufficient to justify any form of compensation or benefit.

In 1965, a meeting of Commonwealth and State Ministers with responsibility for Aboriginal matters reached tentative agreement that the objective of policy should be assimilation; that is:

> that all persons of Aboriginal descent will choose to attain a similar manner and standard of living to that of other Australians and live as members of a single Australian community – enjoying the same rights and privileges, accepting the same responsibilities and influenced by the same hopes and loyalties as other Australians.

No conclusions were reached about what should be done to ensure that

> ... all persons of Aboriginal descent will choose ... to live as members of a single Australian community or to determine whether, and at what

rate and on what conditions they will accept the same responsibilities
... as other Australians.

Since that time there has been a variety of formulations of the assimilation objective, some of which recognised that Aborigines may have views about these matters, but all embodying words ranging from assimilation pure and simple, through to integration, self-management and self-determination. The latter were concerned to delineate the degree to which differences arising from autonomous Aboriginal cultural, religious, economic and political values could be tolerated. However, an objective assessment of the measures actually introduced or proposed reveals a continuing incorporation of Aborigines into those existing institutions – educational, economic, legal, administrative and political – which are concerned to socialise white members of Australian society to conform to the purposes and procedures of its institutions. In other words, they all assume that Aborigines will in due course speak the same language, be educated in the same schools, find a livelihood by employment in white-owned or administered enterprises and institutions, play the same games and have the same heroes as white Australians. All were based on an end to Aboriginal autonomy. Differences in language, religion, values and culture were in theory to be tolerated and in some instances encouraged, but only insofar as they were decorative and did not encroach upon the time, the energy or the dedication demanded by the mainstream and particularly, by its economic system.

What has been written above suggests that such priority for mainstream activities and values may well be incompatible with the Aboriginal processes of growing up the young and of their acquiring knowledge through ceremony. The socialisation required to equip Aboriginal young people for these Aboriginal purposes would almost certainly conflict with that envisaged by white society to fit them into its own institutions. In 1990, in a memo on Aboriginal education for the Royal Commission on Aboriginal Deaths in Custody, I wrote of this fundamental conflict:

> Every aspect of the life of an Aboriginal child confronts him or her
> with this conflict of values – between the assimilationist objectives of

white Australian policies and the deeply ingrained attitudes and patterns of behaviour of Aborigines. In my view this conflict is so fundamental and is internalised so deeply in the minds of Aborigines that it induces in many a state of mental confusion and emotional stress amounting often to psychiatric disorder: a disorder that lies at the heart of many of the issues which underlie the more immediate causes of incarceration and deaths in custody. (Coombs 1990a)

Nowhere in white Australian policies is consideration given to the possible need of Aborigines to reconcile the demands of their own Aboriginal way with those of living in the mainstream. Until we and Aborigines turn our minds effectively to ways of meeting that need, the issues underlying deaths in custody will persist. It is in these deaths that we see most clearly the impact on Aboriginal people of the loss of personal and cultural autonomy and of the conflicting socialisations they face as a result of white colonisation.

Aborigines and the Land

2

The future of the homeland
movement

Originally published as 'Centre for Resource and Environmental Studies Working Paper No. 15', CRES, Australian National University, Canberra, 1979.

The outstation, or homeland movement as I prefer to call it, is, I believe, an Aboriginal response to the problems of contact and an attempt to evolve a lifestyle which preserves the essence of the Aboriginal way along with access to chosen elements from white society. In this description of the early outcomes of the homeland movement I have drawn upon the experience of many communities, extrapolating developments in their early stages where these appear capable of being sustained and likely to contribute to a lifestyle consistent with Aboriginal needs and desires. Inevitably, it is a picture based upon wish fulfilment, upon the expectation of increasingly effective adaptation by Aborigines and upon a political context in Australian society which ensures reasonable support for, and sympathy with, this Aboriginal initiative.

THE GEOGRAPHICAL PATTERN

Already it is possible to discern a geographical pattern in the distribution of the Aboriginal population within regions in which the homeland movement is permitted to operate. This pattern is based upon a series of focal settlements with populations of up to 1,000, linked with a set of decentralised homeland communities at varying

24

distances of up to one hundred miles. Many of these homelands, in turn, have a surrounding periphery of their own smaller satellite locations. Homeland settlements, occupied by rarely more than forty or fifty families, are invariably located in territory with which the group identifies and with surrounding locations which would be places of importance to them, visited from time to time as sites of spiritual significance, as sources of food and materials, or simply as good places for relaxation.

The inhabitants of these groups of homeland communities would be predominantly persons who shared ties of language and religious tradition, together with their spouses. They would also predominantly be those who shared clan or other common descent affiliations. The homelands would be linked by road, air and radio with their focal settlement which would act as a source of supplies and services, and as a centre of common political and administrative action. To a degree, it will be possible to see the central settlements and their satellite homeland communities as a loosely associated federation sharing some elements of common economic, social and political structure.

One can envisage the progressive reoccupation of their traditional lands by Aborigines in such groups of communities as populations grow and resources become available to them. In this process, some of the satellite locations around existing homeland communities would themselves develop into homelands, while some homelands would become larger focal settlements. Physically, homeland settlements will, for some time, be somewhat more sophisticated versions of traditional bush camps. Buildings will be increasingly evident, but for environmental, health and social reasons these will continue to be capable of being moved or abandoned without serious cost.

HOMELAND ECONOMIES

Homeland settlements may, for some time, continue to be largely autonomous and self-sufficient economic units. Production, including hunting and gathering, will be directed to home consumption and the reduction of dependence on imported stores. Exports, except where the community concerned is linked with an Aboriginal-owned cattle property, will generally be confined to art and crafts and occasional surpluses. Imports will be diverse and include white-style food and clothing, fuel, tools and building materials. They will be financed by sales of artefacts and art, by the earnings of those employed in providing government-sponsored services in education, health, town management and so on, by government grants for capital projects and by receipts from social security payments. Homeland economies will be limited by the magnitude of these financial resources. Any reduction in the quantity, variety and cost of these imports seems likely to come mainly from new and improved technology in subsistence production: from the introduction of gardening, domestic poultry and livestock production; from the introduction of exotic species, and irrigation and other techniques from overseas; and from improvement by breeding and selection of the yield of native flora and fauna. An examination of the goods sold in community stores suggests other products which may be capable of domestic production, perhaps with some specialisation between homeland settlements forming part of the same geographic and social network. The local production of such goods is likely to come slowly.

It is unlikely, for some time, that activities directed at the external markets (other than artefacts, art, cattle and perhaps tourism) would prove successful. Their processes conflict with much in Aboriginal tradition and ways of thought, and require a learning jump likely to be too great for tradition-oriented communities. An interesting possibility is suggested by the negotiations for the administration of national parks and wildlife sanctuaries like those at Kakadu and Tanami. As Aboriginal title to land is acknowledged over wider areas, it is possible to conceive of a chain of such parks and sanctuaries in regions of scenic and cultural significance, from which Aborigines could derive not merely opportunities for employment and contract work related to the parks, but income in the nature of rent and royalties for access to them.

POLITICAL ORGANISATION AND ASPIRATIONS

One of the most important effects of the decentralisation movement is the rehabilitation of Aboriginal traditional authority and decision-making structures. With this is coming a political component in

Aboriginal plans; namely, the desire to resume control of those aspects of their affairs where European dominance has most severely weakened the Aboriginality of their lives. The functions most affected are likely to be education, health services and law and order. While contact with whites has brought concepts, patterns of behaviour and agents of authority derived from sources alien to and substantially incompatible with traditional ways, at the same time Aborigines have come to realise that if they are to deal effectively with white society they must devise workable means of performing these functions and incorporate them into their own culture. Thus, in the homelands some distinctive developments in education are occurring. School time has been restricted and the curriculum limited so that while still providing basic skills of literacy and numeracy, scope is left for traditional instruction and to minimise assimilationist influences. There is also occurring a shift of emphasis from concentration on the child to greater involvement of family groups and adults, and an increasing emphasis on training within the region by apprenticeship-style instruction in skills required and chosen by the community. In this context the white teacher becomes an educational adviser to the community, a mobiliser of resources and a support for Aboriginal teachers and aides from the community.

The community emphasis is apparent also in developments in health with white professional and para-professional health personnel becoming a resource to be drawn upon from a distance, or during periodic visits for services controlled by the community and delivered by its members. There is also a growing interest in asserting the right and capacity of homeland communities to administer law and order, with white enforcement and judicial agencies being brought in only in the event of 'big trouble', or when the community feels the need for external support. This interest is likely to express itself in the application of traditional dispute resolution procedures, modified and perhaps formalised in community 'courts' that are set up as required to deal with specific situations, offences or disputes.

In all of this, the source of political authority is the group or community itself. The Commonwealth *Aboriginal Councils and Associations Act 1976*, with its emphasis on the community council as the main incorporated body, seems to have been misdirected. A council is, or should be, merely the executive agency of the community with which ultimate authority should lie. The difficulty of registering fluctuating membership has been exaggerated. There seems no valid reason why a person could not be a member of several communities, at least at different times. Provided questions of eligibility were for the community to decide, problems do not seem likely to be acute. In many smaller communities, the problem of statutory authority being with a council has been evaded by the council functioning, in effect, like a 'town meeting' with all residents free to participate and with special weight being given, especially in matters bearing on traditional law and custom, to the views of the elders. In other words, by ostensibly accepting a white institutional structure, but making it work in an Aboriginal style.

In brief, the homeland movement has strengthened the degree to which Aboriginal Australians are seeking pluralism in Australian society, giving self-management a more political connotation than was probably anticipated among white Australians, even those who sympathised with its objectives. With this trend has come increasing opposition to the demand for strict financial and administrative accountability which has marked the administration of Aboriginal affairs under the Fraser Federal Government. Self-management is an empty concept if it does not carry with it authority to allocate resources, including those provided by the community, in accordance with Aboriginal priorities. Requests for block grants rather than allocations for specific projects and services, as well as the preference for Community Development Employment Projects (CDEP) grants to the community rather than payment of unemployment benefits to individuals, are evidence of this desire to shift effective decision making into Aboriginal hands. Especially for homeland communities, this desire and the capacity to give effect to it is likely to grow.

RENEWED RELIGIOUS VITALITY

There are widespread reports of increasing activity in Aboriginal ceremonial life which probably reflects the stimulus which the homeland movement has given to these activities. Residence at decentralised homelands affords readier and more frequent contact with sacred sites and the Dreaming tracks of ancestral beings. In addition, access to motor vehicles and money for petrol has greatly extended the range of group interaction, so that men and women from ever more distant communities are called to participate in initiation and other ceremonies.

A very interesting aspect of these reports is that they refer to instances where more isolated communities have been involved in 'bringing back the law' to those among whom it has become weak and corrupted. In the Kimberley and the Pilbara regions, elders from the desert are reported to be visiting communities closer to the coast and reviving ancient rituals. Similar processes are occurring in parts of northern and central Australia.

It will be interesting to see how far the effect of this renaissance can offset the influence of white society on the young. It would be idle to believe that the combined effects of European education and the attractions of our consumer goods, films, advertising and the whole content of our materialist society could leave the young untouched. Nor do I think even the most traditional or chauvinistic of Aborigines expect or hope it. If I understand them, they believe that given the security of the homeland context and the confirmation of the Aboriginal way which it may make possible, the young will grow up capable of making use of what white society offers, but remaining essentially uncorrupted by it, being able to take over the most useful items of its technology, to turn to it for occasional excitement and stimulus, but remaining able and happy to return to their own way. In other words, to behave rather like the affluent young Englishmen who used to go off to the Continent to sow their wild oats before settling down in their own society. This may be an optimistic expectation and may underrate the meretricious charms of the 'beer and Coca-Cola' civilisation, but it represents perhaps the only strategy which stands a chance of preserving continuity for Aboriginal society.

CONCLUSION

Looked at objectively, the homeland movement can be seen as an attempt by Aborigines to moderate the rate of cultural change caused by contact with European ways and commodities, and to re-establish a physical, social and spiritual environment in which traditional elements will be once more dominant and the influence of the alien culture made more marginal. In such a context, the learning situation would be realistically more manageable. It would make it possible for the community as a whole to progress from the known to the unknown, to find in their own traditions components with which the new influences can be linked, or in terms of which they could be interpreted. Only if this can be done will social change be achieved without serious disruption, without the polarisation of generations and without denying the young the security and support which membership of a familiar and comprehended group can give.

It is unlikely that this strategy will be universally successful. In any event, the young of the homelands will respond in a variety of ways. Some will break their links with their communities wholly and permanently; others will choose to remain entirely within them; the majority perhaps will lie between these extremes. Almost all will visit major settlements as well as towns and cities. Many will, at times and perhaps for years, seek employment and residence within them or on their outskirts, but keeping in touch by visits and with the intention of returning home more permanently in due course. The balance is impossible to predict, but an interesting pointer is the frequency with which the ablest are choosing to remain, finding in the opportunities offered by self-management and political action through local and regional Aboriginal organisations a more effective stimulus and challenge than they can find in white society. The emergence of men like Ivan Baker, Donald Fraser, Yami Lester, Albert Lennon, Galarrwuy Yunupingu, Wesley Lanhupuy, Gatjil and Walyambula, is significant, not merely directly, but because they provide models of achievable aspiration within their own society which the young can hope to emulate.

Much will, of course, depend upon the attitude of white society to developments in the homelands. It was the Commonwealth referendum in 1967 which opened the way to political action by Aborigines and their friends in white society, and from which the Woodward proposals (1973, 1974) for the settlement of the land rights issue emerged with an apparent consensus for support among political parties in the Federal Parliament. Since then, there has been a retreat and an erosion of the substance of Woodward's proposals and white Australian sentiment is now sharply polarised. A majority, narrow perhaps, continues to favour Aboriginal rights to land and more generous and humane policies, but in those areas of Australia where Aboriginal land claims could prove substantial and where the Aboriginal population is large enough to present a threat to white supremacy, a clear backlash is apparent. Fear of encroachment on white property rights and other privileges has produced attitudes which have much in common with those of white South Africans and Rhodesians.

These attitudes accord well with the interests of mining companies impatient with the need to negotiate with Aborigines. Those who hold these views look back with nostalgia to the authoritarian, paternalistic institutions of mission and government settlements and cling to the assimilationist doctrines of the past that are still dominant in the administration of education, health and law and order. They view the homeland movement as an outcome of the rejection of those doctrines. In Queensland and in Western Australia, at least where mining prospects exist, State Government policies are positively hostile to the modest autonomy the movement seeks. In the Northern Territory, the move to extend the boundaries of cities and towns to extravagant limits so as to frustrate Aboriginal claims to land shows the way they would go if they were free to discard the Commonwealth's land rights legislation of 1976. However, given that the conscience of white Australian society and the pressure of international opinion ensures that the homeland movement is allowed an opportunity to survive and develop, it has the seeds of success within it. Its material aspirations are modest and it accords with and expresses much that is fundamental to the Aboriginal way. Aboriginal faith in it is alive, the ideas on which its future depends are developing and the men and women to express and apply them are emerging.

3

Warlpiri land use and management

Originally presented as a submission to the Aboriginal Land Commissioner, Mr Justice Toohey, for the Warlpiri and Kartangaruru-Kurintji land claim in 1978. Subsequently published as 'Centre for Resource and Environmental Studies Working Paper No. 8', CRES, Australian National University, Canberra, 1978.

BACKGROUND

From my association since 1967 with Aboriginal Australians I have become aware, firstly, of the strength of the association between them and the land with which their clan or family group is identified and secondly, how important it is to them that their title to those lands be acknowledged in Australian law. More recently, as a result of my interest in environmental matters my attention has been drawn to fears held by some conservationists that Aborigines, armed and equipped as they now can be with contemporary weapons of destruction and transporting themselves in motor vehicles, would damage as ruthlessly as white men the environment and the wildlife of land over which they might gain title. These fears have led some conservationists to oppose the acknowledgment of Aboriginal title to lands which have been, or are proposed to be, reserved as national parks or wildlife sanctuaries. Some of them have spoken against the current land claim by Warlpiri and Kartangaruru-Kurintji peoples currently before this land claim tribunal on these grounds. When in 1977, I was elected to the position of President of the Australian Conservation Foundation, I urged the Foundation to establish communication with Aboriginal people in the hope that better mutual understanding would lead to a common approach to the protection of the flora and fauna and the whole physical and spiritual environment of the lands concerned. That communication was established with results which I will outline later.

I would like, before doing so, to refer to some considerations which encouraged me to believe that a common approach was possible and that as part of it, conservationists could support acknowledgment of Aboriginal title as providing circumstances in which their own purposes would be most likely to be achieved.

ABORIGINAL HUNTING TECHNIQUES

Anxiety about Aboriginal land ownership and practice derives predominantly from three main fears:
- that more efficient hunting techniques will endanger or eliminate native species;
- that Aboriginal burning practices will destroy both flora and fauna leading to an extension of desert areas; and
- that Aboriginal plans for the use of lands to which they have sought title are based upon activities copied from white Australians, such as cattle-raising, and would have similar environmental consequences.

I believe the first fear is greatly exaggerated. The late Professor J Marshall, editor and part-author of *The Great Extermination* (1966), a classic and seminal review of the impact of white civilisation on Australian wildlife, believed there was little evidence that any species had been eliminated by being hunted for food or for any other direct use by Aboriginal hunters. When species have been hunted to be sold it was, of course, a different matter and the actual and threatened extinction of many Australian species could be attributed to their commercial exploitation. However with rare exception, Aborigines do not hunt for commercial profit, nor for purposeless destruction. Anyone who has lived among them even for short periods will be aware of the restraints they impose once their immediate needs have been met. Some will argue that while this may have been and still be true of older traditional Aborigines, younger people have become so corrupted by contact with white society and its values that the same cannot be expected of them. There is an element of truth in this, although I believe it is frequently exaggerated. Two points must be made in this regard. Firstly, even when they occur, excesses of the young will represent a marginal increase in the harvesting of the natural resource and, except for already endangered species, are unlikely to be a serious threat. Secondly, recognition of Aboriginal ownership of the land is likely to encourage the re-establishment of small, family-based settlements in which traditional values and practices and the social disciplines associated with them are likely to be strengthened. There is evidence that in the region north-west of Alice Springs covered by this claim, as in the Kakadu National Park in the north, Aboriginal plans for the use of land which includes the Tanami Desert Wildlife Sanctuary will involve its resettlement by such groups.

Considerable attention has recently been given to the work and writings of Professor Messel of the University of Sydney in relation to crocodiles which he believed to be close to extinction in northern coastal waters because of more efficient Aboriginal hunting practices. It is true that widespread commercial exploitation of crocodiles predominantly by white hunters, but in which some Aborigines participated, had seriously depleted their numbers. The termination or severe limitation of this traffic was, in my view, fully justified. But the fears of early extinction were, I believe, exaggerated. At the time when Professor Messel's newspaper articles were attracting public attention I travelled by boat from near Maningrida down the Blythe River to Kopanga, an Aboriginal homeland community near the mouth of that river. On the return journey I counted seventeen crocodiles sunning themselves on mud banks. This observation was not compatible with a belief in imminent extinction. Furthermore, I believe there is now reason to believe that with the control of the traffic in crocodile skins, the population will quickly recover.

In fact, more important than Aboriginal hunting has been the destruction of the environment of many native species by white land use. This has seriously affected, and in many instances eliminated, unique species of both flora and fauna. This destruction has been brought about primarily by the effect of introduced species; particularly cattle, horses, camels, donkeys, rabbits and cats. All of these now exist in substantial numbers in the feral state, acting both as predators on and competitors with native species of flora and fauna. It must be emphasised that Aboriginal hunting is an important control for some of these exotic species, limiting the populations (particularly of rabbits and cats) in areas occupied and used by Aboriginal people. It would be easy, by legislative and administrative measures, to extend this control at relatively low cost to the other introduced, feral species.

Such control, while valuable, is unlikely to be sufficient to prevent the progressive elimination of native species already seriously endangered. On this matter I have three comments to offer:

- Records I have seen of discussions between Warlpiri Aborigines and representatives of the Northern Territory Conservation Commission, between traditional owners of the Kakadu National Park and the Australian National Parks and Wildlife Service, and between CSIRO scientists and Aborigines represented by the Central Land Council, demonstrate that these Aborigines have a deep concern for the survival of these species. They have an extensive knowledge of their habitats, numbers and threats to them, and a willingness to be associated with programs to protect them.
- Involvement of Aborigines in the design and implementation of programs for the protection of these species and their habitats represents the best and cheapest prospect of ensuring their survival.
- Programs which do not have the full endorsement and participation of the traditional owners and managers of the lands in which such conservation programs are to be carried out, have little prospect of being effective.

ABORIGINAL FIRE PRACTICE

Consideration of fears about Aboriginal use of fire leads, I believe, to similar conclusions. It is now widely acknowledged among ecologists that fire is an integral component in Australian ecosystems and that its wise use is critical to national land management and to the protection of the environment. I believe it is also increasingly being acknowledged that traditional Aboriginal burning practices are based upon a profound understanding of the relationship between fire and the environment and are superior to those widely followed by white Australians. Thus, I understand that plans being discussed between the Australian National Parks and Wildlife Service and the traditional owners of Kakadu Park are based not merely on the adoption of traditional fire practices, but the direct involvement of the traditional owners in their design and administration. There is reason to believe that such plans are likely to be more effective and cheaper to carry out than others for which non-Aboriginal manpower would be required. It is also certain that plans to unilaterally impose alien fire practices on resident Aborigines would prove ineffective.

WARLPIRI PLANS FOR LAND USE

Discussions with traditional owners of land covered by the present Warlpiri claim suggest that they plan, when their title is acknowledged, to resettle clan territories with small homeland-style communities. While the lifestyle contemplated involves some non-traditional uses of land, such as the conduct of cattle-raising in appropriate areas, the development of vegetable and fruit gardening, as well as some employment in nearby white enterprises and in the provision of community services, the emphasis is primarily towards community self-sufficiency rather than involvement in large-scale production for the market. For many communities, social security benefits will continue to provide the bulk of the cash income. It must be remembered also that the numbers of the potential workforce will be limited and that the demands of aspects of traditional life, such as participation in ceremonies and subsistence activities, will limit the demands for paid work even further.

Despite these constraints it is possible that Aboriginal land-use plans may involve some potential threat to the environment, although the non-commercial emphasis is likely to set limits to that threat. The contemplated land use will not follow automatically on the acknowledgment of title; it will call for more detailed planning and the allocation and use of external resources in which various government agencies must be involved. Thus, I understand that the Central Land Council has proposed that the CSIRO and other government departments and agencies should collaborate with it in a survey of possible land use in the region covered by this claim and that this should occur within the context of Aboriginal practice and aspirations. It would, furthermore, be normal for the social and economic aspects of the establishment and development of proposed homeland communities to be considered in the context of dealings between the communities concerned and the Department of Aboriginal Affairs.

It would, therefore, be normal for consideration of any environmental constraints on planned land use to be taken into account in the usual processes of government relations with the communities. It would also be important that in these processes the input from government agencies should not merely be negative. If concentration on environmentally sound opportunities would unduly restrict community development, other possibilities should be explored. Involvement in the management and protective aspects of park and sanctuary areas, of the kind contemplated by the Australian National Parks and Wildlife Service for Kakadu, seems capable of providing the bulk of the money income likely to be sought. If activities such as cattle-raising are important to the community, but ruled out as too restrictive in the land claim area, there would be an obligation on the government to acquire additional land for the group concerned. It seems improbable, with existing and anticipated numbers, that such action would be needed.

CONCLUSION

All of these considerations suggest that there is no inherent incompatibility between environmentally acceptable land use, the protection of national park and wildlife values, and Aboriginal ownership. Indeed, the areas of common interest are overwhelmingly predominant. The issue is therefore simply that of identifying the most effective means of achieving that environmental protection and appropriate land use.

To deny Aboriginal title because of lack of faith in Aboriginal integrity, understanding or capacity is to rely upon law and compulsion. To grant Aboriginal title and then to negotiate agreement is to rely upon consultation, mutual education and collaboration in agreed plans. Discussions between the Australian National Parks and Wildlife Service and Kakadu traditional owners, through the Northern Land Council, demonstrate that such agreements can be reached. The discussions between the Australian Conservation Foundation and Aborigines from the Central Land Council to which I referred at the outset of this submission and the statements which, following those discussions, have been formally endorsed by the Northern and Central Land Councils strengthen that conclusion. The willingness of those Land Councils to establish a continuing working relationship with the Australian Conservation Foundation and other conservation agencies and to seek from them professional advice in situations of difficulty, justifies confidence in the processes of mutual education and consultation. Finally, let it be clear that Aboriginal communities and individuals will not feel morally or legally committed to decisions in which they are not fully involved and that unilaterally imposed settlements will be divisive, destructive and ineffective.

4

The implications of
land rights

Originally published as 'Centre for Resource and Environmental Studies Working Paper No. 9', CRES, Australian National University, Canberra, 1978.

THE LAND RIGHTS MOVEMENT

The land rights movement basically expresses the desire of Aborigines to acquire title to, and control of, land which they regard as theirs by traditional right and with which they identify in a complex and spiritually charged manner. By logical extension it comprehends their desire, when links with their ancestral lands have been broken or cannot be demonstrated, to gain title to other land for their own economic and social purposes. Accordingly, it also includes calls to be compensated for the loss of land which was taken from their ancestors by force and without treaty or compensation, and for the destruction of the way of life which had sustained those ancestors for more than 40,000 years.

It is a movement being expressed in political action not merely by Aborigines, but by influential elements in white Australian society. It had initial success during the period of the Whitlam Government when legislation based on the report of the Woodward Commission (1973, 1974) was introduced, but did not become law before that government was replaced. The incoming Fraser Government, however, legislated on substantially similar lines. Since then, the movement has encountered increasing resistance. The Commonwealth Government's land rights legislation of 1976 applied only to the Northern Territory, and the governments of Western Australia and Queensland, where numbers of Aboriginal communities believed they could establish valid claims to large areas, refused to follow Commonwealth policy in this area. In other States, except South Australia where land rights legislation is comparable with that of the Commonwealth and where the north-west reserve forms a major part of the territory of the Pitjantjatjara and related peoples, the destruction of the link between remaining Aborigines and their traditional territory had been almost complete and Aboriginal reserves were small and insignificant and Crown lands had been largely alienated. The Commonwealth Government itself has administered its land rights legislation with decreasing enthusiasm, subordinating Aboriginal claims to the interests of white-owned enterprises, particularly mining companies, and reducing financial allocations for the acquisition and development of land for Aboriginal communities.

The full implications of the movement will depend on whether it achieves legislative changes in other States comparable with those in South Australia and the Northern Territory, on the spirit in which legislation is administered, and on the financial allocations made to it by the Commonwealth. The present situation has a transitory air. It seems likely that either political pressure will generalise more widely the proposals established by the Woodward Commission, or the present backlash will whittle them away, returning Aborigines to their former dependent and powerless condition. Nevertheless, the experience so far is sufficient to support some conclusions about the impact of land rights legislation, both on Aborigines and more generally on Australian society.

ABORIGINAL RIGHTS TO LAND

At present, Aboriginal groups in the Northern Territory can obtain title to land in three ways:
- to land within existing Aboriginal reserves, by demonstrating traditional association with it;
- to unalienated Crown land, by applying to the Aboriginal land

claims Commissioner who hears evidence to determine traditional ownership, considers objections, usually from white interests, and makes a recommendation to the Minister for Aboriginal
Affairs about how the claim should be dealt with; and

- to land which has been alienated, by applying to the Aboriginal
Land Fund Commission which is authorised to consider both
traditional association and social, economic and other needs of
the applicant community and to purchase land on their behalf
from funds available to it from the Commonwealth.

The first two of these means are available only in the Northern
Territory, but the Land Fund Commission may operate in any State.
In Queensland, however, the government has refused to transfer to
an Aboriginal community a pastoral lease purchased for it from a
willing seller, by the Land Fund Commission.

In the first of the two ways above by which Aborigines can acquire
land, the title is inalienable freehold (though with additional
advantages made available under the land rights legislation) and in
the third it would be identical with that held by the previous owner.
However, in some instances, land purchased as leasehold property
has been converted to freehold at the request of the Aborigines
concerned and where traditional association has been established.

The fact that the title is formally held by trustees and land trusts
acting for the traditional owners allows some flexibility to Aborigines
in determining the rights of those owners in relation to other Aborigines. But the absoluteness of our concept of freehold title accords
ill with the complexity of Aboriginal rights to and relationships with
land. While Aboriginal land-owning groups are predominantly
made up of those who share a common patrilineal descent, this is
not always so. There will always be real, if imprecise rights vested
in a range of other persons outside that group. Thus, an Aboriginal
person usually possesses some rights in his or her mother's country
and in many regions, in land within which he or she was born or
conceived, if these events occurred outside the father's territory.
Furthermore, rights of a somewhat different, but nonetheless real kind
seem to exist in groups which have alliances or other special
relationships with patrilineal group owners. Indeed, much of the

politicking of Aboriginal society seems to have been and probably still is concerned with the development and extension of claims to the land of other groups; claims whose potential could become important if the owning group were threatened with extinction. It will be interesting to observe whether the simplicity and exclusiveness of white concepts of land ownership as expressed in freehold title influence the pattern of Aboriginal relationships with, and use of, their territory.

Consciousness of the difficulty of expressing Aboriginal rights to land adequately in any form of European title, together with complications arising from the fact that their territory comprehended land in South Australia, Western Australia and the Northern Territory, has led Pitjantjatjara Aborigines to seek a different approach to the question of title. They point out that some rights in relation to Pitjantjatjara land, in, say, the Northern Territory, will be held by persons normally resident in Western Australia and South Australia and that as the Australian Constitution and law now stands, title to it would be vested in different trustees appointed in accordance with three different pieces of State legislation. Trustees appointed in terms of present Western Australian and South Australian legislation would probably have no links with the Pitjantjatjara peoples at all. They have therefore proposed that the land be vested in all Pitjantjatjara peoples collectively, leaving to their own agencies and procedures the determination of the nature and extent of the rights of any individual or group.

The South Australian Government expressed sympathy with their request and set up a study group to consider ways in which it might be met. The group reported with an ingenious solution. It proposed first that the South Australian lands involved, essentially the north-west Aboriginal reserves and related lands held on Aboriginal behalf by mission authorities and certain cattle properties purchased for Aborigines, should be delimited in the legislation and then vested in the Pitjantjatjara peoples as a whole. The legislation would then go on to define that group as those persons, wherever resident, 'who by Aboriginal law and tradition have rights in the said land'. These peoples would then be authorised to establish their own land council to hold the certificate of title and to act for them in relation to it. The South Australian Government has accepted the report of the study group and proposes to legislate accordingly. The Pitjantjatjara Land Council is now pressing the Western Australian Government, with little effect so far, to legislate similarly and the Commonwealth Government to administer the *Aboriginal Land Rights (Northern Territory) Act 1976* so as to conform with the study group proposals. This plan has the advantage of not identifying exclusive rights to particular areas with specific persons or groups and it would, therefore, be more compatible with the complexity of Aboriginal land ownership.

DEVELOPMENTS IN ABORIGINAL LAND USE AND LIFESTYLE

The widespread tendency among tradition-oriented Aborigines to withdraw from missions and government settlements and to establish homeland communities, preferably within territory which they regard as their own, must be seen in part as a component of the land rights movement itself. It seems certain that this desire to return has always been present to varying degrees, but was inhibited by official opposition and increased dependence on supplies and services available only in the larger settlements. Changes in policy made by the Whitlam Government, increased money incomes (primarily from social security payments) and improved facilities for transport and communications have made it possible for that desire to be met without the same degree of hardship. Furthermore, many felt an increasing need to renew the spiritual links which bound them to their own territory. The move also had political motivation. In the Northern Territory, it established an Aboriginal presence on some lands under claim, thereby giving authority to the claims and lending substance to the argument that they wished 'to make use of' the land; an argument which they knew carried weight with white authorities. In Western Australia and Queensland, the homelands movement similarly represented part of a strong Aboriginal desire to regain control of, and access to, their traditional lands in the face of adamant resistance by the government of these States.

It is in these decentralised communities that one can see being worked out the chosen lifestyle of Aborigines. There are, of course, wide variations in aspiration and achievement, but I believe a pattern is emerging which represents an amalgam of chosen elements of the Aboriginal and settlement or mission ways of life. It gives, I believe, priority to the restoration of essential features of their culture, both in its hunter-gatherer aspects and in those associated with its religious and ceremonial content. Indeed, many observers believe that greater affluence and mobility have contributed to a cultural and spiritual renaissance among these communities.

But hunter-gatherer activities can now rarely meet all their needs and they have become dependent on goods, particularly flour, sugar, tea and tobacco from the store and on the services which the settlement provided. However, even at their poorest there is at these homeland communities some money income from pensions and child endowment to purchase minimum stores. Officialdom also shows a new willingness to provide essential services in a more flexible and decentralised way. Some homelands are able to supplement social security payments by the sale of artefacts and art, and to supplement bush tucker by self-sufficient gardens modelled on those they have seen in the missions and settlements. There are problems though. Some have sought goods and services which call for technology and skills that can be provided only by recreating the white domination from which they had sought to escape. Despite these difficulties and the material hardships involved in the moves, it now seems certain that the homeland movement is here to stay. Among other things, it is an important aspect of the land rights movement and is a genuinely Aboriginal response to the problems of black–white confrontation.

Assuming that the recognition of Aboriginal ownership and the acquisition of land for Aboriginal communities continue, even with halts and fluctuations, it seems certain that those parts of Australia which Rowley (1970, 1971a, b) designated 'Aboriginal' will, outside the major administrative centres and towns associated with large-scale mining, increasingly be occupied by small Aboriginal communities developing their own characteristic lifestyle. The combination of Aboriginal land rights and a rapidly increasing population ensure this.

This does not mean that multi-group communities based on the old missions and settlements will wither away. Rather, they will develop as service centres for the homeland communities around them, providing administrative, commercial, medical, technical and educational services. There will continue to be movement between them, with the outstations making possible a wider range of choice between practicable lifestyles. But the predominant forms of land use will be those adopted by Aboriginal communities and these will not necessarily reflect those of white enterprises. Even where land use appears similar, as for instance in the conduct of cattle enterprises, it is clear that Aborigines envisage these as less highly capitalised, less market-oriented and less intensive. Indeed, they appear to see the cattle rather as an addition to the wildlife resources, drawn upon for subsistence but providing a variable surplus for sale. For a people whose access to capital is minimal, it is not a wholly irrational concept. Some interesting variations are appearing, partly as a result of the homeland movement and partly as a response to the cutting off of government funds for wage payments. At Fregon in South Australia, the herd has been divided between family groups who 'shepherd' them on a semi-nomadic basis. A division of responsibility between the community as a whole and the family groups, for capital and running costs on the one hand and receipts from sales on the other, has been established and the plan appears to be working well. In the homelands around Aurukun where the cattle enterprise consists almost solely of mustering wild cattle, the rights to kill off scrubbers and brand calves have been divided on the basis of land ownership, so that the various family groups work independently of one another except in relation to marketing.

There is a need to study what is happening in Aboriginal land use in the context of land rights and to reorient research so that it is relevant to that use rather than, as at present, exclusively to the needs of white-owned and market-oriented enterprises. The maintenance and increase of native species which are important to Aboriginal nutrition, the improvement in their yields and the domestication of native species for local use and potential export, are lines of research which could contribute to greater self-sufficiency and independence. Similarly, the redirection of adult education services and vocational training facilities so that they meet Aboriginal land needs would be a logical recognition of Aboriginal land rights. Here also there are interesting models. The Uniting Church mission at Ernabella in South Australia has pioneered the development of arid zone agriculture, horticulture and reafforestation, using drip irrigation and run-off technologies and equipment compatible with Aboriginal patterns of belief and lifestyle. This work is now under Aboriginal control and the mission is developing extension and educational functions, and acting as a source of supplies for Aboriginal communities throughout Pitjantjatjara country.

In other words, Aboriginal land use in territories around their settlements and homelands reflects a similar amalgam of selected components from their traditional hunter-gatherer activities and from productive processes which they have observed in settlements and on cattle properties. The methods and technologies in these latter processes are being modified to conform with Aboriginal priorities and there is evidence of creative innovation as well as mistakes. A rich potential exists for research and enterprises accepting the requirements of the Aboriginal way of life.

LAND RIGHTS AND AUTHORITY

An Aboriginal group, socially and ethnically homogeneous and living within its own territory, possessed a political authority structure adequate to conduct its own traditional affairs, to maintain social discipline and to resolve interpersonal and inter-family disputes. It also had processes by which its children were instructed in the skills demanded by their lifestyle, in the culture of their people and generally socialised to fit them for the life they would have to face. Contact with other groups tended to occur on special occasions and seasonally, and their processes for handling inter-group issues and conflicts were then less effective, although there were established procedures by which tensions could be handled before they became wholly destructive. The effectiveness of all these processes derived from the authority inherent in the relationship of people to the land and the primacy of that authority within their own territory.

When different groups were brought together in missions and settlements their internal authority structure was encroached upon by white authority and their own procedures for handling inter-group concerns largely replaced; first by those of officials and sub-sequently by councils and similar bodies modelled on white political institutions. Similarly, the nurturing and education of children became significantly a function of white institutions. These changes were invariably destructive. Aboriginal responsibility was impaired, if not wholly destroyed, law and order became difficult to sustain and vandalism and delinquency became characteristic of Aboriginal child and youth behaviour.

The recognition of land rights, the development of the homeland movement and the adoption, in theory at least, of a policy of self-management for Aboriginal communities have combined to lend power to traditional Aboriginal authority and to introduce an increasing political content into Aboriginal demands and expec-tations in their own communities.

At the homelands, traditional leadership and procedures have tended to re-establish themselves naturally. Within their own territory leaders show a renewed confidence and there is evidence of respect for it and the traditional law. Responsibility for the nurture of children returns to those in whom it traditionally lay and almost universally, the problems of delinquency appear to decline or disappear, though anxiety about the style and content of education appropriate to the homeland context persists. Aborigines generally are conscious that their capacity to deal effectively with white society is dependent on command of the English language, of numeracy and a minimum familiarity with the institutions of white Australia. They therefore wish their children to acquire these skills, but are conscious that in its present form the education provided continues to be assimilationist in its objectives and, in its content, derogatory and destructive of Aboriginal values. Responses vary, but there is increasing demand for greater control of educational content and procedures, for the right of veto on hiring teachers, for the right of their own members to be trained as teachers, for greater educational effort to be directed at vocational skills and at training and retraining adults.

In the larger settlements, the acceptance of white models for developing political institutions is giving way to more varied experiments in amalgamating these with components from their own authority structures. In Yirrkala, these experiments are at an interesting stage. The first development in self-management was the establishment about ten years ago of a mission-inspired town council, largely mission controlled and essentially advisory in function. This was supplemented by the formation of an Aboriginal association to own and manage business enterprises established with government aid and possessing its own elected council of Aborigines. In due course, this council replaced the original town council and was responsible for town management, the receipt and disbursement of funds from mining royalties and all 'whitefella' business. There also existed, without constitution or incorporation, an informal gathering of leaders from each of the clans which was brought together at the request of one or more leaders when matters affecting Aboriginal law, the land or major negotiations with the government were involved. This body's opinions were generally accepted by the association as binding on its action.

Thus, it is to this 'leadership council' that the community looks to evolve and present its views on the question of the relationship between Aboriginal and white Australian law and how far the administration of law and order will become the responsibility of the Aboriginal community itself. This is a question which bears closely upon Aboriginal law itself, of which clan leaders are the acknowledged custodians. Furthermore, many of the problems of Aboriginal responsibility for law and order, such as those arising from the abuse of alcohol, will be rendered more acute in multi-group communities by the nature of group and family loyalties and rivalries. If effective Aboriginal institutions are to be evolved, they must, it seems to me, derive from additional procedures for the settlement of intergroup disputes.

Furthermore, the division of responsibility between the community association and Aboriginal 'leadership councils' does not deal

48

adequately with the demarcation of authority between them on the one hand and, on the other, the leaders of the group who are the traditional owners of the territory within which the settlement of Yirrkala stands. The authority of these owners is, in theory at least, extensive and powerful and has been strengthened by the acknowledgment of land rights and by the role allotted to them in the procedures established by the legislation. Members of other clans or groups, inhibited by their status as 'visitors', are reluctant to set limits to that authority even when they are irked by its exercise. This issue could become explosive at Yirrkala where the land-owning clan is headed by a vigorous and aggressive leader.

Apart from these structural experiments, there is growing pressure for increased power to be accorded to Aboriginal agencies to administer law and order and to apply, with the support of white law enforcement agencies, sanctions of their own devising or derived from Aboriginal tradition and practice. Similarly, there is growing pressure for authority to influence and control educational content and procedures, to control the issue of permits to enter their territory and to exercise a right of veto on government and other personnel appointed to posts within their territory. These demands are essentially political ones for greater self-determination and independence. It is noteworthy that they bear close resemblance to demands being made by indigenous minorities in other countries such as the United States of America and Canada, whose traditional relationship with the land has much in common with that of Aboriginal Australians.

THE IMPACT OF LAND RIGHTS

The recognition of Aboriginal land rights is limited geographically, by the doctrine of Crown ownership of minerals, by the exclusion of lands already alienated, by the economic and political power of mining companies, by the lack of resources to defend Aboriginal rights or to enjoy their benefits and potential, and by political weakness generally. Nevertheless, it is difficult not to conclude from the most superficial observation of Aborigines affected even by this limited recognition, that it represents the most beneficial initiative taken by white Australian society towards Aborigines. Its impact on their self-respect and independence, while as yet in its early stages, is marked and there is reason to be confident about its continued development.

But the effect of the changes it has brought about on white attitudes towards Aborigines and on the relationship between the two peoples is far from encouraging. It is clear that this recognition and its effects provoke some powerful prejudices characteristic of our society. At the moment, they are occurring at a time when there is widespread fear and anxiety about personal and economic security, and when many are seeking a scapegoat onto which they can, with safety, transfer the animosities which these fears and anxieties induce.

Australians generally are a chauvinist people, hostile and suspicious towards people who look, behave, believe or think differently from the conventional image they have of themselves. They can usually be tolerant of those who exhibit these idiosyncrasies, provided they are not forced by circumstance to observe them closely or to accommodate to them. Aboriginal Australians not merely exhibit most of these unwelcome departures from the white norm, but apparently feel no sense of inferiority and little inclination to conform. Furthermore, in many parts of north and central Australia they are increasingly visible, asserting their differences and exacerbating them by emulating or surpassing our own less pleasing patterns of behaviour. It is, therefore, in these parts of the country that opposition to and resentment about Aboriginal land rights is presently strongest and most vocal. Myths about Aboriginal privileges and advantages, and about their moral and social depravities are exchanged freely among white Australians in the north as a means to justify their prejudices. Such expressions serve also to divert attention from the inadequacies of our own society and the failure of its policies towards Aborigines.

Economic growth or development has become an article of blind faith among us. We see it as not merely the major achievement of our civilisation and the source of material welfare, but as an essential requirement for the operation of the economic system and a solution to the problems it creates. That Aborigines should not merely regard it as irrelevant, but presume to stand in its way, provokes hostility more intense than atrocities in Vietnam or Rhodesia. Furthermore, the expectation of spin-off economic benefits to white residents of the Northern Territory from uranium mining are extravagant to the point of absurdity. True, income earned in its mining and refinement can be expected to exert a mutliplier effect on employment and incomes generally, but what is known and can be anticipated of the cash flows which will be generated suggests that the multiplier will be at work in southern cities and overseas, rather than in the Northern Territory. A look at the minimal effect which iron ore has had on Port Hedland should dispel some of these illusions. Nevertheless, they add to the public's conviction that only Aboriginal recalcitrance stands in the way of El Dorado.

The present economic and social climate is one which induces widespread uncertainty and fear that jobs, income and property may be insecure. This insecurity intensifies anxieties from real causes and generates them from imaginary sources. It makes attractive any hypothesis which allocates blame to other groups, particularly if they are in other ways open to suspicion. I recall how, in the early thirties, there were anti-Italian riots in Kalgoorlie as the depression created uncertainty about the future of jobs and indeed, about the future of the mining industry. In other words, Aborigines are serving as a substitute for those enemies we are unable to identify, or who are too powerful for us to attack. The emergence of extremist groups and organisations in the north is not surprising. They represent the lunatic fringe it is true, but they express what many others would assert if they had the courage. These trends are lending bitterness to black-white relationships across the north in Western Australia, the Northern Territory and Queensland to a degree which I have not previously encountered anywhere in Australia.

However, the polarisation of racial groups is, in the Northern Territory, no longer a one-way influence politically. In the last Legislative Assembly elections in the Territory the Aboriginal vote produced a dramatic swing to the Labor Party and, indeed, suggested that if it had been effectively mobilised, it could have defeated the Liberal–Country Party Coalition. It is believed that Aborigines have learnt that at the ballot box they command a powerful political clout and the present Chief Minister has said publicly that if the Coalition wishes to remain in office it must mend its bridges with the Aborigines. Even by the next election the number of Aboriginal voters will be significantly greater, both absolutely and as a proportion of the various electorates, and it seems highly probable that their electoral influence could command the balance of power.

It cannot be doubted that this sudden development of political consciousness is a by-product of the campaign for land rights and the common sense of Aboriginal identity which it has promoted among previously disparate and frequently hostile groups. This consciousness of being Aboriginal as well as belonging to Pitjantjatjara, Warlpiri, Rirratjingu or some other tribe or clan, is relatively new and in its early stages. Comprehending, as this trend does, the more politically activist urban Aborigines, its development may well prove to be the most significant change in Aboriginal society since white occupation.

Aboriginal Lifestyles

5

Economic, social and spiritual factors in Aboriginal health

Paper presented to the 53rd ANZAAS Congress, Perth, 17 May 1983. Subsequently published as 'Centre for Resource and Environmental Studies Working Paper No. 16', CRES, Australian National University, Canberra, 1983.

Since the coming of Europeans the record of Aboriginal health has been one of unmitigated disaster. For 140 years the Aboriginal population plummeted until the race was within sight of extinction. Since then, as population has risen (in recent years rapidly) the record has been one of infant mortality, shamefully excessive by white Australian or world standards, and levels of morbidity which compare unfavourably with those of most societies in the world for which records are available. Even today, despite considerable expenditure on medical research, technology and expertise, the most recent comprehensive review of Aboriginal health can still legitimately describe the situation as one of crisis (Reid 1982).

The variety and emphasis of the diseases and morbid conditions common among Aborigines, ranging as they do through infectious and respiratory diseases, gastroenteritis, sexually transmitted, dental and eye diseases, together with widespread malnutrition, strongly suggest a common set of environmental factors in the context from which these ills emerge. That this should be so for people who have shown themselves capable of achieving physical and psychic health over millennia in diverse and frequently inhospitable habitats suggests that these factors are likely to be found in the changes,

54

physical and other, imposed on them and their habitat by the European invasion.

THE HUNTER-GATHERER LIFESTYLE

Any considerations of the effect of those changes, I believe, must begin from the realisation that Aborigines are closely linked in culture and psychological attitudes to the hunter-gatherer lifestyle of their ancestors. The concept of a lifestyle is convenient, but it is desirable to elaborate its content in order to clarify its relevance to the question of Aboriginal health, or indeed health generally.

The daily life of any individual consists of a series of activities which in a hunter-gatherer community range from sleeping, through the various hunting and gathering processes, to weapon and artefact-making, to cooking and eating, to story-telling, visiting relatives and the conduct of ceremonies. Each of these activities occurs in a specific setting or context forming part of the total environment, partly natural and partly man-made or modified. It is these activity-setting combinations which, in the aggregate, constitute the mode of life or lifestyle of the individual and the group.

The capacity of those combinations to meet the diverse needs of the individual will largely determine their relevance to his or her physical, social and psychic health. Survival demands access to reasonably clean air and water, and to adequate nutrition and shelter. A sense of well-being also requires conditions more difficult to identify with certainty. Membership of, and a recognised role within, a social group which provide collective and personal identity and an assurance of support; competence in the knowledge and skills required by the lifestyle, sufficient to ensure confidence in coping with the common or exceptional challenges it presents; a pattern of belief about the universe and its operation, sufficient to provide a framework for rational or imaginative thought and action; and a sense of purpose with which one can identify; all these seem necessary for, or at least capable of contributing significantly to, an individual's total health.

There seems ample reason to believe that the activities and experience which constitute the hunter-gatherer lifestyle were capable of providing the means to survival and the requirements for a sense of well-being. This is not to say that Aboriginal society was wholly imbued with sweetness and light. While we have no direct knowledge of its pristine state, their own accounts suggest that violence in inter-personal disputes was common and many lived in fear of sorcery. Inter-tribal relations were, it is believed, often marked by suspicion and distrust, and the strong Aboriginal commitment to mutual support and sharing was largely confined to members of the imme-diate extended family. Nevertheless, within the relatively small bands characteristic of most traditional Aboriginal societies, life could be stimulating, secure and rewarding. Furthermore, this quality was achieved by means which brought individuals into direct contact with a largely natural environment with which they were physically and spiritually integrated.

It is common among those who live in contemporary urban civili-sation to think of that and similar lifestyles as inherently poor and degraded; as 'nasty, brutish and short'. There is good reason to question this presupposition. Anthropologists and others who have studied Aboriginal groups living a similar lifestyle have concluded that while infant mortality was probably high relative to that in contemporary Australian society, those who survived infancy were usually healthy and vigorous, with a normal proportion reaching advanced age. Most importantly, they have commented on the evid-ence of a general sense of well-being, of real satisfaction being derived from their lifestyle.

Thus Richard Gould, an American anthropologist who lived with one of the few remaining Aboriginal groups still pursuing a hunter-gatherer existence in the harsh and inhospitable habitat of the Western Desert, wrote:

> ... in the context of the desert environment, the daily lives of the nomadic Aborigines are essentially harmonious and rewarding. An individual grows up realising what is expected of him. By acquiring and developing practical knowledge and skill he learns to fulfil these expectations and is rewarded immediately by his own satisfaction in achievement and in the long-run esteem of his kin. (1969: 90)

Similarly, Betty Meehan, an Australian prehistorian, reported on the Anbarra people who left the government settlement at Maningrida and returned to their traditional territory in the 1970s, noting that apart from introduced diseases, mostly now under control, the health of the Anbarra people living in the bush appeared to be good. They recognised this and visiting health workers frequently commented upon it. Meehan argued that their emotional well-being was enhanced by the fact that they were back on their own territory, rather than living in centralised settlements (1982: 157–8).

That human beings are at home in a hunter-gatherer society is not surprising. They have been adapted to it for more than 500,000 years. By contrast, in those parts of the world where it was succeeded by the nomadic-pastoralist and agricultural eras, perhaps 10,000 years would be the limit of their experience and little more than 200 years since the industrial revolution changed the face of Europe and the lifestyle of its people.

ADAPTING TO A CHANGING ENVIRONMENT

Some students of human ecology argue that if the conditions of life of any species, including humanity, deviate significantly from those in which it evolved, signs of maladjustment will emerge: that it will experience physical, mental and emotional ill health (Boyden 1981). This proposition, in its simplest form, probably underestimates the capacity of the human species to adapt both itself and its habitat. Indeed, the history of the species in those parts of the world where the hunter-gatherer way has been abandoned can be interpreted as a continuous process of mutual adaptation of the species and its habitat to counter the effects of maladjustment as increasing population has combined with technological change to compel changes in the lifestyle itself. This adaptation always involves costs. Thus, Rene Dubos comments:

> Life in a modern city has become a symbol of the fact that man can become adapted to starless skies, treeless avenues, shapeless buildings, tasteless bread, joyless celebrations, spiritless pleasures – to a life without reverence for the past, love for the present or hope for the future. (1965: 278)

The adaptation of which Dubos speaks is primarily cultural, although the dividing line between genetic and cultural change is, in the field of behaviour, not easy to draw. The study of animal behaviour has shown that complex patterns which have at least the appearance of having been learned are sometimes, in fact, inherited. Inherited behaviour patterns can sometimes be strangely distorted in abnormal contexts. Furthermore, in man and other primates at least, what was inherited appears to have been a capacity to learn readily a valuable skill or response to a particular stimulus, especially at an appropriate stage in the individual's development. Despite these qualifications, it is to cultural changes that one must look for the means by which humanity adapted to environmental change. Cultural changes also increased humanity's capacity to alter the environment deliberately, although rarely with full awareness of the limits, or the effects of that alteration.

Aborigines can therefore be seen as having been compelled to adapt, within the lifetime of a few generations, to material and social changes which elsewhere have spread over 10,000 years. These changes were achieved by destructive aggression and forced them out of the productive part of their habitat. The rest of their lands have been ravaged not merely by whites, but by domesticated and feral animals of alien origin. The physical changes themselves may well have been less damaging to the Aboriginal lifestyle and therefore to Aboriginal health than the enormously different social, economic and spiritual character of the total environment which Aborigines had to confront after white colonisation. To them and their forebears, periods of acute scarcity must have been an ever-present threat through the dramatic climatic changes of 40,000 years, but their cultural and spiritual ambience had, through those periods, served as a source of security.

A comparison of the total environment which Aboriginal Australians now confront with that to which they and their ancestors had ever been physically and culturally adapted, makes clear the enormity of their difficulties. Firstly, they came from small communities, all members of which were known and probably kin; communities whose patterns of organisation and relationships, while complex, had been learned by personal experience. They now confront a community which in some respects is worldwide in its scope, which even at its most local level is formed by aspects of institutions much more widely based, deriving their authority from sources unknown and incomprehensible, and demanding patterns of behaviour for which nothing in the experience or wisdom of their elders has prepared them, or can offer any rational explanation.

Secondly, that environment, so far as they have access to it, is no longer capable of meeting their basic needs. Air alone is substantially as freely available, although not of comparable quality with that of pre-contact times. In many places, the waters upon which their lives depended and which figured so splendidly in their mythology have been denied them, or sullied and polluted by alien animals. In many places, they have become dependent on ground water, for access to which they must rely on the bounty of governments and the technology and convenience of their engineers. Many of the seed and fruit-bearing plants that were important sources of food have become fodder for stock, or been eliminated by the combination of drought, overstocking and soil erosion. Many indigenous animal species have been exterminated, or brought close to extinction as their habitats have been destroyed or taken over by competitors.

Thirdly, most of that environment, depleted as it is from an Aboriginal viewpoint, is now closed to them. Traditionally, an Aboriginal family or group within their own territory had free access to whatever their knowledge and skill could command. Even within the territory of other land-owning groups they frequently had subsidiary rights by tradition and kinship ties, or could count upon access by readily available permission and the implied promise of reciprocity. By contrast, Aborigines today confront institutions of property which operate on different principles which are directed not to the care and protection of natural resources, but to the rationing of demand to levels which can be satisfied; that is, to excluding some from the benefits of possession, access or use of any component of the total environment which is scarce. These benefits are reserved to those who possess the key; namely, wealth or influence.

THE IMPACT OF COLONISATION ON
ABORIGINAL HEALTH

Since white colonisation Aborigines have been forced to come to terms with the world economic system. Deprived of the sustenance the land provided they must depend upon the sugar, flour and tea from the store, paid for predominantly from the social security benefits received by the old, the mothers, the sick and the disabled. The poverty inherent in this dependence makes malnutrition inevitable. To gain the maximum from these benefits, to seek paid employment, to find markets for their art and artefacts, to get access to education and health services, Aborigines were forcibly moved or attracted to missions and government settlements.

It was in these white-dominated institutional situations that the basic conflict between Aboriginal needs and aspirations became most apparent and most irreconcilable. Despite the welfare orientation of the administration of these institutions, both physical and psychic health were probably at their worst. Poverty, and stores stocked without reference to dietary principles, ensured that malnutrition remained the rule, especially as opportunities to hunt and gather were restricted increasingly by the depletion of the immediate area surrounding new settlements and by the lack of transport. Inadequate facilities for supplying water to camps, the imposition of a sedentary way of life on a people accustomed to frequent movement and the lack of adequate shelter combined with overcrowding to produce conditions ideal for the generation, transmission and perpetuation of disease. All of these factors intensified problems created by exposure to diseases to which they had no immunity.

Susceptibility to environmentally caused diseases was almost certainly intensified by psychological factors. The populations of many of these settlements brought together Aborigines of different tribal groups and languages, without concern for their traditional compatibility, so that fears, suspicion of sorcery and other forms of mutual hostility often resulted. The residents were usually isolated from their traditional homelands and from the sacred sites which were so important to their ceremonial and cultural life. Indeed, the opportunities to pursue this aspect of their lives were severely restricted and often the subject of deliberate white interference, derision and contempt. The demands of fixed hours of work for sustenance or wages interfered with the traditional pattern of bush activities in which all members of the family participated and so deprived children of the experience and instruction by their elders necessary for their development as Aborigines. In addition to this deprivation, Aborigines saw their children being alienated from them by white teachers, missionaries and others inspired by the assimilationist objectives of government policies, and the role of their elders as teachers and keepers of Aboriginal law depreciated and indeed, denigrated.

All this meant that Aborigines in these settlements were undergoing a life experience utterly inconsistent and incompatible with their own pattern of beliefs about the nature and operation of the universe. It was an experience about which they could not think or act rationally, which denied the validity of all that their ancestors had transmitted and, above all, which isolated them from the natural world as they knew it. It is not surprising that Aborigines in such places seemed utterly alienated, to be sunk in hopelessness and despair. It was in respect of these conditions that Reid and Kerr (1983) commented that Aborigines have been 'trapped in the role of supplicants', that is, in conditions fostering dependency and undermining initiative.

In such circumstances the investment of white knowledge, skills and resources in attempts to 'solve the problems' of Aboriginal health was bound to yield little return. Disease and the conditions which reflected the total Aboriginal environment, even when successfully treated or cured, would almost certainly recur when the patient returned to that environment. Frequently, the treatment involved isolating the patient from his or her family and social group, thereby intensifying the anxieties which derived from an inability to comprehend and cope with the total situation. Furthermore the treatment, even when its purposes were explained, often bore little or no relation to, or compatibility with, the patient's own understanding of his or her physiological processes. In turn, few medical workers showed much interest in the Aboriginal view of health and biology.

In other words, policies directed to the solution of poor Aboriginal health have shared the almost universal experience of welfare policies designed and administered by others for the benefit of target groups. However well intentioned, scientifically planned or generously and humanely administered, they rarely achieve their purposes. Indeed, they frequently seem to intensify rather than ameliorate the problems at which they are directed. Furthermore, as many health workers among Aborigines can testify, they often proved a powerful source of disillusionment among those responsible for giving effect to them (Coombs et al. 1983).

ABORIGINAL HEALTH INITIATIVES

It is pleasant to be able to conclude this paper by reference to some developments which hold promise of altering effectively the direction of change in the health of Aborigines. The first is the land rights campaign and the beginnings of its success. Where in parts of the Northern Territory and South Australia Aborigines have had land restored to them and are in effective control of it, there is already evidence that they are coping more successfully with the problems of contemporary life. To be in their own territory, to be able to restore their relationship with it, to hunt and to gather, to renew their ceremonial life, to instruct their young in the traditional law; these things are the source of renewed strength and confidence. As that experience extends to Aborigines elsewhere, the effects on the psychic health of Aborigines will, I believe, be dramatic.

The second development is the homeland, or outstation movement. Aborigines in settlements and missions have long dreamed and talked of returning to their traditional lands, but were deterred by official opposition and by their dependence on goods and services supplied by those who administered the institutions of which they were inmates. However in the sixties, the desire to return was intensified by the land rights campaign and the need to demonstrate their title to ownership by a physical presence on the land. With the change to a Labor Government in 1972, official policies towards homelands changed. Opposition was no longer general and in some circumstances there was increased willingness to back the movement with resources.

Homelands are characteristically small communities usually between 50 and 200 people, closely linked familially and culturally and by association with the region within which the settlement is made. In homeland centres, groups are attempting to establish a pattern of life which is an amalgam of their traditional lifestyle and chosen elements from their experience of white society. Thus, hunting and gathering provide a substantial part of subsistence for outstation food, although they remain significantly dependent on the incomes derived from social security payments. The importance of the hunter-gatherer component in this amalgam to the nutrition and health of Aborigines has been demonstrated by the recent research of Dr Kerin O'Dea (1988). Dr O'Dea arranged for ten Aboriginal diabetics to return to a traditional dietary and activity pattern for a period of seven weeks. Her study of the group carrying out this experiment revealed a striking improvement in all of the metabolic abnormalities associated with diabetics in this group.

In another interesting development, in some settlements, unemployment benefits available for those who have been members of the employed workforce are voluntarily commuted to bulk payments to the group or community, which can be used for the payment of wages for work done on community projects. These can include the development of vegetable and fruit gardens, tree-planting and other subsistence activities. Generally, homeland communities desire to have educational and health services maintained. This creates the opportunity for their own members to be trained to deliver these services to the community and thus to increase its money income, while preserving its social independence. As with Aborigines resident on and controlling their own cattle enterprises, homeland populations, despite very difficult problems and acute scarcity of resources, show resilience and increasing capacity to cope. The prevailing tone is cheerful and confident. It is a context in which physical health is likely to improve.

The third significant development is the emergence of Aboriginal-controlled health services. These began as a self-help activity amongst

Aboriginal groups living in the crowded inner suburbs of Sydney and Melbourne, to give support to families in need. This initiative was able to attract support from medical and other professional areas and, in due course, from governments. From the outset, the principle has been that the services are controlled and administered by Aborigines. Non-Aboriginal medical and paramedical practitioners are employees and increasing emphasis is placed on having Aboriginal health workers as the members of the team in closest communication with the patient and his or her family.

The idea was taken up vigorously by the Central Australian Aboriginal Congress, a political instrument of Aborigines in that region which has organised an extensive and comprehensive health service for Aborigines in and around Alice Springs. Its success has led to a spawning of similar services for other Aboriginal communities in the Northern Territory, South Australia and Western Australia.

The principles on which these health services are developing include:

- Aboriginal control;
- emphasis on positive environmental aspects of health;
- emphasis on the Aboriginal health worker in the community as the primary instrument of service delivery;
- full use of western medical technology and personnel as far as possible on a visiting basis; and
- respect for, and use of, traditional Aboriginal medical knowledge and traditional healers.

The success of these services and the growing pressure from communities to have their own, is a measure of their appropriateness for the Aboriginal context. It has also influenced official thinking and practice. The Department of Health in the Northern Territory has recently introduced changes in its own organisation which incorporate some of the same principles. The Department of Health in South Australia proposes to hand over the administration of health services in what was the north-west Aboriginal reserve to an agency of the Pitjantjatjara Council.

CONCLUSION

Changes are in process which are beginning to restore to Aborigines command over the lifestyle they choose to live. Critical to the success of that lifestyle will be the relationship which it establishes between Aboriginal ways of gaining a livelihood and the market-oriented national economy, and the degree to which Aborigines are enabled to develop under their own effective control the institutions they need, in accordance with their own view of the world and its purposes.

It is interesting to note that the World Bank, after nearly forty years of pursuit of development for tribal peoples, now urges that 'immediate integration of tribal populations [into the economic system] can only swell the numbers of the rural and urban poor'. A recent report states:

(a) National Governments and international organisations must support rights to land used or occupied by tribal people, to their ethnic identity and to cultural autonomy.

(b) The tribe must be provided with interim safeguards that enable it to deal with unwelcome outside influences on its own land until the tribe adapts sufficiently.

(c) Neither the nation nor the non-tribal neighbours should compete with the tribal society on its own lands for its resources.

(Goodland and Ledec 1986: 28)

In Aboriginal Australia, the scope for progressive evolution of autonomous economic and social institutions has been greatly preempted by history. The base from which their successful development can begin must, to some degree, be re-established. These institutions will not be easy for Aborigines to design; their roots must be in Aboriginal society, but they must function also in the mainstream society itself. However the examples I have given, taken from the field of health, indicate that Aborigines, given scope, are capable of significant political and managerial innovation and competence. If we are prepared to trust to that capacity, the investment of human and material resources in Aboriginal health need no longer be wasted.

6

Aboriginal education and the issues underlying Aboriginal deaths in custody

Paper presented to Commissioner P Dodson, Underlying Issues Unit of the Royal Commission into Aboriginal Deaths in Custody, 1990.

It is not possible to consider the significance of education in shaping the social conditions out of which Aboriginal deaths in custody emerge, without taking into account the whole traditional process by which Aboriginal children are socialised to grow up as Aboriginal people; to acquire the beliefs, the patterns of behaviour, the values and the role models which they will express in their adult lives. These socialisation processes are comprehensive and coherent, involve every activity of the group and are geared to the lifestyle needs and purposes of its members. They are not separated and devolved upon particular members of the group, or delegated to external authority. This close integration of the educational process with the life of the group means that when the circumstances of the group are radically changed, the pattern of those processes adapts slowly. Where those changes are powerful and demand radical adjustments in relationship with other groups, conflict can emerge between the need to achieve those adjustments and the responses inculcated by traditional socialisation.

The hypothesis which I wish to put forward is that such a conflict exists between the assimilationist objectives of white Australian policies and the deeply ingrained attitudes and patterns of behaviour of Aborigines. Many of the events and patterns of behaviour being examined by the Royal Commission into Aboriginal Deaths in Custody are symptoms of that conflict.

THE IMPORTANCE OF ABORIGINAL SOCIALISATION

Much of the discussion of possible issues underlying the apparent frequency of Aboriginal deaths in custody has tended to concentrate on specific behavioural patterns which appear to lead to situations in which incarceration is a likely outcome or response; for example, drunkenness and violence sometimes including murder or suicide. Some observers have intuitively believed that it is inadequate to see these patterns as independent phenomena, but that rather more accurately, they can be seen as symptoms of a more comprehensive syndrome amongst Aboriginal people. Abuse of alcohol is perhaps the most widely canvassed single cause or predominant factor. This tends to be popular, I consider, because it is most visible to whites and places blame most specifically with Aborigines themselves.

The Commission into Aboriginal Deaths in Custody should view such simplistic approaches with scepticism, if only immediately because Aboriginal drinking patterns echo closely those of white society with its emphasis on binge drinking, especially those of rural itinerant labourers, and because Aborigines, both as individuals and as groups, have shown at least as successful a capacity to come to terms with the abuse as white Australians where they wish to do so. Both their moves to exercise greater social control and their analysis of the problem itself, for instance in the Tangentyere (Lyon 1990) study of the problem in Central Australia, are evidence of such a capacity.

Two considerations in particular suggest that understanding must be sought more deeply and particularly in the destructive impacts of colonisation on Aboriginal social control and socialisation. The first consideration is the degree to which similar problems, such as petrol sniffing, often emerge first among the young and apparently serve as a kind of transition to alcohol and other abuse. The second, is that in groups and communities where these problems are emerging there is strong evidence of a breakdown in traditional Aboriginal educational practices, especially in the socialisation of the young by their elders and in participation in daily activities as part of their step-by-step cultural and religious training. Certainly, older men and women frequently emphasise the link they believe exists between the failure of contemporary Aborigines to fulfil the obligations and observances of Aboriginal law and the marked increase in these behavioural problems. Aboriginal patterns of socialisation are subjected to enormous pressures by current assimilationist objectives of government policies, causing severe mental confusion and emotional stress among many younger Aboriginal people and their families.

In the socialisation of Aboriginal children and young people, great importance is placed upon the timing of particular experiences and the preparation necessary to ensure that the young are equipped to handle the problems and confrontations involved in those experiences. The succession of initiation ceremonies is designed both to protect those not yet ready and to ensure that readiness is socially symbolised and expressed. Thus, Aborigines 'bring up' boys and girls together when they are very young, separate them in the years leading up to puberty and maturity, and bring them together again later. Similarly, among the Pintubi and perhaps other groups, young people are excluded from responsibility for dealings with 'people from far away'; a responsibility which is reserved for mature-age people and for which training is reserved to appropriate stages in the succession of ceremonial life.

I mention this for several reasons. Firstly, because it could well be that some of the conflicts which form part of the underlying issues being investigated by the Royal Commission arise from Aboriginal children and young people being called upon to adapt to a contact situation before they are ready, and in particular, before they are effectively socialised into their own society, with their Aboriginal identity well established. Similarly, some experience of the virtues of diversity and of the potential of multiculturalism could be valuable before mainstream educational authorities are given decision-making powers in a mixed and colonised community. I offer no positive judgements on these issues, except to say that they are matters about which Aboriginal groups hold strong views and about which they are entitled to the right of participation in decisions.

CONTINUITY AND CHANGE

From 1788 competent observers of Aboriginal society have been impressed by the continuity of that society and its capacity to adapt to change: physical change, continental in its magnitude; climatic change as dramatic as ice ages and the greenhouse effect; and social change as absolute as the dispossession of their land, the widespread slaughter of their people and the acceptance of servitude as the alternative to extermination. This adaptability has not been confined to pre-white contact situations. Thus, for instance, the decision of Aborigines to bring the 'killing time' to an end in the Kimberley by 'coming in' to the pastoral stations and accepting the role of unpaid labour for the cattle industry was an Aboriginal initiative. Furthermore, the design of the lifestyle in that relationship – with its use of the annual stand-down period to return to the bush for a period of traditional life, for ceremony, for care of the land, and for the instruction and socialisation of the young – was theirs also. It recognised that there existed the basis of a compromise with pastoralists embodying some mutually advantageous components.

Recent studies in the Kimberley (Coombs et al. 1989; Dixon and Dillon 1990) have demonstrated that in similar adjustments in black–white economic relationships, such as in dealings with the diamond mining industry, it has been Aboriginal ingenuity which has identified their basis. Descriptions by anthropologists of changes in the structure and practice of Aboriginal religion in the Kimberley also reveal skilful adaptation to accommodate movement into the region of different tribal groups with potentially conflicting religious interests and responsibilities.

Why then has Aboriginal adaptability failed to deal more effectively with a problem which could be seen as a failure of morale and of Aboriginal people's own social organisation? Why has this failure apparently become more acute in recent years?

Evidence suggests that in this century, it is only in the period since the end of the Second World War that there has been extensive and profound interaction between the two societies of Aboriginal and non-Aboriginal Australians. After the dispossession of Aboriginal people from their land and when indiscriminate violence had been brought under apparent control, the two tended to live separately in space (and in time, as in the largely pastoral country) so that accommodation between them in a day-to-day sense was unnecessary. Aborigines camped on the fringes of towns and settlements, moving from place to place, in mission or government institutions, in city ghettoes, or in distant lands not occupied by whites. A large proportion of the white population was unlikely even to meet or to have met with an Aboriginal person, family or community. Aborigines and whites were protected from each other by isolation, by their own mutual distrust and by the 'great white Australian indifference'.

A major change began with the Second World War and the threat of Japanese invasion. Whereas in the early stages of the war the military were, to say the least, unenthusiastic about Aborigines being enrolled in the armed forces, when that threat developed such significance Aborigines were recruited into the paramilitary, semi-civilian, construction, coast-watch and similar groups. Their experience there was seminal. For the first time they experienced some degree of equality: in food, working conditions and most importantly, often in earnings.

When the war ended, return to pre-war status on the pastoral properties began to be resisted. Industrial trouble emerged in the Pilbara region of Western Australia and in properties touching upon the north-south highway in the Northern Territory. These troubles and humanitarian concerns also emerged internationally and as issues in the media. Aborigines were pushed off cattle stations as they began to demand payment in wages and other award conditions, and moved increasingly to larger population centres seeking paid employment or government support. Changes to some State laws allowed Aboriginal people access to citizenship, the Commonwealth extended their eligibility for social security benefits and in the 1967 referendum, the Constitution was amended to give the Commonwealth responsibility, in parallel with the States, for Aboriginal affairs and to provide for their inclusion in population censuses.

The Aboriginal population had been co-opted into the Australian nation! In the lead-up to the 1967 referendum there were discussions between the States and the Commonwealth about the basis on which this co-option should be made effective. The earlier period of the 'killing time' had been followed by an expectation that Aborigines would rapidly 'die out' and that government, mission and public policy should be to 'smooth the dying pillow'. As it became apparent that this expectation was unlikely to be realised, the policy passed through various stages of Aboriginal tutelage and institutionalisation designed to direct Aborigines into the, hopefully, kindly care and service of their actual or potential employers.

In this pre-referendum period, more humanitarian influences and increasing awareness of international opinion concentrated the choice between Aborigines as wards of the State and an alternative, distant objective of assimilation. The State and Commonwealth Governments expected that Aborigines would choose to live by the same standards, accepting the same obligations as the rest of the Australian community. This offer of assimilation was widely felt to be humane, progressive, indeed generous.

MAINSTREAM EDUCATION – SELF-DETERMINATION OR ASSIMILATION?

Precisely the same interpretation is currently being made by the authors of the Commonwealth Government's National Aboriginal Education Policy (NAEP), who apparently cannot understand why Aborigines are not pleased with a policy which offers them equality – equality of access, of continuance and of performance in relation to education provided by mainstream providers (mainly government schools) – when what they seek is authority to design, administer and deliver an education based upon and compatible with the values and purposes of their own society.

If Aborigines say, 'We ask you for bread for our children and you offer us a stone', we can reply, 'but it's not just a stone – it's the same stone which we give our own children'.

However, with the Woodward Commission's land rights reports (1973, 1974) and the activities of the Whitlam Government (1972–5), there seemed to be a growing recognition that the just and most expedient course would be to recognise the reality of Aboriginal rights in the resources of the land and that they possessed a strong and legitimate culture entitled to be accommodated in a multicultural society. When the Fraser Government endorsed this integrationist approach in its land rights legislation in 1976, in the protection of the Barrier Reef and negotiations with the Torres Strait Islanders for greater autonomy, the way forward seemed clear. But the rise of economic rationalism after the defeat of Malcolm Fraser's Liberal Government saw the return of assimilationist policies. Although the Hawke Government has preserved the words of the Australian Labor Party's statements of policy, in fact its actions accorded with those of Northern Territory and State conservative opinion in withdrawing resources from Aboriginal autonomous action, mainstreaming the provision of services and abandoning its commitment to self-determination, or even self-management, in a significant form. Under the guise of accountability, Aboriginal communities and groups have been flooded with bureaucratic procedures, intrusive inquiries and guidelines for viability, until the purposes of their initiatives have been denied and their autonomy undermined.

The procedures by which the recently launched (26 October 1989) National Aboriginal Education Policy has been developed, its content, its provisions for the allocation of resources and the sanctions to be used to impose its purposes on Aboriginal groups and communities, demonstrate its bureaucratic and assimilationist character. Thus, while Aboriginal consultative groups were encouraged to prepare submissions about the form and content of the policy, their recommendations have been almost wholly ignored; no explanations for the decisions made have been provided to these groups and no genuine negotiations have been conducted.

The NAEP identifies education with what is provided in mainstream government and Catholic schools. There is no provision for the development of alternative programs designed to meet the needs of Aboriginal communities and equip their children for lives which are compatible with and express their own culture. There is no provision for the control of the content of the curriculum by locally-based Aborigines.

There is strong evidence that Aboriginal educational practices developed in their traditional socialisation processes are based on different principles from the instructive style of European education. Aborigines should be free to choose not merely the content of the curriculum, but the media and the teaching methods by which it is presented. The assumption that European procedures are inevitably superior is unwarranted.

The procedures contemplated for the provision of resources amount to the imposition of financial sanctions to ensure the acceptance of assimilationist education. Under the NAEP, agreements will be required between providers of education to Aborigines and the Commonwealth. In accordance with such agreements, supplementary grants (over and above what is provided through the States) will be made on the condition that an education which conforms to the mainstream pattern is delivered and which satisfies periodical reviews by the Commonwealth and States' educational bureaucracy that results equal to those of mainstream providers are progressively being achieved. This is education for a monocultural society where parents and communities are denied the right to determine how their children are to grow up; where innovation, experiment and diversity are suppressed in the interests of commercial corporations. It is to be hoped that Aboriginal parents, communities and teachers will demand that: no provider of education can enter into an agreement with the Commonwealth without effective negotiation (not just consultation) with them; no agreement will be approved which denies them a choice of educational styles, including schools controlled by local Aboriginal residents; and that when agreement cannot be reached by negotiation, independent arbitrators would be appointed who have had educational experience in multicultural societies.

The NAEP demonstrates the arrogant presumptions of our decision makers that we have nothing to learn from Aborigines. In fact, some of the most intellectually stimulating and innovating thinking about education is coming from Aboriginal educators and it is among them that some of the most profound philosophical issues involved are being explored. Above all, the unwillingness of white educators to take effectively into account the view of Aborigines on the socialisation and education of their children is a significant contributor to the conflicts which are producing the severe mental confusion and emotional stress that underlies the problems with which the Royal Commission is concerned.

As a consequence, I propose the following series of recommendations:

- That the NAEP be withdrawn for reconsideration and negotiation.
- That a joint Aboriginal and non-Aboriginal task force be appointed to negotiate a revised basis for the NAEP compatible with the objective stated above.
- That this task force should include, or have effectively available to it, anthropologists and other experts familiar with the socialisation processes of Aboriginal society and with educational experience in multicultural societies.
- That the application of the policy to particular communities be determined by negotiations in which the local Aboriginal people effectively participate.
- That this task force should report, in the first instance, to the House of Representatives Standing Committee on Aboriginal Affairs, on the content and conclusions of its study.
- That pending the revision and renegotiation of the NAEP, agreements under Part Two of the *Aboriginal Education (Supplementary Assistance) Act 1989* be concluded only after negotiations in which appropriate Aboriginal representation has been involved.
- That the task force should, as a separate and prior task, recommend a structure for such agreements to include protection for the rights of Aboriginal groups and for making recommendations in relation to the content and style of the education to be provided under the agreements.

CONCLUSION

The historical process of colonisation has seriously weakened, indeed threatened with destruction, the strong and effective traditional

74

Aboriginal processes of educating and socialising the young. This, and the related failure of the Australian educational system to prepare young white Australians adequately for life in a multicultural society, are major sources of the conflicts which underlie the problems which the Commission is investigating.

The Commonwealth Government has a moral and constitutional obligation to provide Aboriginal groups and communities with resources under their own control to re-establish a system which will maintain and strengthen Aboriginal culture and identity, and equip them with the skills necessary to design their own strategies for life in a multicultural society. The National Aboriginal Education Policy will not serve these purposes and is more likely to intensify than to ameliorate the present conflicts. Strong Aboriginal communities, confident in their own culture and identity, and functioning within a multicultural society which values and respects diversity, should be the objective of Commonwealth, State and Territory educational policy.

7

Aboriginal work and economy

Paper presented to Commissioner P Dodson, Underlying Issues Unit of the Royal Commission into Aboriginal Deaths in Custody, 1990.

There is an assumption continuously propagated by white Australian authorities to Aboriginal people that there are 'jobs' available and that those jobs alone can offer the rewards of the lifestyle Aborigines seek. It is an assumption certainly not proven and its reiteration by whites is designed to persuade Aborigines to accept assimilation into the Australian and international economic systems. It also ignores the probable consequences of such assimilation which often carries with it the social and personal relationships that those systems establish between employer and employee and which, at least tacitly, demand patterns of behaviour and values appropriate to their relative status within it.

There is substantial evidence (Altman 1987; Coombs et al. 1989) that Aborigines often make substantial sacrifices to avoid accepting these relationships and their implications. What can be said is that Aborigines, like other people, want to be purposefully occupied, that they seek and welcome contexts and opportunities which enable them to demonstrate their energy, skills and judgement, and thereby to acquire status among their peers. Anyone who doubts the capacity of Aborigines to work skilfully, purposefully and sustainably should read *Raparapa,* Paul Marshall's (1988) account of the working lives of Fitzroy River Aboriginal drovers, or Anne McGrath's (1987) description of the work undertaken by Aboriginal stockmen and women in the Northern Territory. What can also be said is that Aborigines are generally conscious that in a society in which practically all transactions are articulated through money, they need money to sustain themselves, to fulfil their obligations to their kin and other members of their society, and to achieve their other purposes. They need income, real and in money.

There are, of course, forms of income other than those such as wages and salary which derive from a job; namely, from employment in an enterprise owned by, or conducted for, someone else. More generally, incomes come largely from the proceeds of goods and services sold in the local or the world's markets and it is increasingly clear that a steadily declining proportion of those proceeds go to people employed in their production and distribution, and that a decreasing proportion of the population is dependent wholly on wage income. To illustrate, a pastoralist will breed and pasture cattle on his property and sell them at the market price. He will employ and pay wages to stockmen and others to work for him in these activities. But before he knows whether he has made a profit himself, he must also make payments to others. Besides his employees, he probably hires a helicopter and pilot to muster his cattle; he may contract with a transport company to carry them to the abattoir or point of sale. The charges for these services will include something for wages, but also for the use of the capital equipment. The pastoralist will almost certainly hire an accountant whose fee will depend upon the special skills and knowledge he possesses. He will almost certainly borrow from a bank and possibly from suppliers of equipment and will pay interest and other charges for his loans. In other words, apart from wages and salary for being employed, people can receive income as payment for a service rendered and for the use of property such as land, other natural resources, capital and knowledge. There are some similarities, but also crucial differences between these contractual labour and capital arrangements and the relations to work that Aborigines seek to establish.

ABORIGINAL WORK; WHITE EMPLOYMENT

In Aboriginal society there are transactions or exchanges analogous with those outlined above, which are articulated by the establishment of rights and obligations between the parties concerned. In what way do such Aboriginal transactions differ from those articulated by the wage contract between employer and employee? Transactions within Aboriginal society are generally part of ongoing relationships in which obligations accepted are to some extent mutual and open for renegotiation at any time. Aborigines who work for an Aboriginal 'boss' of an area of land or of a ceremony, expect that person also to 'look after' them in the sense of having an obligation to advance their interests and welfare when called upon. An employer in white society has no such generalised obligation to an employee outside the specific terms of the wage contract.

On the other hand, an Aboriginal employee will be under strong social pressure to accept a whole western work ethic which establishes absolute priority for the demands of the job, requires regularity, dependability, loyalty to one's employer, which encourages the virtues of thrift and accepts the right of the state to extract support for its activities from his or her earnings and to determine the relative value of one kind of work compared with another, indeed, to determine what work is and what must therefore be paid. Aboriginal employees will also be expected to take their place in a hierarchical social structure based upon values alien to Aboriginal society and to place those values ahead of any originating in their own.

As the final report of the East Kimberley Impact Assessment Project emphasises:

> Aborigines do not face the Australian economy with their time fully available for employment or divided simply between 'work' and 'leisure'. Rather they come with their time significantly allocated to Aboriginal purposes and activities. Employment or other involvement in the Australian economy involves a trade-off between the potential to earn cash and a range of such other Aboriginal activities. In some instances the strength of obligations dictated by Aboriginal custom, for example attendance at ceremonies, are in principle absolute, in many powerful and in almost all at least persuasive. (Coombs et al. 1989: 85–6)

In some instances such trade-offs may require the sacrifice of 'real' income: food, materials for artefacts and direct enjoyment of the environment. Judgement concerning these trade-offs is the more difficult to the extent that Aborigines have been dispossessed of land and of access to it, and so have to accept that their traditional way can no longer wholly sustain them and that they no longer possess property which previously enabled them to conclude deals from which they could obtain such sustenance indirectly.

The issue is more important than merely the need to identify a work context which Aborigines find more congenial. Employment, with its involvement in the economic system and the tacit acceptance of white values which it demands of those who accept it, is the most powerful and successful instrument of assimilation. Many Aborigines appear to accept a general drift to being assimilated and to judge their own and their peers' performance by its degree of success within the mainstream economy. But such success does not eliminate the tension which their acceptance creates between their acquiescence and the personal and group autonomy which is part of their heritage. There are also many for whom that autonomy is dominant and who see involvement in mainstream employment as incompatible with Aboriginal identity.

Neither this position, nor that at the other extreme which sees the Aboriginal economic role inevitably and naturally as that of the landless proletariat, need be accepted. There is already evidence that in territories where Aborigines have land rights and the power to negotiate the sharing of resources, mutually acceptable agreements have been made between traditional owners and the corporations wishing to use those resources in ways clearly to the general benefit of the regional mainstream economies within which those lands and resources lie. Also, in contexts closer to wage-style employment, Aborigines are slowly but increasingly earning money incomes as 'self-employed producers', especially in activities based upon traditional Aboriginal skills – as painters, sculptors, designers and potters – creating art and crafts and offering them for sale with increasing financial success and cultural esteem. They appear increasingly as performers – as singers, dancers, instrumentalists and sometimes as participants in more public ceremonies – where the traditional rewards for their participation have been partly commuted into cash. These activities, deriving from Aboriginal skills in the visual, material and performing arts, form a field in which Aboriginal cultural impact on the mainstream society grows daily.

Aborigines, both as individuals and as members of groups, are progressively attempting to Aboriginalise the circumstances of their work. For example, they accept contracts for the performance of rural work on the basis of a fee for the whole job which allows the timing of the work to be at the discretion of the contractor. This procedure involves Aborigines in fencing, the repair and maintenance of wells and windmills, in dam construction, bore sinking, clearing land of feral animals, culling cattle and so on. Increasingly, Aboriginal-controlled resource agencies are acting as brokers in relation to such arrangements, identifying opportunities and individuals or groups who can take advantage of them, and assisting in the negotiation of the terms and conditions of contracts.

LOCAL ABORIGINAL ECONOMIES

Within Aboriginal society itself, services and exchanges which traditionally would have been articulated by the establishment of obligations capable of being called upon, now often have a money element as part of the total deal. In regional centres to which home-land residents come, there are appearing specialist brokers (often relatives), who advise on contacts, procedures and sources of information. It seems that such brokers are often rewarded, in part at least, in money terms. Such micro-enterprises are part of the informal or 'black' economy, providing services which in the mainstream would be included in the service industry sector, be taxed and incorporated into the gross national product. They are of growing importance, both as components in the Aboriginal economy and as instruments whereby, at the margin, that economy filters into and modifies that of the mainstream.

Of special importance can be the activities made possible by the existence of the Community Development Employment Projects

(CDEP) scheme, a community-oriented program sometimes referred to as 'work for the dole'. The uses made of this scheme enable Aborigines to be paid the equivalent of welfare entitlements for work on a part-time basis, while leaving them time to pursue subsistence hunting and gathering and other activities. It also enables the community to acquire valuable capital and equipment from the additional payments in the form of on-costs supplementing the unemployment benefit component. The uses to which the resources of the CDEP scheme have been put range from the unimaginative mission-style work teams cleaning up the immediate camp environment, to activities which not merely add to wage-style money incomes, but which also add to supplies of traditional and other foods and materials, as well as occasional cash from transactions with other groups and the market economy.

There is evidence of intelligent opportunism and structural innovation in the responses of individual CDEP communities to opportunities created by their own needs and interests, and by those observed in the interstices of the mainstream society. The part-time character of CDEP employment offers scope for shared employment and makes it possible for jobs to be divided between persons from different families and groups. These opportunities have been seized upon in many communities and have included:

- support for subsistence hunting and gathering activities, including seed-gathering for sale;
- support for land-care activities including burning, the reduction of feral animals, rounding up uncontrolled stock, and protection and restoration of wildlife resources;
- support for arts and craft training, and production and marketing in the areas of painting, sculpture, screen-printing, fabric and clothing design;
- support for enterprises based on indigenous species such as emu and crocodile farming, and gathering seeds and medicinal plants;
- establishment and conduct of gardens producing foods to supplement and replace imports;
- training, experience and employment in the provision of services

to communities such as in the areas of education, operation of stores, child-care, health work, and building and construction;

- conduct of commercial enterprises including air and other transport services, usually in association with non-Aboriginal charter and contract enterprises; and
- the increasing employment of women in clerical, accounting, administrative and similar work in Aboriginal councils and stores as well as in the extension of culture-based creativity in education, literature and theatre.

These examples suggest that for groups desiring to live in the relative isolation of a homeland context, it is possible with the help of the CDEP scheme to design an economic livelihood which, in addition to providing a minimal cash income, can also achieve greater self-sufficiency and add to the flow of goods and services within the community, so enriching its quality of life. These mini-economies would function in parallel with the mainstream and should not be regarded as a return to some pristine, pre-capitalist way of life. Such small-scale, local economies would certainly identify ways of interacting with the mainstream economy which were compatible with the degree of autonomy different groups seek. Such groups would, for a considerable time, probably be less materially affluent than those more closely incorporated into the mainstream, but this could be offset by greater local control and autonomy. On the other hand, there are homelands in East Arnhem Land which in many ways are materially as rich and also a focus for intellectual innovations that are distinctively Aboriginal.

It is important that these qualities of autonomy and the growing Aboriginalisation of work in such local informal economies be protected from white intrusion in the name of accountability, efficiency and bureaucratic guidelines. The cost of such intrusion in money terms, apart from its social impact, probably far exceeds the benefits. Aborigines still need time to adapt the checks and balances inherent in their own culture to the requirements of a market context, but they are more likely to make them effective than to accept the authoritarian, intrusive intervention of bureaucratic and politically motivated inquiries and studies.

CONCLUSION

The growth of an Aboriginal economy at a more sophisticated level calls for measures to make available to Aboriginal groups a significant share of proceeds of resource-based enterprises currently under non-Aboriginal ownership and control; to restore Aboriginal ownership and access to land; to design the delivery of community services such as education, health, child-care and so on, so that the personnel engaged are Aborigines from the community itself; and generally to establish Aboriginal property rights in the indigenous resources of the continent, enabling them to share in their use and to receive a rental payment from non-Aborigines as a source of capital for their own development. The establishment of such measures could be achieved by agreements between Aboriginal land owners and developers wishing to exploit the relevant resources. Sanctions already available to governments are adequate to ensure that such agreements could be successfully negotiated under the potential supervision of arbitrators.

The recent report of the East Kimberley Impact Assessment Project (Coombs et al. 1989) examines the scope in the Kimberley for measures of these kinds. The resulting changes in the control and use of resources there would not merely strengthen local Aboriginal economies, but would ensure a substantial increase in the benefits to the mainstream economy in the region. In a society of this kind, 'income' would be flowing into the region and into Aboriginal communities in various forms and to different groups and individuals. This flow would strengthen Aboriginal organisations and add to their capacity to provide opportunities for paid activities and for more substantial enterprises on the fringes of the mainstream economy. Such incursions would be made from a position of security not endangering the stability which the homeland movement seeks.

The Aboriginal economy envisaged here would function in parallel and close interaction with the mainstream, not as set apart from it. It would probably be materially less affluent, but would have its own cultural emphasis choosing its own stream of development and the points at which it enters and seeks to influence the mainstream.

The Yirrkala people of East Arnhem Land describe the two streams who make up the Australian people as being like the two streams which flow side by side into Caledonian Bay, one from the sea and one from the land, merging little by little until they both enter the large lagoon but each, even there, retaining much of its own composition and character. This image sees Aborigines as like the gulf stream which flows through the chilly Atlantic, but even after reaching the north-western coast of Europe is influential enough to change the climate of those lands from frozen wastes to green and pleasant land.

Western history is a record of grandiose and expensive programs of migration, land settlement and industrialisation backed by subsidy and protection in the interests of growth. These have depopulated large areas of the Australian continent, driving off the only people who have successfully demonstrated how to live and work there. They have brought those people and an ancient culture to the verge of extinction. It is time we restored to them the right to use the land and its resources in their own fashion. That restoration would go far to restore also the lost balance between their personal and group autonomy and the demands of their social and economic obligations; a loss which lies at the heart of many of the problems facing Aboriginal people today.

Aborigines, Resources and

Development

8

The ideology of development in the East Kimberley

Edited version, originally published in H C Coombs, H McCann, H Ross and N M Williams (eds), 'Land of Promises', Centre for Resource and Environmental Studies, Australian National University and Aboriginal Studies Press, Canberra, 1989.

DEVELOPMENT IN THE EAST KIMBERLEY

In 1988, white Australians promote an illusion that the entire continent of Australia was brought under British control 200 years ago. The East Kimberley region was 'settled', very sparsely, by white Australians just over 100 years ago. Since that time, Aborigines have faced three waves of intensive development which have transformed their existence.

In the first wave during the 1880s, the establishment of pastoral properties, the Halls Creek gold rush and associated services were accompanied by the massacre of many Aborigines and the appropriation of nearly all of their land. The gold rush was short-lived, but the service towns of Wyndham and Halls Creek remained. Aborigines were gradually incorporated into the pastoral operations and small service industries as an unpaid workforce. This lifestyle, though hard, at least allowed them to continue occupancy of their lands and maintain cultural continuity.

During the second wave in the 1950s, large agricultural developments were planned around the damming of the Ord River to create

Lake Argyle. This is the country's largest artificial lake, yet agricultural production based around it has been marginal. Miriwung and Gadjerrong people lost much of their land, including sacred sites, under the lake and through associated works programs. They became marginalised residents of the town of Kununurra, built in the 1960s as the service centre. Kununurra grew, not as an agricultural centre but as an administrative base, largely because it housed the regional airport. As the pastoral industry declined, the Wyndham meatworks closed and port traffic lessened. With the administrative and service role transferred to Kununurra, Wyndham Aboriginal people along with whites suffered the loss of jobs as business revenue and services decreased.

Inland, the accommodation reached between Aborigines and pastoralists was shattered by declining viability and structural change in the pastoral industry, coinciding with legislative change requiring the compulsory payment of award wages from 1968. While the changes for non-Aborigines were gradual, Aborigines felt their impact very suddenly in the mid-1970s when a number of station owners evicted most of the resident workforce and their families. Hundreds of people moved to the fringes of the towns and to a small area of Crown land at Turkey Creek. This had tremendous psychological impact, as it left people without continuous access to their traditional lands, without jobs and at first, without incomes. Again, Aborigines were forced to build up new communities and had to adjust to life as dependants on government welfare payments, given the lack of other sources of income.

In the third wave from 1979, Aborigines were faced with a development boom which began with a burst of exploration activity across the East Kimberley and the development of the Argyle diamond mine. This was followed by rapid growth in tourism, the 'discovery' and promotion of the Bungle Bungles region and growth in the non-Aboriginal population of the area. Aborigines are now contending with these changes while still struggling to re-establish themselves after their removal from the pastoral industry and at the same time dealing with the escalated role of government in the management of their daily affairs.

Aboriginal people of the East Kimberley are determined to avoid being overtaken by changes which are beyond their control. The East Kimberley Impact Assessment Project (EKIAP), with which I was closely involved, arose from their approach to the Centre for Resource and Environmental Studies to find out more about the process of development and for assistance with strategies to deal with the rapid changes occurring in the region. Development in the East Kimberley has resulted in conflict over control of the resources upon which development depends; about the purposes towards which development is and should be directed; and about the relationship between the inhabitants' present needs and their responsibilities for future generations. This continuing conflict has demonstrated that Aborigines and other Australians think about these matters in radically different ways, using concepts which at times seem incommunicable to one another.

THE CREDO OF THE FAITHFUL

What then is meant by development? In its original meaning the word refers to the way a potential is realised. Thus, a child will develop into an adult and a seedling into a mature plant. In these instances the process is inherent, but there are others where action is necessary to achieve realisation, or where it can increase that potential. Thus, a composer can take a melody and develop it into a complex musical pattern. In a similar fashion, Aborigines know that children will not grow properly into adults unless they are 'brought up' and learn from their elders.

The use of the term development in relation to economic matters is relatively new, but in the last few decades it has become dominant in the study of the economy as a system: the ways in which it is organised, responds to external influences and can be modified to change its potential. Processes which are believed to promote an increase in that potential are referred to as development. The conviction that such an increase can be pursued consciously has been based on the experience of the major industrial powers of Britain, Western Europe, North America and Japan. In these economies,

greatly increased material production has been achieved and the subsequent benefits shared by a substantial proportion of their populations. These achievements reflect the ready availability of financial
capital and natural resources, the use of sophisticated technology,
large-scale operation and sophisticated marketing. They also reflect
the benefits these countries, particularly Britain, derived and continued to derive from their leadership in the 'discovery' and the opening
up to trade of the lands of the New World. That trade made possible
great increases in accumulated wealth which provided the financial
capital to launch and sustain the development of the British and
European economies and ensured their continued domination of the
economies of the New World. In effect, the European powers incorporated into their own economic systems much of the productive
potential of the countries of the New World which they colonised
economically and politically.

So impressive have been the effects of this process on these countries
that there has grown up a pattern of beliefs, an ideology, that it could
bring affluence to all countries which apply it. Economists wrote
about it, emphasising the constructive components such as the
accumulation of capital, the growth of organisational and managerial
skills, the development of a science-based technology, and the mobil-
isation of the world's resources and human capacities. Less emphasis
was given to its origins in gross colonial exploitation and to its effects
on the local populations. Economists also drew attention to the
advantages of growth in the scale of operation of an economy not
merely in increasing total output, but in easing the problems in its
management, foreshadowing an age of plenty plagued only by
problems of excessive leisure time. In effect, they became advocates
and apologists of the development ideology.

This advocacy has been so influential that development and
growth have been made the objectives of the economic policies of
practically all governments in the world, including those of Australia,
irrespective of political affiliations. Similarly, policies advocated after
the Second World War by the agencies of the United Nations were
inspired by this ideology. Apparently, it was assumed that to the
extent that unindustrialised countries could be given access, on

appropriate commercial terms or as generously subsidised aid, to the capital, technology and skills of their Euro-American counterparts, they too would match their productive performance. The World Bank, wealthier governments and some commercial banks, particularly those of the United States, joined in lending to third world countries and developing plans to spread the use of contemporary technology. Private firms opened subsidiary and joint enterprises in colonial economies, continuing the process of their incorporation into the expanding, interdependent world system. A form of colonialism also operates within nations, whereby developed regions extract resources and profits from less developed ones. This is referred to as internal colonialism and the East Kimberley is an example.

Historically, the development ideology has been a powerful intellectual and political force. It has changed and is changing the face of the world, including regions such as the East Kimberley. It is important that we understand its rationale and assess the validity of its assertion that development is 'good for everyone'. The foundation of this conviction can be summarised in a series of propositions. It has been said that development brings into production resources previously idle or inadequately used. These resources can be material, such as land and mineral deposits; intellectual, such as inventions and technology; or physical, such as labour capacity and skill. Such production, it is said, adds to goods and services which increase the gross national product and makes possible higher personal incomes and therefore, material wealth.

The benefit of this addition goes first to those involved in the new production as proprietors, providers of financial capital, organisers, workers, sellers of equipment, materials and specialist services and so on; all of whose incomes will tend to be increased. This addition is seen as only the first round of benefits. As shareholders, debenture lenders, employees and suppliers spend their increased incomes they add to the demand for goods and services, generally spreading the benefits through the economic system. These indirect benefits are referred to as multiplier effects. Some whose income is increased, especially those who share in the profits from the new production, will save part of that income, adding to the funds available for investment and making possible a still higher level of production and national wealth. The increased production and related incomes will, according to these propositions, make possible higher yields from income taxes and from royalties charged for the use of publicly-owned assets such as minerals. The proceeds can be used by governments for public purposes, or to reduce other taxes. The effects of this process in the short run will tend to be concentrated in areas and communities where those directly involved in the development reside, but gradually as the indirect effects spread more widely they will, in theory, 'trickle down' to the poorest and most dispersed members of the world economic community.

These propositions provide persuasive support for the development ideology which has been the motivating force for the emergence and growth of the world industrial economy. It has generated material goods of a diversity and on a scale unprecedented in human history and has, for many, provided the basis for a life both rich and satisfying. It continues to underlie the economic policies of most governments and finds wide acceptance among academics, the media and the community generally.

DOUBTS AND HERESIES

Despite this acceptance, development ideology is now being subjected to serious questioning. This questioning is, of course, not entirely new. Classical economists such as Adam Smith, John Stuart Mill, Marx and others all expressed concern about the inevitability of declining levels of profit which would weaken and ultimately destroy the stimulus to investment. Debate about the possibility of a viable 'stationary state' was a consistent part of the literature of their time. The issue was pushed into the background by the colonisation of the New World with its untapped resources and potential markets, but as the frontiers of that world were progressively closed, doubts about development ideology returned with increasing strength. This was greatly stimulated by exercises like those of the Club of Rome, which drew attention to the limits to growth imposed by the now obviously finite natural resources. Boulding, Daley, Commoner,

Henderson, Hirsch, Mishan and others have explored the implications for economic theory and policy, turning back for intellectual stimulus to their classical forebears, while writers like Schumacher, Mumford and Illich have emphasised the adverse human and quality-of-life implications of growth.

In both the United States and Canada, a substantial literature has emerged exploring the potential for consciously applied conservationist policies directed at achieving a sustainable pattern of resource use (see Valaskakis et al. 1977). The report of the World Commission on Environment and Development (WCED 1987) *Our Common Future*, the World Conservation Strategy (IUCN 1980) and the National Conservation Strategy for Australia (Australia 1984) are more recent examples of this concern. This questioning has raised a series of criticisms. In particular, the assumption that increased production of material goods and services will increase well-being is far from proven. The gross national product which purports to measure the output of the economy does not bring into account the loss of exhaustible resources used in achieving that output, nor that parts of the system and perhaps, in the long run, the system itself are inherently non-sustainable:

> Many present efforts to guard and maintain human progress, to meet human needs, and to realise human ambitions are simply unsustainable .... . They draw too heavily, too quickly, on already overdrawn environmental resource accounts to be affordable .... . They may show profits on the balance sheets of our generation, but our children will inherit the losses. (WCED 1987: 8)

It is clear that significant environmental and social costs of the production fall on individuals; resources and institutions external to the enterprise concerned are not paid for from its proceeds and are therefore borne by the community. The increased incomes and wealth from development are concentrated among the owners of property and investable funds, and their influence on the pattern of production does not reflect the desires or needs of the community generally. This concentration often makes previous productive systems obsolete. The people who had been dependent on them are thus condemned to the role of a propertyless proletariat, unequipped for the new system which involves the loss of traditional skills, the destruction of the physical and institutional capital and their rich cultural by-products.

The expectation that the multiplier effect will, in due course, bring about a 'trickle down' of widespread material benefit is not justified; indeed, it appears to lead to increasing affluence at one extreme and a wider spread of poverty and dependence at the other. The world economy which development is creating therefore is characterised by marked contrasts of material welfare; by the destruction of societies based upon hunting and gathering, peasant farming, handicraft and simple manufacturing; by the increasing incidence of unsaleable surpluses in some parts of the world while famine devastates others; and by vast cities growing in population and poverty while the countryside is denuded and degraded.

Judgements about the validity of these criticisms and the weight which policy should give to them will vary widely among persons, communities and social groups. These criticisms are valid and policy changes should be directed at least to mitigate them. However, there is little commercial incentive to the proprietors of the relevant enterprises to introduce or support such changes. As it stands, Aborigines and other residents of the East Kimberley are poorly placed to benefit from the development process in their region as it at present occurs, or seems likely to occur if its course remains unaltered.

ABORIGINAL IDEOLOGY AND DEVELOPMENT

Aborigines in the East Kimberley bring to their experience of development a set of beliefs which carries the authority of religion and ancestral law. Reflecting these beliefs, Aborigines emphasise the continuity of their present experience with that of the past and seek meaning for the present in terms of the past. This often leads them to speak of their environment and lifestyle as essentially immutable and to be suspicious of change, especially when it is rapid, unexpected or immediately obvious in its effects.

Yet Aboriginal life has always been lived in a context of change of varying degrees of intensity. Over millennia the Australian landscape

93

has undergone significant changes not merely in the cyclical fluctuations of drought and rainfall, but also in the coastline itself, the size and location of rivers and the composition of the wildlife and vegetation. In some of these changes Aboriginal activities, particularly the use of fire, have been significant causal factors. To an important degree, the traditional Australian landscape is an Aboriginal artefact, maintained in its 'pristine' form by conscious Aboriginal management.

Aborigines are aware of these changes and their involvement in them. They do not see such awareness as a contradiction of their view of the landscape as immutable. They interpret these large long-term changes as part of the 'working out' of the original intentions of the spiritual and ancestral creators. Their own involvement is seen as giving effect to their responsibility to care for the land established by those creators.

This obligation of stewardship largely determines Aboriginal people's response to environmental change caused by development. Destructive and sudden changes, especially those which contravene the ethics of environmental management prescribed by ancestors, are resented. They are seen as a breach of property rights when their purpose is unknown and permission has not been sought. They also interfere with the proper performance of a duty imposed by spiritual authority. Traditional owners, when they fail to prevent damage, fear retribution by spiritual forces in the form of death, illness or natural disaster. Where damage has happened by inadvertence, or where Aboriginal people have been compelled to accept it, they still see it as a wrong which, in Aboriginal law, should be acknowledged and for which compensation should be made.

Anxiety about environmental damage is intensified by the religious relationship with the environment and its creatures. It is seen as 'wounding' and is responded to emotionally. No one who has witnessed the response, particularly of older Aborigines, to the sight of unexpected damage to the landscape, for instance by bulldozed tracks or test pits, could doubt the obvious pain it engenders.

Where change has the appearance of being 'natural', Aborigines are more likely to accept it. Thus, the progressive degradation of grazed lands in the Ord River catchment region seems to be accepted as 'natural'. It may be that Aboriginal people are aware of the degradation and its causes, but 'play them down' because they too wish to use the land for cattle pasturing. Aborigines in the region appear to accept the presence of introduced animals, some of which have become feral, particularly cattle, donkeys and horses. One reason is that some of these animals have helped fill gaps in the Aboriginal diet previously held by native species now threatened or extinct. They also concede the benefit derived from use of these animals. This is not to suggest that Aboriginal people are unaware of the effects of introduced animals on the environment.

Far from being hidebound by tradition and hostile to change, Aborigines are innovative, flexible and pragmatic. Positive value is attached to change in many aspects of Aboriginal social life, including new art forms and intellectual concepts. Variations in traditional social relationships and religious ceremonies have been passed from group to group. Non-Aboriginal technology has been selectively adopted. Rifles, vehicles for hunting, social and religious purposes and the increasing use of communications media are good examples. Non-Aboriginal social and political organisations have been incorporated into Aboriginal practice and adapted to their own purposes (Sullivan 1988).

Aboriginal people's concern about non-Aboriginal development enterprises, especially their impact on land, is not based exclusively on a sense of possessiveness about resources. Their concept of responsibility for the land has much in common with contemporary principles of sustainable development. The Aboriginal system of land ownership and management encourages access and sharing of resources, provided proprieties are observed and due deference is shown to traditional owners. Resistance is due largely to the unwillingness of non-Aborigines and their governments to respect the prior rights of Aborigines to ownership of the land and to a partnership or reasonable share in its use and benefits, and an unwillingness to recognise the reality of Aboriginal responsibility and stewardship for its care and protection. East Kimberley Aboriginal people have shown themselves willing to consider and often to support development when the proponents approach them correctly.

SUSTAINABLE DEVELOPMENT

Both economic excesses in the exploitation of resources as outlined earlier, and Aboriginal reservations about the proper treatment of the environment, could be avoided through the adoption of principles of sustainable development. According to the report of the WCED:

> In essence, sustainable development is a process of change in which the exploitation of resources, the direction of investments, the orientation of technological development, and institutional change are all in harmony and enhance both current and future potential to meet human needs and aspirations. (1987: 46)

The achievement of sustainable development would require concentration on renewable resources, avoidance of degradation and reliance on forms of development which benefit the local economy and people in preference to the national or international one. It also requires long-term maintenance of the stock of biological resources and the productivity of agricultural systems, stable human populations, limited growth economies and an emphasis on small scale and self-reliance (Brown et al. 1987).

Many natural resources are exhaustible; their use involves a reduction of the economy's capital. Current accounting practices and pricing regimes, by failing to include this reduction, provide government and industry policy makers with false signals and give an impression of substantial economic growth when in fact the region and the country may be becoming poorer in real terms. To assess income properly in the national accounts, the value of the reduction of existing resources should be deducted from the proceeds of the sale of the extracted resources. Only if the resources remaining are vast or renewable would the deduction from income be unimportant. As Repetto (1985) points out, a country could exhaust its mineral resources, cut down its forests, erode its soils and hunt its wildlife and fisheries to extinction, but measured income would rise steadily as these assets disappeared.

This description could be aptly applied to developments in the East Kimberley. The WCED (1987: xii) has characterised much development in the industrialised nations as 'clearly unsustainable'. It is perhaps not too late for a new way to be found in the East Kimberley that incorporates principles of sustainable development.

> A conserver society, which could evolve from our present society, would develop its economy in harmony with, rather than in opposition to, our environment ... based on the ethic of stewardship, a feeling of responsibility for conserving the natural resources .... [T]here would still be selective economic growth ... [and] a commitment to sustainability. (Chittleborough and Keating 1987: 50)

FUTURE PROSPECTS

The analysis here suggests that if development in the East Kimberley continues in its present pattern, and especially if that pattern is encouraged and supported by government, there is a risk that it may result in the denudation of many of the region's natural resources. It is also probable that the bulk of the current benefits of activities associated with development and the possible capital assets it could finance would flow to other parts of the Australian and international economies. This risk is independent of the probable damaging effect on Aboriginal people. There is a clear need, from the point of view of the Australian economy as a whole, for a reconsideration of the principles on which the development of the East Kimberley and other parts of the north are based. This is particularly so given, as stated earlier, that all options for resource development are not yet known.

The present is not a time for dramatic action, but rather for careful study of experience so far and for basic research and small-scale experiment to test possible options. In the selection of such options, primary emphasis should be given to the long-term environmental and economic sustainability of each activity being tested. Approval of any proposal to exploit exhaustible natural resources should be dependent on evidence that a significant proportion of its proceeds will flow to the East Kimberley region and will be available as capital for sustainable enterprises there and in the Australian economy generally. To this end, special royalties could be imposed on the exploitation of exhaustible resources with exemption for proceeds devoted to the development of sustainable alternatives. There is need for extensive research into the potential for exploitation of the indigenous species of the region, both as a direct source of livelihood and as a source of cash income for the inhabitants.

Development in the East Kimberley has resulted in conflict over control of the resources on which development depends, over the purposes of such development, and about the relationship between Aboriginal people's present needs and their responsibilities for future generations. Further, the East Kimberley Impact Assessment Project's research indicates that if the present pattern of development continues with the support and encouragement of governments, there is a risk amounting almost to certainty that it will result in the denudation of the region's natural resources; benefits will flow to other parts of the Australian and international economies; and that damage to the prospects of a sustainable economic future for the Aboriginal and other residents of the region will continue.

CONCLUSION

Clearly, Aborigines in the East Kimberley would be unwise to rely heavily on the expectation of increasing employment and other benefits from the contemporary pattern of enterprises in the region. These are capital intensive, technologically and administratively complex and their focus of decisions will continue to be elsewhere, in places to which the major proportion of the rewards will flow. Aboriginal skills and preferences will find little scope within them.

A wide range of EKIAP–sponsored research revealed that the probability of economic development bringing the human and material resources of the Kimberley region and the country into the interdependent world system, in ways which would increase the financial and material well-being of local Aboriginal communities, was grossly overestimated. The project's final report (Coombs et al. 1989) emphasises that sustainability must weigh more heavily in the economic criteria of policy, not merely for Aborigines, but for Australians generally.

As a policy and action-oriented study, EKIAP advocated that:
- the techniques of impact assessment – economic, environmental and social – can be valuable if employed in the context of regional plans before and during new developments;

- Aborigines should be involved in the assessment programs and account taken of their needs and aspirations, their knowledge and their skills;
- assessments conducted by, or for, the protagonists of commercial and government projects are frequently biased;
- there is a need for universities and other independent research agencies to develop the techniques of these assessments, to stand ready to conduct them and to subject their results to competent peer assessment; and
- there are increasing benefits in transferring control of social programs such as those concerned with education, health and housing to local community-based Aboriginal organisations with access to adequate resources. This is not to suggest that their programs should be free from financial and other forms of accountability, but to recognise that improvement in performance must come from within them.

Central to Aboriginal concerns in the East Kimberley is a practical consideration of the options open both to the Aborigines themselves and to governments to develop a comprehensive strategy for progressively reducing their poverty and dependence and increasing their capacity to control their own lives. Fundamental to this strategy is the restoration of the means to a livelihood of which dispossession robbed them and the establishment and support of political and administrative instruments under Aboriginal control necessary to give effect to their strategies. If economic development is to benefit Aborigines in the Kimberley region and throughout Australia, it must incorporate activities under their own control, making use of their own skills and it must be compatible with Aboriginal concepts of just relationships between people and with their choice of lifestyle.

9

Aborigines and resources: from 'humbug' to negotiation

Edited version of the second Kenneth Myer Lecture presented to the Friends of the National Library of Australia, Canberra, 29 October 1991. Subsequently published in the Friends of the National Library of Australia Series, Canberra, 1991.

CONTROL OF RESOURCES

The first phase of the battle between Aborigines and settlers for the control of resources was concerned with the widely ranging pastoral lands. The victory, apparently at least, has been with the settlers. Right across the south and east they occupied the country changing its character from open woodlands to pastured rangelands while the Aboriginal population was progressively being substantially eliminated by disease, by killings and by despair. In those areas, Aboriginal people survived as fringe dwellers, the fragments of once-vigorous societies on the outskirts of white society, their culture and coherence often destroyed or seriously impaired. In the north, the outcome was slightly different. In the face of defeat Aborigines in effect offered a compromise: to share the right of occupation and to accept the role of an unpaid, but supported workforce.

This compromise enabled them to continue their traditional hunter-gatherer way of life for significant periods during the year and to continue their religious, ceremonial and cultural life relatively unhindered. Their compromise allowed them to maintain their own sense of identity with the land and its physical and spiritual components. For the rest, a relatively stable quiescent relationship emerged enabling Aborigines the choice of withdrawing into relative isolation from the white community, or being drawn into it to live on its fringes. They camped on distant parts of pastoral leases and Crown lands practically ignored by all; they camped on the fringes of towns or crowded into city ghettoes, and in some areas were brought into missions and government settlements. These marginal environments ensured their virtual invisibility and that they could be ignored by the non-Aboriginal population.

This relative separation of white and black continued until the Second World War. When the threat of invasion by Japan developed they were freely recruited, mainly into auxiliary units engaged in paramilitary, coast watch and construction and, interestingly, into special 'irregular' units secretly recruited and commanded by two anthropologists, Bill Stanner and Donald Thomson. In these activities they often experienced substantial equality in food, working conditions and occasionally pay. When the war ended, this experience made impossible a simple return to their pre-war status, especially on cattle properties. In the Pilbara, Aborigines 'walked off' the stations, resuming a hunter-gatherer way of life supplemented by the proceeds of small-scale alluvial mining under the guidance of the legendary Don McLeod. On cattle leases in the Northern Territory they began to demand money wages. The practice spread. Aborigines 'pushed off' by pastoralists unwilling to meet these demands were moving, or being moved, to larger population centres seeking paid employment or government assistance.

Of more importance was the change in the management of the pastoral industry stimulated by technology acquired through wartime experience, and the influence of practices of large corporate enterprises from abroad and the access to capital which that brought. Fenced and bore-watered paddocks, the use of motor vehicles and an impersonal cash relationship with a greatly reduced workforce was a more attractive proposition than the paternal and personalised responsibility of owner-manager pastoral leases where the relationship was more intimate and mutually dependent. Properties with corporate management whose decision makers were distant and guided by more financial criteria were especially reluctant to accept any responsibility for the families and dependants of the Aboriginal workers (Berndt and Berndt 1987). By such historical processes of dispossession, Aboriginal people were progressively marginalised from their traditional control of land and its resources in many areas of Australia.

LEGISLATING FOR ABORIGINAL RIGHTS

Ad hoc government responses hinted at the direction of change without providing a clear basis for policy. Commonwealth, State and Territory Governments extended Aboriginal access to social security benefits and citizenship rights. The entry of the Commonwealth into Aboriginal affairs as a new source of funding led to special action to improve Aboriginal children's access to education and health, and to provide funds for Aboriginal enterprises, including the purchase of land for pastoral and community enterprises. But in the meantime, movement towards a political settlement began to emerge from the acknowledgment that prior discovery and long occupation had provided a basis for the recognition of Aboriginal proprietary rights. Judge Blackburn, despite his adverse judgement in the Gove case (Milirrpum and others v. Nabalco and the Commonwealth) in 1971, gave his support for political action to satisfy the claims of the Yirrkala clans to the land concerned.

With the election in 1972 of the Whitlam Government and the report of the Woodward Commission, the *Aboriginal Land Rights (Northern Territory) Act 1976* legislation was enacted by the Commonwealth. A new consideration had, in the meantime, shifted the focus of attention from Aborigines in relation to the pastoral industry, to demands of mining enterprises for access to Aboriginal land. The rapid growth already underway and the anticipation of a resources boom which was exciting great commercial interest, both within Australia and among the multinational corporations operating around the world, was establishing the basis for massive developments here.

The Northern Territory land rights legislation recognised certain Aboriginal rights to land and granted them inalienable freehold tenure to lands previously reserved for their use, and it afforded

Aboriginal people the right to claim unalienated Crown lands to which they could establish title under specific criteria. It required that the traditional owners of the land concerned understand the nature and purpose of any proposed development project and, as a group, consent to it, and further required that any Aboriginal group or community 'affected' by the proposed development be consulted and have an adequate opportunity to express their views. While preserving the traditional right of the Crown to title in all minerals, the legislation established, in effect, an Aboriginal right to a share in royalties paid by miners to the government and the right to negotiate for an additional share as the price of their acquiescence to development on land in which they had rights. Part of the Aboriginal share in the royalties was to be available to land councils representing the traditional owners, especially in negotiations with miners.

THE MINING INDUSTRY RESPONSE

The Northern Territory legislation was met with great hostility by the mining companies. They resented the impact on their profits of the need to share their proceeds with Aboriginal traditional owners and they especially resented the use of their payments to support land councils which were showing that in negotiations they could mobilise expertise and bargaining capacity to match those of the companies themselves.

Highly organised and expensive campaigns based upon material which many observers found distasteful were stark examples of the mining industry's capacity to resort to 'humbug' in defence of their depredations. Furthermore, in Western Australia they demonstrated in the negotiations leading to the so-called Argyle Diamond Mine Agreement that, in the absence of the support of a land council and without access to professional advice, Aborigines were left to deal with the persuasive might of a multinational company and induced to accept a 'beads and axes' settlement. This settlement does not begin to approach standards set by companies negotiating under the Northern Territory land rights legislation, or in comparable conditions in other countries such as the USA, Canada and Papua New

103

Guinea. Indeed a recently published book, *Aborigines and Diamond Mining*, edited by R A Dixon and M C Dillon (1990), both independent observers of the events leading to that agreement, raised grave doubts about the legality and professional propriety of actions occurring during those processes. A number of these instances were brought to the attention of the Royal Commission on Government and Commercial Enterprises in Western Australia, but generally were thought to be outside the Commission's terms of reference.

An aspect of the political campaigns being conducted on behalf of the mining industry is the frequent misuse of statistical information to exaggerate the contribution of the industry to the Australian economy. The outstanding example is the use of the total value of mineral exports as a measure of foreign exchange earned and available to finance imports and other charges. In fact, the industry itself is an extensive user of foreign exchange for purchases of equipment, stores and services abroad; for the payment of royalties for foreign-owned patents, processes and similar rights; and for the service of borrowings and the remittance to foreign shareholders of dividends representing a major share of the profits. The net foreign exchange earned would be substantially less than the gross proceeds from the sales of the minerals exported. In addition, those earnings would have been derived from the sale of non-sustainable capital assets. Some of these, such as gold and some of the diamonds, appear to have a very high degree of potential for recycling, but the proceeds of those used by industry or sold abroad and used to finance current expenditure, represent a reduction in the national wealth of the country and reduce our future productive capacity.

There is currently, I note, extensive propaganda urging the expansion of investment (especially by foreign capital) in mining as a stimulus to employment. It should be noted that measured by jobs per unit of capital costs, the location of minerals prospected, the capital-intensive processes of both the mining itself and the processing of the raw products, money spent in expanding the mining industry produces a minimum of jobs. Some years ago, a competent economic study (O'Faircheallaigh 1986) of the effect on employment and economic activity of the uranium industry on the economy of the

Northern Territory concluded that the only significant benefit to that economy came from the expenditure by Aborigines and their organisations of the money paid to them by mining companies under the terms of the Commonwealth's land rights legislation. Those wishing to see our economy providing more employment opportunities would do better to emphasise the expansion of solar, wind and tidal sources of energy which are labour and skill-intensive and which would reduce our and the world's dependence on exhaustible, environmentally threatening and health-damaging products of the mining sector.

It is characteristic of the skilful use of 'humbug' by our new corporate colonisers that they have been able to dominate our governments, their bureaucracies, the media and political organisations; that they can propagate these 'misunderstandings' so favourable to their current corporate financial interests; and that they can apparently be questioned no more than holy writ. Or perhaps it is simply that information which might call them into question is held by them and access to it is denied. Attempts by academic researchers to obtain access to this information about the patterns of mining company expenditures which would give some precision to, for instance, their net foreign exchange contribution to the Australian economy, referred to above, have been met with blunt refusal or 'the cold ignore' from companies, even when they have Commonwealth or State Government backing. In fact, both Commonwealth and State Governments seem to be behaving as if they were departments of the bureaucracy of a united transnational corporation aiming for the exhaustion of the mineral and energy resources of the earth.

SIGNS OF CHANGE?

Recently, there have been signs of change. Some mining companies have at last realised that many Aboriginal communities are not opposed absolutely to mining, but on the contrary, are anxious to negotiate with them for participation compatible with the protection of their environmental, spiritual and economic concerns and are demonstrating this in their responses to mining enterprise approaches.

Also, a recent report from the Commonwealth Industry Commission (1991) has proposed:

- the legal recognition of Aboriginal title to minerals within Aboriginal land;
- the modification of the land rights laws to encourage direct negotiation between mining enterprises and Aboriginal traditional owners; and
- that land councils should be financed directly from the Commonwealth, not by payments as equivalents to a share of royalties received by the government, but directly for the performance of functions (such as identification of relevant traditional owners in particular instances) and that they should no longer be the agent for the conduct of negotiations on behalf of Aboriginal communities.

There is potential virtue in each of these suggestions, but also evidence of the clever use of 'humbug'.

The recognition of Aboriginal ownership would certainly create conditions which would maximise the chances of early and extensive access by miners to known and presumed reserves of minerals. There could be benefits from negotiations between mining enterprises and Aboriginal communities and there is no reason why payments to land councils for the performance of functions imposed on them by the Commonwealth Parliament should be linked with, or dependent upon, royalties received. They should logically be met from consolidated revenue on a scale comparable with standards set by public service practice. However, it is clear that:

- Aborigines, their organisations, environmentalists and economists (other than the so-called 'economic rationalists') fear that those measures will succeed in maximising the rate of access to mineral reserves, depleting their availability for the long-term future and maximising the environmental damage and disruptive effects on Aboriginal society;
- Aborigines, their organisations and their friends fear that mining companies in the conduct of direct negotiations will take advantage of their overwhelming bargaining capacity to achieve agreements which no reasonably informed or equipped

community would accept; that is, that negotiations would probably be accompanied by activities of at best doubtful propriety and could, at worst, provide temptation for bribery, secret access, political intervention and corruption of public officials and professional experts;

- Aboriginal communities and their organisations fear that through these direct negotiations companies would seek to establish relationships with individuals and groups in those communities of the kind which would enable the companies to exercise an influence incompatible with Aboriginal autonomy and the maintenance of Aboriginal cultural life; and

- land councils and other Aboriginal-controlled organisations fear that the proposal to finance their functions directly from the Commonwealth budget would be used, as it has been in the past, as an instrument to whittle away their independence and competence and indeed, weaken all parts of the Aboriginal-controlled administrative and executive structures financed from the budget.

In the meantime, in Western Australia almost the whole of the Aboriginal, Crown and leased lands in the north, centre and eastern shires of the State are the subject of applications from mining companies to explore or to mine. Community after community is being pressed into direct negotiations and there are disturbing, but often unverifiable reports and rumours about 'humbug' behaviour reminiscent of practices described by Dixon and Dillon (1990). It is a situation which can best be described as a failure of society to provide a framework for peace, order and good government in the relationship between black and white Australians in those regions.

NEGOTIATING FUTURE RIGHTS

It is a matter of extreme urgency that procedures be established to control the activities of corporations seeking access to lands or resources in which Aborigines have proprietary interests, which will avoid or prevent their 'humbug' practices and establish a basis for negotiation. Such procedures would need to ensure that Aboriginal groups and communities have access to information and expertise comparable with that available to miners and that scope was provided for the consideration of public environmental and sustainability concerns.

Aborigines are not absolutely opposed to mining, even if they would prefer that it did not occur. They have, I believe, developed a pattern of response to mining projects which, in the light of their fears, is rational and comprehensible. Evidence suggests that they want to:

- control the use of the land with which they identify so as to prevent intrusion into areas important to their cultural and ceremonial life;
- limit the non-Aboriginal presence to numbers which do not threaten the realities of their relationship with the land;
- conduct their own affairs essentially at arm's length from those involved in the mining project with an emphasis on residence in, or the opportunity to escape to, homeland communities where they have substantial privacy and autonomy and where the traditional component in their lifestyle can be maintained;
- be satisfied that their environment is adequately protected in its physical and spiritual aspects; and
- be compensated financially at levels consistent with fair practice in comparable situations elsewhere in Australia and internationally.

Acceptance of these objectives is not, in my view, incompatible with the development of a program of resource exploitation. To some extent, their achievement by Aborigines will require time. They cannot withdraw to homelands if these are unable to sustain them, and minimum facilities will be required before mining activities can fairly begin. This minimum need not be extravagant: an ensured water supply, radio communication with centres providing essential health, education and similar services and basic means of transport would be sufficient for a start. But, without them, the independence necessary for Aboriginal people to consider the issues will be lacking.

If the Aboriginal interest in land and resource rights is to be recognised and if their priorities are to be accommodated so that programs of resource exploitation can be carried out with their freely-given consent and collaboration, the basic requirement is for a change in the attitude of white society, its government and its commercial institutions. Such a change will need to show itself in a recognition of Aboriginal rights to land, in a respect for their traditional values and culture, in a willingness to deal with them frankly and fairly and to stand by commitments. Such a change of attitude would mean national legislation by the Federal Government recognising Aboriginal land rights. It would mean the restoration of an effective Aboriginal right of veto to mining proposals (subject only to a genuine emergency national interest provision), the establishment of procedures which would guarantee Aboriginal land owners and affected communities the time and information necessary to fully understand such proposals, and the time and resources to give effect to their own plans to protect the integrity of their own society before mining activities occurred.

Whether or not such action is taken by government, enterprises wishing to undertake resource exploitation within land with which Aborigines identify would be wise to proceed as if such changes had been made. I suggest that they would need to:

- acknowledge and support Aboriginal claims to title to land of which they can demonstrate ownership in Aboriginal law and tradition;
- identify through appropriate representative organisations the traditional owners of the land with which they are concerned and work out effective and respectful relationships with them and any organisations they establish;
- arrange with those land owners for any exploratory teams to be accompanied by the owners' representatives to tell them where they can go without intrusion and to be guided by this advice;
- find out what plans Aborigines themselves have to deal with the effects of the enterprise's plans and to support these plans, without seeking to take them over;
- delay developments if necessary to allow Aborigines to give effect to these plans, at least to the minimum degree necessary to ensure their subsequent practicability; and

- arrange for independent monitoring of the impact of their activities on Aboriginal communities and be willing to adapt their activities to take account of the results so monitored.

A policy based upon these principles of negotiation would appear exceptional only by contrast with present practice. In comparison with the knowledge, intelligence and resources which are frequently devoted to the solution of technological, marketing and public relations problems, its costs would be minor. It calls primarily for a willingness to modify the ethnocentric arrogance of western society and for a realisation that the purpose of economic activity is the welfare of human beings. I wish I could see signs of such willingness.

10

The McArthur River
development: a case in point

Edited version, unpublished paper originally presented at the Centre for Aboriginal and Islander Studies, Northern Territory University for the 20th anniversary of the North Australian Research Unit, Australian National University, Darwin (1993).

ISSUES OF CONCERN

At the conclusion of a comprehensive, multidisciplinary study of the impacts of resource development on Aboriginal communities in the East Kimberley region, the project researchers recommended that:

Approval of any proposal to exploit exhaustible natural resources should be dependent on evidence that a significant proportion will flow to the East Kimberley region and will be available as capital for sustainable enterprises there and in the Australian economy generally. (Coombs et al. 1989)

In stark contrast to this recommendation, the discussions following the High Court's judgement on the Mabo case have almost exclusively been conducted with a view to establishing the effect of native title upon the mining industry. This single-issue focus has had the result that many other concerns, both environmental and social, have been ignored in the process. This is clearly evident in circumstances surrounding the McArthur River mine development, near the settlement of Borroloola in the Northern Territory Gulf country, where

111

Mount Isa Mines plan to exploit massive lead and zinc deposits. Reports of preliminary discussions between Aboriginal land owners and government and community lawyers, have led to the provisional conclusion that an agreement with the company could be possible without requiring extinguishment of native title.

But concern about the possible impact of the project on native title is only a part of the problems posed by the McArthur River project. It would profoundly affect the natural environment and a number of other authorities express great concern about the social and physical condition of the Aboriginal community, their traditional culture, way of life and especially the health, education and livelihood prospects of the children (Altman et al. 1993; Niblett 1993). Furthermore, it remains uncertain whether the project is compatible with a strategy for a sustainable economic future for the region, even if it is capable of full development.

FAST-TRACK DEVELOPMENT

It is apparent that environmental and related concerns have been overridden in government and private sector zeal to fast-track the process (a euphemism for ignoring all considerations other than those raised by the mining company). The official environmental impact assessment took only nine weeks to carry out and has been 'roundly condemned by environmental scientists, academics, environmentalists, Aboriginal organisations and commercial fishing groups' (Jackson and Cooper 1993: 8).

There has been no attempt to assess the social impact of the mine upon the Kurdandji, Mara and Yanyuwa people who use the area and frequent the isolated settlement of Borroloola. This emphasises the ill-considered process within which this 'agreement' has been generated. Evidence of any long-term economic benefit has not been presented or examined. There has been only the assumption that this kind of development is to the economic and financial benefit of all Australians. Indeed, the Federal and Northern Territory Governments, in their zeal to facilitate the corporate arrangements, appear to have found it necessary to offer concessions to the developers likely to cost taxpayers many millions of dollars (ibid.: 8).

The assumption that mining is of automatic cost-benefit is one that needs to be questioned closely and about which mining enterprises continue to deny access to information. The environmental costs too, in many cases, have yet to be factored into the cost-benefit equations. Examples of the Territory Government's existing relationship with the mining industry and the environment provide a grim track record not only of environmental damage, but of financial and political corruption and financial costs to the community as well. The uranium development at Rum Jungle was abandoned early in its projected development, leaving the area a wasteland, the Finnis River biologically dead for some 75 kilometres and requiring a clean-up and rehabilitation program costing the taxpayer some $16.2 million that is, as yet, incomplete (Coombs 1990b: 99–102). The area of Captains Flat near the Australian Capital Territory required similar recuperative measures to attempt to abate the heavy metal pollution of the Molonglo River, with associated costs to be borne by the New South Wales and Commonwealth Governments. The damage to the environment is serious enough, but the neglect of these and similar costs to the taxpayers should be added to them.

Whose responsibility is it going to be to clean up after the McArthur River development? In the government's haste to fast-track the development approval process, we have yet to see an undertaking from the mining venturers that any such costs can and will be borne by them. In many other instances where no specific provision has been made about responsibility for the clean-up operations, the burden has fallen on the taxpayer or has simply been ignored, leaving an environmental wasteland with soils and waters poisoned by the residue of chemical processing. The valley of the Mongarlowe, near Braidwood in New South Wales (an erstwhile gold mining township), provides an example where local shires fear the impact of that poisoning on possible future developments.

A PREFERRED PROCEDURE

The procedures required for permission to conduct mining developments are inadequate to satisfy responsible economic, social and environmental standards. For these reasons I have set out below a series of procedures which I feel should be followed before any negotiations about resource and other developments with traditional owners of land take place. Before any negotiation with traditional owners takes place it is important that the following procedure should be followed:

- Any enterprise seeking permission to conduct a mining development should be required to submit detailed estimates of the economic, financial, social and environmental costs and benefits to the region, Australia and to the rest of the world. Thus, estimates of the gross proceeds from minerals expected to be produced annually for the first decade should show the payments which would provide income for employees, suppliers of materials and equipment, commercial and professional services, and shareholders in corporations providing capital who are residents of the region, Australia and the rest of the world. Professional opinion should be provided as to whether those estimated incomes to be received would cover costs of insurance against possible future compensation claims for damage to health and disturbance to environment and property, and whether they would provide an adequate benefit to the levels of regional and national employment and income, to justify the benefits sought by the company.

- Any mining enterprise wishing to explore within lands in which Aborigines have interests shall apply to the relevant Aboriginal and Torres Strait Islander Commission (ATSIC) regional council for permission to negotiate with the responsible Aboriginal group or community.

- The elected members of that council shall, in consultation with the group or community concerned, satisfy itself that the appropriate traditional owners have been fully consulted; that it is the wish of the group or community that the negotiations proceed; and that the group or community will be represented by an appropriate Aboriginal-controlled organisation, such as a land council or other independent body with access to a range of professional advice.

- Further, to ensure that all environmental and economic considerations have been properly assessed, it should be made clear that the grant of approval to explore an area for minerals should carry no automatic right to an approval to mine; that before an approval to mine is granted tenders should be called for applications for such approval; that a tender should be accepted only from enterprises which have concluded an agreement with the traditional indigenous owners of the land, in terms equivalent to the best international practice; and should only be accepted on condition that the enterprise demonstrates a willingness to accept environmental standards set by appropriate regulatory authorities and a guaranteed capacity to bear an appropriate share of the audited costs of the exploration.

- If so satisfied, the ATSIC regional council shall inform the appropriate Aboriginal land trust (currently operating over Aboriginal lands in the Northern Territory, but potentially Australia-wide subsequent to the enactment of the *Native Title Act 1993*) of its recommendation, for their consideration of any application for a permit to enter the relevant lands. The council shall require that it be kept informed of the progress of the negotiations and of the terms of any provisionally agreed settlement, before the settlement is confirmed.

- The council will refuse to endorse or recommend acceptance of any provisional agreement not conducted in accordance with the above principles and will make its refusal known to the Commonwealth and State Governments and their agencies, to other ATSIC regional councils and Aboriginal land councils in the State.

- Any agreement between a mining enterprise and an Aboriginal group or community will be registered with the relevant regional council and be accompanied by a statutory declaration on behalf of the enterprise that no payments or other benefits have been made, delivered or promised to any person, for any reason, in respect of the agreement other than those specified in the agreement.

- Any Aboriginal person or group believing that an agreement

115

has been improperly reached, or denies them natural justice, may lodge a complaint with the regional council concerned which shall consider the complaint and may refer it to an appropriate judicial authority for action.

- All information arising from such exploration should be fully available to the government concerned and the applicants for a permit to mine. In the event of a failure to reach agreement with the traditional owners of the relevant land, an enterprise may appeal to arbitrators agreed to by the parties and approved by a tribunal constituted by agreement.

CONCLUSION

None of these issues, post-Mabo, can be properly considered when the debate continues to focus outside the important areas. In the long run, you cannot speed up the process of resolution by ignoring the data available, or by ignoring the issues. When the appropriate procedures are in place and the proper standards set up, then and only then, should negotiations between Aboriginal people and developers proceed. Minerals will not cease to be valuable and available for future generations if they are left in the ground. The capital to be employed in their exploitation in haste can usefully be employed elsewhere in sustainable economic enterprises and to reduce the interest and related cost of other forms of development.

Aborigines, Law and the State

11

The Yirrkala proposals for the control of law and order

Edited version of chapter nine from H C Coombs, M M Brandl and W E Snowdon, 'A Certain Heritage: Programs for and by Aboriginal Families in Australia', Centre for Resource and Environmental Studies Monograph No. 9, CRES, Australian National University, Canberra, 1983.

ABORIGINAL SOCIAL CONTROL

There is a strong tendency among members of white Australian society to think of the maintenance of law and order exclusively in terms of its own processes: of a codified set of laws, enforced by a State police and judicial system, with the ultimate sanction of the State's exclusive right to impose punishment by violence and even death. However, many smaller societies achieve the order and regularity necessary for social life without such mechanisms and in ways which place greater emphasis on consensus and less upon coercion. In such societies there is often no ruler or body exercising apparent authority and no clearly stated rules or laws. In them, order depends upon an understanding of how the day-to-day activities are to be arranged and of what are acceptable and unacceptable forms of conduct. There must, for instance, be socially accepted norms regulating interpersonal violence, sexual relations, sharing of food and the management of scarce and valuable resources. These norms reflect the structure of the society: how relationships between people are traced; whom they do and do not marry and the ways in which status and property devolve. This understanding develops in individuals as part of the process of growing up; the process of socialisation which leads up to the transition to adult status and continues through life. Ceremonies form an important component of this process. They serve not merely to enable individuals to acquire the necessary understanding, but also to smooth the path through difficult transitions and so cement the unity of the group.

Traditional Aboriginal societies were of this kind. In them, a mutual assessment of individual opinion and reactions was an important regulator of behaviour. Fear of disapproval expressed through ridicule, loss of prestige, physical retaliation, sorcery, the withdrawal of valued co-operation, or even through total ostracism, provided the basis of self-regulated conduct. Of course all is not sweetness and harmony in such societies. They vary widely in the degree of conflict which is tolerated. In some, aggressiveness within acceptable limits is given a positive value, but generally those limits are clear and prevent cumulative violence likely to disrupt the unity of the group. But in all there will be disputes and processes for their resolution, generally based upon social pressure exerted on the offender to conform to acceptable patterns of behaviour.

Thus, in a small traditional Aboriginal community an aggrieved person would rise early in the camp, parade up and down between the bush shelters, proclaiming loudly the nature of his grievance and charges against those responsible, rattling his spears and beating on his shield to lend emphasis to his words. In all the shelters there would be discussion of this proclamation and families would confer about it. Gradually, a consensus would develop about what had in fact happened, who was culpable and what should be done about it. Leaders in the development of this consensus would include senior members of the families or clans of the alleged offender and of the aggrieved party. In due course, the content of the consensus would be made clear and the action expected communicated to the parties. The consequences of failure to act in conformity with the consensus, in terms of disapproval expressed in a variety of ways, would usually be sufficient to resolve disputes.

Disputes between groups or communities were more difficult to settle, but occasions when groups came together for shared ceremonies were regarded as opportunities for their resolution. Senior men and women of the groups concerned met to discuss the issues in the conflict and to evolve a basis for agreement. The objective was not so much to determine guilt and allot punishment, as to restore normal relationships between the groups and to remove the source of potential conflict in the future.

THE IMPACT OF WHITE LAW

In Aboriginal society elaborate, complex and well-established mechanisms and procedures exist to maintain social orders. These systems of customary law have been gravely interfered with by the legal system prevailing in wider Australia, to which Aborigines have been made subject. The now historically entrenched and tragic relationship (or misunderstanding) that Aborigines have with the white Australian legal system has had several destructive results on the once effective Aboriginal measures of self-control, including:

- the power of Aboriginal families and groups to apply self-regulation has declined, sometimes because their social control mechanisms are viewed with repugnance or as illegal, and sometimes because their function has been inadequately usurped by white laws;
- our insistence, even in law, on the rights of the individual over the rights of the family or the clan has brought conflict at times, and distress between younger Aborigines seeking to assert themselves and older Aborigines seeking to assert Aboriginal law;
- Australian laws applied against Aborigines use power without accepting responsibility for the consequences of its use;
- the high rates of imprisonment among Aborigines and their consequent absence from the socialising influences of kin. The life of their families – parents, spouse, children – are likewise disrupted. Additionally, Aborigines who value their rights to be with kinsfolk regard with repugnance our punishment by imprisonment. Their repugnance is arguably better founded than ours, where corporal punishment is concerned. Death excepted, a physical punishment involves a short-term distress. Imprisonment,

separation from one's social network and isolation (physical and cultural) cause long-term distress;

- the anti-social consequences of imprisonment upon institutionalised Aborigines where they are socialised into prison behaviour, not re-integrated or re-socialised as they would be under Aboriginal customary law;
- inadequate legal representation until the advent in the last decade of Aboriginal legal aid services;
- the still inadequate linguistic representation in court for many people from remote Aboriginal communities; and
- the non-recognition of Aboriginal customary law has often resulted in an Aboriginal being punished twice for the same offence and conversely, sometimes escaping punishment altogether.

The Yirrkala proposals which follow are a contemporary Aboriginal reaction to the impact of this social control by outsiders. They show how the leaders of one community have set about correcting the imbalances in legal justice applied to them and their people.

LAW AND ORDER AT YIRRKALA

The Yirrkala community in East Arnhem Land has had some experience of applying traditional procedures in difficult circumstances and is attempting to define a place for Aboriginal customary law within the white legal system. The community itself is composed of members of about sixteen separate clans each with its own homeland territories in the region. Brought together at Yirrkala by the missionary authorities, some of these clans were traditionally suspicious of each other and fears of sorcery, disputes over presence on and use of the resources of another clan's land, and rival marriage claims, intensified the problems of maintaining reasonable harmony. Over a period, however, the traditional processes of resolving inter-group disputes were modified to enable these problems to be dealt with. When necessary, clan leaders met informally to resolve disputes; on the whole effectively. These leaders believe that Aboriginal and Balanda (white Australian) law are broadly compatible and should support one another; that in the event of apparent incompatibility the process of

121

a search for consensus will be able to resolve it. They believe that what is lacking in the present administration of law and order is trust in Aboriginal processes by white authorities who do not understand them, or are able to think about the issues only in terms of their own culture and its processes.

I became aware of the views of Yirrkala groups on these matters while chairman of the Council of Aboriginal Affairs in the early seventies and have acted in relation to them as a kind of intermediary between those communities and white Australian law enforcement agencies intermittently since then. The reference by the Commonwealth Government to the Commonwealth Law Reform Commission in 1977 for a report on recognition of traditional Aboriginal law and the involvement of Aborigines in the administration of Australian law made possible a more comprehensive consideration of the Yirrkala ideas. Since then, there has been a number of exchanges between the Yirrkala groups and the Law Reform Commission in which I have acted as scribe and as a kind of cultural interpreter between them and the Commission. Thus, in May 1980 at the request of the elders, I outlined for the Commission the arrangements for the administration of law and order which I understood those groups to desire. These were described (not wholly accurately) in the Commission's recent discussion paper (Australia 1980). Subsequently, the Commission raised a number of queries about the proposals and these have been discussed by the elders of the clans and responses agreed to. I have participated in those discussions.

The procedure which was followed in developing these proposals closely followed traditional practice. A series of discussions among the elders of the various clans was spread over a period of months. These were essentially discussions about law and order problems which were giving the community concern and how they should be dealt with, and about the inadequacies and ineffectiveness of Balanda processes, particularly in their failure to resolve disputes and to re-establish offenders within the society. From these discussions emerged the idea of community rules to supplement traditional law and custom, and the establishment of formal procedures for their enforcement by the community itself.

My role in these discussions was to listen, assisted by the Yirrkala Council officer, to ask questions and to draw attention to relevant Balanda attitudes and concepts. Thereafter, I was authorised to try to write down what I understood the elders to want, both in respect of community rules and of procedures for the enforcement of those rules, Aboriginal law and Balanda law. This task proved difficult. My first attempt carried over too much of my own cultural inheritance of concepts, language and institutions. This became clear when I sought to have it translated into one of the local languages. The interpreter found much of it impossible to translate and I was forced to revise the text so as to use the simplest possible language and to avoid concepts that were alien to the elders. However, an acceptable text gradually emerged and was typed and recorded on tape. The tape was used as a basis first for discussion with the elders and when their agreement with it, in modified form, had been achieved, with the community as a whole at a kind of 'town meeting'.

THE YIRRKALA PROPOSALS

Briefly, the Yirrkala proposals envisage:
- A law council composed of elders of the clans in Yirrkala and the related homelands.
- This council would:
  - make (subject to community endorsement) rules governing the maintenance of social order;
  - name members of the community to constitute a community court to seek to resolve any dispute and to deal with alleged breaches of those rules, or of traditional Aboriginal law;
  - name members of the community to be responsible for ensuring that punishments or settlements agreed upon by the community court are carried out;
  - advise magistrates and judges about the facts of any case before them involving a member or members of the community; the community's attitude towards the issues involved; the content of Aboriginal law which may have bearing upon the case; and the form and degree of compensation or punishment; and

with the approval of the magistrate or judge, conduct preliminary hearings of the case concerned so as to be able to advise the magistrate or judge appropriately.

- The law council would also appoint and control a group of 'orderlies', with police functions which would include the power to arrest and imprison overnight any person believed to be threatening or endangering peace and good order.
- A community court would be established for each dispute or alleged offence and would include senior members of the families or clans of the alleged offender and of the complainant, as well as others chosen for their wisdom and standing in the community. The court's objective would be to devise a consensus settlement in which, ideally, both the offender and complainant and their respective families would concur.
- If the settlement involved compensation to an injured party or punishment of the offender, it would, subject to the supervision of the law council, be the responsibility of the clan or family to which he or she belonged to see that the punishment was carried out or the compensation paid, and that the terms of the settlement were adhered to.

The rules which the law council envisaged would be general and concerned primarily with the maintenance of social order, apart from some omnibus rules relating to Aboriginal and Balanda law. In discussions over a number of visits, the community suggested the following general rules:

- It is wrong to do anything which will, or could, injure another person.
- It is wrong to take or damage anything which belongs to somebody else.
- It is wrong to go where other people have a right to be by themselves.
- It is wrong to do anything which will cause great noise or violence and will make other members of the community frightened and unhappy.
- It is wrong to behave outside the community in a way which will offend members of other communities or will cause trouble with them.

- It is wrong to do anything forbidden by Aboriginal law or which will make that law weak.
- It is wrong not to do those things which Aboriginal law and tradition says should be done.
- It is wrong to do anything forbidden by Balanda law.

The most common breaches of rules with which the community courts would have to deal are:

- violence and threats of violence while under the influence of alcohol;
- offences against Aboriginal codes of behaviour while under the influence of alcohol, including using the names of recently dead people, offensive language, references to secret ceremony and interference with the sacred objects of other clans;
- failure to carry out traditional obligations to relatives, especially the care and nurture of children, old people and the sick;
- unwillingness to accept traditional marriage partners;
- juvenile delinquency, including petrol sniffing and petty theft, and failure to perform parental and other family responsibilities.

ABORIGINAL ATTITUDES TOWARDS PUNISHMENT

Aboriginal attitudes towards punishment differ from those of white society. They see punishment as directed to the restoration of normal relations between the parties and within the community and to the prevention of future offences. It is therefore, in their eyes, important that an injured party should be satisfied that his or her injury has been 'paid for'. Traditionally, in interpersonal disputes, a 'spear through the thigh' was a common form of resolution and in extreme and rare instances of offences of a sacrilegious nature, sometimes death was the penalty. The elders state that these forms of punishment have gone into disuse and that they do not seek authority to impose them.

It is possible, of course, that the 'spear through the thigh' could remain as an unofficial component in the settlement of interpersonal disputes. Our unwillingness to tolerate such punishment, it seems to me, is ethnocentric. Certainly, Aborigines feel that prolonged imprisonment where the offender is isolated from his family and clan from which would derive the influences likely to prevent future offences and which exposed him to alien and probably criminal associates, is both counterproductive and unconscionable.

There is an increasing tendency for 'pay-back' type penalties to be commuted to compensation as the central component in the punishments which the community courts would impose. However, to preclude wholly 'pay-back' in the form of physical injury would leave the risk that a dispute would remain essentially unresolved and therefore could recur. It would seem wise to allow the passage into disuse of this form of 'pay-back' to occur by the increasing use of other forms of compensation. If it is feared that recognition of this form of punishment would encourage its use, it would be sufficient to provide a general appeal to a magistrate against any punishment on grounds of undue severity. The community courts could be required to inform the offender of this option. This would make it possible for relevant considerations to be taken into account by the magistrate; in particular, the possibility of double punishment and the risk of the dispute remaining unresolved. Furthermore, the prospect of an appeal would mean that such punishments would be used only when they were part of an agreed settlement and were accepted by the offender concerned. Thus, already, compensation has become the standard resolution to the problem of a young girl who is unwilling to marry the man to whom she was 'promised' and who persists in this refusal despite social pressure. The deprived husband-to-be is compensated by the girl's family for the material resources he may have contributed to the girl and her family over the years since the betrothal, and probably with some addition for injury to his dignity.

A problem exists in relation to offences arising from alcohol abuse. Aborigines at Yirrkala have a strong sense that such offences are subject to reduced responsibility and that punishment is not appropriate. At the same time, they are greatly concerned about their frequency and the disorder they cause. It is for this reason that they seek authority to arrest and confine overnight a person threatening or endangering the peace and good order of the community. They do not see this as punishment and, generally, no charge would be made against the arrested person.

Apart from this protective arrest and various forms of compensation, the Yirrkala Council envisages the following forms of punishment:

- commitment of the offender to the care of an older member of the clan for re-socialisation; often combined with
- compulsory residence at a homeland settlement;
- fines;
- work on a community project; and
- temporary banishment from the community.

These emphasise either remedial action or the provision of time for 'cooling off'. They are, in effect, the return of the offender to an earlier stage of socialisation.

THE LAW REFORM COMMISSION

In its discussion paper the Law Reform Commission (1980) expresses interest in the Yirrkala proposals, but raises a number of issues about which I sought further information. The most important of these were:

- the possibility of community courts imposing punishments abhorrent by white Australian standards, or in conflict with international conventions about human rights;
- whether the Commission has been sufficiently informed about the content of Aboriginal law to recommend its endorsement by white society;
- whether the authority the proposals entrust to elders would be endorsed by all sections of the community;
- whether women are adequately represented in the proposals;
- what would be the limits of the jurisdiction of the Aboriginal law councils and their rules;
- the relationship of the proposed community courts to the law enforcement agencies of Australian governments; and
- what sanctions would stand behind the consensus upon which the proposals rest.

The following comments on these matters report the responses of the Yirrkala elders in discussion of the Law Reform Commission's queries.

Punishments

Judgement about what forms of punishment are abhorrent or unconscionable are obviously ethnocentric and there can be no objective
basis for judging white standards superior. However Yirrkala Aborigines accept, at least ostensibly, that they must in this matter defer to
the prejudices or preconceptions of the dominant society. They do
not, therefore, seek authority to impose penalties involving physical
injury or death; a privilege we ourselves have not wholly abandoned.

Content of Aboriginal customary law

Yirrkala Aborigines reply that it would be difficult to codify Aboriginal law and that it is not necessary to do so, provided a procedure
is established for determining what is the content of that law in the
case under consideration. This, they point out, can be done by reference to those members of the law council best qualified by seniority
and knowledge acquired by training and experience – a procedure
not different in principle from that followed in our own courts, at
least in respect of the common law. The query appears to me to reflect
a desire to impose the concepts of our own law on Aboriginal society.

Authority of the elders

The elders in Yirrkala assert that the community generally, including
women and young men, endorse that in respect of the law, authority
should be with the elders, subject to endorsement by the community
in relation to rules and the decisions of community courts. It is my
firm impression that this claim would be validated by meetings of
the whole community.

The role of women

The division of function and responsibility between the sexes in
traditional Aboriginal society was clear and firm, although it has
been affected by contact with white Australian society to the detriment
of the status of women. However, the law council in Yirrkala confirms
that there are important issues of law and order which are the concern
of women. They assert that where these were involved they would
confer with senior women and that any community court appointed

in relation to offences or disputes arising from them would include, or be composed, of women. This view was endorsed by women, senior and younger, who talked to me about it. They did not think a separate women's council necessary, although I specifically sought their views on this issue.

To some extent this might reflect their desire to keep women's activities outside the area of white male political and bureaucratic intervention. Personally, I would like to see any legislative action keep open the option of a separate women's law council if it is sought by women in a particular community.

Jurisdiction of the law councils
The Yirrkala proposals envisage the authority of the law council, its rules and its community courts, extending to the residents of Yirrkala and the homeland settlements of its constituent clans. They presume that other communities would establish their own law councils and community courts and make their own rules. Where the dispute or defence concerned only members of a homeland community, the community court would be constituted from the members of that community. They believe that white residents and visiting Aborigines should accept the authority of the local law council and its courts, and that acceptance should be a condition of a permit to enter or to reside in the community's territory.

Relationship with Australian law enforcement agencies
The Yirrkala proposals envisage that the local machinery would be responsible for most law and order matters arising from Aboriginal law and from the council's rules. This would not preclude action by police and other State or Commonwealth law enforcement agencies if those authorities considered the circumstances warranted it, especially in 'big trouble' such as homicide.

However, the proposals envisage that in any case before a magistrate or judge in which Yirrkala Aborigines are involved, the magistrate or judge would authorise the law council to appoint a community court to conduct a preliminary hearing and to advise him or her in relation to:

- the facts;
- community attitudes to the alleged offence or dispute;
- Aboriginal law involved; and
- the form and degree of punishment or compensation.

If such a preliminary hearing were not conducted, the proposals would require that the law council should be asked to nominate members of the community to sit with the magistrate or judge so as to provide advice on these matters.

Ultimate sanctions

The proposals contemplate that the backing of white Australian law and its agencies would be given to the Yirrkala law council, its courts and their decisions. This would not preclude the possibility of appeal in some circumstances, for instance against the severity of punishments, but the Yirrkala community doubt whether such appeals would be made. They trust in the desire to strengthen Aboriginal law and the fear of social disapproval, to ensure this support from their own community; even from those on whom punishments are being imposed.

CONCLUSION

My own view is that the proposals are moderate, compatible with normal Australian practice and likely to strengthen the prospects of orderly change and continuity in Aboriginal communities within Australian society. Accordingly, I would recommend legislation which would provide that: a community could seek authority to establish its own law council or councils (if they desire a separate women's council) and community courts, in accordance with general principles based on the Yirrkala proposals. There should be a registrar of Aboriginal courts backed by a consultative body of Aborigines to provide resources for these councils and courts, and to watch over their development and report periodically to Parliament. This consultative body should report on applications for authority to establish a law council so as to satisfy the registrar that the community as a whole endorses the application and the proposed rules, and has the social coherence necessary to ensure their effectiveness.

130

12

Aboriginal political leadership and the role of the National Aboriginal Conference

Edited version, published originally in H C Coombs, 'The Role of the National Aboriginal Conference', Report to the Honourable Clyde Holding, Minister for Aboriginal Affairs, Australian Government Publishing Service, Canberra, 1984. Commonwealth of Australia copyright reproduced by permission.

REVIEWING THE NAC

The initiative taken by the Minister for Aboriginal Affairs in 1983, in sponsoring a review of the structure and functions of the National Aboriginal Conference (NAC) provides an opportunity to achieve significant change. The Minister expressed the desire to see a representative Aboriginal organisation at the national level which would be acknowledged in Aboriginal and non-Aboriginal quarters as an effective agent of Aboriginal political initiative and to which he could turn for meaningful advice and debate. He also indicated a willingness to entrust greater power to this organisation; indeed, to make its operations a significant step towards self-determination. The Minister has drawn an analogy between the Aboriginal organisation he envisages and the Australian Council of Trade Unions (ACTU), the national political instrument of the industrial labour movement, and has suggested that there is a need in the Aboriginal movement for a similar overarching organisation whose relationships with other Aboriginal organisations would presumably be similar to those of the Federal Council of the ACTU to its constituent unions and State councils.

Such a body would be very different from the National Aboriginal Conference as at present structured. The ACTU is not composed of elected members. Rather it is a loose federation of trade unions, individually and in groups, each of which continues to operate independently in the interests of its members and reserves the right to deal directly with employers, arbitration authorities, governments and their agencies. This federation provides the means by which they come together for combined political or industrial action when this seems to be necessary. The national council of this federation is composed of delegates nominated by the constituent unions whose delegates are presumably accountable to the unions which nominated them.

An overarching national Aboriginal organisation could be designed on similar lines with its members being chosen by, and accountable to, other existing or emerging Aboriginal organisations. Each of these would, if the ACTU model were followed, continue to have its own independent purposes, administrative and executive structure, retaining substantial autonomy in relation to them but sending delegates to the overarching organisation for consultation and common action. This model has attractions for some Aborigines and their organisations and it has been argued that it seems closer to traditional Aboriginal processes than those based upon the models of representative parliamentary institutions.

It is a model which warrants study, but consideration of it and other options must take account of Aboriginal attitudes towards political processes and decision making generally. For this purpose it will be useful to consider the structure of organisations which have already emerged in Aboriginal society for their own political and related purposes, the role of Aborigines working within government agencies and the influence of the Aboriginal political struggle on the attitude of Aborigines to government-sponsored agencies.

ABORIGINAL LEADERSHIP AND DECISION MAKING

Aboriginal processes of decision making and Aboriginal attitudes towards elected representatives are markedly different from those of European Australians. While Aborigines follow processes which are,

I believe, basically democratic, the European concept of representative government seems incompatible with their culture. The basic unit of contemporary Aboriginal decision making, in situations where the means to decision are not clearly established by tradition, or where decision does not lie within the authority of individuals by virtue of structural considerations within Aboriginal society itself, seems to be the local community or group meeting. Issues are discussed, but decisions are rarely made at once if the matters are important. Discussions are often interrupted and may be spread over several meetings to allow time for discussions within families and other smaller groups, or for consultation with other people of authority and influence. During these intervals influential members of the community often move around to ensure that issues are understood, to identify the lines of emerging consensus and perhaps to support particular ones.

Thus, the meetings of the Central Land Council, which are composed of delegates of communities, are generally open to others. Meetings organised by the Kimberley Land Council in which I participated were conducted in this way also. If persons are chosen to take part in discussions with other communities or with government and other agencies, it is my understanding that their nomination is not an authority to decide, or in other ways to act for, or represent the community without reference back to it, but rather to serve as two-way 'messengers' on its behalf between it and the other parties. The ambiguity and difficulties inherent in such a role are witnessed by the fact that very often such individuals do not adequately feed information back to their community or, conversely, unknowingly misinform them and invariably cannot make decisions binding on the wider community.

Another important aspect of Aboriginal decision-making processes in many regions is the complementary division of ritual responsibility between separate, but related groups. For example, the complementary relationship between 'owners' of land and ceremonies, and the 'guardians' or 'managers' – those with responsibility to see that traditional duties are properly performed – is now increasingly understood. It is the same expectation of reciprocity and fulfilment of mutual obligations that generally characterises social relationships between the generations and, in particular, serves as the basis of authority and leadership in many Aboriginal societies. In particular, if individual leaders or 'bosses' are given deference or respect, then it is as a person who 'looks after' and 'works for' others and who will transmit to subordinates valued knowledge and experience. Authority to command or to effect decisions continues to be accorded only to those who observe reciprocal obligations and is given within an ideology of egalitarianism and traditionally, within the context of Aboriginal law. Thus conceptualised, '... legitimate authority is without despotic or personal overtones, taken on as a responsibility to ensure the security and benefit of its objects' (Myers 1980: 206).

This concept of interlocking balance and complementarity would be valuable in contemporary Aboriginal political affairs if a way could be found to incorporate reciprocal accountability into institutional structure. While these attitudes towards authority and decision making seem to be found in urban Aboriginal communities as well as in rural and traditional ones, the idea of elected representatives appears to be more valued in the former and in some of them considerable interest has been expressed in the mechanics of electoral processes, such as qualifications for candidature, preferential voting versus 'first past the post', compulsory voting and so on.

To the extent that these general comments on Aboriginal political processes are accurate, it will be apparent that the NAC charter establishes processes incompatible with practices of Aboriginal society. NAC representatives are not accountable to and are rarely 'instructed' by, or perceived as 'working for', their community. Even if they assess its attitude and wishes correctly, they can express them only in a forum meeting at long intervals, are not required to report back to it and rarely do so. The decisions of the representative forum are only advice to the NAC executive which, in turn, has the certain opportunity to advise the Minister for Aboriginal Affairs only if the issue has been referred to it by the Minister. Even then, the NAC executive is not bound to advise the Minister in accordance with the wishes of the full conference membership. Clearly, there is an enormous communication gap between the government and Aboriginal communities, groups and organisations which the NAC, as it is presently structured, can do little to bridge.

Aborigines identify most strongly with Aboriginal organisations which are active within their own context. Even when critical of them, they almost invariably see land councils, Aboriginal legal services, Aboriginal health and welfare organisations, Aboriginal service agencies like Tangentyere in Alice Springs, Aboriginal housing associations and similar functional bodies, as more relevant to their affairs than the NAC. Indeed, it is to such organisations that Aborigines turn for advocacy of their claims for funding and for new or more comprehensive programs, rather than to the NAC. They certainly would distrust a requirement which precluded those organisations from having direct access to Ministers or to agencies within their portfolios.

ABORIGINAL POLITICAL PROCESSES

It seems clear, therefore, that the NAC is unlikely in its present form to develop into a political instrument with which Aboriginal groups and communities will identify, or which would be acknowledged by them as capable and having a legitimate right to speak for them to the government. This conclusion is supported by some aspects of the contemporary Aboriginal political scene. Aboriginal activists have consistently been suspicious of official advisory, consultative or representative bodies. With some justice they see them as composed of 'tame cats' and designed to quiet Aboriginal discontent, rather than to express it effectively or to force action to remove its causes. Their experience has demonstrated that concessions to Aborigines have followed outbursts of protest in one form or another, rather than persuasive co-operation through officially established channels.

Thus, political leadership among Aborigines generally, with the exceptions of ritual or ceremonial arenas and through membership of government agencies, has increasingly come to be exercised by activists who have found in Aboriginal-controlled functional and service organisations, outlets for their executive capacities and increasingly, a base from which to conduct political campaigns. Land councils, both official and unofficial, Aboriginal-controlled health, legal, welfare and other service organisations provide examples of this tendency.

To some of these leaders this situation has other attractions. Contemporary Aboriginal politics can be said to be characterised by factionalism and segmentation. It is sometimes claimed that activists coming to leadership through Aboriginal-controlled organisations seek to mobilise these into personal or family empires. Disputes between rival factions competing for such power as can be commanded are not infrequent and at times factions will seek support from sources of power within white society against their Aboriginal rivals. However, this divisiveness should not necessarily be seen as a negative quality; indeed, it would seem to be in character with the long-term nature of Aboriginal social and territorial organisation in general. If factionalism reflects significant cultural divisions within Aboriginal society and represents a valid political process whereby individuals establish, maintain and perhaps lose necessary support, then it is important that this is also positively acknowledged and that political organisations provide a framework within which any detrimental conflict that might arise can be usefully resolved.

To the extent that factionalism has a recognised political and social value, the leaders of factionally or family-controlled organisations are unlikely to be attracted to proposals which would bring them and their empires under official control or influence, even if that control is apparently exercised by Aborigines, or if they have a constitutional right to share in it. Even if the negative effects of Aboriginal factionalism can be overcome it seems most probable, as one perceptive Aboriginal observer commented, that militant leaders will continue to be influenced by the knowledge that Ministers and governments have in the past responded 'more frequently, faster and more sincerely to black militant protest than to organised approaches through the correct channels' and therefore will continue to resist incorporation into any official structure and to rely on direct pressure at Ministerial level.

THE ROLE OF ABORIGINAL ORGANISATIONS

Since the referendum of 1967 which brought the Commonwealth into Aboriginal affairs at a national level, there have been some important institutional developments affecting the capacity of Aborigines to exercise power. The most widely influential of these developments has been the process of legal incorporation of Aboriginal groups and their executive agencies.

Professor Charles Rowley, in his seminal work on Aboriginal society (1970, 1971a, b), saw incorporation as providing a 'carapace' within the protection of which Aboriginal groups could experiment with the development of mechanisms which might enable them to devise an acceptable working relationship with white society. This idea was seized upon in 1967 by the newly established Council and Office of Aboriginal Affairs and continued to influence the practice of the Department of Aboriginal Affairs when it was established in 1973. Incorporation gave to Aboriginal groups an identity within the Australian legal system and with it the potential for greater autonomy and future self-determination. It made it possible for such groups to own property in accordance with Australian law, to enter into contracts, to sue and be sued. They could therefore undertake their own programs, negotiate with governments about these, receive grants and establish their own councils, housing and progress associations and business enterprises for the conduct of their own affairs.

A relatively recent development among both government and Aboriginal-sponsored corporations is the tendency for them to form loose federations. Thus, Aboriginal health, legal aid and other service organisations have established the National Aboriginal and Islander Health Organisations (NAIHO), the National Aboriginal and Islander Legal Service (NAILS) and equivalent joint agencies. These federations are designed ostensibly to facilitate co-operation and joint action to lobby governments in the interests of their services, but generally have a positive and politically active stance on wider Aboriginal issues. The Federation of Land Councils is an interesting example, since it brings together government-sponsored councils with others formed independently by Aborigines to protect their traditional lands and to fight for recognition of their title. Member organisations generally wish to preserve their right to autonomy and to limit the authority of federations. Not all Aboriginal organisations apparently eligible to belong to these federations in fact do so. Some see them as evidence of the 'empire building' of individual leaders and family groups, and they are sometimes racked by factional disputes. Others say that incorporation is not necessarily a good thing for Aborigines; that it is a white structure which has served white rather than Aboriginal interests. However, still another view is that Aborigines have often achieved political success precisely by being able to control and manipulate white structures.

Despite dissensions, or possibly because of them, these federations of Aboriginal corporations represent a growing force in Aboriginal political life and already exercise considerable influence, sometimes reluctantly conceded, on government and its agencies. Plans for the development of Aboriginal political institutions within Australian society which ignore Aboriginal-controlled service bodies are, in my view, likely to risk the institutions they create being by-passed.

THE BLACK BUREAUCRACY

Another growing Aboriginal influence on government and the pattern of Aboriginal development has been the Aboriginalisation of the official agencies within the Minister for Aboriginal Affairs' portfolio. While the Department of Aboriginal Affairs (DAA) is still headed by a non-Aboriginal secretary, there has been a slow but significant increase in the numbers of Aborigines employed, including some in positions of influence and responsibility. The Aboriginal Development Commission (ADC), a statutory corporation, is managed by a commission of Aborigines appointed by the Minister on a broadly regional basis and its full-time chairperson, who is in essence the managing director, is also Aboriginal. The chairperson exercises a widely influential role as an adviser to the Minister and independent political commentator. There seems to be a trend for the Commission to be given even wider executive functions, sometimes at the expense of the DAA, and sometimes at that of other, previously separate, Aboriginal corporations.

Aboriginal Hostels Pty Ltd, a government-owned enterprise incorporated as a company to own and administer hostels and other accommodation for Aboriginal students, workers and transients, is managed by a board nominated by the Minister, all but one member of which is Aboriginal. Its chairperson and general manager are both Aboriginal. The Australian Institute of Aboriginal Studies is headed by a council of academics and Aborigines elected by the members who are predominantly anthropologists, prehistorians, archaeologists and others engaged in studies relating to Aboriginal societies, as well as nominees of the Governor-General. In 1981, for the first time, the principal of the Institute is Aboriginal.

All of these agencies have direct access to the Minister for Aboriginal Affairs and under the present Minister exercise significant influence on his judgement. A recent development has been the establishment of informal portfolio meetings at which the heads of these organisations confer with the Minister at intervals of a few weeks. These meetings seem designed to keep the Minister in touch with current events and to advise him about them, but it seems probable that they will exercise significant influence on the longer-term development of policy.

These organisations are part of the machinery of government, and recruitment and promotion to positions of influence within them are predominantly by public service-type procedures, or by Ministerial or Cabinet decision. The organisations are accountable to the Minister, although those with statutory powers and funds under their own control (particularly the ADC) have significant autonomy. There does not seem to be any effective line of accountability to Aboriginal communities. The NAC has the authority to comment to the Minister on the annual report of the ADC and is to be given power to nominate some of its commissioners, but its influence on government policies and decisions appears to have been negligible.

The apparently growing strength of this bureaucratic form of Aboriginal influence on government and the power which it appears to give to individuals successful within it is by no means universally welcomed by Aborigines. Some see it as the emergence of a black bureaucracy concerned primarily with its own power and the personal advancement of its members. It is criticised as being almost as isolated from Aboriginal communities as the white bureaucracy it is gradually replacing. Fear is expressed that its effect is integrationist; that it will come to identify itself progressively with the white bureaucracy and to accept its methods and ways of thought, ceasing in any real sense to be an instrument of Aboriginal self-determination.

On the other hand, some argue that the experience of European education and of the machinery of government which these Aboriginal officials have acquired makes it possible for them, to the extent that they continue to identify strongly as Aborigines and preserve their links with their society, to play the role of brokers between Aboriginal and white authorities. In this role they can help governments and their agents understand Aboriginal aspirations and help Aborigines frame their demands in ways most likely to be understood and sympathetically received by white authority. This role has, in the past, been performed by sympathetic members of white society inside and outside government with varying degrees of understanding and success. In some respects at least, Aborigines will be better qualified to perform it, if mechanisms ensuring their accountability to Aborigines can be established and maintained.

Whatever judgement is reached about the relative importance of these considerations, it would certainly be a mistake to expect that a growth in the power and influence of the black bureaucracy would of itself satisfy Aboriginal demands for progress towards self-determination. The capacity of the black bureaucracy to help satisfy those demands will depend on the degree to which it is felt to be accountable to, and identified with, Aboriginal communities as an extension of their own political institutions.

CONCLUSIONS

Aboriginal society is composed of many substantially separate communities which often do not readily work together except for specific and limited purposes and periods of time. Aboriginal assessment of the performance of individual Aboriginal leaders, of institutions and of government policies tends to be dominated by their immediate implications for the Aboriginal communities to which the assessors belong. The self-management or self-determination which Aborigines seek is primarily local in its form and purpose, and involves the power to create and control their own institutions; to manage their own domestic affairs; to hold accountable those who exercise power among them; and to receive and administer resources necessary for Aboriginal purposes.

Apart from the NAC itself, the years of Commonwealth participation in Aboriginal affairs have seen a dramatic and significant development of Aboriginal political institutions, the more important being:

- the incorporation of Aboriginal communities and executive agencies set up by them, such as councils, housing and progress associations, business enterprises and so on;
- the establishment, by Aboriginal initiative, of Aboriginal-controlled agencies to provide services, such as health, legal aid and welfare, for their communities;
- the establishment of land councils, both officially recognised and unofficial, to work for land rights, conduct claims for land and negotiate with governments and developers in relation to land;
- the tendency for these Aboriginal organisations to join in loose federations to co-operate more effectively and to strengthen their capacity to influence or negotiate with governments. These federations are sometimes based on geographical or tribal association, for example the Pitjantjatjara Council, and sometimes on common functions.

Parallel with this institutional development there has been a significant and continuing Aboriginalisation of government agencies within the Minister's portfolio, with influential positions increasingly being held by Aborigines and with articulate spokespersons emerging. Any consideration of the future of the NAC, or any other national Aboriginal political structure, must take account of these other instruments of Aboriginal power and the attitude of Aboriginal communities towards them. Provisionally, these conclusions suggest that any organisation designed to give Aborigines an effective influence on government policies must:

- be firmly based on, derive its Aboriginal authority from, and be accountable to, local groups and communities and their organisations;
- integrate with itself, but without impairing their essential

141

autonomy, Aboriginal-controlled organisations through which Aboriginal political initiative is already being significantly exercised;

- have access to expertise necessary for the formulation of policy on matters of concern to Aborigines; and
- be given and accept significant responsibility for decisions about the total funding and its allocation for expenditure on Aboriginal Affairs.

13

Aborigines and the Treaty of Waitangi

Originally presented as part of the Boyer Lecture Series by the Australian Broadcasting Corporation, 1988.

THE NEED FOR A TREATY

In June 1979 I spoke in an Australian Broadcasting Commission *Guest of Honour* series about the need for the Australian Government to negotiate a treaty with the Aboriginal people of Australia. I pointed out that until this was done, our occupancy of this land, our very right to be here, is tainted by the aggression against the Aborigines by which it was established. Since that time there have been important changes in public awareness of that treatment and the status of Aborigines in our society. Evidence accumulates that international opinion judges our performance to fall far short of civilised standards. A series of reports by internationally respected bodies, including the World Council of Churches and agencies of the United Nations, shames us before the world. Our name is linked with South Africa and other nations whose lack of respect for human rights is widely condemned. Such judgements could well lead to action, political and economic, seriously detrimental to our international standing. It is inconsistent with our dignity as a civilised people to wait for such pressure to be mobilised against us.

Within Australia there has been a growing awareness of the injustices inflicted upon Aborigines by our forebears and of our own failure to act effectively to correct them. On the other hand, there have been active campaigns against any such action from a racist minority and those who profit from the injustices. Widespread indifference to the human suffering that our neglect continues to create has made effective government action difficult. However, in June of this year [1988], the Prime Minister, the Honourable Mr Robert Hawke, at the Barunga Festival, celebrating the survival through 40,000 years of Aboriginal culture, made an historic commitment to the negotiation and conclusion of a treaty between the Commonwealth and the Aboriginal people. In making that commitment, he expressed a preference for a treaty in general terms and simple language, and invited the Aboriginal people and their organisations to consider what the content of such a treaty should be.

It would be presumptuous for me to suggest how Aborigines should respond; that is for them to consider and decide. But the suggestion that the treaty might be in simple and general terms – a statement of principles supported by mechanisms to ensure their application – draws attention to the Treaty of Waitangi which governs the relationship between the Maori people of New Zealand and the New Zealand Government. This Treaty is in such a form. After a history of fluctuating ineffectiveness, it has recently been judged by the highest New Zealand legal authority to be a binding commitment on the Crown in the New Zealand Government and to provide an effective protection for Maori interests, especially in relation to land. It may therefore be useful to review briefly the form of that Treaty, its history in operation and to assess its contemporary value as a basis for the relationship between the Maori and the Pakeha (white) people of New Zealand.

THE TREATY OF WAITANGI

The circumstances in which, in 1840, the original Treaty of Waitangi was negotiated resembled those existing in New South Wales during the decades following the first white settlement. There was an increasing flow of migrants from Britain and Europe who were encroaching on Maori land and its resources in ways which Maori land-owning clans were unable to control. No other established authority existed. There were fears that France and possibly other European powers would establish settlements and so add to the Maoris' problems. On the other hand, indigenous political authority existed in the persons of clan chiefs recognised by Britain. This made negotiations easier to arrange. An emissary of Queen Victoria offered to guarantee to those chiefs and their clans, in return for Maoris accepting British sovereignty:

> ... the full exclusive and undisturbed possession of their lands and estates, forests, fisheries and other properties and ... the pre-emptive right of the Crown to purchase such lands and properties as the proprietors may be disposed to alienate, at such prices as may be agreed upon.

The chiefs faced a difficult choice: an uncertain and perhaps temporary continuance of rights they could not enforce, or a partnership with a stronger power on whose good faith they believed they could rely.

The intentions of the British negotiators seem to have been reasonably benign. Similarities can be seen in the provisions of the Treaty they proposed and the instructions to the Governor of South Australia embodied in the Letters Patent, round the same time. The content and the language of both documents had been influenced by liberal Christian reformers then politically influential in Britain.

In South Australia, as earlier in New South Wales, colonial Governors were quite unable to control or prevent the seizure of land by settlers and soldiers, even when they wished to do so. Similarly, in New Zealand, the Treaty failed to control the greed and ruthlessness of the settlers. Maori land was taken or purchased at prices not conforming to the terms of the Treaty. Formal war was declared against clans which resisted the taking of their land. Although subsequently, an official inquiry declared such war to be unjust and Maoris entitled to compensation, the amount awarded was trifling and the Treaty ceased to have significant effect. Rather, it was interpreted as no more than a vague expression of goodwill with no legal significance.

In recent years there have, in New Zealand, been significant legal and legislative changes. In 1975, the *Treaty of Waitangi Act* provided that the Crown was bound by the Treaty's commitments, thus reasserting its validity and contemporary relevance. It also established a tribunal with authority to hear Maori claims and grievances and to make recommendations to the government for action in response to them. This authority was to relate to any claim or grievance arising from any action since 1840, the date of the conclusion of the original Treaty. Furthermore, the tribunal was given exclusive authority to determine the meaning of the Treaty which had been embodied in two texts, one in English and one in the Maori language, and to decide issues raised by differences between them. The work of the tribunal has, in the years since 1975, exercised significant and increasing influence.

In 1986, the New Zealand Parliament passed a law which enabled the government to transfer Crown lands to corporations established to conduct commercial enterprises. It included provisions to ensure that such transfers would not breach 'the principles' of the Treaty of Waitangi. This led to a review of the *Treaty of Waitangi Act* by the Court of Appeal to clarify what were 'the principles of the Treaty' and to determine whether the proposed transfer of lands was inconsistent with them. This review developed into a comprehensive examination of the purposes of the Treaty and the commitments it imposed on the New Zealand Government. The results were embodied in the judgements of the Court which were unanimous in supporting the Maori assertion that land should not be transferred until the possibility of its being the subject of a Maori claim had been appropriately determined. It also reached conclusions about 'the principles' of the Treaty of Waitangi of profound significance not merely for New Zealand, but for any nation contemplating a treaty with its indigenous people.

These conclusions can be summarised as follows:
- The original Treaty of Waitangi established and symbolised a special relationship between the Maori people and the British Crown. With New Zealand self-government, the Crown in the New Zealand Parliament and Government inherited the obligations of that relationship. The relationship can best be described as a partnership between the Maori and Pakeha

146

peoples in New Zealand, in which the partners undertake to act in good faith in relation to their obligations towards one another.

- The obligation of the Crown is not passive, but requires positive measures to extend to Maori people the rights and privileges of British subjects and actively to protect them:
  - in the use of their lands, waters and related resources; and
  - in the custody and care of matters significant to their cultural identity in trust for future generations.
- The obligations of the Maori people are:
  - a duty of loyalty to the Crown and the acceptance of duties under its Constitution in New Zealand; and
  - the acceptance of the Crown's government through its responsible Ministers and reasonable co-operation with it.
- Both the Crown and the Maori people have an obligation to:
  - accept and respect the role of the tribunal as the interpreter of the principles of the Treaty and as the arbiter in disputes which may arise in relation to their application. Thus, if the tribunal finds that a breach of those principles has occurred and recommends redress, the Crown will grant redress unless, in very special circumstances, there are grounds justifying a reasonable partner, in good faith, withholding such redress.

IMPLICATIONS FOR AUSTRALIA

The distinguishing features of the approach taken by the New Zealand Government to the Treaty are:

- the principle of a flexible partnership;
- the embodiment in it of general principles as to the purposes of the partnership;
- the establishment of an independent tribunal to work out the precise action which, from time to time, should be taken to apply those principles.

It would be possible to construct a treaty embodying these features which would meet the Australian Government's expressed preference for a treaty in general terms and simple language. Given an appropriately structured and competent tribunal and the genuine commitment of the parties to the concept and principles of the partnership, such a treaty could have advantages. It could move, step-by-step, towards full realisation of the purposes of the treaty. It could propose applications of its principles which would take account, for instance, of the varying circumstances of different Aboriginal groups and communities. The results of action taken could be reviewed from time to time and modified in the light of experience, consistently with the principles of the treaty.

Perhaps most important, from the Australian point of view, is the use of a tribunal; a practice we have used extensively in the past. Thus, for instance, the division of resources between the States and the Commonwealth has been the continuing subject of study by Commonwealth Grants Commissions, and the present land rights legislation in the Northern Territory reflected the work of a judicial tribunal.

The critical issue for Aborigines in their consideration of such a proposed treaty must be how far they will feel able to rely on the Australian Government and non-Aboriginal people to accept the commitment to partnership and to act in good faith. They may argue that the history of the Waitangi Treaty itself, for most of the period since 1840, has been a record of refusal by Pakeha and their governments to act in accordance with its principle, and that the good intentions embodied in the present legislation have not yet been seriously tested against the pressure of vested interests.

It may well be easier to reach agreement about a statement of general principles than about the complex details of their application to particular issues. Many of these will bear upon the interests and prejudices of individuals and groups. It is probable that such applications would be made more consistently with the principles of any general agreement and, from a Maori or Aboriginal point of view, more sympathetically, if considered in the context of judicial procedure rather than in political negotiations.

ABORIGINES DENIED NATIVE TITLE

The major difference between the New Zealand position and that which faces Aborigines in Australia is that in New Zealand both the

Parliament and the legal system accept that Maori title to land, as it existed prior to 1840, was valid in international and New Zealand law and continues so except where it has been ceded voluntarily. This principle has been accepted also in the USA, Canada, New Guinea and indeed, in most countries previously British colonies. That acceptance has been confirmed in New Zealand by the *Treaty of Waitangi Act 1975* and by the recent judgement of the Court of Appeal. In Australia, the prevailing legal view has been that native title did not exist. The issue has not yet been dealt with effectively in the High Court.

This difference means that Aborigines fear that in any negotiations they will start from a position of weakness; that they will be engaged in a debate which takes the present status quo for granted and will have to bargain for every departure from it as a concession. In their view, the proper starting point is the status before settlement began; as if Captain Cook had obeyed his instructions and negotiated with the various Aboriginal land-owning groups for the acquisition of land for the purposes of the British Government.

Aborigines are aware that it would be both impracticable and unjust to penalise the present non-Aboriginal inhabitants who have no personal responsibility for Aboriginal dispossession. Their leaders have made it clear that they accept and are prepared to validate the title of those who now hold land and property in other resources. Their claims are, and will be, to unalienated Crown lands and resources and for fair compensation for what has been lost. They believe that they have, in this, already made a tremendous contribution to their side of any bargain. They look for evidence that the Commonwealth Government is prepared to match their contribution. Some have said that they will not enter negotiations until they have seen that evidence. What evidence would be adequate is not clear. Some would accept national land rights legislation as sufficient; others talk in terms of formal recognition of Aboriginal sovereignty. It is doubtful whether the issue can be resolved simply by legislative action, as the threat of the Federal Opposition to 'tear up' any treaty or compact amply illustrates.

Essentially, it is a matter of fundamental law whether – by international law or by the protection of property rights inherent in the common law of Britain which we inherited – Aboriginal land-owning groups were legally protected against arbitrary or forceful dispossession. Only a judgement of the High Court, or of the International Court of Justice, would give security to any recognition accorded by a government of the day. It is vital that this matter be resolved. This could be done if the Commonwealth Government sought an advisory judgement from either of these judicial bodies.

THE ISSUE OF SOVEREIGNTY

Another aspect of the New Zealand arrangements which may well give concern to Aboriginal groups is the absoluteness of the acceptance required from Maoris of the sovereignty of the Crown and its New Zealand Government. The ultimate constraint on that sovereignty is only what the government may impose on itself as a result of its undertaking to respect the recommendations of the tribunal except where, in its interpretation of the responsibilities of a good partner, circumstances justify its doing otherwise.

Some Aborigines are interested in sovereignty, perhaps unrealistically, and some non-Aboriginal opponents of the treaty see any agreement as a threat to the sovereignty inherent in our Constitution. But the doctrine which the New Zealand Treaty seems to embody, that sovereignty is indivisible, must surely be rejected. Here in Australia we divide it through our Constitution between the Commonwealth and the States, on criteria based on a combination of territory and subject matter. We apparently divide it between the Parliament and the Commonwealth Government on the one hand, and the sovereign or her representative on the other, through the convention of the reserved powers of the Crown. Certainly, there are matters which many Aboriginal groups believe should not be dealt with other than with their consent, especially those relating to Aboriginal culture in which they believe the views of Aborigines directly concerned should prevail. There are other matters which they believe should be the responsibility of Aboriginal-controlled agencies established by Aborigines on bases of their own choosing. There is no insuperable barrier to a treaty which divides sovereignty, if the political will exists.

NEGOTIATING A TREATY

A major problem facing both parties in relation to the negotiation and conclusion of a treaty in Australia is to decide who has the authority to negotiate for the parties and, even more importantly, to accept the commitments negotiated. In New Zealand, the fact that in 1840 there existed a set of clan chiefs with recognised authority to speak for their members and a system of clan government which would enable the chiefs to give effect to their commitments, made the conclusion of the original Treaty of Waitangi practicable. While it is now known that territorially-based Aboriginal groups had a system of laws and of social control effective within their own lands, this knowledge was not general in the years after 1788. Even if it had been, the system of Aboriginal law did not provide a simple focus of authority, comparable with that of the New Zealand chiefs, with whom negotiations could have readily been conducted. Furthermore, the colonial governors, the settlers and even more, the military upon whom law enforcement depended, had powerful incentives not to seek out Aborigines with whom negotiations could have been conducted.

Today, these problems continue to exist on both sides. The pre-1788 Aboriginal political structure of small, largely autonomous groups identified with specific areas of land has, over much of the country, been destroyed by dispossession and the dispersal of many of the Aboriginal people. However, there remain strong regional and local loyalties in relation to land, language and culture, and pan-Aboriginal sentiment and institutions are only recently beginning to emerge. It is far from clear who Aborigines would wish to authorise to negotiate on their behalf, or how they would wish to go about deciding the matter.

Partly as a result of the increasing interest in the negotiation of a treaty, some liaison of representative Aboriginal organisations which are territorially or functionally based has developed. An informal coalition of Aboriginal organisations has been formed and could be the instrument for overcoming the lack of a representative body to act in relation to the treaty. At present, the coalition itself would lack the legitimacy to undertake this task. It resembles, rather, those citizens' organisations operating at the beginning of the twentieth century which mobilised support for the formation of the Commonwealth of Australia and shared in its planning. In this capacity, the coalition could reasonably organise an Australia-wide convention to which all Aborigines and their organisations could be invited. Such a convention could nominate a continuing body to provisionally negotiate the draft terms of a treaty which could then be returned to a later meeting of the convention for decision. It is possible that the convention would decide that, before it could properly make a decision, it should refer the draft to land-owning groups with continuity of authority and to other organisations established to act for Aborigines in various regions. If Aborigines wish, they could, by this or other means, devise a procedure to enable them to act collectively. At present, the coalition of Aboriginal organisations appears to possess sufficient legitimacy and effectiveness to be given that responsibility.

ADMINISTERING A TREATY

Problems also exist on the non-Aboriginal side. At present, the Commonwealth and the States share constitutional authority for Aboriginal affairs. Furthermore, the matters which would need to be covered by a treaty, including land tenure, compensation and responsibility for services, raise issues of concern to the various levels of government. Whatever authority is entrusted with the negotiation of the treaty itself, there will need to be close consultation with the States and other agencies. However, the referendum of 1967 placed the ultimate responsibility with the Commonwealth. The conclusion of a treaty would be easier if it held that responsibility exclusively, as soon as possible. The sharing of responsibility leads to confusion and inefficiency. The Commonwealth should be the sole financial source for the conduct of programs by and for Aborigines. This is not to suggest that it should administer these programs. Administrative responsibility for them should be placed with appropriate existing State, local or Commonwealth Government agencies and, progressively and increasingly, with Aboriginal incorporated agencies. The transfer of power and related resources from the agencies of various governments to Aboriginal organisations would need to be negotiated. These considerations strengthen the need for a tribunal to help develop the muscles which must give effectiveness to the bare bones of any treaty.

There will, inevitably, be problems in the administration of a treaty even if the parties accept the responsibilities of partnership and good faith: the treaty may, by mutual consent, need revision; one party or the other may seek amendment of its obligations or amendment of the decisions of a tribunal, or may even wish to repudiate the treaty itself. It would be desirable that the treaty commit the parties to negotiation in such events, under the supervision of an independent authority. Possible choices for such an authority could be the tribunal itself, the High Court or an instrument established by the Secretariat of the British Commonwealth or by the United Nations. The emphasis in the Treaty of Waitangi on the link between the Maori people and the Crown, as distinct from the government of the day, could suggest that this role as protector of the treaty might be added to those powers reserved to the Crown in the person of the Governor-General.

CONCLUSION

Let me bring together the major conclusions which seem to me to derive from this consideration of the New Zealand experience with the Treaty of Waitangi. Firstly, the idea of a treaty in the form of a statement of basic purposes and principles, supported by the establishment of a tribunal to interpret those principles and to guide their implementation, is essentially workable given the political will of Aboriginal and non-Aboriginal people to achieve it. Secondly, for such a treaty to be effective, it would require that:

- the validity of Aboriginal title to their traditional lands be recognised by the Australian legal system;
- exclusive legislative and financial responsibility for Aboriginal matters be in the power of the Commonwealth Parliament;
- the property rights of non-Aboriginal citizens at the time of the negotiation of the treaty be protected against Aboriginal claim;
- a tribunal constituted on a basis agreed by the Commonwealth

and a representative coalition of Aboriginal organisations be established:

- to supervise and to act as arbitrator in negotiations leading to a treaty; and
- to act as interpreter of the principles of the treaty and to advise on its implementation.

Whatever the outcome, the coming together of Aboriginal and non-Aboriginal Australians to work out a constitutional-style basis for their living together in this continent represents, in my view, the most exciting political and social adventure in the history of the continent. Its success could provide a model for the many nations whose progress so far has been at the expense of their indigenous peoples and would be a noble expression of the political and social genius of the Australian people, black and white.

Asserting Autonomy:
Recent Aboriginal Initiatives

14

Aboriginal initiatives
on the land

The anthropologist W E H Stanner has argued that ever since it became apparent that Europeans were here to stay and that Aborigines lacked the fire power to prevent them, Aborigines have had a conscious agenda directed at a 'composition' with the invaders. There was then no way that this agenda could be articulated as a basis for negotiation and in any case, the fire power was generally in the hands of an enemy interested only in final solutions. However after killing, disease and starvation had eliminated major resistance, the needs of the pastoralists made it possible for the Aboriginal agenda for a composition to be expressed increasingly in Aboriginal actions – in what they did and what they refrained from doing.

In this chapter I draw attention to some instances of Aboriginal initiative and innovation which provide information about the Aboriginal agenda for the achievement of such a composition. It is only when white society becomes aware of that agenda and its purposes that reconciliation can become a meaningful objective. There could be many instances which would serve that purpose. Those which I have chosen are instances where their character and their compatibility have to some extent become clear. They are also ones in which I personally have been involved. This is not to suggest that my involvement was especially significant, but that it ensured that my account of the instances is based to a greater or lesser degree on personal observation.

ABORIGINES IN THE PASTORAL ECONOMY

In 1971, I was a member of the Gibb Committee appointed jointly by the Commonwealth Ministers for the Interior and for Aboriginal Affairs to report on the condition of Aborigines living and working on cattle leases in the Northern Territory. My contribution to the work of the Committee was highly critical of existing policies, yet somewhat to my own surprise, I wrote as part of a draft for the Committee's report:

> In many ways the relationship between the Aborigines and the pastoral industry is appropriate and appealing. The Aborigine has a genuine economic function to perform . . . some aspects of which he can perform as well or better than white employees. This employment offers him some social security and self-respect. Furthermore, this work he can do while living in the fashion he prefers. (Coombs in Gibb 1973: 40)

The pastoralist offered surviving Aboriginal groups access to desired goods – meat, flour, tea, sugar, tobacco and often medical and other social care – and was often required by the terms of his lease to allow free access to game, bush tucker and surface waters (requirements progressively less fully honoured). In return, the pastoralist received at little and sometimes no financial cost the services of increasingly competent young Aboriginal men and women.

Especially important in this composition was the long 'stand-down' in the wet season when stock work was suspended. During this period Aborigines resumed their traditional lifestyle with its access to the land and its resources, its opportunities to maintain and instruct the young in traditional skills and to share in the rich social life of cultural gatherings and ceremonies. The pastoralists' demands did not appear any longer to threaten Aboriginal survival, the maintenance of their cultural and religious heritage, or their capacity to raise their children to acquire and carry on that heritage; these were the non-negotiable components of the composition they sought.

This idealised description of the pastoral scene illustrates what Aborigines sought and, I believe, seek in any composition with white society in addition to the right of survival; that is, to live in the fashion they prefer, with access to the land, its resources and its creatures, with time and opportunity to care for the land, to practise their religious and cultural heritage, and to bring up their children to maintain and continue it. The relationship between them and the pastoral industry could be seen as appropriate and appealing because, until the technological pattern of the industry's husbandry was transformed after the Second World War, it enabled pastoral lessees and managers to obtain what they sought in labour, skills and local knowledge without denying these non-negotiable elements of the Aboriginal image of an acceptable composition.

Generally since then in Australian society, neither the economic system nor the governments which serve it have been prepared to explore seriously the possibility of an economic role for Aborigines which accommodates these non-negotiable elements. The brief period of the Whitlam government, during which assimilation policies appeared to be yielding to humane influences and giving way to policies designed to recognise Aborigines as a separate and respected component in Australian society, was merely an interlude. The objective became to transform Aborigines into the drably uniform and acquiescent labour force demanded by economic rationalism. Under this latter approach Aborigines must abandon their differences, particularly their identification with the land and their metaphorical knowledge of the habitat that they, the pastoralists and their cattle inhabit, to become the landless, powerless proletariat competing with their white compatriots for the increasingly scarce employment opportunities in a technological, capital-intensive and corporately-owned economy.

Since the referendum in 1967 which gave the Commonwealth Government active responsibilities for the conduct of Aboriginal affairs, there have been at least three separate group agenda seeking to determine the pattern of black–white relationships in Australia regarding access to, and use of, the land. None has been precisely articulated, but their motivations and respective patterns progressively have become clear.

The first is the agenda of the multinational and national corporate sector, led by resource-hungry pastoral and mining enterprises, which has become the instrument to complete the dispossession of Aborigines. The second agenda is that of the Commonwealth, State and Territory Governments and their bureaucracies, in uneasy competitive partnership, to establish the hegemony of their individual and professional power bases in Aboriginal affairs and to facilitate at government level the corporate agenda, while maintaining the appearance of a neutral arbiter between it and that of Aborigines. The third is the agenda of the Aborigines themselves. Aborigines have not, I believe, abandoned their desire for a composition; for a role or roles in our society which they can fill to mutual benefit while continuing to maintain their connections to the land and live in the fashion they prefer. But that fashion is not unchanging. Aboriginal initiatives, including those reviewed in this chapter, are rich in evidence of adaptation to a world of change, of the capacity to take from white society ideas, institutions and technology and to modify them creatively so that continuity with the Aboriginal past and its traditions is maintained. What *is* unchanging is firstly, the demand for personal and group autonomy and secondly, the identification with, sense of responsibility for and care of the land, indeed for the whole nature of the environment.

HOMELANDS: A CONTINUING ABORIGINAL INITIATIVE

Since the 1967 referendum, Aboriginal groups have been quietly pursuing their separate, but similar agenda to achieve components of a 'composition' by their own actions, rather than by violent protests or by appeals to judicial courts, governments or international agencies. These agenda have become especially evident in action to:

- reassert Aboriginal ownership of the land and its resources by claiming it, gaining access to it, by using and occupying it wherever this has been physically possible;
- reassert their cultural heritage and their right to maintain, express and develop it;
- maintain, formalise and adapt their control of the education and

socialisation of their children to the changes in lifestyle forced upon them;

- diversify their sources of income, real and financial, and to demand a share in the proceeds of exhaustible resources; and
- create Aboriginal-controlled institutions to provide their own services and to manage their domestic and political affairs.

At the time the Council for Aboriginal Affairs was established (1967), Aboriginal occupation of their traditional lands was close to its lowest ebb. Aborigines had increasingly and often forcibly been brought into institutionalised contexts, often far from their traditional territory. It was during an early visit to Yirrkala in 1968 that I became aware of the effects of the institutionalisation on Aborigines and of their hostility towards it. Even in Yirrkala, where clans were closely related and had long-established reciprocal obligations and effective dispute settlement procedures, there were tensions. Long periods of residence and resource use on other people's lands is frequently a significant source of conflict and of stress affecting both Aboriginal visitors and host communities.

Daymbalipu, leader of the Djapu clan and at that time chairman of a community council of clan leaders, explained to me that the clans had originally come to Yirrkala 'to help the Mission get established', an objective which they felt had been substantially achieved. It was time, he said, that they returned to their own lands and received the reciprocal help to which they felt entitled, in order to establish comparable facilities on their own lands. 'Why', he asked, 'did the government prevent them returning?'

Discussion with the Director of Welfare in the Northern Territory confirmed that the administration was strongly opposed to the return to homelands because it was seen as contrary to the then official policy of assimilation, 'weakening mission and administration control' and 'likely to make health and education programs ineffective'. On my next visit to Yirrkala I informed Daymbalipu of this response, but said that if they felt strongly about returning, the government administration could not legally stop them and in my opinion would have to accept and adapt to the decision if they 'just went'. That, I believe, was the significant beginning of the return to country in that area.

Not long afterwards, I visited Elcho Island where I found that under the influence of the intrepid mission aviator Sheppardson (Sheppy) the communities had been encouraged to remain on their own territory, rather than to move to the mission, by his willingness to 'service' them by air despite the lack of adequate landing facilities. This initiative similarly encouraged the homeland movement and, progressively, mission and Aboriginal involvement in local and regional air services.

Since then, and despite government reluctance, Aboriginal initiative has tended increasingly towards returning to traditional lands wherever possible: on unalienated Crown lands; on lands granted to Aborigines under Commonwealth and State land rights legislation; and on land within pastoral and other leasehold areas, either as excisions from the lease agreed to by the lessee, or within national parks and other reserves. The movement was often initiated by unilateral Aboriginal action, or by negotiation with government through the Department of Aboriginal Affairs. It has emerged as a major element in Aboriginal strategies to return to their lands, especially as a range of funds from the Commonwealth has become available to support those decentralised settlements.

The combination of access to land and to financial resources was not readily or easily achieved, as resistance from mission, pastoral and government sources, and differently motivated Aboriginal anxieties had first to be overcome. However, Aboriginal flexibility and ingenuity progressively made it possible for them to take advantage of official policies to achieve the objective of 'returning to country' and at the same time, to resolve conflicts between the requirements of those policies and of Aboriginal traditional behaviour. Access to traditional land was fundamental to almost all items on their agenda. In 1979, I wrote optimistically of the potential for the homeland movement (Chapter 2). Some ten years later, a report of the Standing Committee of the House of Representatives on Aboriginal Affairs drew attention to the remarkable growth in the number of homeland settlements, enumerating 588 such communities and over 100 pastoral excision communities in the Northern Territory alone (Blanchard 1987: 281–308).

THE INTRODUCTION OF UNEMPLOYMENT BENEFITS

During the 1950s and 1960s in Arnhem Land and Central Australia, missions and many government officials opposed the acceptance by Aborigines of unemployment benefits ('sit down' money) as encouraging Aboriginal 'idleness'. In view of the lack of employment opportunities in those areas and the pressure on subsistence resources because of the concentration of Aboriginal groups in missions and government settlements, this attitude seemed unduly puritanical, but I was surprised to find that it was often shared by Aborigines themselves. Their reasons were, however, different.

Aboriginal society was, and is, based very much on mutual and reciprocal sharing of resources. The acceptance of gifts or help implied the acceptance of an obligation to reciprocate when called upon. Unsolicited gifts, especially if repeated, generated doubts about the wisdom of acceptance, especially if persons outside the kinship structure were involved. There was a widespread reluctance to become heavily indebted by obligations to pay back, because of the uncertainties it created.

Where did this 'sit down' money come from? What form of repayment would be demanded and how were Aborigines to find the means to satisfy any such demands? These were reasonable questions, not easy to answer. I, for one, was inclined to believe that assimilation into the workforce and easy 'white' access to resources was the return which the Northern Territory administration and Commonwealth Government consciously or unconsciously expected, and that the Aboriginal fear that their independence was threatened by acceptance was not without foundation. Nevertheless, I urged Aboriginal leaders and the missions to explore ways to enable Aborigines to accept, without this sense of indebtedness, income support which was the right of Australian citizenship and desperately needed in many instances.

During the 1950s, welfare benefits were progressively paid to Aboriginal people indirectly through governing welfare authorities, missions and employers; it was felt that they needed to 'learn' how to deal with money first. It was only during the late 1960s that this paternalistic attitude changed and pressure was exerted to have welfare transfers paid directly to Aborigines (Altman and Sanders 1991a).

CDEP: 'SIT DOWN' MONEY OR REGAINING AUTONOMY?

The idea of commuting the right of Aborigines to unemployment benefit into an alternative form of payment, especially when they were living or wished to live in remote circumstances, seems to have emerged roughly simultaneously in regions where the homeland movement was strongest, especially in East Arnhem Land and in the Pitjantjatjara lands. This was due partly to the influence of some concerned community advisers and missionaries who saw it as a way of enabling homeland establishment and community work to be done by Aborigines working for part-time wages, rather than purely voluntarily, and so remaining independent of the 'indebtedness' of unemployment benefit. It was in these circumstances that the Community Development Employment Projects (CDEP) scheme was established by the Commonwealth Government in 1977. Under the scheme Aboriginal communities were able to request the payment of welfare entitlements (due as individual payments) to the community as a whole. Individuals would then obtain a CDEP 'wage' in return for work given priority by the community. The idea helped Aborigines escape from the fear that the money they received was an unrequited gift carrying a potential obligation to repay, and to escape from the dependencies of welfare.

The idea also had attractions for government. Such a program would make it possible for part of the establishment costs of new communities such as the homelands to be met from funds which it would have had to use for social service benefits and at the same time, to stimulate Aboriginal self-management and local 'community development'. There have been problems: trade unions have, at times, been critical of conditions which they see as undermining award pay standards; some local Aboriginal and white administrators of the scheme managed to use it as a means to advance their own personal and family monetary advantage and as an instrument of social power;

and some human rights critics saw it as a denial of Aboriginal rights as Australian citizens to an income support legally available to all (see Altman and Sanders 1991b; Sanders 1988). All of these criticisms were to a greater or lesser degree valid and some areas call for reform, but amongst most Aboriginal groups and communities they were outweighed by the fact that CDEP funding was the only significant source of funds under their own control.

For this reason, Aboriginal acceptance and use of the program widened and strengthened during the late 1980s, especially when the Commonwealth Government supplemented the unemployment benefit equivalent component with grants to the administering Aboriginal councils to help pay for materials, tools and equipment. Acceptance of CDEP scheme moneys has always, in theory, been an Aboriginal option; groups and individuals could refuse to participate or could withdraw, preserving their right to personal unemployment benefit. Growth of the scheme was constrained, since funds to be available for it were determined in the annual Commonwealth budget and communities often had to wait until funds were available and also to 'demonstrate commitment', before being allowed to participate. Nevertheless, year by year, the number of Aboriginal communities – including homelands and urban communities – involved in the scheme has grown.

The praise given to the scheme in more recent times by the Royal Commission into Aboriginal Deaths in Custody (Commonwealth of Australia 1991) has led the Commonwealth Government to increase its financial allocation to the scheme substantially, so that funds allocated to it now constitute the major program expenditure in ATSIC's budget. The praise was directed especially to the stimulus to Aboriginal autonomy and the sense of purpose promoted by the scheme, as well as to the direct contribution to health and quality of life. The Royal Commission saw scope for still greater achievement, especially that resulting from the increased involvement of women and in the use of the scheme to support self-sufficiency activities and other small-scale enterprises. The number of communities seeking admission to the CDEP scheme has continued to increase. In 1993, some 165 Aboriginal communities across remote, rural and urban

Aboriginal Australia have elected to join the scheme, with approximately 19,000 participants working on community-initiated work programs. There is little doubt that one of the attractions for Aboriginal people in the scheme is that it enables an Aboriginal definition and control of work, and in remote areas supports the movement to decentralised homelands.

THE ABORIGINALISATION OF WORK

In a note for the Royal Commission into Aboriginal Deaths in Custody in 1990, I wrote:

> The uses made of this (CDEP) scheme enable Aboriginal participants to be paid for work on a part-time basis while leaving them time to pursue their traditional hunting and gathering and other activities, and also to acquire valuable capital equipment and materials for community use . . . . The uses to which the resources of this scheme have been put range from the unimaginative 'mission-style' work teams clearing up the immediate camp environment, to activities which not merely add to wage-style money incomes, but which add to supplies of traditional and other foods and material, as well as occasional cash . . . .

There is evidence of intelligent opportunism in the responses of individual CDEP communities to the scheme, reflecting their own needs and interests. In particular, the opportunity available under the scheme to Aboriginalise work has been seized upon by a number of participant communities and includes:

- support for traditional hunting and gathering, including some activities directed at commercial markets;
- contracts for land-care activities;
- support for arts and craft production;
- preparation and printing of educational materials;
- commercial enterprises based on indigenous species such as emu and crocodile, and on gathering medicinal herbs and seeds;
- conduct of gardens;
- training and employment in providing services to the community; and

- the training of previously unemployed women in a wide range of clerical and administrative services.

In the context of this wide variety of activities, the need for a fresh appraisal of the economic and work circumstances in many Aboriginal communities is apparent. For example, there is a common refusal to regard Aboriginal food collection as income, yet as Altman (1987) has demonstrated, when bush production is valued at market replacement prices it can account for over 60 per cent of income in remote outstations. Similarly, when hunting, fishing and gathering activities are quantified and regarded as employment, their contribution is significant (Altman 1987; Meehan 1982). Looking at the situation of central Arnhem Land, it can be shown that:

> ... if employment were re-defined to include informal activities and recognising that adult work participation rates were 100 per cent, then the people at Momega outstation were fully employed, even by the standards of wider society. (Altman and Taylor 1989: 67–8)

These data all suggest that Aboriginal groups wishing to live in a homeland context, or in a pattern of movement between a homeland and an associated service centre, can with the help of the CDEP scheme and of training and employment in the provision of government-financed services like health and education, design an economic livelihood with a modest group cash income and greater self-sufficiency while adding to the flow of goods and services within the economy as a whole. While such a livelihood may be less materially affluent than that theoretically available through employment in the mainstream, it could offer a preferred form of Aboriginal work and greater personal autonomy. It represents a serious option and one which is not confined to the remote areas of Australia.

A recent innovation has been the decision of urban Aboriginal groups, such as those at Redfern (an inner Sydney Aboriginal enclave), to seek entry to the CDEP scheme. As an urban Aboriginal woman commented to me:

> We get exasperated by white people telling us we should be proud of being Aborigines. Here we are all Aborigines. Our kids now don't have

to be told – they recognise each other and themselves for Aborigines. I am a Koori – I know I am. (Coombs 1978: 120)

The Redfern decision has attracted significant and enterprising membership, developing mini-enterprises and providing services of a local government and community service character such as gardening, waste disposal and child-care. These add to Aboriginal money incomes and to services available to Aboriginal and non-Aboriginal residents. It will be interesting to observe the effect of this development, if its success is sustained, on other urban Aboriginal groups and perhaps on the urban unemployed white population. There is little doubt that in remote, rural and urban communities Aboriginal initiatives taken under the umbrella of the CDEP scheme have the potential to support greater local control and autonomy.

AN ABORIGINAL ROLE IN MULTI-FUNCTION PARKS

Aboriginal and white ways of thought have come more closely together in recent years over the concept of national parks than over any other issue. Areas of Aboriginal land have, with their co-operation, been set aside as national parks and wildlife reserves. The best known examples of these are Uluru–Kata Tjuta and Kakadu National Parks in the Northern Territory, where Aboriginal freehold land has been leased back to the Australian National Parks and Wildlife Service (ANPWS). In the case of Uluru, the Mutitjulu people have a majority of members on the board of management and important input into decisions over which parts of the park will be accessible to tourists, what kinds of infrastructure will be constructed for tourist support and how the Aboriginal people resident there will be involved in the day-to-day practicalities of park management (Altman 1988). This has included employing Aborigines as rangers and establishing programs of instructional walks in which Aborigines teach small groups of tourists about social, economic and therapeutic resource use, as well as other aspects of Aboriginal life at Uluru.

Decisions over access to ritual and other important sites are an important responsibility of Aborigines in park management. In addition, Aboriginal know-how about burning has been used by ANPWS and occasionally by pastoralists, to assist the regeneration of the environment. Park authorities also employ Aboriginal knowledge in reintroducing and restoring species previously eradicated or under threat.

But despite recognition of Aboriginal ownership of the land and their knowledge of the ecosystems and environments of these parks, and despite the occasional establishment of joint management arrangements, national parks remain essentially white institutions. Generally, the primary purpose of the parks is seen and justified by governments as an adjunct to the tourism industry and as a source of international and domestic income for the economy as a whole.

The problems of reconciling conflicting interest groups under the umbrella structure of a national park means that Aboriginal subsistence activities and other initiatives are sometimes threatened. For example, Altman and Allen (1991: 8–10) have argued that the impact of tourists may be greater than the direct pressure of numbers. They have pointed out that:

- some species are vulnerable to the impact of tourist visitation and that Aboriginal people may be in direct competition with recreational fishers;
- to avoid environmental damage, visitors are sometimes encouraged to disperse which can run counter to the economic interests of traditional owners who are then left with less area than if visitors are concentrated; and
- in the concern of sustainability, zoning areas for Aboriginal hunting and foraging by limiting access to resources may be unnecessary and result, paradoxically, in overuse of particular areas.

At present, white Australians and international tourists are most visible in and benefit most from these parks. Despite effective information services and the increasing presence of Aboriginal park rangers, it is hard for a visitor to experience any significant sense of sharing in an Aboriginal culture in action, or to be aware of the strength and persistence of the Aboriginal 'way'. This is changing slowly. Under the contribution to management and the enthusiasm and skills of Aboriginal rangers, programs are progressively being initiated which throw light on the richness of the Aboriginal cultural heritage. Those programs touch only marginally on the power and complexity of the views of the environment which traditional Aborigines share with the other indigenous peoples of the world. As Altman and Allen note:

> Despite a great deal of lip service paid to 'traditional' activities, the issue of subsistence is generally marginalised in policy debate and the comparative economic advantages that Aboriginal people in remote areas enjoy in such activities are either ignored or tolerated, but are rarely encouraged. (1991: 9)

A recent report of the National Estate Enquiry strongly commended a great extension and diversification of national parks and other reserves. Clearly, a valuable component of that process would be the establishment of specifically Aboriginal reserves, or parts of reserves, dedicated to the preservation of the culture of the various tribal groups linked with the Aboriginal territories in which the parks are located. At least one such major reserve should exist within the territory of every significant tribal or language group. It is well known that Aborigines rarely identify themselves simply as Aborigines, but rather as Nyungah, Wiradjuri, Warlpiri, Yolngu, Murri, Koori and so on, and that they value the differences in language, beliefs, histories and customs which mark those more specific identities. Reserves identified with such groups and with their territory, presenting their history and their culture, would command valuable Aboriginal involvement and management and help express the cultural diversity on which Aboriginal society is built.

Such reserves, and indeed all reserves such as those which protect and preserve nature for forest, for genetic diversity, for the protection of water sources and quality and for scientific inquiry should be based upon the Uluru model of Aboriginal ownership and joint management shared with the authority professionally dedicated to the 'white' purpose for which the reserve is established. A key Aboriginal participation and management role should be established at all times and be evident in all activities, and each reserve administration should recruit and provide training for resident Aborigines for employment as rangers and members of management teams.

Although Uluru and Kakadu National Parks are still essentially white institutions, the concept and function of joint management within them could provide an owner-management model at a regional and civic level upon which reconciliation and composition could be built. The development, for instance, of a chain of coastal and marine national parks circling the continent would be a material contribution to the vexed problem of coastal environmental protection and management which cries out for creative action. A special Aboriginal study could be conducted of the potential of regional national parks to add to the education of young Aboriginal children and to their involvement in the traditional culture of their tribal and language groups. Special camps and tours during holidays could have an especially important role in such a development. I commend the idea of such a study and the experimental organisation of such camps and tours to Aboriginal education authorities and to the Council for Reconciliation.

Multi-function parks, used in these ways, could support Aboriginal economic and cultural initiatives and effectively help offset losses incurred by Aborigines from the dispossession of their land. Such parks could form a valuable component in the equipment of Aboriginal education at all levels. Managed with full Aboriginal participation, these parks could be compatible with, indeed enhance their use for tourists, scholars and others interested in the regional environment and its role in Aboriginal society. They may also usefully support small-scale Aboriginal economic enterprises and attempts at greater self-sufficiency. Importantly, they would provide substantial redress to urban and rural Aboriginal people for whom the homelands movement is problematic, if not impossible, because of their historical removal from their traditional land and ongoing alienation from access to it. Aboriginal initiatives in the homeland movements, in their attempts to assert control and management over their work context, in their enterprise initiatives on their own lands, in land management roles in national parks, all attest to their continuing attempts to seek a 'composition' with white Australia on terms which maintain and strengthen Aboriginal culture and autonomy.

15

Initiatives in Aboriginal political organisation

SOME EARLY GOVERNMENT INITIATIVES

After the referendum of 1967 I was approached by the then Prime Minister, Harold Holt, for advice about an appropriate organisation to guide his government in the much neglected area of Aboriginal affairs. In relation to this new responsibility I recommended that the government should not rush a decision on this matter of organisation, but should initially appoint a small council supported by an office with a strong research basis, to study the nature of the problems it would face and advise the government in relation to policies and the administrative and executive means by which they might be carried out. My early contact with the administration of Aboriginal affairs in the Northern Territory and Queensland, in both of which the tendency for separatism and paternalistic dominance seemed strong, convinced me that unless the council and office were free of executive responsibility they could not avoid being identified with the status quo and would, as a consequence, be inhibited in the advocacy of change. I hoped the council could develop an independent but influential role, seeking to mould policy and administration widely by the quality of its research, knowledge of and links with Aborigines and by persuasiveness, rather than authority.

Accordingly, in September of 1967 the Council and the Office of Aboriginal Affairs were set up and I was appointed chairman. Although I had little formal experience of Aborigines outside my work as a teacher in country schools in Western Australia, the need and opportunity for reform were abundantly clear and the potential to redress some of the injustices suffered by Aborigines associated with the settlement of Australia seemed compelling.

Despite the excellence of my colleagues on the Council – the anthropologist, Professor W E H Stanner, and Barrie Dexter, then Australian Ambassador to Laos – the history of the Council between the referendum and the end of 1972 might be seen as a record of failure: marked by its growing rejection of assimilation as an appropriate basis for policies affecting Aborigines and by its unsuccessful struggle to persuade successive governments to accept the right of Aborigines to choose the nature and extent of their involvement in Australian society (Coombs 1978). It became the objective of the Council, having accepted Holt's challenge, to try to establish that right and to enable Aborigines to make that choice a reality.

One area of change that seemed particularly imperative was that Aborigines needed to be empowered to take an active role as agents in negotiations with Federal, State and local governments and other bodies (especially corporations from the private sector), which were impinging on their lives. Too often they were allowed to act only as passive institutionalised recipients of services, reacting as beneficiaries or victims. In 1971, I wrote to the Minister urging the benefits of establishing incorporated councils representing the interests of Aborigines in particular areas, in response to a Department of the Interior submission which sought to expand its establishment to provide additional services on Aboriginal settlements. I argued that:

> It is our provisional view that both missions and settlements should be developed as incorporated communities under the control of the residents (most, but not all of whom would be Aborigines) being assisted by professionally trained managers and community development workers. (Coombs 1971)

The idea of legal incorporation was eventually seized upon by the Whitlam Government and continued to influence the practice of the Department of Aboriginal Affairs (DAA) after its establishment in 1973. More importantly, Aboriginal groups and communities began to recognise the opportunity that incorporation afforded for greater local self-management and autonomy.

INCORPORATED ABORIGINAL ORGANISATIONS

Initially, the idea of legal incorporation into associations made little impact, but gradually its benefits (and its difficulties) became evident to some Aboriginal groups and those working with them. The difficulties of reconciling the European basis of these incorporated bodies and the traditional practices of Aboriginal society were acute and the early years of their development provided a record of confusion, dissension, trial and error, failures and new beginnings. But the spread of the Aboriginal incorporated association is evidence that its adoption encouraged a greater degree of Aboriginal self-management. By the time the Commonwealth introduced the *Aboriginal Councils and Associations Act 1976* to allow Aboriginal communities and groups to incorporate, the process was rapidly gaining ground.

Incorporation allowed for a new relationship between Aborigines and those in white society who possessed knowledge and expertise; a relationship in which Aborigines were increasingly in greater control, where they took the initiative as employers with the right to hire and fire. Thus, incorporated communities often employed advisers of their own choosing, rather than continue in sole dependence on departmental officers. Housing associations employed architects, contractors and building supervisors. Resource organisations hired community development officers, educators and artists. Royalty associations hired accountants, lawyers and administrators. Many of these relationships suffered from the fact that Aboriginal inexperience exposed them to exploitation and incompetence, whilst advisers often didn't know how to represent Aboriginal interests. Also, initially, the level of incorporation often omitted smaller groups such as the residents of outstations and pastoral stations.

However, those in white society whose expertise was so desperately needed were not always motivated by exclusively commercial considerations. There were professional men and women willing to work with Aborigines as employees to assist them to develop and administer services under Aboriginal control. Thus, in urban centres there developed legal, health-care and welfare services designed by Aboriginal people and with sympathetic professional men and women willing to accept employee status. These services gradually extended to rural and remote areas and became a significant focus for Aboriginal activism and service delivery. The Aboriginal men and women given authority in these organisations found them a source of administrative experience and a valuable base from which to conduct more widely-directed political campaigns.

Sometimes, the initiative for incorporation came from government. Thus, the informal land councils established by Justice Woodward to provide a basis of consultation with Aborigines in the Northern Territory about his report to the Whitlam Government on land rights were subsequently incorporated by statute and given significant powers and responsibilities. However, Aboriginal leaders within these and other incorporated organisations have shown a capacity to use their positions for purposes beyond those conferred upon them by their statutes. Sometimes, these are merely logical extensions to meet the obvious needs of their constituent communities, but often and increasingly, they represent an Aboriginal assertion of political and executive power in relation to, and through the medium of, Aboriginal affairs more generally.

ABORIGINAL-PREFERRED MODELS

There is no field of Aboriginal–white relationships where the differences between the respective concepts of authority and decision making seem so fundamental and where conflict or passive resistance are so persuasive, as in those institutions concerned with political and administrative management. It is therefore important that we become aware of the nature of these differences by looking closely at the organisational structures which Aborigines themselves favour when they are able to make their own decisions, establish the principles on which such structures function and define the circumstances within which they do so. Perhaps one of the best examples can be seen in the emergence of the Tangentyere Council, the incorporated agency of the Aboriginal groups setting up semi-permanent camps on the fringes of Alice Springs, although there is evidence of Aboriginal-preferred models of political organisation elsewhere, as well as in other aspects of Aboriginal life, especially at local and regional levels. I have put forward some of these models below, as examples of the type of creative political organisations being developed through Aboriginal initiative.

THE PITJANTJATJARA LAND RIGHTS MODEL

In 1971, a group of Aboriginal people from Amata on the north-west reserve set up a permanent camp at Puta Puta, marking the beginning of negotiations with the South Australian Government for recognition of their title to the lands of that reserve. They were represented in the negotiations by the Pitjantjatjara Land Council which was constituted by delegates of the Councils of the Yankantjatjara, Pitjantjatjara and Gnanatjara peoples who were insistent that this jointly-based Council had no role in the domestic affairs of those separate peoples, but for this specific purpose. It existed solely for the purpose of negotiating a united basis for land rights and their development into a functioning system.

A very significant result of this Aboriginal concept of the role of the jointly-based council was that the South Australian Parliament, at Pitjantjatjara insistence, legislated in 1981 not to establish a procedure by which Aborigines would have to separately claim and establish their title to the lands of the north-west reserve, but simply to declare the land within that reserve to be Pitjantjatjara land and to vest title in 'those persons who in Aboriginal law and tradition (wherever they may live) have rights in it'. It is interesting to speculate on how different the administration of the Northern Territory land rights legislation (and the incomes of lawyers and anthropologists) would have been if the Commonwealth Parliament had pursued a model similar to the South Australian one.

This model of the informal federation of autonomous groups for specific shared purposes, accompanied by a reservation of the independence of the individual groups forming the federation, seems to be a characteristic feature of Aboriginal political thought. A number of such examples of what might be called a 'bottom-up' federation of groups of organisations seems to have emerged; for example, in Aboriginal legal, health and other service areas. It is possibly from this approach that Aboriginal understanding developed of the role of land councils established in the Northern Territory under the Commonwealth's land rights legislation. Aboriginal attitudes towards such councils tend to resist the recognition of hierarchies within them and the right of their bureaucracies to determine or advise on more local issues.

THE CROCODILE HOLE CONFERENCE

In October 1991, a very successful conference organised by the Kimberley Land Council and the Waringarri Resource Centre at Crocodile Hole in the East Kimberley region reviewed the effect of resource development on local communities as a follow-up to the study reported in *Land of Promises* (Coombs et al. 1989). More than 500 Aborigines from the Kimberleys and Western Desert communities set up a working party composed of nominees of various Aboriginal-controlled organisations in the region to prepare an outline strategy for Aboriginal action.

The structure of the Crocodile Hole working party, I believe, shows the path chosen to be followed. The working party is the instrument of the Aboriginal-controlled organisations. Its members are in close touch with the Aboriginal and Torres Strait Islander Commission (ATSIC) regional council of the Kimberley and its report has gone to that council. When that communication is strengthened – when the regional councils have become effectively the agents of the Aboriginal-controlled organisations within the region – there will be the beginning of a 'bottom-up', representative political structure.

When the link between the regional councils and the Commission of ATSIC is similarly modified, Aborigines could reasonably identify with the regional councils and work to control them. They would then have the means to fight for their rights and to negotiate with governments and corporations with some prospect of orderly relationships in their conduct and significant change in their outcome, and to achieve this without significant sacrifice of autonomy in their local and domestic affairs.

I believe that the 'bottom-up' federalism concept is a realistic political option for Aboriginal self-government; an alternative to government by elected representatives holding plenary powers during their term of office. At a time when the place of Aborigines in the Australian Constitution is a matter of serious concern it is important to examine institutions created by Aboriginal initiative, including those which appear to be based on this principle. It is, as an example of that option, that I wish to comment more fully on the origins, developments and implications of the Tangentyere Aboriginal Council.

THE TANGENTYERE COUNCIL MODEL

Tangentyere Council is a good example of an organisation of different Aboriginal groups which are federated, yet retain their autonomy. The groups represented within the umbrella organisation have memberships which are geographically and culturally distinct and retain the right to withdraw from the combined Council at any time.

The way this organisation came into existence owes something to the shifting emphasis between the recommendations of the Woodward Commission and the passing of the Commonwealth's land rights legislation in the Northern Territory in 1976. Originally, Woodward had recommended that urban Aborigines such as those resident in the camps around Alice Springs, who were unable to claim land on the basis of traditional ownership, be able to apply for leases in perpetuity over vacant Crown land, on a needs basis. In October 1975, the Whitlam Government prepared a land rights Bill based on Woodward's findings and an interim Land Commissioner, Mr Justice Ward, was appointed to hear submissions, including 'town claims' in Alice Springs (Heppell and Wigley 1981: 92).

After the appointment of the Fraser Government, the Bill lapsed and hearings were terminated. In 1976, the Liberal–Country Party Government introduced an amended Bill which, after lobbying by the Northern Territory Government and others, dropped the needs basis. The Department of Aboriginal Affairs subsequently became involved in negotiating leases for town camp residents in Alice Springs with the Administrator of the Northern Territory, on the same basis as application for land by members of the general public.

Heppell and Wigley's *Black Out in Alice* details the complicated steps involved as the town campers attempted to secure tenure to the land on which they were camped:

> By the end of 1975, all that had been provided for the many permanent homeless Aboriginal people living in and around Alice Springs were a few ablution blocks and five small units built at Charles River. (1981: 106)

Lack of security of tenure over land was a severe impediment to development of any facilities such as housing, water supplies and sanitation.

It is an irony that the Tangentyere Council grew from an association that had been originally established by non-Aboriginal initiative. Townspeople considered the Aboriginal town campers, for the most part, as public nuisances impairing the tourist image of the town. Throughout the 1960s, after numerous complaints to the *Centralian Advocate* newspaper, citizens formed into action groups to consider ways to remove the town campers and only after a decade of futile efforts did people realise that their 'problem' would not simply go away. In response to the situation, in 1974, the DAA called a meeting of non-Aboriginal people associated with the town camps to form a housing association called Tangatjira. They co-opted one town camper on the committee, but Aboriginal support for the Association was token. The town campers did not see the relevance of the Association and by the end of the year Tangatjira was non-existent.

By the time the town campers became ineligible to claim land under the land rights legislation, only two of the camps had made leasehold applications. The campers began negotiations with the

DAA and were asked by the Department to develop a schematic plan to support the leasehold applications. Geoff Shaw of the Mt Nancy camp and Eli Rabuntja of Ndapa camp in Alice Springs, although politically opposites, were the first to recognise the benefits of co-operative organisation for town camp residents. In the growing expectancy generated by the passing of the land rights legislation, town campers held meetings throughout 1976 with representations from the thirteen town camps, the Central Australian Legal Aid, the Central Land Council and the Central Australian Aborigines Congress, where they resolved to form into a corporate body 'like Tangatjira'. The aims of such a body would be to:

- establish and support town land claims;
- have a body that can talk with and help lobby politicians; and
- ask for processes to help them meet their needs and to deal with the Department of Aboriginal Affairs. (Heppell and Wigley 1981: 177)

Mt Nancy was the first group which received assistance from the Aboriginal Housing Panel, a McMahon Government initiative intended to provide advice to government on low-cost housing for remote Aborigines. Architect Julian Wigley, recognised that without an ability to work in close contact with the community and listen to what the Mt Nancy people really wanted, the project, like earlier ones, would be unsuccessful. It is perhaps paradoxical, although on reflection logical, that after consultation with the Mt Nancy Housing Association, Wigley discovered that housing was not as urgent as the need for fencing, lighting and an ablutions area providing hot and cold water for showers, toilets and laundry. How the construction of such an amenity led to the community making decisions about civic responsibility, banking, community purchasing, plumbing and electricity supplies is well detailed in Heppell and Wigley (ibid.: Chapter 7).

But the situation at Mt Nancy demonstrates the futility and arrogance of attempting to force a political or social structure upon Aborigines. If, as in the Mt Nancy situation, Aboriginal people are sufficiently consulted so that they can express their needs and priorities for themselves, they can then begin to manage their affairs with some degree of autonomy. That is not to suggest that Aboriginal people should be abandoned. It is clear in the Mt Nancy case that the very good advice supplied by Wigley was a contributing factor in its success. But it is neither desirable, nor useful, to impose constraints upon Aboriginal communities based on non-Aboriginal priorities and expect the outcome to be good.

By 1977 there were signs that some progress had been made by the town campers. The leases of Ilparpa and Mt Nancy camps were granted and in August a town campers' newsletter was produced. Here, I believe, can be demonstrated the particular nature of Aboriginal political organisation at its most flexible. It could be argued that the Central Australian Aborigines Congress could have served the function of advocate for the town campers, yet there is evidence that the town campers did not believe that such a central organisation would have fully represented their requirements adequately (ibid.: 178).

By early 1978 a renewed Tangentyere Council was operational, thus saving the expense of establishing a separate incorporated body. Although primarily established as a housing association, the Council began to influence events in other directions as well. In February 1978, it conducted a census of each of the town camps to determine what skills people had to contribute. Housing was designed which would be both multifunctional and relatively simple to erect and by the end of 1978, seven buildings had been completed by the Tangentyere work force. The Council also began to provide other services for the camps, beginning with a rubbish collection service and rapidly expanding into other activities including a fencing and welding gang, a hygiene gang for maintaining plumbing and landscaping, and others for carpentry and town camp design. This progressive development made Tangentyere a valuable source of advice and expertise. Town resident, Agnes Mathews commented:

> Tangentyere helped us. Got everything for us. We were only living in tin sheds and tents out in the rain. We carried water in buckets from the creek and wells on the farm. Never had taps. We were flooded out every time it rained. We stuck chewing gum in the holes in the tin to stop the leaks. It was like living in a shower. Now we have these houses. It's beautiful. (Tangentyere 1984: 4)

However, Tangentyere was initially opposed by the Alice Springs City Council, disliked by residents and suspected by the government officials. Nevertheless, it has continued to grow and expand operations and is now a very successful organisation with increasing support from local government and the wider Alice Springs community. In 1985, the constitution of the Tangentyere Council listed its objectives as follows:

- to assist the development of member communities;
- to act to improve the living conditions and meet the needs of Aboriginal people who form the member communities; and
- to co-ordinate action of the member communities with each other and with service agencies and other bodies dealing with member communities. (1985: 44)

These objectives all reflect the fact that while in its original and early development, Tangentyere was primarily a planning, design and construction organisation concerned with the physical context of the town campers' environment, it is now also concerned with social problems affecting the camps. The Council currently services not only the permanent and transient occupiers of town camps, but also town camp members who are away visiting relatives in remote areas and communities. It provides a range of services, including mailing and banking facilities, the installation and maintenance of children's playground facilities, the establishment of parks and the provision of transport and advice (Tangentyere 1990: 12). Since 1982, the Council's liquor committee has been the largely successful opponent of new take-away liquor licences in Alice Springs (since 1980 only one new take-away licence has been granted in the town). They continue to lobby for an inquiry into the *Northern Territory Liquor Act* and Liquor Commission. After long lobbying, the Tangentyere liquor committee succeeded, in October 1989, in gaining land and funds for Alice Springs' first Aboriginal social club (Lyon 1990: 151, 153). The Council has also initiated a social behaviour project which aims to develop a consensus among local Aboriginal elders for the establishment of a code of behaviour appropriate for visitors to camp communities and to the town.

So within the primary concern of providing housing, Tangentyere Council has filled a hiatus in government and community services provided to Aboriginal people in town camps in Alice Springs. To understand the particular circumstances of its success, there is a need to look at the way the Council developed. In particular, there was strong support from the individual members of the council, and they hired good independent professional advice. Within the structure of the organisation a forum was provided for the members; for the first time the various town camp groups talked to one another. They were also fortunate to have very good Aboriginal leaders.

'BOTTOM-UP' FEDERALISM

In their structure, the Tangentyere and Pitjantjatjara Councils are good models of 'bottom-up' federalism and of a pattern for the development of local and regional government. Aboriginal society traditionally was composed of small groups whose relationships with one another were frequently suspicious and hostile. From time to time, groups who shared a common language or religious and ceremonial traditions came together for specific purposes. There was, however, little sense of a common identity between the various groups where ceremonial and language affiliation was not shared.

It has only been since white colonisation and the emergency need for groups, however separate and mutually suspicious, to work together to resist a common danger, that some sense of identity between diverse Aboriginal groups has begun to emerge. This amalgamated sense of identity has found structural expression in the Tangentyere Council which includes representatives from Arrernte, Warlpiri, Pitjantjatjara, Loritja, Anmatjira, Alyawarra and Kaititja people. It is, I believe, a model for the type of Aboriginal political organisation which will become more common.

A commonality of purpose, coupled with the expedience of having to provide specialist services to Aboriginal communities and a strong desire for cultural expression outside white Australian hegemony, will increasingly find a voice in these incorporated and informally federated organisations. These organisations, because of their 'bottom-up' federal structure, do not compromise the identity or culture of individual groups, but give common purpose and considerable effectiveness to Aboriginal aspirations and political action.

These examples of preferred organisational structures are not presented as comprehensive of contemporary Aboriginal society generally, but I believe they demonstrate a remarkable capacity in Aborigines to adapt to the need to live as autonomous groups within a racially complex and culturally diverse society; to maintain continuity with their past and its traditions; to modify non-Aboriginal experience and its institutions to serve their own autonomous purposes; and to design and give effect to their own agenda. They represent a remarkable achievement in creative political organisation.

THE ROLE OF ATSIC

It is within this context that we must consider the role and political effectiveness of the Aboriginal and Torres Strait Islander Commission since its establishment by the Commonwealth Government in 1991. The most debilitating element in the present organisational structures for Aboriginal participation in the processes of government is the misleading presentation of ATSIC as an Aboriginal organisation. This representation by the Commonwealth Government, its bureaucracy and by ATSIC itself is often accepted by the media as accurate, but is an example of contemporary 'double-speak'; of the official 'humbug' which has characterised government tactics throughout the history of Aboriginal affairs.

ATSIC was established as an instrument of government consultation; that is, of listening (or appearing to listen) to carefully selected Aborigines to create the appearance of consent, or at least conscious acquiescence, while continuing to make unilateral decisions. It is an expression of the racist assumption, so strongly criticised by the Royal Commission into Aboriginal Deaths in Custody, that we, the 'superior' race know best what is good for them, the Aboriginal people. This is not to suggest that there are not able and dedicated men and women in various parts of the existing ATSIC structure, or that their decisions and advice are likely to be wrong or improperly motivated. It is simply a necessary judgement that the Commission is not, as yet, an Aboriginal organisation working for and accountable to Aboriginal society and importantly, that it is not thought of as such by many Aborigines. Rather, it continues to be seen by many as the instrument of the Commonwealth Government and of the central ATSIC bureaucracy in Canberra. It does not, therefore, adequately serve the purposes of either government or Aborigines.

If ATSIC is to become a genuinely representative Aboriginal organisation its structure must reflect the debates conducted and decisions made by Aboriginal society through its legitimate agents at the local level. It would be relatively easy to modify ATSIC's organisational structure, especially at the regional council level, in order to achieve this local co-ordination. Indeed, it is part of ATSIC's corporate philosophy and legislative intent to see greater decision-making powers devolved downwards to the regional councils. But fundamental reorganisation is required at the regional level to effectively lock the councils into the well-established, existing network of local incorporated Aboriginal organisations.

As a means to achieve this, negotiations between the elected members of the present regional councils and the nominees of Aboriginal organisations within each region could put forward a structure for each council, acceptable to both elected delegates and other Aboriginal organisations. There is no necessity for every regional council to be constituted in precisely the same way. After all, the councils were supposed to be a reflection of the important cultural and other differences existing within the Aboriginal population (Smith 1993). Some councils seem to prefer to have fully elected representatives and others to have delegates nominated by regional organisation. A balance of these two models may possibly also have supporters. Councils comprised of delegates of local organisations or of elected representatives are both legitimate democratic structures with historical origins. The critical matter is whether the structure is determined, and accepted as appropriate, by Aborigines and their chosen and accountable representatives.

Similarly, an ATSIC Board of Commissioners, itself consisting either wholly of Aboriginally-elected commissioners or wholly of delegates nominated by their regional councils (alone or with other Aboriginal organisations) would be acceptable in Australia and internationally if it were the product of negotiated agreement among

Aborigines. The important thing is for the choice of representation to be clearly an act of Aboriginal self-determination. The decision to make ATSIC accountable at its various levels to Aboriginal communities and organisations would enable it quickly to become accepted by Aborigines generally, as their legitimate mouthpiece and as their potential negotiator.

The difficult problem is what to do with the ATSIC bureaucracy. It consists partly of survivors of the Department of Aboriginal Affairs and its related organisations, though it also includes a growing proportion of Aboriginal officers. This cannot be interpreted as establishing the new organisation as an effective instrument of Aboriginal autonomy. However interested and sympathetic to Aboriginal attitudes the staff are, they remain formally accountable to the Commonwealth Government and legally required to serve its purposes. Unlike Aboriginal land councils and resource agencies, the ATSIC bureaucracy often does not make clear in action that Aborigines are their 'bosses' and that non-Aboriginal employees, however highly paid and trusted, must accept accountability to those bosses when they make decisions. Such recognition of accountability to Aborigines is fundamental to the wider acceptance of the ATSIC bureaucracy as a source of advice and guidance. In this regard, my conclusions concerning the role of the Aboriginal bureaucracy in the National Aboriginal Conference hold true for its counterpart in ATSIC:

> ... it would certainly be a mistake to expect that a growth in the power and influence of the 'black bureaucracy' would of itself satisfy Aboriginal demands for progress towards self-determination. The capacity of the black bureaucracy to help satisfy those demands will depend on the degree to which it is felt to be accountable to, and identified with, Aboriginal communities and the degree to which it is seen by those communities as an extension of their own political institutions. (Coombs 1984: 30–1)

Reform of the central and regional office administration is urgent. Immediate changes in top management must indicate the change in lines of accountability; in particular, decision making, recruitment and training need to be regionalised. There should be an urgent commitment to strengthen ATSIC's Aboriginal and regional composition and its identification with an ideology of autonomous Aboriginal self-government.

There is potential for ATSIC to make a significant contribution to developing a workable partnership between Aboriginal and other Australians in this country. But that potential can be realised only if the ATSIC bureaucracy can be transformed into an accountable structure located within the network of existing local and regional Aboriginal organisations. Only if it is seen as such by Aborigines and their organisations at all levels and by the government, will it be able to strengthen, as opposed to undermining, Aboriginal autonomy.

16

Education: taking control

EDUCATION AS ASSIMILATION

At present, the education system is felt by Aborigines to be an instrument of assimilation: children are there to be changed; to unlearn what their parents and kin have taught them; to be weaned away from the loyalties that have made them Aboriginal. The result is evident in the fundamental conflict that characterises black–white relationships throughout Australia. The importance of this source of conflict within the education system was highlighted by a task force of Aboriginal women who reported:

> Differences in cultural values between the home and school manifest themselves on the very first day of school. The gaps in learning begin then and widen as Aboriginal children progress through schooling. (Daylight and Johnstone 1986: 5)

There is a widespread demand among teachers, especially Aboriginal teachers and those who are training them, for an independent professional review of the Aboriginal educational system. There are serious doubts about the wisdom of a system which places the highest levels of decision about education in the hands of politicians and their officials who see its purposes almost solely in terms of the needs of industrial and commercial employers for acquiescent employees, narrowly skilled to meet their needs, or who see education as the instrument to impose the drab uniformity of the managerial industrial society on all who pass through the school system. There is need for an educational charter which would establish the right of parents, children and teachers to choice; which would identify the school as an instrument of healthy diversity; and recognise that for Aborigines, it should be seen and developed as a continuation of the traditional educational and socialisation practices of their family-based society.

While Aboriginal schools and their teachers remain formally part of the State and Territory Education Departments and continue to be dependent on them for resources, the funding agencies will continue to dictate on all matters of policy. Furthermore, the criteria embodied in current policy assume that the educational process will be conducted in school, in age or performance-based groups; that European instructional-style pedagogy will be used; and that the curriculum, at least in its core subjects, will be the same as in non-Aboriginal schools. It assumes that commitment and performance can be measured by attendance and continuance to higher levels of educational institutions.

Among Aborigines these assumptions are being actively questioned, indeed disputed. Aboriginal teachers express the problem in the following way:

We thought that the institution of schooling was a threat to Blekbala [Aboriginal] ways of talking about things, relating to one another, and to appropriate ways of teaching. We took the children to a place called Ten Mile Creek ... the children could swim there; and there was an abundance of wildlife, plants and animals which were the focus of the lessons at the time. At Ten Mile Creek, the classes were separated into language groups led by language teachers. They talked about plant, animal and natural formation names in their languages, and explained to the children the basic significance of each in the Blekbala world. This significance was in terms of the Blekbala world view.

What we were trying to do was to get the children away from seeing the world in the Munanga [white Australian] way. We were working towards decolonising the minds of the Warlamirri children. This means sitting obediently behind desks, writing Munanga ideas and language, and being told what to do by the Munanga teacher out at the front of the class. In other words, we were trying to get away from Munanga teacher-centred learning. (Bindarriy et al. 1991: 166)

This form of educational assimilation is an option which should be open to the voluntary choice of Aborigines: the way in to the mainstream and the welcome should be clear. But assimilation by compulsion, by the destruction or the denial of the resources for the development of Aborigines' own traditional educational processes, or by the deliberate cultivation of conflict, is cultural genocide.

There is no doubt that denial of resources and the cultivation of conflict characterise the patterns of official government policies towards Aboriginal education. The results can be seen especially in the conflict which has been internalised in the minds of many Aborigines and which shows itself in severe mental confusion and emotional stress. In many individuals these symptoms form part of the syndrome which underlies many of the events and conditions reviewed by the Royal Commission into Aboriginal Deaths in Custody (Commonwealth of Australia 1991).

TOWARDS 'TWO-WAY' EDUCATION

The case for a high-level professional review of government policies towards Aboriginal education is powerful. Such a review should be directed at the achievement of self-determination in education and the protection of Aboriginal culture in its broadest sense. It should guarantee to every Aboriginal community the right of choice for its children between a government school, a private or religious-based school, or an independent Aboriginal school responsible to the community it serves. Such independent schools should have access to resources, to research facilities and training on a basis fully comparable with those available to government schools. Every homeland community should have educational facilities under its own control, at least at a level achievable by a combination of partially-trained teachers drawn from its own families. They should be supported, where necessary, by regular visits by fully qualified teachers from the nearest community school and by 'education at a distance' services of the kind originally developed by Schools of the Air, but now more widely available in effective and economical forms.

John Bucknall noted that an essential part of the process was communication between Aboriginal communities and education departments:

> There is an argument that the presence of formal and informal networking is a key component in areas such as morale, the development of an esprit de corps and the encouragement of innovative and effective strategies at a school based level. (1991: 9–10)

Part of this communication process is the recognition that Aboriginal education is a 'two-way' process. Traditionally, Aboriginal children came to understand the world they lived in and acquired the knowledge and skills it demanded of them by sharing from infancy in the daily lives of their parents and kin, learning by observation and experiment, and by accepting almost from infancy a role within the group appropriate to their age and gender. This style of education is now impossible in a society where parents and kin must dedicate many of their waking hours to mainstream employment to earn a living and where the State requires that Aboriginal children attend school for a major part of their time. There they are instructed by non-Aboriginal teachers to prepare them for employment in a world vastly different from that in which their parents grew up.

But Aborigines have not become wholly isolated from that world. Wherever they have access to it, however limited, they continue to use and enjoy the bush, its tucker, its medicines, its creatures and its solitude. Whatever white attitudes and lifestyle they may adopt or accept, the great majority retain relationships, loyalties and obligations which derive from their perhaps half-forgotten kinship system. In their homes, their children continue to hear at least fragments of dead or dying languages, ancient stories, songs and vocabularies, and to acquire patterns of behaviour and the bases of moral judgements which tie them irrevocably to the Aboriginal world. When they get to school they become progressively aware that they are there to be changed: that a battle is being fought over their minds and their souls; that acceptance requires that they cast off their past and their kin.

I know of no Aboriginal parents who do not wish their children to have effective command of English and numeracy: to understand and to be competent in the white man's world. At the same time, I know almost no Aboriginal parents who do not strongly value their identity as Aborigines and wish their children to continue to share it. It is for these reasons that where Aborigines control, or wish to control, their own schools and strive to devise their own curricula and their own pedagogic style, they think and talk of 'two-way' education where they will have the opportunity to involve parents, kin and elders in its design and practice, calling upon the knowledge and wisdom of their own experts. It is for these reasons, too, that much of this education is delivered, not by instruction in a classroom, but by participation in carrying out real activities in the community and the bush. Like the great educationist Ivan Illich, they believe that knowledge of both white society and their own can be learned by participation and by reflection on that experience, but cannot be taught simply by instruction. Aboriginal education, to a significant degree, must be de-schooled and made 'two-way'.

INITIATIVES IN THE PILBARA

The possibility of independent Aboriginal education emerged not long after the 1967 referendum which brought the Commonwealth into Aboriginal affairs. The possibility formed part of the agenda of the campaign for control of their own domestic affairs among the Aborigines of the Pilbara region of Western Australia who were influenced by the legendary Don McLeod. McLeod's training and experience as a mining prospector had enabled clans in that region to develop skills for the mining and concentration of rare metals like titanium which had become important and expensive in the making of munitions and in the burgeoning aviation industry of the time. Briefly, McLeod's 'mob' began to accumulate substantial cash holdings and were entering the market for the purchase of pastoral leases. McLeod was insistent that the authority of the elders and the

Aboriginal law should be maintained and that this unexpected affluence should be directed to strengthening traditional ways.

Under McLeod's guidance, the Western Australian Education Department's proposal for a school under the authority of white teachers was rejected by the Aborigines. Instead, they demanded funds for a school under their own control and amenable to the peripatetic life of the various families on their seasonal journeys. It was an issue which came to the attention of the Council for Aboriginal Affairs which was sympathetic to many of McLeod's ideas. The Council supported the group's submission to the Commonwealth for funds for an independent Aboriginal school, as part of the experimental educational activities sponsored by the Commonwealth Office of Education. McLeod was able to mobilise support also from trade unions, some religious groups and foundations interested in education experiment, and was able to get an Aboriginal-controlled school operating on independent and innovative lines.

The school was staffed by volunteer non-Aboriginal educators working together with the elders and those members of extended families with responsibilities for training of the young. The school had a difficult birth and development, being partly dependent financially on trade union, church and similar sources of support. The mobile character of the school has been maintained and has influenced the pedagogy and curricula styles of the education and the changing staff.

In Western Australia, the movement has continued to grow, especially in the north-western and desert communities. There are now about twenty such schools forming the Nomads Charitable and Educational Foundation which provides some research backing and battles for resources for equipment and training. A recent and vital development is the entry of this organisation and its members into a network linking them with centres of innovation such as the Aboriginal teacher training centres at Mt Lawley College, Perth, and Batchelor College, NT, and with universities like the John Curtin University, Perth, which have substantial Aboriginal student populations.

INITIATIVES AT YIRRKALA

In the early 1980s, the East Arnhem clans in and around Yirrkala began a campaign to Aboriginalise their schools. They formed a

192

school council consisting solely of Yolngu clans, to meet and discuss in their own languages the school policies and to make decisions for themselves. This council involved parents, Yolngu teachers and community leaders. They wanted their school to be a continuation of their traditional pattern of socialisation based upon their vision of the world as an extension of their family structure, and to become a familiar Yolngu institution, rather than an instrument of mainstream society.

It quickly became apparent that the existence of the council alone could not achieve this. Indeed, they progressively realised that in the school, as elsewhere, every aspect of its administration, its staffing policy, use of languages, curriculum, ways of teaching and its attitude towards children's participation in family and group life, were the instrument of Balanda (white) power. They also realised that if their aim of making the school an expression of Yolngu life was to be achieved, they must establish control of all those aspects. Wesley Lanhupuy of the Yirrkala community and Member for Arnhem in the Northern Territory Assembly articulated the problem in a speech to the Assembly in 1991:

> The strong Balanda cultural orientation of the [school] and the dominating position of Balanda teachers and administrators inevitably work to influence the minds of children in ways that undervalue the Aboriginal heritage. Aboriginal people now understand that if schools are to service the political, social and economic purposes of their own people, the school as an institution, needs to be accommodated within Aboriginal society itself. Only when the cultural orientation of the school becomes Yolngu will schools become integral to the movement of Aborigines towards self-determination. The decolonisation of schools in Aboriginal communities is the challenge for Aborigines now.

In 1984 the Yirrkala people established a Yolngu action group made up of all the Yolngu school staff; from the principal to the janitor, all were to be equal. Whites were sometimes invited. Decisions were made about staffing, curriculum, problem children, problem white people, attendance at school programs and special activities. The Aboriginalisation of all such decisions had become the immediate objective, to be worked for day by day in the school, at school council meetings, in dealings with the principal, white staff and with the education bureaucracy.

But the major tasks of Aboriginalisation and educational reform still had to be faced. The school would not be a Yolngu institution until the majority of the teachers were themselves Yolngu, until the content of what was taught (the curriculum) and the way in which it was taught (the pedagogy) also reflected Aboriginal life, provided Aboriginal knowledge and met Aboriginal needs – including the need to be skilled and competent in the white aspects of life at Yirrkala – and until Aboriginal autonomy replaced white authority in all aspects of decision making in the school's affairs.

It was in response to these tasks that the Yirrkala people began 'two-way' education. Yolngu children in the traditional past had acquired the complex body of Yolngu knowledge with its responsibilities for appropriate behaviour, almost unconsciously, by progressively increasing involvement in activities with their family, clan and community members. Formal instruction was rare and then subtly provided without destroying the child's sense of personal competence. But the intrusion of western lifestyles, with members of the family being employed elsewhere for much of the day or week and therefore not necessarily available to be observed and learned from as a model, made it necessary for the school to take over some of the educational and socialisation functions previously performed by members of the extended family. This meant that the form of much of what was to be learned had to be changed. Also as white teachers and administrators wished or needed to learn Yolngu languages and culture, especially to understand relationships and behaviour, it became necessary for the information to be abstracted, formalised and recorded in appropriate oral and printed form.

If the school was not to become an even more insidious instrument of the mainstream desire to change and assimilate Yolngu, it was important that it should quickly and in all essential ways become more integrated with Yolngu culture. It was also important that the necessity for it to perform some of the functions previously carried out by children's relatives should not isolate those children from the activities in which they would traditionally have been involved. In addition to this integration, the school had also to accept substantial responsibility for introducing Yolngu children to the non-Aboriginal aspects of the world around them. The children must be made aware that there were two cultures functioning within their community: one with which they and their kin identified and one which they must understand, recognising its differences and acquiring the skills necessary to be competent in dealing with it.

To achieve such a transformation was and remains a mammoth task, a fundamental part of which was to develop a philosophy for the school and its management to serve as a guide for action and a basis for progressive reflection upon its outcome. This could be achieved only by having staff of high intellectual quality with a wide grasp of educational theory, establishing links with other institutional centres with comparable interests and relevant resources. It was decided that within the Yolngu community the important links were with the Dhanbul and Lanhupuy Councils responsible for self-management within the Yirrkala and homeland communities respectively, and that the school council and the internal action group should develop and maintain programs of communication with these councils and with the parents and community groups for which they spoke.

Externally, important links were established with the Education Faculty at Deakin University, with the History and Philosophy of Science Unit at the University of Melbourne, with the Training College at Batchelor in the Northern Territory and with other interstate teacher training centres. These institutions, in association with Yolngu schools, conducted research directed at comparisons of Aboriginal and western knowledge systems and educational theory and practice. A pattern of regular visits and consultations between the school management and those institutions has progressively been developed.

An early outcome of these linkages was the targeting of specific staff positions to be filled as priorities by Yolngu and the development of training programs linked with periods of understudy for the individuals selected. This has enabled dramatic success in the Aboriginalisation of staff at senior levels and has been supplemented by basic programs for trainee teachers within Yolngu territory, thus strengthening and speeding up the progress towards Aboriginal-isation of homeland schools. The first Yolngu principal of an Aboriginal school in Australia (who died in December 1989 and so I will not give her name), with a staff composed completely of Yolngu teachers, was a graduate of Deakin University and worked hard to provide leadership in the school and understanding of the way in which the school interacts with the community.

Separately from changes in the school itself, more recent developments in the community include setting up an educational resource centre, designed primarily to produce material to support the activities of homeland schools but also more generally for the community's educational activities. This centre serves as a focus for the progressive development of the school's curricula and its academic and social philosophy. The establishment of the resource centre, together with the return of a Yolngu graduate from the History and Philosophy of Science Unit in the University of Melbourne, has made possible a triumvirate as the focus of leadership in the educational structure at Yirrkala, consisting of the principal of the school (at present his deputy while he is on leave), a manager with especial responsibility for dealing with the Northern Territory Government bureaucracy, and the director of the education resource agency. It will be interesting to observe the effects of this departure from the traditional European hierarchical structure of educational authority, towards one more consensual.

There is a quality of enthusiasm, almost of exuberance, about Yolngu education at present. Increasingly, 'school' activities are being conducted as part of community life, sometimes simply by participation, as part of a cultural studies program and sometimes in planned and structured workshops. Such workshops often extend over days, or even weeks, and are followed by exercises to record their purposes, their processes and their outcome. These records provide a basis for subsequent reflection and review.

CONCLUSION

The precise meaning of 'two-way' in relation to education is disputed, even among its advocates. To some, it is no more than a bilingual instruction in English and the mother tongue; to others it means education for two separate domains of living, in both of which the student must acquire competence. Still others envisage that teacher and student occupy and fill both roles as teachers and learners. But increasingly, it means that Aboriginal children must learn from the beginning the separate foundations of their own culture and understand and value its differences from that of the white man's world, which they must also comprehend. But in all of these interpretations of 'two-way' there is an assertion of, and a demand for, respect for the Aboriginal 'way'.

Furthermore, it is generally accepted among Aboriginal teachers and parents that attendance cannot usefully be compelled and that the options chosen by those who do not attend may at least possibly be educationally valuable. This is not to suggest that absence, particularly sustained, can be ignored, but rather that its significance and alternative positive courses of action for dealing with it need to be explored and reflected upon by decision makers. It is noteworthy that attendance is markedly higher in homeland schools where activities are more closely integrated with those of the resident families, than is possible in the main Yirrkala school, but that in both, attendance is believed to be numerically better than that of Aboriginal children in most European-style schools.

These experiments in curriculum content and in pedagogic style are being, and will continue to be, closely monitored. Of particular interest will be whether the success of introducing Aboriginal children to numeracy by emphasising the structural similarity of the European number system to the genealogical pattern of generational relationships within families with which Aboriginal children acquire an early familiarity, will continue into their introduction to arithmetical and other mathematical processes. Similarly, the return to a more natural acquisition of basic skills by participation and imitation, rather than by formal drilled repetition, will be tested in practice.

The development of a wider support network that links Aboriginal-controlled schools with the staff and students of teacher training institutions and with the research activities of universities generally, means that Aboriginal educational institutions and practice provide a focus for research and innovation capable of influencing not merely other aspects of Aboriginal independent development, but also the theory and practice of pedagogy generally. It is an outstanding example of the creativity which Aboriginal autonomy can unleash.

The Recognition of Native Title

17

The Mabo decision: a basis for Aboriginal autonomy?

FROM *TERRA NULLIUS* TO EXTINGUISHMENT

In 1983, when writing in support of the need for a treaty between the Australian Government and Aboriginal peoples, I noted that in Australia, 'the prevailing legal view has been that native title did not exist' and that 'the issue has not yet been dealt with effectively in the High Court' (see Chapter 13). I argued strongly that only such a judgement 'would give security' to Aborigines and that 'it is vital that this matter be resolved'. Some ten years later the High Court made such an historic decision in respect to the Mabo case put to it by the Meriam people of Mer Island in the Torres Strait. It is a moot point, however, as to whether this judgement and the national legislation subsequently presented by the Commonwealth Government will provide either the land rights or the political and cultural autonomy that Aboriginal people have long sought.

The High Court judgement was handed down in June 1992 and received a favourable initial response from Aboriginal people, the Prime Minister and much of the public and media. A valuable analysis of the judgement by Professor Garth Nettheim (1992) of the University of New South Wales incorporates a useful summary by

Justice Brennan of the present state of Australian law relating to Aboriginal land rights and refers also to changes in the historical foundations of Australian law affecting Aborigines. Perhaps the most important of these changes were:

- that the doctrine of *terra nullius* was false. (It had asserted that the territory of Australia, prior to British occupation and assumption of sovereignty, was 'waste and substantially unoccupied' and without legitimate owners with right and power to govern);

- that the British Crown had acquired sovereignty and radical title to all that territory by 'acts of State' begun in 1788 and by subsequent occupation and dispossession, and that the validity of that acquisition of sovereignty and radical title could not be questioned in an Australian municipal court; and

- that native title to the lands of the territory of Australia had existed from time immemorial, prior to the acquisition of sovereignty by the British Crown, and had survived that acquisition, but had been and could continue to be extinguished by legislation and other valid grants of title by the Crown in the States, Territories or the Commonwealth, to the extent that the continuance of native title was inconsistent with the terms of the title granted. Extinguishment could occur provided the Acts making the grants were not in conflict with existing Commonwealth legislation and in particular, the Commonwealth *Racial Discrimination Act 1975*.

A Federal Court judgement in September 1993 in regard to land granted under the *Aboriginal Land Rights (Northern Territory) Act 1976* emphasised that a grant of other title to land previously or currently held by Aborigines extinguishes native title only to the extent of any inconsistency between the terms of that grant and the continuance of native title. This judgement, together with the High Court's view that an intention to extinguish native title cannot be presumed or lightly inferred, suggests that the imposition of any limitation on the duration of a lease, constraint on the purposes for which the leased land can be used, or indeed any other reservation to the Crown of a right to qualify or change its lease terms – for instance, by imposing obligations on the lessee to conform to a regional or other development plan – could be prima-facie evidence of intention that native title was not to be extinguished. It would therefore appear logical to conclude, unless clear and unambiguous intention to the contrary exists, that any pastoral or other special purpose lease could continue together with native title. However that title would, for the period of the lease, be subject to the provisions of that lease, but be fully restored thereafter (see *Janice Pareroultja, Dulcie Jukkadai, Elfreida Ungwanaka, Magdeline Ungwanaka v Robert Tickner and Kunmanara Breaden and Max Stuart*). It is not logically necessary that native title be extinguished to enable grants of more specific title to be granted. This includes grants under other land rights legislation and leases for mining developments (which already operate in parallel to all other existing land leases). The view of the High Court on these matters was not made clear in the June 1992 judgement.

When, after the Norman conquest, the radical title of the Crown was established, it was a title which accepted and was burdened with the obligation to recognise and protect all previously existing titles established by ancient laws and customs. (It is true there were exceptions of a punitive character, but the principle held true.) *Even freehold title was held to be derived from the Crown and the Crown was committed to protect it.* Somewhat similarly, prior to white occupation of Australia, Aboriginal title to land was inalienable, but rights to allow use could be granted simply by asking and receiving permission, or reasonably presuming it to have been granted, that is, the request, in itself, is an acknowledgment of native title. Thus, when the Pintubi wished to leave Papunya in the early 1970s they were given permission by the relevant Loritja traditional owners to live at Yayayi, which was not Pintubi territory.

The inalienability of land title is sacrosanct to Aborigines, but their practice shows that they saw and see no inconsistency between the preservation of that title and it 'being burdened with' obligations to protect rights agreed to by them and established by valid exercise of their sovereign power. The consistency of leasehold, or even free-hold, with native title may seem to non-Aborigines to be a legal contradiction, but logically it is less so than extinguishment. Extinguishment means in fact alienation to the Crown and, furthermore, makes land available for alienation to other owners. Aborigines generally wish to honour the recent promises their leaders have made to respect other people's rights to their backyards. But to do so, it is not necessary that they should have to deny the existence of an ancient and special identity between them and the land of their forebears.

LIMITATIONS OF THE MABO JUDGEMENT

The High Court judgement on what is now known as the Mabo decision was designed to clarify and give greater precision to the laws concerning Aboriginal people and their rights to land. It did not deal with Aboriginal rights or claims to other forms of property or to social, political, human and other rights. Nor, indeed, did it deal with more general legal questions raised by the European occupation and dispossession of Aboriginal land that are potentially important to the resolution of disputes between Aboriginal people and white society. In particular, the questions of:

- whether a fiduciary obligation of care and protection for indigenous Australians had been established by the process of the Crown acquiring sovereignty and radical title to the land, or by the various individual and corporate acts by which that title was historically extended, and
- what were the limits to sovereignty as it existed in the various manifestations of the Crown and by what processes were such limits established or changed.

These are issues about which Aboriginal people have expressed strong opinions and which, subsequent to the Mabo decision, remain vexed and emotionally charged. They will be important in continuing negotiations between government and indigenous leaders and their communities and groups.

Government discussion following the Mabo judgement was dominated largely by private consultations conducted by the Prime Minister and his immediate advisers with selected groups and individuals presumably seen by them as representative of important special interests. Such a process marginalises Aboriginal people, whose rights and future are at stake, as merely one of the special interests which the government must consider. Their rights should in fact be the prime focus in the key issue in dispute between indigenous people and Australian society generally; namely, the resolution of the conflict created by white occupation in 1788 and the continuing dispossession and genocidal destruction of Aboriginal peoples and their society.

The Commonwealth must at least resume its long-respected role of the Crown as arbiter, in the interests of peace, order and good government, between the conflicting special interests attempting to exercise control over the resources of the land and water. It should not ignore the fact that the original white occupation and subsequent dispossession was effected in defiance of official instructions to Cook, and to Phillip and other early governors, to acquire land with 'the consent of the natives'. Neither should it ignore the fact that the physical acts of dispossession and dispersal – 'clearing the land of the natives' – were predominantly illegal acts of private settlers and their agents. In most instances, official action was confined to ex-post facto validation of a dispossession that had already been carried out, often brutally, by such settlers on the moving frontier of contact.

Since white 'discovery' and settlement began in 1788, and throughout the successive transfers of administrative and legislative powers to Australian States from the British Crown, there were occasions when the option of negotiation could have been chosen. Despite evidence in official documents that the Crown in the British Government at various times was concerned that a fiduciary obligation of care for indigenous people existed, but was not being and would not be honoured (indeed was already being grossly repudiated), at no time was significant action by Australian governments taken to explore this option. This was amply demonstrated in the exchanges between the British Government and the authorities in Western Australia which made clear that the final willingness of the British Government to grant white hegemony in a sovereign State emerged because it had been persuaded that the Western Australian

Government could be trusted to honour a fiduciary obligation to protect and care for the indigenous people in that State. It was similarly demonstrated in South Australia, where the British Secretary of State for the Colonies insisted that Robert Torrens should make arrangements to purchase land needed for white settlement from the Aboriginal landowners, before he would issue Letters Patent to allow Torrens' colonising venture to proceed (Reynolds 1994). The purchases were not undertaken. There are, then, many such historical, legal and other considerations which the High Court decision left unresolved.

THE CROWN'S FIDUCIARY DUTY

The High Court's failure to clarify adequately the claim that a fiduciary obligation to protect the rights and interest of indigenous people exists in the Crown is a great disappointment. Such a fiduciary relationship between the Crown and the Maori of New Zealand is now acknowledged. The New Zealand Court of Appeal has declared that the negotiated Treaty of Waitangi is binding on the Crown. The processes for clarifying the implications of that Treaty demonstrate impressive progress in advancing reconciliation between Maori and Pakeha (whites). The acknowledgment of an equivalent obligation towards indigenous Australians would almost certainly serve a similar purpose.

Of the seven judges involved in the Mabo case, only Justice Toohey made specific reference to the existence of a fiduciary duty to Australian indigenous people. He argued, in effect, that the power to extinguish their rights carried with it an obligation to protect and compensate those who suffered from that extinguishment. Natural justice could scarcely require less, especially as the power to extinguish has so often been exercised in defiance of Crown instructions to acquire land 'with the consent of the natives' and has been effected by illegal individual actions.

The High Court, as a whole, seems to have paid effective attention only to those problems presented to it which could be dealt with within the limits of Australian laws relating to Aboriginal rights to land. It seems to have considered political action necessary to amend those laws by agreement, in order to strengthen Aboriginal rights to land or to give effect to social justice programs, as beyond the scope of legal issues raised by the Mabo case itself. In the light of events subsequent to its judgement, such a limitation would seem to be a dereliction. The issue of Aboriginal rights (not only in land) is perhaps the most important political issue now facing the Australian community. If, as Justice Toohey stated, a fiduciary duty exists, the Commonwealth and the Australian community have the right to know. If it exists and requires political action to honour it, the High Court has a duty at least to refer to the possibility of negotiating an agreement about such action. It is a sad comment that it has taken Aboriginal initiative in the form of the Wik people's claim to traditional lands in western Cape York Peninsula, to bring the moral issue of the Crown's fiduciary obligation forward for legal assessment.

THE STATUS OF SOVEREIGNTY

Similarly, the High Court failed to clarify the question of sovereignty; that is, the right and power to govern. It cannot be denied that before 1788, sovereignty was exercised by the various family-based groups of indigenous people who occupied this continent. No act ceding that right to govern was, or has since then, been made by them. Many Aborigines and other Australians believe that in the absence of such an act of cession, their sovereignty persists morally and in international law.

The closest the Court came to dealing with this issue is in its judgement that the acquisition of the Australian continent by the British Crown and sovereignty over it cannot be challenged in an Australian municipal court. That judgement cannot be disputed. However, it leaves unanswered the question of whether there is, or could be, any international court or other agency in which it could be challenged and so provide the means by which that power to govern can be changed or divided. The implication is that the Court considers sovereignty to be unchangeable except by force of arms. Such a belief is clearly untenable. In Australia, sovereignty is divided territorially and by subject matter: between the Commonwealth and

States by the Constitution; between the Commonwealth and its various Territories by agreement validated by Commonwealth legislation; and between the Commonwealth and certain Aboriginal communities and their incorporated organisations.

The Commonwealth's sovereignty and consequently that of the States is qualified also by Commonwealth acceptance of the right of the International Court of Justice to adjudicate certain matters, and by the Crown becoming party to a number of internationally negotiated covenants addressing a wide range of social and economic commitments. These could possibly include a covenant recognising a range of rights of indigenous peoples. An even more important precedent is Australia's participation in the Bretton Woods Agreements and the General Agreement on Tariffs and Trade negotiated as part of the post-World War II settlement which granted effective power to United Nations (UN) institutions like the International Monetary Fund to influence and, to some degree, control economic policies of member nation states. Less precise, but of increasing importance, is also the apparently growing authority of the Security Council and other UN agencies to impose policies on nation states and, where that Council thinks it necessary, to enforce them by sanctions including armed force. There is, then, a growing international audience attending the domestic processes that purport to deal with indigenous rights.

Furthermore, the political reality is that multinational corporations are now so economically dominant in their impact on nation states that even the most powerful governments take account of their interests and wishes. The legal and economic significance of these political facts has, I understand, been strengthened by the International Court of Justice accepting responsibility for adjudicating disputes between the parties to certain agreements between international corporations and nation states. Thus, the realistic condition of sovereignty in Australia is that it has been significantly limited, divided and varied in its history by High Court decisions, by constitutional change and by acts of the Crown, often following agreements with other governmental or corporate authorities. Clearly, sovereignty can be changed if the political will exists. The option of negotiation and agreement endorsed by legislation and if necessary constitutional change is, at least in theory, always available. A refusal to use it could well be seen as justifying violent resistance by Aborigines to their dispossession. Similarly, the legal assertion and acceptance of the right to govern does not necessarily carry a corresponding capacity to govern. On the other hand, the power to impose and to govern does not necessarily imply a right to govern.

Most existing agreements between nation states and their indigenous people have, in effect, been an exchange of an act of cession of the power to govern in return for constitutional-style guarantees of self-government within agreed limits, and for the recognition of indigenous social, political and property rights. In some instances, compensation has also been guaranteed where title has been granted elsewhere. To confidently withstand international challenge, an agreement that embodies such an exchange between the Commonwealth and indigenous people would need to occur as an 'act of self-determination' by those peoples. Such acts are not unheard of in Australia. The Australian Government afforded the Malay people on the Cocos Islands an 'act of self-determination' on 6 April 1984 that was witnessed by a UN visiting mission. This process eventually saw Malay people vote for integration with Australia, but under conditions that continued '... to protect the Islanders' rights and traditions' and gave the community the right to '... manage its own affairs to the greatest extent possible, without interference in its culture, traditions, religion and land use' (Commonwealth Grants Commission 1989). In the absence of such an 'act' for indigenous Australians, the continued exercise of sovereignty by the Crown in Australia will continue to be tainted by the aggression by which it was originally achieved. It certainly raises the question of whether to deny the right to an 'act of self-determination' to Aboriginal people, while granting that right to its citizens of Malay origin, is not discriminatory.

There is no insuperable barrier to an agreement between Aborigines and the Crown to divide sovereignty so as to allow Aboriginal communities the power to govern, to live in a style they prefer and have title to property in forms and quantity sufficient to provide for that lifestyle. Equally, such an agreement could be reached about the procedures which should govern access to, and use of, the resources of lands and waters previously Aboriginal property. The independent function of the judiciary to determine what is the precise state of Australian law in respect to Aboriginal rights in land has not yet been completely performed. Until it is clear how far the continuance of native title is compatible with other possible grants of title; until it is known whether and to what extent a fiduciary obligation exists in the Crown towards the dispossessed; until questions such as those referred to above about sovereignty and the right of self-determination are answered, the task of the judiciary remains unfinished. In other words, the Commonwealth's native title legislation is unlikely to resolve certain key issues for Aboriginal people. A series of test cases may well arise and need to be heard by the High Court in order for a firm basis for legislative action to be established.

THE LIMITATIONS OF NATIVE TITLE LEGISLATION

It is not surprising that indigenous peoples around the world continue to deny the legitimacy of legislation and agreements which purport to recognise or grant them native title to land they believe has always been theirs. This is especially the case when a primary purpose has in fact been to validate earlier dispossessions and to ensure that remaining land continues to be subject to alienation by compulsion.

It is clear that such a purpose is inherent in the native legislation put forward by the Keating Government in late 1993. It is equally clear that the legislation responds to the agenda of powerful corporations in the mining industry (though not responsively enough according to mining interests) and to particular State interests, and that other significant economic and social interests, especially those arising from ecological and environmental aspects of the use of natural resources, were substantially subordinated in the preliminary discussions held about that legislation.

If the High Court itself focused only on particular legal issues and, as a consequence, limited its findings to that degree, then subsequent Commonwealth legislation proposes even more specific conditions upon the recognition and exercise of native title. What is being granted by Commonwealth legislative largesse is an Aboriginal native title engineered to suit white proprietary interests. One has to ask then, is not the survival of native title in its legislative form simply another mechanism for the progressive extinguishment of Aboriginal title? For the legislative survival of native title differs radically from its pre-contact nature and therefore is not a survival, but a form of alienation, indeed of extinguishment. Prior to European occupation, Aboriginal land ownership was by its very nature, inalienable. Through legal extinguishment, alienation to the Crown establishes a mechanism for further alienation. If native title survives in law as the High Court has so judged, surely it can be alienated (or extinguished) only with consent, in accordance with Aboriginal procedures; that is, by an Act of Self-determination.

The claim that uncertainty for miners and other development interests is intolerable and requires the extinguishment of native title is unwarranted. It is the product of the continuing unwillingness of many resource-exploiting enterprises to concede that they will have to negotiate with Aboriginal people and accept their right to hire expertise to secure reasonable equality of bargaining power. In 1979 (see Chapter 2), I commented on the pressure created by mining companies who were impatient with the need to negotiate with Aborigines. They were similarly impatient at Noonkanbah and in the Argyle area of Western Australia in the 1980s (Dixon and Dillon 1990; Hawke 1989) and have become no more patient in the 1990s. Yet dealing with uncertainty is what entrepreneurs are rewarded for. Furthermore, there are cheaper, less bureaucratic and less intrusive ways to resolve uncertainty about access to resources than to require the establishment of a register detailing individual Aboriginal owners, with public access to private and confidential information. The Pitjantjatjara were not required to present detailed lists of individual owners or to establish historical proof of continuous association in order to secure Aboriginal title under land rights legislation. When development applications are proposed, then the Pitjantjatjara identify, by their own traditional processes, appropriate individuals who will participate in negotiations with prospective developers. The

Pintubi had no certainty that they would be given the right to live at Yayayi. They asked the owners and no doubt negotiated. Let miners do likewise. Aborigines are not isolated by apartheid and they have organisations to represent them. The continued unwillingness of mining corporations to provide information about the use and distribution of the proceeds of their output – to whom, where and for what purpose those proceeds are used – denies Aborigines information vital to fair negotiation and the Australian community information vital to the formation of economic policy.

There is a saying that what is done in haste will be repented at leisure. This is especially true of what is done with land. The Commonwealth has, in the operation of its land rights legislation in the Northern Territory, a model which has functioned effectively for almost two decades, producing a steady flow of negotiated agreements. The overwhelming majority of these agreements allow access to Aboriginal land for exploration and for mining on terms which have been accepted as protecting Aboriginal interests. Generally, in other States, wherever resource developers have been prepared to adopt a negotiating stance, agreements have also been achieved. The demand by companies for special action to expedite approval for mining and other development projects reflects, primarily, the desire to escape from the justified concerns of regulatory agencies to ensure that general economic, social and environmental welfare is protected. If we allow such irresponsibility in haste, our children will repent in perpetuity.

At the most, the tribunals operating under native title legislation should not assume, but rather test the need for special measures to expedite development processes. Such tribunals should include members of financial, economic and environmental regulatory authorities and community organisations concerned with these aspects of our future, with access to the best contemporary scientific knowledge and awareness of international practice. These tribunals could examine claims for special 'expediting', satisfying themselves that genuine negotiations between Aboriginal and development interests have been conducted without an agreement being reached.

There would be value in the Commonwealth fulfilling its long-deferred promise to enact national land rights legislation and set in train negotiations for a comprehensive agreement concerning all social and political issues in dispute; not simply pushing a land deal to satisfy the greedy. National land rights legislation would need to accept, as some settlements of claims have done in the Northern Territory, that the narrow basis for Aboriginal claims based on verifiable evidence of descent and continuing identification needs to be broadened to accommodate the realities of historical dispossession and the diversities in contemporary Aboriginal society. The success of the Pitjantjatjara land rights legislation in South Australia demonstrates that within a broad recognition of native rights in land, there is room for diversity in the form of identification used as the bases for decisions. At one stage in late 1992, the Minister for Aboriginal Affairs supported the running of a small number of test cases across Aboriginal Australia in order to more fully understand the forms of title and range of possible legal issues involved in native title. But in 1993, in the government's haste to end 'uncertainty' and enact legislation speedily, these test cases have not proceeded, with the exception of the Wik case. The world experience of attempts to impose final solutions on the relationships of peoples to one another and to land is a recipe for divisiveness and conflict. Let us take note and let the Crown resume its role as arbiter calling the contending interests to the negotiating table.

Many Aborigines fear that acceptance of Commonwealth native title legislation would require them to accept less protection for their traditional rights in land than the High Court judgement has already decided exists. It would also require them to allow their native title in land subject to lease to be extinguished where the rights granted by the lease are limited in time and purpose and are subject to Crown covenants, thereby requiring them to accept more permanent and destructive dispossession than they have already suffered. They would have to do this without knowing whether the Commonwealth Government is to accept an obligation of trusteeship; without clear provision of the legislation for increasing self-government at local, regional or national level; without knowledge of what will be contained in proposed social and economic packages; and without any commitment of opposition parties and interests. Aborigines may make gains from these packages, but as yet we can pass no judgement. This is where the uncertainty exists and it threatens Aboriginal survival.

There has, as yet, been no formal consideration of an official Aboriginal response to the High Court's Mabo judgement. Indeed, there have been no formal meetings between the Commonwealth Government and legitimate delegates of *all* Aboriginal Australia; no exchange of documents; and no program to open ongoing and comprehensive negotiations on anything approximating the terms proposed in the Eva Valley Statement (see Appendix). The negotiations the Prime Minister held during October of 1993 with representatives of some key Aboriginal organisations, valuable as they were, cannot be seen as providing for the Act of Self-determination which, at some time, the United Nations Charter may require. The absence of a procedure by which the concerns of delegates of all legitimate Aboriginal organisations could be dealt with has been a serious obstacle which the Government and the bureaucracy have done little to overcome. Though the Aboriginal negotiating team acted with great skill, integrity and leadership in representing their respective Aboriginal constituencies, the Commonwealth Government's insistence, under pressure, to hasten into legislation has inevitably seen consultation with a wider cross-section of Aboriginal interests neglected.

The Commonwealth's native title legislation arising from the High Court decision must be judged within its limits. While it may well make for considerable gains for some Aboriginal people, it has had powerful corporate interests, political lobbies, various bureaucracies, the media and the public all asserting their particular influences. The many expectations of Aboriginal people, especially that the High Court decision and subsequent legislation would open the way for greater land rights, will undoubtedly be disappointed if the piecemeal nature of legislated native title rights and the reality of progressive dispossession are, in fact, confirmed. Historically, it has been Aboriginal practice to seize any opportunity to influence legislative and other government action affecting their interests, but to abstain from identification with its terms; to take what benefit can be gained, but to avoid providing legitimacy to externally established decisions which continue to deny the ultimate reality and truth of Aboriginal identification with the land. Clearly, the Aboriginal negotiating team has displayed a preparedness to take gains from, and fight for amendments to, the Commonwealth's legislation. But equally, some Aborigines will, and almost certainly should, make specific their reservations concerning the legislation. Many Aboriginal people have not had adequate opportunity to reach an informed assessment of either what the judgement and the Commonwealth's legislation mean, or what they mean for them and their children. The precedents set by the past actions of Australian governments and their colonising international associates are not encouraging. At least they are entitled to time to continue the learning process begun so impressively at Eva Valley.

THE IMPORTANCE OF THE EVA VALLEY MEETING

The initiative of the Council for Aboriginal Reconciliation and the Aboriginal and Torres Strait Islander Commission (ATSIC) in sponsoring the first meeting at Eva Valley in August 1993 of delegates of Aboriginal organisations from across the country, to discuss the Mabo decision, was a seminal one. That Eva Valley could be the birth-place of a national Aboriginal political movement is suggested by:

- the statement prepared by the delegates and presented to the Commonwealth Government which could be seen as the draft for a political manifesto;
- the decision made that future meetings of delegates would be held to organise a national Aboriginal response to Mabo and be responsible for the nomination of smaller, regionally-based groups of delegates authorised to conduct preliminary nego-tiations, thus providing the nucleus of the movement's structure;
- the attempts to resolve divisions on issues which became apparent during the Eva Valley meeting, indicating a developing negotiating strategy; and
- discussions arising between groups of delegates about procedural problems created for delegates by pressures arising from travel

and attendance at meetings while maintaining their own organisations, indicating an intention that the structure must be flexible, but with a firm regional base.

The significance of the Eva Valley meeting can be assessed in the light of the tendency of Aboriginal society to reflect local level interests and priorities over regional and national ones. Aboriginal society is not homogeneous; it is culturally diverse and localised. Apart from the traditional divisions of tribe, language group, clan and family, with their complex linkages through marriage and shared territory, different patterns of relationships have also been imposed on them by the consequences of their dispossession. Men and women from different, sometimes hostile, traditional groupings were thrown together in and around towns, settlements and institutions, in schools, prisons and in the work place; in all the various sites of assimilation. In these contexts they often shared a more intense dispossession not merely of land and resources, but of their identity, culture and relatedness. Some of these new groupings have made more difficult the growth of common Aboriginal attitudes towards community and political problems. Indeed, in certain situations they have been consciously used by non-Aboriginal agencies as a means to preserve their own dominance. Sometimes, the success of this 'divide and rule' strategy has been facilitated by an Aboriginal unwillingness to accept leadership from outside familial or local groups and a reluctance to work together nationally for solutions of common problems; insistence on autonomy can stand in the way. The very preliminary efforts at Eva Valley established a potentially strategic unanimity between many diverse interests to a degree not previously seen and, as such, represented a significant political development.

The Eva Valley Statement produced out of this meeting played an important role in representing the strength of Aboriginal concerns over the Mabo debate and the various government proposals for native title legislation. The decisions made by Aboriginal people at the Eva Valley meeting informed the directions subsequently taken by key Aboriginal leaders in negotiating greater Aboriginal involvement in the Mabo debate. The meeting was crucial in asserting Aboriginal rights to participate in decision making but, more importantly, placed onto the political agenda the fact that their rights were absolutely central to future legislative proposals put forward by the Commonwealth Government. For these reasons, both the Statement and the procedural decisions arising from the Eva Valley meeting are reproduced below (Appendix).

MABO AND THE QUEST FOR ABORIGINAL AUTONOMY

The High Court decision and subsequent Commonwealth Government legislation have presented a crucial test to Aboriginal people as to whether their traditional and historical divisions, and the need to maintain local autonomy, could be balanced with the real and urgent need to develop national strategies asserting rights and priorities on behalf of all of Aboriginal Australia.

Discussion amongst Aborigines, politicians, academics and in the media had made clear that despite the death of *terra nullius* and the survival of native title,

- the Mabo judgement was concerned more to extinguish native title than to protect or extend the lands held under it and provided the mechanism for that progressive extinguishment;
- some States would challenge the power of Commonwealth legislation which might overrule existing or newly introduced State legislation and limit State power to extinguish Aboriginal rights; and
- national and multinational corporations (led by mining companies) would continue to mobilise their financial and political influence on States, the media and the public, to use native title legislation to complete the dispossession of Aboriginal people, not merely of their rights in land, but also in other forms of property and in civil and political matters.

In these circumstances there can be little doubt that the continuing battle is for Aboriginal survival and their capacity to achieve increasing autonomy.

As has been evident from events subsequent to the High Court decision, the task facing the Aboriginal political movement is enormous, but the required human and intellectual resources exist to be mobilised. All students of the judgement and its implications are indebted to Paul Coe, Michael Mansell, Michael Dodson, John Ah Kit, David Ross, Peter Yu, Noel Pearson, Marcia Langton and many other Aboriginal leaders for their contribution to the clarification of the judgement's significance and the hidden purposes which its language made, or failed to make, clear. Government and public discussions about extinguishment of native title, about sovereignty and its complexities, about fiduciary obligation and its achievements in other countries and its potential here, have been better informed and more creative as a result of their work. The considerable ability of these leaders to command access to and the attention of the media gave both government and Aboriginal groups a valuable reminder that the Mabo judgement posed problems which could not properly be considered and certainly not resolved, except in the context of a comprehensive settlement that would provide a basis for effective Aboriginal self-government.

Michael Mansell (1993) has commented that 'the policy approach of the Mabo case appears to protect those fortunate Aboriginal groups less affected by white contact'. However, it is evident already that Aborigines across the country are attempting to use the discussions following the judgement as an opportunity to secure more long-term and comprehensive solutions to end the injustices affecting all their people. While confusion and divisions have arisen owing to the haste in which the Commonwealth and some other governments rushed to proceed with legislation, the momentum for co-operation afforded by a national Aboriginal leadership on behalf of wide regional constituencies has done much to keep Aboriginal interests and rights in the political arena. Perhaps what we are seeing is the beginning of a national coalition or federation of Aboriginal organisations, accountable through its member organisations to Aboriginal communities and groups. Certainly, we saw evidence of such a supra-organisational alliance prepared to use its respective resources on a broader national front during the negotiations carried out prior to the Commonwealth native title legislation. Such a coalition will be sorely needed in the future as the complex implications of the High Court decision and of government legislation continue to require strategic action and resolution for the purpose of securing Aboriginal autonomy. A willingness to work together despite differences is critical to success in the short and longer term.

With the Commonwealth's native title legislation, Aborigines seem to have won the right to be cautiously optimistic. Their negotiators have performed with distinction and a number of Aborigines apparently feel encouraged to go along with the legislation, as a first instalment along the road to self-determination and autonomy. However, the future outcomes of legislation will be subject to necessary clarification, perhaps by the High Court, of fundamental issues like the rights of Aboriginal people to self-government, the existence of the Crown's fiduciary obligation, the compatibility of existing land titles with native titles and the exact content of proposed social and economic packages. Legal action to bring before the judiciary issues which call for prompt action (like the Wik and Wiradjuri claims) may still be necessary despite the justification for cautious optimism. There were considerable and real pressures exerted on Aboriginal people to endorse the speedy passage of a legislative resolution of native title. Given the limitations of consultation and of the legislation, there remain many good grounds for arguing that mechanisms for ongoing review of, and reflection upon both the legislation's many complex implications and upon the original High Court judgement itself are essential.

Michael Dodson, Commissioner for Aboriginal and Torres Strait Islander Social Justice, has rightly pointed out that whatever political settlement arises out of the Mabo decision, it will almost certainly represent a compromise and perhaps assist only a small number of people (1993: 16). Neither the High Court decision, nor the subsequent Commonwealth native title legislation, provides a *clear* basis for future Aboriginal autonomy; though they do provide an historic potential.

Conclusion

18

Negotiating future autonomy

THE ABORIGINAL DESIRE FOR AUTONOMY

Ideally, this final chapter should return to the two themes which seem to me to dominate Aboriginal society, their ways of thought and their plans for the future. These are, firstly, the autonomy which they see as vital to their own personal existence and, secondly, the reciprocal obligation to nurture and care for others within the social groups in which their Aboriginal identity will emerge and develop. Contemporary Aboriginal history can be viewed as a continuing effort to balance the personal and group tensions inherent in these two key principles of autonomy and nurture, and to realise and maintain them in the colonised pattern of life which dispossession has imposed on that history. The earlier chapters of this book, I believe, demonstrate that Aboriginal society remains strongly committed to the pursuit of autonomy for its people in their diverse individual and corporate lives, and to the acceptance of respect, responsibility and accountability for the rights and autonomy of others.

The events and initiatives described in these chapters demonstrate that in the years since the apparent 'consensus' in approach by the Whitlam and Fraser Governments, the direction of change has inexorably been towards greater independence for Aboriginal Australians. Despite the repudiation of that 'consensus', Aborigines have made by their own initiatives, intelligence and dedication, remarkable progress in the achievement of a lifestyle more healthy, more creative and more characteristically Aboriginal than has previously been possible since their dispossession. To assess the quality of that lifestyle and the compatibility of its institutions with those necessary for the development of a multiracial, multicultural Australia is the task which confronts the Australian peoples, irrespective of the outcome of the contemporary debates about the content and impact of government legislation to give effect to the High Court's recognition of native title.

In 1977, I attempted to discuss with an audience of economists the question of whether the same precision could be given to the concept of quality of life (as an alternative basis for economic and social policy), as that currently given to the pursuit of economic growth and the gross national product. My suggestions made little impact, but their further consideration had led me to see the contemporary economic system not as inherent in the nature of things, but as an historical artefact of the 'arrangements of society'; an adaptation to the earlier conscious change of arrangements which, at one time, were based upon the patterns of behaviour of hunter-gatherer societies. I concluded that:

- the quality of life reflects the capacity of its lifestyle to satisfy humankind's physical and psychic needs;
- whatever level of material affluence is achieved, psychic needs will remain critical and seem to require:
  – a balance between security and challenge;
  – a balance between personal identity and one derived from involvement with groups of various sizes and objectives;
  – the sense of continuing purpose in human life; and
  – the opportunity for privacy and effective choice;
- these qualities emerge as by-products of activities of men and women in the environmental settings in which they live;
- a diversity in the environmental settings available and a real choice between them are components of the quality of life. (Coombs 1990b)

Since then, I have been particularly concerned to examine the contemporary 'arrangements of society' as they affect both Aboriginal and non-Aboriginal Australians. In that process I have become increasingly convinced that these non-material considerations, rather than the apparently measurable economic qualities, are embodied more effectively and persistently in Aboriginal decision-making processes than in those of white society, and that despite its relative poverty in material terms, Aboriginal society may well be capable of providing a superior quality of life. Through their decisions, Aboriginal people have continued to pursue an autonomous lifestyle compatible with their diverse physical and intellectual activities and rich cultural experience. By contrast, contemporary industrial society seems to contribute little to these non-material needs and indeed tends to eliminate alternative lifestyles and the reality of choice and to threaten the survival of life itself.

Aboriginal decisions about their preferred lifestyles are, in part, based on the Aboriginal ethic of accountability to others. Social accountability is required by their commitment that autonomy, at a personal and group level, will be exercised so as to ensure that what is done contributes to the care and nurture of others with whom they are related; so that personal behaviour remains socially grounded. This commitment, in effect, builds a 'fiduciary obligation' into social relations, and into the individual right to make decisions and to act in accordance with them. The nature of this obligation requires, in turn, an accountability from those who exercise that right. This sense of mutual obligation is not due to an external agent, like that sought by white authority, but to the group as a whole. The instances I have cited in this book of initiatives taken by Aborigines in relation to land, to education, health, law and order, economic activities and to administrative instruments of control, demonstrate the reality and general acceptability of the 'fiduciary obligation' internal to Aboriginal society, and of the mechanisms for its performance.

The mechanisms for what might be called accountable autonomy are facilitated by the binary structures of traditional Aboriginal social organisation. All their societies show structural divisions into complementary pairs, based upon different criteria by which the power to act and responsibility are divided. Thus, in relation to the conduct of ceremony there is both an 'owner' of the ceremony who acts, and a 'guardian' or 'manager' whose approval or consent is required for decisions affecting all group members involved in the ceremony. There are similar arrangements for decision making and mutual accountability in respect to many other matters: like for example, those concerned with the land; with education and socialisation of the young; the use of resources where men and women have separate, but at the same time, shared concerns; and with relations and responsibilities between the generations and within families. In other words, the ethic of autonomy and nurture are crucial sustaining factors within traditional and contemporary Aboriginal societies, and not simply the reactive product of resistance to white colonisation.

Currently, in some of these matters, Aboriginal mechanisms for accountability and autonomy between the various social and kin categories have been, to some degree, impaired by decision making and structures imposed or significantly influenced by white authority; by the incorporation of non-Aboriginal processes into their Aboriginal affairs; and by issues new to Aboriginal society demanding decisions where no appropriate organisational division of responsibility and accountability seems possible. Thus, Aboriginal people face the problems of abuse of alcohol, of increasing male domination of family and clan matters sometimes by violence, and the encroachment of men into matters previously regarded as the primary (but not exclusive) responsibility of women, all leading to major disruptions to family life. Aboriginal society is already actively considering whether there is a need to revitalise the internal processes of mutual accountability upon which the harmony of family and group life depends, to deal with these issues. As noted in earlier chapters, there is evidence that active initiatives to resolve these problems are already underway and there is much progress.

It is important that these issues be resolved within Aboriginal society by the application and adaptation of its own mechanisms and capacities; in accordance with people's preferred lifestyle and cultural priorities. On the other hand, the assertion of accountability to external white authority frequently provokes resistance. Proposals like those for the administration of law and order advanced by the Yolngu clans of East Arnhem Land show that their autonomy and concern for each other are an adequate basis for decision, when they are allowed to exercise it. Social and other change is affecting also the operation of white institutions for the management of closely related problems. Their processes and attempted solutions seem in no way superior.

A PAUSE FOR REFLECTION

Given the strength of Aboriginal identity and desire for autonomy described in these chapters, it must be argued that the Commonwealth native title legislation is not wholly relevant to the developing domestic and international opinion, or to the Aboriginal directions of change. Michael Dodson, the Aboriginal and Torres Strait Islander Social Justice Commissioner, in his first report to Parliament has rightly pointed out that the immediate practical implications of the Mabo decision, while of great importance, do not adequately convey the essential significance of the decision. The recognition of native title 'is not merely a recognition of rights at law'. Rather, it '. . . provides a catalyst for a further, deeper act of recognition which embraces our entire experience since colonisation' (Dodson 1993: 16–18). It is towards this 'deeper act of recognition' that the ongoing Aboriginal struggle for autonomy has been directed, and will continue to be pursued as the dust of government native title legislation settles.

Legislation to establish and define 'native title' must therefore be seen as a provisional first step along the road. To identify the direction of that road there is a need for key constitutional and political issues, including those arising from the High Court judgement, to be tested by carefully selected cases, to make clear, in the Court's view:

- whether governments must make their decisions in the light of the Crown's 'fiduciary obligation' to Aborigines arising from both the fact and the means of the dispossession of Aboriginal land and other property;
- whether dispossession and the radical title judged by the High Court to confer immunity from challenge in a domestic court,

does not carry with it an obligation to re-establish the implied promise to act with 'consent' which was denied with the assumption of that title;

- whether the Crown's radical title is not subject to and burdened with an obligation to protect the inalienability of traditional Aboriginal ownership except by due Aboriginal process and consent;
- whether Aboriginal title can be extinguished by the grant of other title in circumstances where inconsistency has been assumed or inferred, rather than demonstrated beyond reasonable doubt and, importantly,
- whether the divisions of sovereignty (the power to govern) can be divided as arranged and agreed upon, between Aboriginal and non-Aboriginal Australians.

These are the real uncertainties and it is because of them that there is a need for a pause for reflection. To create this pause, there should be a moratorium on legislative action; though this moratorium should not prevent the initiation of the legislative processes. What is needed is an Act of the Commonwealth (preferably with State and Aboriginal consent) to provide that no State or Territory legislative or other Act affecting Aboriginal rights or title in land should come into operation until after it has been passed through both Houses of the Commonwealth Parliament. This would allow time for a series of test cases dealing with the unresolved issues referred to above and in Chapter 17, to be determined by the High Court.

A moratorium for reflection would not exclude or preclude reform of the law flowing from negotiations in the context of wide and informed community debate: indeed, it would increase the probability of such an outcome from negotiations. The expressed need for certainty about the extent of Aboriginal ownership and the implications of native title are largely fictional. Existing procedures are providing the necessary answers routinely to those prepared to deal with Aboriginal owners and claimants. The most that is required is access to a tribunal with powers, such as referred to in Chapter 17, to conciliate and arbitrate in cases where one party or the other is withholding information to which the other has a legitimate or reasonable need, or is not prepared to adapt a negotiating stance.

More generally, the contemporary debate covers the whole question of the status of Aboriginal Australians within the federation of Australia and within the international body of the 'United Nations'. This issue is not exclusively the concern of Australian Governments, their citizens and 'special interests'. The nature and extent of rights of groups of peoples to self-determination and authority to manage their own domestic affairs are increasingly part and parcel of the subject matter of international law and custom.

A 'DEEPER ACT OF RECOGNITION'

Aboriginal right to autonomy and self-determination is recognised in international law by the International Covenant on Civil and Political Rights, as we have been reminded by the recent report of the Aboriginal Social Justice Commissioner. That right entitles Aboriginal people to 'freely determine their political status and freely pursue their economic, social and cultural development' (Dodson 1993: 41). It is towards the practical realisation of this fundamental right that 'a deeper act of recognition' must be directed. Importantly, I would argue that any action by a State to grant, recognise or with-hold recognition of Aboriginal people's right to autonomy must be validated by the participation of the holders or claimants of those rights, in a formal Act of Self-determination.

On 27 April 1993, Aboriginal representatives from a number of land councils and legal services presented to the Prime Minister, on behalf of the organisations to which they were accountable, the Aboriginal Peace Plan. The Plan proposed principles by which Aboriginal rights could be recognised and protected. In the post-Mabo context, the focus of public debate has been concentrated towards land and other property rights. However, the Aboriginal Peace Plan emphasised that a long-term settlement, if it was to be acceptable to Aborigines, must be negotiated via a process in which all Aboriginal and Torres Strait Islander peoples were involved and must deal comprehensively with a much wider range of issues. Arguably, it is only in such a negotiated longer-term settlement that the deeper recognision of Aboriginal autonomy will be identified.

Serious consideration should be given to establishing clear procedures by which such a settlement could be initiated and negotiated. Such processes must lead to an Act of Self-determination in a form recognised by the United Nations and be binding on future Australian Commonwealth and State Governments. The recent Act organised by the Commonwealth and the Malay peoples of Cocos Island, with its careful protection of the independent culture of the Malay people and their right to self-government, and the similarity between their circumstances and those of many Aboriginal and Torres Strait Islander peoples, has established a valuable precedent.

The process of arranging an Act of Self-determination must be an exercise of participatory democracy. I have suggested that a number of test cases must still be put to the High Court to clarify the implications of the Mabo decision for future legislative action. Such classification is a necessary, but not sufficient, first step. Legal decisions and processes will be binding only in a society that is already working together, providing for diversity within unity. We are not yet in sight of that objective. It may well be that judgements by the High Court will be acceptable to Aborigines generally; but they may not. Certainly, members of the negotiating team which has been the Prime Minister's point of contact have emphasised that they do not have authority to speak for other than the organisations which have sponsored them. The widely based meetings of delegates proposed at Eva Valley have not been held and the limited gatherings since then have revealed significant divisions. This is not evidence of irresponsible Aboriginal hostility. It is, rather, evidence of the fundamental importance of some of the issues and of the fact that any binding agreement must come from free and informed consent.

We have, jointly with Aborigines and their organisations, to plan and implement a process which will provide a basis for genuine, informed acceptance by Aborigines of resolutions to key issues affecting their autonomy, according to their own decision-making procedures. Only then will there be the mandate for an internationally recognised Act of Self-determination. Such a course of action will probably look very much like the one which led to the tentative acceptance of the agreed statement at Eva Valley in mid-1993. That is, a process which starts with Aboriginal people and their organisations at the local level, holding a series of regional meetings which any Aboriginal-controlled organisation is entitled to attend, to discuss the settlement of fundamental regional issues relating to local government, self-determination and sovereignty. What Aboriginal people want in this respect must come out of regional meetings where, alone at that stage, they are in reasonable charge of what is happening.

Recent proposals from a Kimberley coalition of Aboriginal organisations for a negotiated regional agreement with the Commonwealth may be embryonic evidence of such a process. Given the significant role played by ATSIC in the hectic Aboriginal negotiations leading up to national native title legislation, it may be appropriate for proposals for such regional agreements to come from meetings that could best be co-ordinated by ATSIC regional councils. These councils, in association with the elected ATSIC Commissioners, the Council for Aboriginal Reconciliation and the Social Justice Commissioner, could prepare supporting material for an agenda determined in the light of the community discussions.

From these regional meetings of Aboriginal people and their representative organisations could come reports on key issues and opinions for further discussion. To continue this exploratory process, participants at such meetings could nominate regional delegates to take their concerns and settlement resolutions up at the national level. This nominated, national negotiating team could put to the Commonwealth Government a schedule for future autonomy, including a timetable, a series of objectives, principles and the hopeful outcomes. This suggested process closely resembles the 'bottom-up' approach to political organisation which, in earlier chapters of this book, I argue is characteristic of Aboriginal political process. It matches the informal federalism which Aboriginal people around the country have shown to be a preferred model for collective action.

Given the diversity of Aboriginal lifestyles today, it would not be surprising if regional settlement proposals differ considerably. There must be room for such differences. In other words, what is important is establishing a procedure whereby Aborigines can, in a participatory democratic way, have time to work their various approaches out. Such a negotiation schedule may well take some years and need the continuing protection of a 'moratorium' on legislation attempting to determine the nature of Aboriginal rights. But as the record of the last twenty years demonstrates, there will continue to be scope for independent and agreed changes in the administrative and policy procedures which are provisional, providing an experimental basis for longer-term action, but subject to periodic pause for review and reflection. It does not, therefore, imply that development and other social and economic proposals cannot continue to emerge, but that any legislation defining Aboriginal rights should be within the arena of discussions occurring between Aboriginal groups and with the Commonwealth. The existence of the tribunal proposed in Chapter 17 would ensure that economic activity could continue normally, with Aboriginal agreement, as it has since the Commonwealth *Northern Territory Land Rights Act* has operated and in all areas where negotiating procedures have been followed.

The objective at the end of the period of negotiation would be to reach an agreement about possible options for self-determination that would be put formally to the Aboriginal population. Such options could include agreed divisions of responsibility and powers between Aboriginal Australians and the Commonwealth on a regional basis, similar to those negotiated between the Commonwealth and the Northern Territory, the Australian Capital Territory and other Territories including the Cocos Islands, where diverse cultural groups exist. Australia has an incomparable range of experience in innovative federalism. Flexibility and diversity are achievable if the political will exists.

AN ACT OF SELF-DETERMINATION

Essentially, what is being suggested is the establishment of a legitimate process of negotiation by which Aboriginal people with sundry views can be brought together in such a way that they will

229

not be coerced into unwilling acceptance or browbeaten into uniformity, but so that their needs and desire for autonomy can be fully recognised.

The Yolngu people of East Arnhem Land have a metaphorical image to illustrate the coming together of 'peoples from far away'. Two streams of water flow into a coastal lagoon: one stream is tidal and salt from the sea; the other fresh from the rain on nearby hills. As the streams enter the lagoon there is, on the surface, the chaotic froth of their interaction which gradually establishes a recognisable pattern as the streams merge with the lagoon. But their separate identity is not wholly lost. At various levels the streams continue to exist, influencing and changing, but not destroying the diversity in the character of the lagoon. It is perhaps an image which Australians, white as well as black, could well incorporate into that of the Australian nation – of unity expressing and protecting diversity and autonomy.

Appendix: The Eva Valley Statement

1. Aboriginal and Torres Strait Islander people held their first national meeting at Eva Valley in the Northern Territory, 3–5 August 1993, to formulate a response to the High Court decision on native title. It was resolved to present the Eva Valley Statement to the Prime Minister.
2. There is an urgent need for this Statement which follows to be considered by all Aboriginal and Torres Strait Islander people. We reject the Commonwealth Government's position on the proposed legislation. We want legislation based on native title to advance Aboriginal rights to land. The Federal Government proposal does not. The government must only move on this issue with the support of Aboriginal and Torres Strait Islander people. The development of any legislation regarding the Commonwealth Government's response to the High Court's decision on native title will need the full and free participation and consent of those peoples concerned.
3. We want the Commonwealth Government to take full control of native title issues to the exclusion of the States and Territories. We want a national standard for our people, not numerous different standards.

4. We demand that:

    4.1 The Commonwealth honour its obligations under international human rights instruments and international law.

    4.2 The Commonwealth agree to a negotiating process to achieve a lasting settlement with and for the benefit of all Aboriginal and Torres Strait Islander people. Since time immemorial we have owned, occupied, used and enjoyed this continent and its islands in accordance with our laws and customs, to the exclusion of the whole world. Since the arrival of non-indigenous people, our political and territorial integrity has been violated and that violation continues. This settlement process must recognise and address these historical truths. It must also redress the impact of our dispossession, marginalisation, destabilisation and disadvantage, including financial and material recompense.

    4.3 The Commonwealth take action in response to the High Court's decision on native title in accordance with the following principles:

        4.3.1 The recognition and protection of Aboriginal and Torres Strait Islander rights.

        4.3.2 The Commonwealth Government acknowledge that Aboriginal and Torres Strait Islander land title cannot be extinguished by grants of any interest.

        4.3.3 No grant of any interest on Aboriginal and Torres Strait Islander title can be made without the informed consent of all relevant title holders.

        4.3.4 Commonwealth declaration of Aboriginal and Torres Strait Islander title in reserves and other defined land.

        4.3.5 Total security for sacred sites and heritage areas which provides for Aboriginal and Torres Strait Islander people's absolute authority.

5. The Aboriginal and Torres Strait Islander people have nominated a representative body to put forward their position in these matters, including the necessity to consult and negotiate with Aboriginal and Torres Strait Islander people about these principles.

6. To ensure there is equity in and ownership of the negotiation process, it is essential that this body be provided with the resources to carry out the wishes of Aboriginal and Torres Strait Islander people.

7. We call upon the Commonwealth Government to acknowledge what the High Court has stated concerning the way in which Aboriginal and Torres Strait Islander people have become dispossessed and disadvantaged.

8. The resources to enable full and informed negotiations with Aboriginal and Torres Strait Islander people should be over and above, and distinct from, the limited resources presently provided to address the gross disadvantage which arises from our dispossession.

PROCEDURAL DECISIONS AT EVA VALLEY

The following courses of action were resolved at the end of the Eva Valley meeting:

1. To reject the legislation at present proposed by the Commonwealth.

2. To issue:

   2.1 a press statement embodying this decision on the grounds that the Commonwealth Government has a duty to protect the Aboriginal rights recognised by the High Court and to restore the rights of which Aborigines have been deprived by their long dispossession (the proposed legislation does neither), and

3. To affirm that:

   3.1 the form of the Eva Valley meeting – a meeting of delegates of legitimate Aboriginal organisations of all kinds, from all parts of Australia – was appropriate for a continuing body to arrange meetings and to manage negotiations with the Commonwealth Government;

   3.2 funding should be arranged to finance two such meetings, even more widely representative, to be held in the months following August, to continue the debate among Aboriginal people and to arrange negotiations with the Commonwealth; and

3.3 delegates should report to their organisations and be accountable to them throughout the meetings.

4. To nominate at least two delegates from each of the various regions represented at Eva Valley as a provisional management team to organise subsequent meetings and negotiations arising from them.

5. To have arranged funding paid to the Coalition of Aboriginal Organisations as a trust fund to be administered by it for the purposes of the provisional management team in the conduct of the proposed meeting.

6. To exclude from the summary statement (see above) reference to issues on which significant differences existed in the Eva Valley debate, but to instruct the provisional management team that these issues should be high on the agenda for the next meeting and that information and discussion papers should be prepared about them, to enable groups to consider them and if they wish, to instruct their delegates.

Eva Valley, 5 August 1993

References

Altman, J.C. 1987. *Hunter-Gatherers Today: An Aboriginal Economy in North Australia*. Canberra: Australian Institute of Aboriginal Studies.

———— 1988. *Aborigines, Tourism and Development: The Northern Territory Experience*. Darwin: North Australia Research Unit, Australian National University.

Altman, J.C. and Allen, L.M. 1991. 'Living off the Land in National Parks: Issues for Aboriginal Australians'. *Centre for Aboriginal Economic Policy Research Discussion Paper No. 14*. Canberra: Centre for Aboriginal Economic Policy Research, Australian National University.

Altman, J.C. and Sanders, W. 1991a. 'From Exclusion to Dependence: Aborigines and the Welfare State in Australia'. *Centre for Aboriginal Economic Policy Research Discussion Paper No. 1*. Canberra: Centre for Aboriginal Economic Policy Research, Australian National University.

Altman, J.C. and Sanders, W. 1991b. 'The CDEP Scheme: Administrative and Policy Issues'. *Australian Journal of Public Administration* 50(4): 515–25.

Altman, J.C. and Taylor, L. 1989. *The Economic Viability of Aboriginal Outstations and Homelands*. A Report to the Australian Council for Employment and Training. Canberra: Australian Government Publishing Service.

Altman, J.C., Ginn, A. and Smith, D.E. (assisted by L.M. Roach). 1993. *Existing and Potential Mechanisms for Indigenous Involvement in Coastal*

235

Zone Resource Management. Report for the Resource Assessment Commission. Canberra: Australian Government Publishing Service.

Australia. Department of Home Affairs and Environment. 1984. *National Conservation Strategy for Australia: Living Resource Conservation for Sustainable Development*. Canberra: Canberra Publishing for the Department of Home Affairs and Environment.

Bell, D. 1983. *Daughters of the Dreaming*. Sydney: McPhee Gribble and George Allen and Unwin.

Berndt, R.M. and Berndt, C.H. 1987. *End of an Era: Aboriginal Labour in the Northern Territory*. Canberra: Australian Institute of Aboriginal Studies.

Bindarriy, Yangarriny, Mingalpa and Warlkunji. 1991. 'Obstacles to Aboriginal Pedagogy'. *Aboriginal Pedagogy* pp. 163–179.

Blanchard, C.A. (chairman). 1987. *Return to Country: The Aboriginal Homelands Movement in Australia*. Report of the House of Representatives Standing Committee on Aboriginal Affairs. Canberra: Australian Government Publishing Service.

Boyden, S.V. (ed.). 1970. *The Impact of Civilisation on the Biology of Man*. Canberra: Australian National University Press.

Boyden, S.V. 1981. 'The Triangle of Human Ecology: Lessons from the Hong Kong Human Ecology Program'. In Hill, S. et al. (eds.). *Development with a Human Face: The Human Implications of Scientific and Technological Development*. pp. 84–97. Proceedings of the UNESCO Regional Workshop, Leura, Wollongong. Canberra: Australian Government Publishing Service.

Brown, B.J., Hanson, M.E., Liverman, D.M. and Meridith, R.W. 1987. 'Global Sustainability: Toward Definition'. *Environmental Management* 11(6): 713–719.

Bucknall, J. 1991. 'Access to Education for Aborigines Living in Remote Areas of Western Australia'. Unpublished paper. Osborne Park, WA: Independendent Community Schools Support Unit.

Chittleborough, R.G. and Keating, F.M. 1987. *Western Australian Environmental Review*. Perth: Department of Conservation and Environment.

Commonwealth Grants Commission. 1989. *Second Report on Cocos (Keeling) Islands Inquiry 1989*. Canberra: Australian Government Publishing Service.

Commonwealth of Australia. 1991. *Royal Commission into Aboriginal Deaths in Custody National Report Vols 1–4*. Canberra: Australian Government Publishing Service.

Coombs, H.C. 1971. 'Correspondence to Minister regarding Northern Territory Resource Allocation on Aboriginal Settlements'. Canberra: Council of Aboriginal Affairs, 6 December 1971.

–––––– 1978. *Kulinma: Listening to Aboriginal Australians*. Canberra: Australian National University Press.

–––––– 1984. *The Role of the National Aboriginal Conference*. Canberra: Australian Government Publishing Service.

–––––– 1990a. *Education, Socialisation and the Underlying Issues*. Unpublished Paper for the Royal Commission into Aboriginal Deaths in Custody, Canberra.

–––––– 1990b. *The Return of Scarcity: Strategies for an Economic Future*. Cambridge: Cambridge University Press in association with the Centre for Resource and Environmental Studies.

Coombs, H.C., Brandl, M. and Snowdon, W. 1983. *A Certain Heritage: Programs for and by Aboriginal Families in Australia*. Centre for Resource and Environmental Studies Monograph No. 9. Canberra: Centre for Resource and Environmental Studies, Australian National University.

Coombs, H.C., McCann, H., Ross, H. and Williams, N.M. (eds). 1989. *Land of Promises: Aborigines and Development in the East Kimberley*. Canberra: Centre for Resource and Environmental Studies, Australian National University, and Aboriginal Studies Press.

Daylight, P. and Johnstone, M. 1986. *Women's Business*. Report of the Aboriginal Women's Task Force. Canberra: Australian Government Publishing Service.

Deakin University. 1982. *Nature and Human Nature Series*. School of Humanities and Ganma Research Project, Yirrkala. Geelong, Victoria: Deakin University Press.

Dixon, R.A. and Dillon, M.C. (eds). 1990. *Aborigines and Diamond Mining: The Politics of Resource Development in the East Kimberley, Western Australia*. Perth: University of Western Australia Press.

Dodson, M. (commissioner). 1993. *Aboriginal and Torres Strait Islander Social Justice Commission First Report 1993*. Canberra: Australian Government Publishing Service.

Dubos, R. 1965. *Man Adapting*. New Haven, Conn.: Yale University Press.

Gibb, C.A. (chairman). 1973. *The Situation of Aborigines on Pastoral Properties in the Northern Territory*. Report of the Committee of Review, December 1971. Parliamentary Paper No. 62. Canberra: Commonwealth Government Printing Office.

Goodland, R.J. and Ledec, G. 1986. *Neoclassical Economics and Principles of Sustainable Development*. Washington: World Bank.

Gould, R. 1969. *Yiwara, Foragers of the Australian Desert.* London: Collins.

Hamilton, A. 1981. *Nature and Nurture: Aboriginal Child-Rearing in North-Central Arnhem Land.* Canberra: Australian Institute of Aboriginal Studies.

Hawke, S. 1989. *Noonkanbah: Whose Land, Whose Law.* Mundaring, Western Australia: Corke Books.

Heppell, M. and Wigley, J.J. 1981. *Black Out in Alice: A History of the Establishment and Development of Town Camps in Alice Springs.* Australian National University Development Studies Centre Monograph No. 26. Canberra: Development Studies Centre, Australian National University.

Industry Commission. 1991. *Mining and Mineral Processing in Australia.* Report No. 7. Canberra: Australian Government Publishing Service.

International Union for Conservation of Nature and Natural Resources (IUCN). 1980. *World Conservation Strategy: Living Resource Conservation for Sustainable Development.* Gland, Switzerland: IUCN.

Jackson, S. and Cooper, D. 1993. 'Coronation Hill Pay-Back: The Case of McArthur River'. *Arena* Oct/Nov 1993: 6–8.

Law Reform Commission. 1980. 'Aboriginal Customary Law Recognition'. *Law Reform Commission Discussion Paper No. 17.* Sydney: Australian Law Reform Commission.

Lyon, P. 1990. *What Everybody Knows About Alice: A Report on the Impact of Alcohol Abuse on the Town of Alice Springs.* Alice Springs: Tangentyere Council.

Mansell, M. 1993. 'Native Title in Australia: 100 Years Too Late'. Unpublished paper, July 1993. Hobart, Tasmania.

Marshall, J. (ed.). 1966. *The Great Extermination.* London: Heinemann.

Marshall, P. (ed.). 1988. *Raparapa Kulall Martuwarra: Stories from the Fitzroy River Drovers.* Broome: Magabala Books.

McGrath, A. 1987. *Born in the Cattle: Aborigines in the Cattle Country.* Sydney: George Allen and Unwin.

Meehan, B. 1982. *Shell Bed to Shell Midden.* Canberra: Australian Institute of Aboriginal Studies.

Mudrooroo Narogin. 1965. *Wild Cat Falling.* Sydney: Angus and Robertson.

Myers, F. 1980. 'The Cultural Basis of Pintupi Politics'. *Mankind* 12: 197–213.

———— 1986. *Pintupi Country, Pintupi Self: Sentiment, Place and Politics Among Western Desert Aborigines.* Canberra: Australian Institute of Aboriginal Studies and the Smithsonian Institution Press.

Nettheim, G. 1992. 'The Mabo Case – As Against the Whole World.' *Australian Law News* 27(6): 9, 14.

Niblett, M. 1993. 'The MIM–McArthur River Mine Development: Assessment of Impacts on the Aboriginal Population of Borroloola Township and Region'. Unpublished report prepared for Mabunji Aboriginal Resource Association and the Northern Land Council, Darwin.

O'Dea, K., White, N. and Sinclair, A. 1988. 'An Investigation of Nutrition-Related Risk Factors in an Isolated Aboriginal Community in Northern Australia: Advantages of a Traditionally-Oriented Life-Style'. *Medical Journal of Australia* 148(4): 177–180.

O'Faircheallaigh, C. 1986. *The Economic Impact of the Northern Territory Mining Industry: A Report to the Northern Land Council.* Darwin: North Australian Research Unit, Australian National University.

Reid, J. (ed.). 1982. *Body, Land and Spirit.* Brisbane: University of Queensland Press.

Reid, J. and Kerr, C. 1983. 'Trends in Aboriginal Mortality'. *Medical Journal of Australia* new series 1(8): 348–350.

Repetto, R.C. 1985. *The Global Possible: Resources Development and the New Century.* New Haven, Conn.: Yale University Press.

Reynolds, H. 1994. 'The Origins and Implications of Mabo: An Historical Perspective'. In Sanders, W. (ed.). *Mabo and the Recognition of Native Title: Origins and Implications for the Institutions of Aboriginal Australia.* Monograph by the Centre for Aboriginal Economic Policy Research and the Reshaping Australian Institutions Project, Australian National University. Canberra: CAEPR, Australian National University.

Rose, D.B. 1992. *Dingo Makes Us Human. Life and Land in an Australian Aboriginal Culture.* Cambridge: Cambridge University Press.

Rowley, C.D. 1970. *The Destruction of Aboriginal Society. Aboriginal Policy and Practice* Vol. 1. Canberra: Australian National University Press.

—— 1971a. *Outcasts in White Australia. Aboriginal Policy and Practice* Vol. II. Canberra: Australian National University Press.

—— 1971b. *The Remote Aborigines. Aboriginal Policy and Practice* Vol. III. Canberra: Australian National University Press.

Rowse, T. 1992. *Remote Possibilities: The Aboriginal Domain and the Administrative Imagination.* Darwin: North Australia Research Unit, Australian National University.

Sanders, W. 1988. 'The CDEP Scheme: Bureaucratic Politics, Remote Community Politics and the Development of an Aboriginal "Workfare" Program in Times of Rising Unemployment'. *Politics* 32(1): 32–47.

Smith, D.E. 1993. 'What's the Difference? The Role of the Aboriginal and Torres Strait Islander Commission in Representing Aboriginal

Diversity'. Unpublished paper to Australian Anthropology Society Annual Conference, Melbourne University. Melbourne, 29 September 1993.

Stanner, W.E.H. 1979. *White Man Got No Dreaming*. Canberra: Australian National University Press.

Sullivan, P. 1988. 'Aboriginal Community Representative Organisations: Intermediate Cultural Processes in the Kimberley Region, Western Australia'. *East Kimberley Working Paper No. 22*. Canberra: Centre for Resource and Environmental Studies, Australian National University.

Tangentyere Council. 1984. *Tangentyere Council of Alice Springs Housing Associations Newsletter*. January 1984. Alice Springs: Tangentyere Council.

———— 1985. *Interim Report of the Committee to Review the Operations and Funding of the Council*. 20 September 1985. Alice Springs: Tangentyere Council.

———— 1990. *Tangentyere Council v the Commissioner of Taxes*. Decision of 12, 16, 19-20 March, Alice Springs; 4 May 1990, Darwin.

Valaskakis, K., Sindell, P.S. and Smith, J.G. (compilers). 1977. *Conserver Society Project: Report on Phase II, Vol. 1. The Selective Conserver Society*. Montreal: University of Montreal and McGill University.

White, I., Barwick, D. and Meehan, B. (eds). 1985. *Fighters and Singers: The Lives of Some Aboriginal Women*. Sydney: George Allen and Unwin.

Woodward, A.E. 1973. *Aboriginal Land Rights Commission: First Report, July 1973*. Canberra: Australian Government Publishing Service.

———— 1974. *Aboriginal Land Rights Commission: Second Report, April 1974*. Canberra: Australian Government Publishing Service.

World Commission on Environment and Development (WCED). 1987. *Our Common Future*. Oxford: Oxford University Press.

Select Bibliography of work by H.C. Coombs on issues regarding Aboriginal Australians

This bibliography presents a selection of the major publications, newspaper articles and some public lectures and addresses written by Dr H.C. Coombs on issues concerning Aboriginal Australians. The listing covers the period commencing 1977 – the year prior to the publication of *Kulinma: Listening to Aboriginal Australians* – to 1993. The bibliography is not comprehensive; a great number of smaller unpublished papers, public lectures and official reports have not been included. The majority of references listed below are held by the library of the Australian Institute of Aboriginal and Torres Strait Islander Studies, Canberra.

1977 *The Pitjantjatjara Aborigines: A Strategy for Survival.* CRES Working Paper No. 1. Canberra: Centre for Resource and Environmental Studies, Australian National University.

1977 *The Quality of Life and its Assessment.* CRES Working Paper No. 2. Canberra: Centre for Resource and Environmental Studies, Australian National University.

1977 *The Application of CDEP in Aboriginal Communities in the Eastern Zone of Western Australia.* CRES Working Paper No. 3. Canberra: Centre for Resource and Environmental Studies, Australian National University.

1977 *Aboriginal Australians 1967–1977*. CRES Working Paper No. 4. Canberra: Centre for Resource and Environmental Studies, Australian National University.

1977 'The Commission Report'. In Hazlehurst, C. and Nethercote, J.R. (eds). *Reforming Australian Government: The Coombs Report and Beyond*. pp. 49–52. Canberra: Royal Institute of Public Administration.

1977 'The Future Bureaucracy'. In Hazlehurst, C. and Nethercote, J.R. (eds). *Reforming Australian Government: The Coombs Report and Beyond*. pp. 53–57. Canberra: Royal Institute of Public Administration.

1977 *Aboriginal Australians 1967–1976: A Decade of Progress?* Walter Murdoch Lecture No. 3. Perth: Murdoch University.

1977 'Aborigines Have the Right to Choose: That is the Point!' *National Times* 4/9 April: 22.

1978 *Some Aspects of Development in Aboriginal Communities in Central Australia*. CRES Working Paper No. 5. Canberra: Centre for Resource and Environmental Studies, Australian National University.

1978 *Aggression and the Aboriginal Movement*. CRES Working Paper No. 6. Canberra: Centre for Resource and Environmental Studies, Australian National University.

1978 *Scarcity, Wealth and Income*. CRES Working Paper No. 7. Canberra: Centre for Resource and Environmental Studies, Australian National University.

1978 *Submission to the Commission on the Warlpiri Land Claim*. CRES Working Paper No. 8. Canberra: Centre for Resource and Environmental Studies, Australian National University.

1978 *Implications of Land Rights*. CRES Working Paper No. 9. Canberra: Centre for Resource and Environmental Studies, Australian National University.

1978 *Australia's Policy Towards Aborigines 1967–1977*. Minority Rights Report No. 35. London: Minority Rights Group.

1978 *Kulinma: Listening to Aboriginal Australians*. Canberra: Australian National University Press.

1978 'President's Report'. In *Australian Conservation Foundation Annual Report 1977–78*. Melbourne: Australian Conservation Foundation.

1978 'Aggression and the Aboriginal Environment.' In *Aggression: Second Australia–Asian Pacific Congress of the Australian Academy of Forensic Sciences 1977*. Sydney.

1978 'Aboriginal Nutrition and the Eco-systems of Central Australia: Summing up.' *Aboriginal Nutrition* 2: 2–3.

1979 *Is Democracy Alive and Well?* CRES Working Paper No. 10. Canberra: Centre for Resource and Environmental Studies, Australian National University.

1979 *Aboriginal Land Rights Teach-In.* CRES Working Paper No. 11. Canberra: Centre for Resource and Environmental Studies, Australian National University.

1979 *Science and Technology – For What Purpose?* CRES Working Paper No. 12. Canberra: Centre for Resource and Environmental Studies, Australian National University.

1979 *Guest of Honour Talk: Australian Broadcasting Commission.* CRES Working Paper No. 13. Canberra: Centre for Resource and Environmental Studies, Australian National University.

1979 *The Proposal for a Treaty Between the Commonwealth and Aboriginal Australians.* CRES Working Paper No. 14. Canberra: Centre for Resource and Environmental Studies, Australian National University.

1979 *The Future of the Outstation Movement.* CRES Working Paper No. 15. Canberra: Centre for Resource and Environmental Studies, Australian National University.

1979 *A Treaty with Aboriginal Australians.* CRES Working Paper No. 16. Canberra: Centre for Resource and Environmental Studies, Australian National University.

1979 'President's report.' In *Australian Conservation Foundation Annual Report 1978–79.* Melbourne: Australian Conservation Foundation.

1979 'A Treaty with Aboriginal Australians.' *Social Alternatives* 1(6/7): 63–64.

1979 'Aborigines and the Law.' Parts 1 and 2. Transcript of radio interview from the Parliamentary Library. *Broadband.* 30 August.

1980 'The Future of the Outstation Movement.' In Coombs, H.C., Dexter, B.G. and Hiatt, L.R. *The Outstation Movement in Aboriginal Australia.* Australian Institute of Aboriginal Studies Newsletter 14: 16–23.

1980 *The Impact of Uranium Mining on the Social Environment of Aborigines in the Alligator Rivers Region.* CRES Working Paper No. 18. Canberra: Centre for Resource and Environmental Studies, Australian National University.

1980 'Towards an End to 200 Years of Aggression and Injustice'. *National Times.* 10 June.

1980 'Government Should Negotiate a Treaty as Guarantee of Rights and Security of Aborigines.' *Catholic Leader* 13 July: 3–4.

1980 'The Impact of Uranium Mining on the Social Environment of Aboriginals in the Alligator Rivers Region.' In Harris, S.F. (ed.). *Social and Environmental Choice: The Impact of Uranium Mining in the Northern Territory.* pp. 122-135. Canberra: Centre for Resource and Environmental Studies, Australian National University.

1980 'Signing an Australian Peace Treaty.' *Social Alternatives* 1(6/7): 63-64.

1980 *Technology, Income Distribution and the Quality of Life.* The John Murtagh Macrossan Endowed Lecture. Brisbane: University of Queensland.

1981 *Trial Balance.* Melbourne: Macmillan.

1981 'Yirrkala Law Council'. *Social Alternatives* 2(2): 36, 60.

1982 'On the Question of Government.' In Berndt, R.M. (ed.). *Aboriginal Sites, Rights and Resource Development.* Proceedings of 5th Academy of the Social Sciences in Australia Symposium, 1981, Canberra. pp. 227-232. Perth: University of Western Australia Press.

1982 'The Case for a Treaty.' In Olbrei, E.K. *Black Australians: The Prospects for Change.* pp. 57-60. Townsville: James Cook University Students Union.

1982 'The Three Waves and Aboriginal Identity.' *Aboriginal Treaty News* 4: 9.

1983 *The Yirrkala Proposals for Law and Order.* CRES Working Paper No. 1983/11. Canberra: Centre for Resource and Environmental Studies, Australian National University.

1983 Coombs, H.C., Brandl, M.M. and Snowdon, W.E. *A Certain Heritage: Programs for and by Aboriginal Families in Australia.* Canberra: Centre for Resource and Environmental Studies, Australian National University.

1983 *Economic, Social and Spiritual Factors in Aboriginal Health.* CRES Working Paper No. 1983/16. Canberra: Centre for Resource and Environmental Studies, Australian National University.

1984 'Land Rights Must Give Control over Mining.' *Age.* 20 December.

1984 'Tourists on Black Lands: Opportunity or Threat?' *Age.* 20 December.

1984 *The Role of the National Aboriginal Conference.* Report to the Hon. Clyde Holding, Minister for Aboriginal Affairs. Canberra: Australian Government Publishing Service.

1985 'The Yirrkala Proposals for the Control of Law and Order.' In Hazlehurst, K.M. (ed.). *Justice Programs for Aboriginal and other Indigenous Communities: Australia, New Zealand, Canada, Fiji and Papua New Guinea.* Proceedings of Aboriginal Criminal Justice Workshop No. 1, 29 April-2 May. pp. 201-205. Canberra: Australian Institute of Criminology.

1985 Coombs, H.C., Bin-Sallik, M.A., Hall, F.L. and Morrison, J. *Report of Committee of Inquiry into Aboriginal Employment and Training Programs.* Canberra: Australian Government Publishing Service.

1985 'Where Do We Go From Here.' In Wright, J. (ed.) *We Call for a Treaty.* pp. 284–307. Sydney: Collins and Fontana.

1986 *Towards Aboriginal Independence.* Transcript from Science and Technology and Aboriginal Development Workshop, November 1985. CRES Working Paper No. 1986/5. Canberra: Centre for Resource and Environmental Studies, Australian National University.

1986 'Towards Aboriginal Independence.' In Foran, B.P. and Walker, B.W. *Science and Technology for Aboriginal Development.* pp. 38–43. Alice Springs: Centre for Appropriate Technology.

1986 'Betrayal of Trust: The Hawke Government and Land Rights'. *Age.* 14 March.

1988 'Foreword.' In McBryde, I., White, I. and Wilson, J. (eds.). *Making a Treaty: The North American Experience. Aboriginal History* 12: 7–26.

1988 *Aborigines and the Treaty of Waitangi.* Boyer Lecture Series, Lecture No. 6. Canberra: Australian Broadcasting Corporation.

1989 'Black Society is Not Mired in Failure.' *Age.* 10 March.

1989 'Aboriginal Enterprises Demand New Criteria.' *Canberra Times.* 20 April.

1989 'Aborigines are Greening Australia's Dead Heart.' *Canberra Times.* 6 July.

1989 'Miriwoong on the Way Back.' *Canberra Times.* 24 September.

1989 'Aborigines Tackling Present and Future.' *Canberra Times.* 4 December.

1989 'Aborigines and the Treaty of Waitangi.' *Land Rights News* 2(12): 18–20.

1990 Coombs, H.C., Dargavel, J., Kesteven, J., Ross, H., Smith, D.I. and Young, E. *The Promise of the Land: Sustainable use by Aboriginal Communities.* CRES Working Paper No. 1990/1. Canberra: Centre for Resource and Environmental Studies, Australian National University.

1990 'What Happened to Self-determination?' *Canberra Times.* 20 June.

1990 'Coalition Policies "Risky" for the Poor. Coombs Slams Aboriginal Policies.' *Canberra Times.* 19 March.

1990 'Aborigines Have to Weigh ATSIC Carefully.' *Canberra Times.* 20 September.

1990 'New Cause for Aboriginal Concern in Federal Review.' *Canberra Times.* 30 October.

1990 Coombs, H.C., McCann, H., Ross, H. and Williams, N.M. (eds.). *Land of Promises: Aborigines and Development in the East Kimberley.* Canberra:

245

Centre for Resource and Environmental Studies, Australian National University and Aboriginal Studies Press, Australian Institute of Aboriginal Studies.

1990. 'Aborigines Tackling Present and Future. What the Traditional Land Owners are Doing to Protect their Resources.' *Canberra Times.* 4 December.

1990 *Return of Scarcity. Strategies for an Economic Future.* Cambridge: Cambridge University Press and the Centre for Resource and Environmental Studies, Australian National University.

1990 'Aboriginal Education, Socialisation and the Underlying Issues.' Report to the Commissioner, Mr P. Dodson, Royal Commission into Aboriginal Deaths in Custody.

1990 'Aboriginal Employment – the Underlying Issues.' Report to the Commissioner, Mr P. Dodson, Royal Commission into Aboriginal Deaths in Custody.

1991 *Aborigines Made Visible: From 'Humbug' to Politics.* Kenneth Myer Lecture II, 29 October. Canberra: Friends of the National Library of Australia.

1992 'Banana Republic? No Banana Colony.' *Australian Business Monthly.* March.

1992 'A Sundered Country.' *Australian Business Monthly.* April.

1992 'Last Things First.' *Australian Business Monthly.* May.

1992 'Black Deaths – Who has Custody?' *Australian Business Monthly.* June.

1992 'Towards a New Federation.' *Australian Business Monthly.* July.

1992 'Multi-Function Parks.' *Australian Business Monthly.* September.

1992 'How the West Was Won.' *Australian Business Monthly.* November.

1993 'Independence or Bust.' *Australian Business Monthly.* January.

1993 'Grasping the Mabo Options.' *Australian Business Monthly.* August 1993.

1993 *Issues in Dispute: Aborigines Working for Autonomy.* Darwin: The North Australia Research Unit, Australian National University, *Age* and *Canberra Times.*

1993 *Willowra.* Darwin: North Australia Research Unit, Australian National University and the Nugget Coombs Forum for Indigenous Studies.

Index

Aboriginal and Torres Strait Islander
Commission (ATSIC) 114, 115, 164,
176, 183-6, 214, 228
Aboriginal Councils and Associations Act
27, 28, 173
Aboriginal Development Commission
(ADC) 138, 139
*Aboriginal Education (Supplementary
Assistance) Act 1989* 74
Aboriginal Hostels Pty Ltd 138
Aboriginal Land Fund Commission 41
*Aboriginal Land Rights (Northern
Territory) Act* 43, 102, 201, 229
Aboriginal Peace Plan 226
agriculture, arid zone 46
alcohol 15, 18, 19, 67, 181
Altman, J.C. 76, 112, 167; and Allen,
L.M. 168, 169; and Sanders, W. 163,
164, 166; and Taylor, L. 166
Alyawarra people 182
Anbarra people 57
Anmatjira people 182
Arbitration Court 18
Arremte people 182
arts and crafts 15, 25, 26, 44, 79, 80, 81
Aurukun community 45
assimilation, Aboriginal 20-2, 27, 31,
47, 61, 66, 68, 70-1, 72, 76, 79, 158,
160, 172, 187-91

Australian Conservation Foundation
32, 38
Australian National Parks and Wildlife
Services 35, 36, 38, 167

Baker, I. 30
Balanda 121-4, 193 *see also* law
Bell, D. 13
Berndt, R.M. and Berndt, C.H. 102
Blanchard, C.A. 161
Boyden, S.V. 57
Bretton Woods Agreements 207
Brown, B.J. et al 96
Bucknall, J. 190

Central Australian Aboriginal Congress
64, 179, 180
Central Land Council 35, 37, 38, 133, 179
ceremonial life 3, 12-13, 19, 28, 36, 44,
62, 68, 69, 100, 157
see also lifestyles
ceremonies
importance of 8-9, 17, 78, 95, 133,
223; initiation 7, 8, 12, 29, 68
male/female roles 11-12, 13
Chittleborough, R.G. and Keating, F.M.
97
Cocos Islands
self-determination for 208, 227
Coe, P. 217

247

colonisation 16, 19, 22, 40, 48-9, 54-5, 57-8, 60-2, 69, 73, 74-5, 86, 88-9, 91, 100, 105, 145, 182, 203, 204-5
Commonwealth Industrial Commission 106
Community Development Employment Projects (CDEP) 28, 80-1, 82, 163, 165, 166, 167
Council for Aboriginal Affairs 14, 160, 172, 192
Council for Aboriginal Reconciliation 214, 228
Crocodile Hole Conference 176
CSIRO 35, 37
cultural change 29, 58, 69, 101
culture, traditional Aboriginal 9, 26-31, 44, 58, 61, 63, 68, 72, 75, 79-80, 86, 100, 112, 157, 158, 159, 168, 169-70, 189, 194, 195, 197

Daylight, P. and Johnstone, M. 187
Department of Aboriginal Affairs (DAA) 14, 37, 38, 137, 138, 173, 178-9, 185
development see resource development; see also economy, economic enterprises; mining industry
Dexter, B. 172
diet, traditional 60, 63
Dixon, R.A. and Dillon, M.C. 69, 107, 210
Dodson, M. ix-x, 217, 218, 224, 226
Dreaming, the 3, 8-9, 12, 29
Dubos, R. 5, 57-8

East Arnhem Land 163, 224
East Kimberley project 78, 83, 86-90, 96, 98
economy, Aboriginal; economic enterprises 25, 45, 48, 76-9, 79-82, 83-4, 88, 95, 100, 162-7, 170
    hunting techniques 33-5
education, Aboriginal
    as assimilation 47, 187-9; mainstream 27, 31, 46, 47, 68, 71-5, 102, 166, 187-98; in a multicultural society 68, 73, 75; and numeracy 10, 27, 47, 197; in the Pilbara 191-2; 'two-way' 189-91, 194, 196-8; traditional 7-12, 66, 68, 72-5, 112, 159-60, 187-91, 192-8; at Yirrkala 192-6
employment see economy, Aboriginal

environment
    Aboriginal relationship to 8-9, 30, 32-8, 57-9, 94-6, 97, 108, 159, 221; coastal 170; destruction of by colonisation 34-5, 59; effects of mining and pastoralists on 112-16 see also mining industry, pastoralists
Eva Valley Statement 213, 214-16, 227, 228, 231-4

family 3, 5, 7, 8, 14, 15, 16, 17, 25, 30, 34, 45, 47, 59, 61, 81, 119, 120-1, 124, 138, 192, 223 see also social relationships
fauna
    conservation of 45-6, 168; threat of extinction to native 32, 33, 34-5, 59
Federation of Land Councils 137
fire, Aboriginal use of 35-6, 168
Fraser, D. 30
Fraser government
    on Aboriginal affairs 28, 220; on land rights movement 39, 72, 178

Gadjerrong people 87
Gatjil 30
gender roles 11-14
Gibb Committee 157
Gnanatjara people 175
Goodland, R.J. and Ledec, G. 65
Gould, Richard 56
government policies
    impact on Aboriginal society 19-22, 31, 39-40, 42-3, 61, 62, 68, 71, 72, 74, 97, 102-3, 144, 157, 158, 159, 163, 171-86, 208, 209, 220, 226-9
    see also assimilation; land rights; self-management

Hamilton, A. 6, 14
Hawke government 72, 144
Hawke, S. 210
health, Aboriginal 27, 31, 55-7, 65, 102, 164; effect of environmental change on 57-9; effect of mining on 112; effect of colonisation on 54-5, 58, 60-2, 68, 74; initiatives 62-4; services 62-4, 174 see also diet
Heppell, M. and Wigley, J.J. 177, 178, 179
heritage, Aboriginal 3, 79, 157, 158, 159, 168, 193

Holt government 171, 172
homelands
  defined 24–5, 63; economies of 25–6,
    162, 163, 164–5, 170;
  establishment of 34, 36, 37, 43–6, 47,
    62–3, 159–61, 170, 175;
  political organisation 26–8; State
    government policies on 31
housing 16, 101, 179–81 *see also*
  Tangentyere Council

identity, Aboriginal 3, 6–7, 13, 17, 19,
    21–2, 84, 101, 119, 159, 166
  contemporary 18, 52, 62, 68, 75, 182;
  traditional 3, 17, 26, 34, 47, 56,
    66–7, 68, 75, 79, 215, 220, 221, 222,
    224 *see also* socialisation
initiation *see* ceremonies
International Covenant on Civil and
  Political Rights 226

Jackson, S. and Cooper, D. 112

Kaititja people 182
Kakadu National Park 35, 36, 37, 38,
    167, 169
Kartangarurru-Kurintji people
  land use by 32
Keating government 209
Kimberley region 29, 69, 86–99, 111, 176,
    228
kinship *see* family; social relationships
Kit, John Ah 217
Kurdandji people 112

land
  Aboriginal relationship to 3, 17, 32–8,
    40–3, 84, 93–5, 100, 151, 158, 159,
    160, 202–3, 214;
  management 35, 36, 93–7, 170;
  women's responsibilities to 12
  see also environment; homelands
land rights
  authority and 46–8, 65, 79, 83, 84, 86,
    102–3, 105–10, 137, 149, 151, 159,
    160, 168, 175–8; Commonwealth
    Government legislation 31, 40, 72,
    102–3, 105, 109–10, 161, 177–9,
    200–14, 216–18, 224–5; and native
    title 148–50, 200–6, 209–14, 216–18,
    224–5, 228; and fiduciary duty of
    Crown 205–6, 208–9, 210, 217, 218,
    224–5; impact of 49–52, 62, 71–2;
    movement 30–1, 39–40, 43, 137, 159;

and status of sovereignty 206–9,
    217, 225
  see also mining industry; treaty;
    Woodward Commission
Langton, M. 6, 15, 217
Lanhupuy, W. 30, 193, 195
law, Aboriginal 3, 13, 19, 29, 48, 61, 62,
    68, 118–21, 134, 151, 192;
  administration of 27, 31, 47, 48, 49,
    118–30, 138–42; impact of white
    120–30, 137
  women's 16, 128–9
  see also punishment
Law Reform Commission 122, 127–30
leadership, traditional 16, 47–9 *see also*
  political organisation, Aboriginal
Lennon, A. 30
Lester, Y. 15, 30
lifestyles, Aboriginal 3, 5, 17–18, 24, 34,
    36, 46, 221, 222; hunter-gatherer
    55–7, 58, 62, 63, 100, 101, 165, 221;
  traditional 26–31, 34, 43–6, 61, 63,
    64, 66–7, 68, 81, 93, 100, 107, 112,
    157, 160, 194
Loritja people 18, 202
Lyon, P. 67, 181

McArthur River mine 111–16
McGrath, A. 77
McLeod, D. 101, 191
McMahon government 179
Mabo case 111, 200, 213, 216–18, 224,
    227; Eva Valley Statement 213,
    214–16, 227, fiduciary duty of
    Crown 205–6, 217, 218; limitations
    of 203–5
Macassan islands 15
Maningrida community 57
Mansell, M. 217
Mara people 112
marriage *see* social relationships
Marshall, P. 76
Meehan, B. 57, 164
Meriam people 200 *see also* Mabo case
mining industry
  clean-up costs 113; and land rights
    102–4, 105–10, 111–16, 159, 202, 209,
    210–11, 216; procedures for
    development 113–16; *see also*
    McArthur River mine; East
    Kimberley project
Miriwung people 87

mobility
for men 14-15; for women 15-16
Mundrooroo 15
Mutitjulu community 167
Myers, F. 6, 134

National Aboriginal and Islander
Health Organisations (NAIHO)
137
National Aboriginal and Islander Legal
Service (NAILS) 137
National Aboriginal Conference (NAC)
131-2, 134, 135, 139, 141, 185
National Aboriginal Education Policy
(NAEP) 71, 72, 73, 74, 75
national parks
Aboriginal and white concepts 167;
management of 168, 169-70; marine
170
native title see land rights; Mabo case
Nettheim, G. 200
Nganyintja 15
Niblett, N. 112
Northern Land Council 38
Northern Territory
land rights legislation 31, 40-1, 42,
43, 102-3, 160, 174, 175-6, 177,
178-9, 212, 229; relationship with
mining industry 113

O'Dea, K. 63
O'Faircheallaigh, C. 104
Oodgeroo Noonuccal 15
outstations see homelands

Papunya community 16, 202
pastoralists
Aboriginal relations with 17, 19-20,
69, 77, 86, 87, 100, 101, 156, 157-9
Pearson, N. 217
Pilbara region 29, 70, 191
Pintubi people 14, 16, 68, 202, 211
Pitjantjatjara people 15, 40, 42-3, 46, 64,
163, 175-6, 182, 210, 212
political organisation, Aboriginal 26-8,
39, 43, 46-9, 51-1, 65, 131-42, 151,
160, 172-7, 179-80, 182-6, 200, 208,
212, 214, 216-18, 226, 227, 228-30
population, Aboriginal
census 70; distribution of 24-5
punishment, Aboriginal attitudes
towards 125-7, 128

Queensland
land rights legislation 31, 41, 43

Rabuntja, E. 179
Racial Discrimination Act 1975 201
racism see white Australian attitudes;
referendum
referendum (1967) 14, 30, 70, 171-2
Reid, J. 54
and Kerr, C. 61
religion, Aboriginal 7-13, 28-9, 44, 68,
69, 100, 157, 158
see also ceremonies; Dreaming, the
Repetto, R.C. 96
resource development 79, 84, 88-93,
93-5, 96-8, 100-2, 105-10
Reynolds H. 205
Roberts, P. 14-15
Roper River 14
Rose, D.B. 6, 9, 10
Ross, D. 217
Roughsey, D. 15
Rowley, C. 44, 137
Royal Commission into Aboriginal
Deaths in Custody 21-2, 66-7, 164,
165, 183, 189
and socialisation of Aboriginal
children 67-8

sacred sites 17, 29, 87
Sanders, W. 164
self-management 21, 28, 30, 47-9, 72,
140-2, 163, 170, 173, 177, 195
settlements, government 60-1, 70, 101,
160
Shaw, G. 179
Smith, D.E. 6, 184
social relationships
Aboriginal consciousness of 3, 6, 8;
conflict in 69, 215; kinship 3, 6, 7,
8, 14, 56, 58-9, 63, 120, 193, 197, 215
social security 28, 62, 68, 70, 102, 162-4
socialisation 8, 17, 19, 21-2, 47, 78, 220
of males 11-13, 68; of females 11-13,
68; influence on personal
autonomy 13; traditional 66, 67-71,
73-5, 88, 119, 157, 160, 188-9, 190-4,
197, 223
society
Aboriginal 5-22, 26-9, 30, 34, 46-8,
56, 58, 74, 78, 118-21, 128-30, 132-5,
140, 162, 169, 170, 182-3, 193, 215,

220-4; impact on mainstream society 79-80; white society influence on Aboriginal 29-30, 47, 49-50, 52, 58, 59, 60-1, 67, 69-70, 71-2, 74, 100, 120-1, 128, 129, 137-8, 140, 157-9, 172, 173, 179, 182, 183, 187-9, 191, 192, 194, 203-4 *see also* family; social relationships

South Australia
land rights legislation 40, 42-3, 175, 212

Stanner, W.E.H. 6, 9, 101, 156, 172

Stanton, V. 15

Sullivan, P. 95

Sutton, P. 6

Tangentyere Council 175, 177-82

terra nullius 201, 216

Thomson, D. 101

Tonkinson, R. 6

Torres Strait Islanders 72

treaty
administration of 152-3; implications for Australia 147-8, 150, 153-4; need for 143-4, 200, 205; negotiating a 151-2, 154

Treaty of Waitangi 144-7, 150, 151, 153, 205

Uluru-Kata Tjuta National Park 167, 169

United Nations
on rights of indigenous people 207, 213, 226, 227

urban Aborigines 166-7, 170, 177

von Sturmer, J. 6

Warlpiri people 32, 182
land use by 32-8

Walyambula 30

Watson, J. 15

welfare, Aboriginal 19-20 *see also* government policies

Western Australia
land rights legislation 31, 40, 42, 43, 103-4, 107

white Australian attitudes 6, 19-22, 26-30, 44, 47, 50-2, 69-75, 107, 143-4, 156, 159, 171-2, 221

White, I. et al. 13

Whitlam government
on land rights movement 39, 102, 174, 177; policies 43, 71, 158, 173, 220

Wigley, J. 177, 178, 179, 180

Wik people 206, 218

Williams, N. 6

Wiradjuri people 218

Woodward Commission 30-1, 39, 40, 71, 102, 174, 177

work, Aboriginal *see* economy, Aboriginal

World Commission on Environment and Development (WCED) 92, 96

World Conservation Strategy 92

Yankantjatjara people 175

Yanyuwa people 112

Yayayi community 16, 202, 211

Yirrkala people 48-9, 84, 102, 160, 191-6; law and order 121-30

Yolngu people 7, 169, 193-6, 224, 230

Yu, P. 217

Yunupingu, Galarrwuy 30

Printed in the United Kingdom
by Lightning Source UK Ltd.
1169